CUSTER

The Life of
General George Armstrong Custer

by JAY MONAGHAN

With illustrations

UNIVERSITY OF NEBRASKA PRESS • LINCOLN/LONDON

ISBN 0–8032–5732–5 pbk.
ISBN 0–8032–3056–7
Library of Congress Catalog Card Number 59–5937

First Bison Book printing: February 1971

Most recent printing indicated by first digit below:
        8   9   10

*Bison Book edition reproduced from the first (1959) edition
published by Little, Brown & Company by arrangement
with the author.*

Manufactured in the United States of America

Dedicated to
MILDRED
with the wish that I might word my
affection with Libbie Custer's skill

Contents

ILLUSTRATIONS APPEAR BETWEEN PAGES 326–327

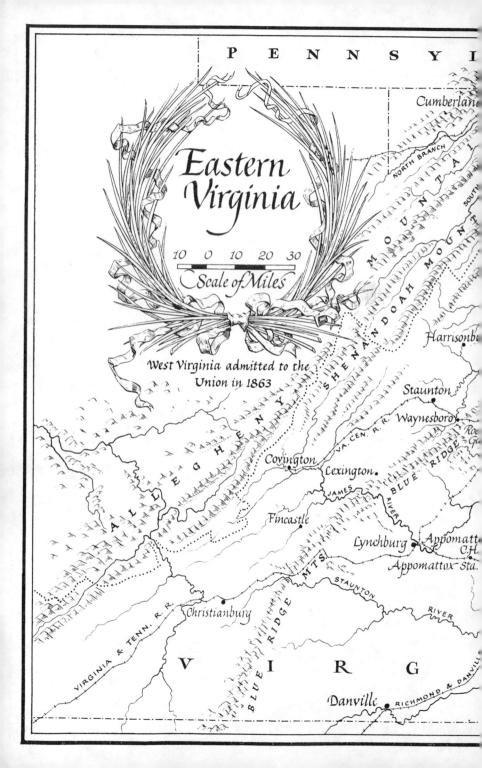

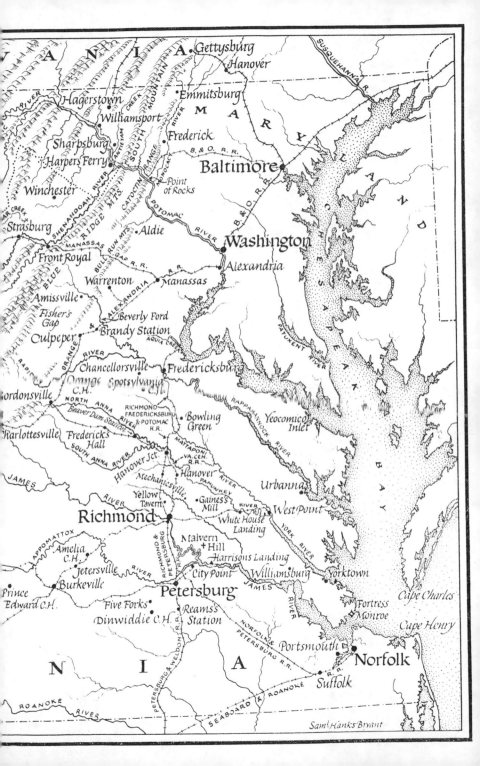

CUSTER

The Life of General George Armstrong Custer

1 "We May All End under Generals' Epaulets"

LITTLE GEORGE ARMSTRONG CUSTER'S JAW HURT. HE CLENCHED HIS FIST AS his father led him out of the dentist's office and along the street to the hitching rack. "Father," he piped, looking up at the bearded man whose thick, horny hand held his little one, "I and you can whip all the Whigs in Ohio, can't we?" *

Emanuel Custer roared with laughter, shaking the long hair which curled over the collar of his rusty frock coat. He was a blacksmith at New Rumley, a community of houses on a hilltop three miles from the town of Scio, Ohio, where the dentist lived.

Driving home, Emanuel stopped everybody on the road to tell about little freckle-faced George Armstrong's bright saying. The curlyheaded youngster had a sharp, fox nose and sparkling blue eyes. Childlike, he laughed when others laughed. It was amusing to picture that redheaded chick rushing off to slay an overwhelming number of his father's Whig enemies. And the joke fitted Emanuel, too, for he would rather talk politics than eat when hungry. He had cast his first vote for Andy Jackson and had opposed the Whigs ever since — didn't care who knew it, either, and expressed his opinions on all occasions.[1]

* Emanuel Custer wrote this story to Libbie, February 3, 1887, and it was printed in her *Tenting on the Plains*, pp. 287–290. He quoted the boy as saying "You and me" and he placed the incident in Monroe. The story is also well known at Cadiz and Scio, Ohio, where Armstrong lived as a little boy, and it seems more appropriate there. It is more probable, too, that Autie said, "I and you." [1] Numbered references are to Notes section at end of book.

The last mile of the road home slanted up a steep hill. Drivers stopped their teams at least once during the pull. Emanuel probably retold George Armstrong's boast to himself as the horses rested. If so, father and son both laughed again. No doubt they enjoyed the prospect of telling the story once more to the family when they reached home.

At the summit, they could look over the horses' ears and see, along the road, the first of the double row of homes known as New Rumley. There was no post office or store. Behind the houses the green hills of eastern Ohio rolled away in every direction — a magnificent panorama. Emanuel's uncle, who had founded this hamlet in 1812, must have appreciated fine scenery. The team trotted down the road and turned into the yard behind a big, plain, two-story clapboard building, which, like the other residences, stood close to the dirt road. Little George had been born in this house on December 5, 1839.

Emanuel unhitched near the blacksmith shop and led his son to the kitchen door. Inside the Custer house there was always an uproar — a happy, stamping, yelling, joke-playing hubbub. Somebody was inevitably sitting on a bent horseshoe nail or having a chair pulled out from under him.

Emanuel Custer had married twice. His first wife died in 1835, leaving him three children. Within a year he married Widow Maria Kirkpatrick, who joined him with her two. The couple then proceeded to add seven curlyheads to these five. The first two of the new family died in infancy. The third, George Armstrong Custer, survived and became the pet of his parents as well as of his older brothers and sisters. He was called "Armstrong" by his father, but the name was soon shortened to "Autie" — his own baby pronunciation. In due time Autie was followed by Nevin J., Thomas Ward, Boston, and finally Margaret. Nevin was an invalid, too delicate to romp with the boys although he outlived them all. Tom, born in 1845, was vigorous. Six years younger than Autie, he grew up imitating everything his older brother said and did — a habit which he never completely outgrew.

Emanuel Custer was as noisy as any of his boys. He romped and scuffled with them, making one, then another the butt of some practical joke. His children, on their part, were always watching an opportunity to turn the tables on their father, no matter how roughly. In such a household a child had to be alert to hold his own. None of them knew the meaning of discipline or restraint. They felt little respect for their parents' authority but were closely bound to them by an everlasting love. The loyalty and affection of this motley tribe was the most remarkable thing about it. Never could anybody truthfully apply to this bubbling household the old saw: "Ma's kids and Pa's kids are fighting Ma's and Pa's kids." Quite the reverse! No member of the Custer family ever cared whose child belonged to whom, and George Armstrong Custer, as a grown man, always considered them all one family. Only with a conscious effort could he remember their diverse parentage.

Mother Custer was a handsome woman — thin, frail, with regular features and a calm expression. She hid her curls with a cap that covered her ears and was tied under her well-molded chin. Like many successful mothers, she believed that every good little boy must be bad at least part of the time. And when she looked over the tops of the little spectacles she wore for knitting and watched her romping brood, she confessed that red-haired Autie fitted her definition. If any prank had been played he was sure to be at the bottom of it and Tom was never far behind. If Autie stamped into the kitchen from the washbench on the back porch with a towel around his middle like a wild Indian's breechcloth and the tin basin on his head, Tom was sure to toddle behind him with the dipper on his towhead. When Autie sang — which he did almost continually — or beat time with his foot, Tom in his highchair tapped an accompaniment with a spoon in his baby fist. Rhythm pulsed with the lifeblood of all the Custer children.

Father Emanuel was one of the "good men" of the community. He did not drink or play cards, and used tobacco only in a pipe.[2] His one weakness was the strength of his voice. He talked politics constantly, and, in church, sang louder than all the congregation. He never accumulated much wealth, but he had enough to be independent, self-sufficient, and proud of what he had. His children ranked with the best in New Rumley and Armstrong never forgot the boyhood friends he made there. During his busy years at West Point he would shade the gas jet after lights were ordered out and write about those happy days when he and the neighbors' children all pretended to be grownups, dressed in their parents' clothes, and strutted around calling each other Sam McCullough, Johnny Kimmel, Poff, Pen, Dotts.[3] Loyalty to the friends of his youth was always one of his characteristics.

During Autie's boyhood, his father moved the family from the big house to a log cabin on a small farm two miles away. The older children left home for various jobs or marriage. Nine-year-old Armstrong was apprenticed to a cabinetmaker in Cadiz, the county seat, a much bigger settlement than Scio. The courthouse square sloped like a barn roof, for this was still hill-country. The neat brick houses on all four sides displayed an air of prosperity which impressed the young Custers. Here for the first time he heard the thump of a printing press, smelled the fumes from a tannery, saw the glare and felt the heat of an iron foundry.

Two important politicians, Edwin M. Stanton and John A. Bingham, had practiced law in Cadiz. Stanton moved to Steubensville the year Armstrong was born, and Bingham went to Congress in 1855; so it is unlikely that either of them could remember the slim stripling who turned the big foot-lathe in Hunter's furniture shop, although both would take considerable interest in him a few years later.[4]

Armstrong was popular with his fellows, especially with the boss's son, who recalled that he made play out of his work. Father and Mother Custer drove down from New Rumley — a day's trip in the buggy — to see how he fared and to show him a new baby sister, Margaret (another example of the closeness of Custer family ties).

His parents evidently did not approve of the apprenticeship, for when Armstrong was ten they sent him to live with his half-sister, Lydia, who had married David Reed in Monroe, Michigan, twenty-five miles north of Toledo, Ohio. Monroe was another small town, having less than four thousand inhabitants, but it differed greatly from the villages Armstrong had known in Ohio. Monroe was closer to the outside world, could be reached by lake steamer as well as by railroad. The residents believed themselves cosmopolitan. They were snobbish. Many belonged to old military families, aristocrats by tradition. One of them remembered, later, "We did not associate with the [Reeds and] Custers. They were quite ordinary people, no intellectual interests, very little schooling." [5]

Armstrong's "new father," David Reed, was in the draying business. He owned plenty of horses and had prospered enough to have money loaned at interest, but the fact remained that he was a Methodist while all the "acceptable people" in Monroe were Presbyterians. The Custers had attended Presbyterian services in Scio — but that was different. In Monroe Lydia felt more at home with the Methodists.

Armstrong lived at Sister Lydia's home for five or six years. Father Custer drove over from the Ohio hill-country at least once for a visit. The trip consumed more than ten days each way. Good enough! A man could talk a lot of politics to his team as it jogged along the country roads. After the first day's drive, winding uphill and down, bouncing across "thank-you-ma'ams" on every grade, he reached the straight, level roads crossing northern Ohio's fat farm lands. What a change! He loosened the quarter-straps on the team's breechings and spanked along for hours, wheels spinning between solid walls of corn. Most of the farmers up here seemed to be Whigs who leaned toward the new Black Republican Party, but Emanuel dared talk to all of them: Did they want their daughters to marry "niggers"? Sometimes arguments cost him an extra day or two, but what of that!

Thus Armstrong grew up in two communities, dividing his time between his mother's and his sister's households. This may have given him a feeling of superiority, a certain youthful maturity. Certainly it made his education irregular and his scholastic record in both Ohio and Michigan excelled only in the skill with which he evaded study.

After he became a famous general, one chronicler remembered that Custer used to smuggle a copy of Charles Lever's popular military romance concerning Charles O'Malley of the 14th Light Dragoons [6] to school and hide it under his geography. Lever's comical character, Mickey Free, was a favorite with him. If this story is true, it seems to have been the extent of young Armstrong's military interest, although his father may have taken him to the militia muster when Autie was a toddler.

In Monroe, Armstrong began going with girls. Soon he was playing the female field in both Michigan and Ohio. Girls liked the smiling curlyhead. He had traveled more than his comrades and a date with Autie was exciting. He kept the crowd laughing, was usually planning a practical joke, and his friends never knew what was going to happen next. For example, once on a bright winter day at New Rumley, he and Joe Dickenson decided to take the neighborhood belles sleigh-riding in a straw-filled wagon box on runners. They packed the girls in under buffalo robes where it was warm, cozy, and lots of fun. But Autie kept reminding Joe about another lass on the next farm and the team jingled over the snowy roads to stop at her kitchen door. Finally so many girls were packed in the sleigh that Joe had to ride one of the horses. Out in the cold, he concluded that Autie had planned this prank from the beginning as a joke on him. Joe decided to get even. He whipped the team along the road and at the first sharp turn rolled the laughing load into a big drift. Armstrong was somewhere at the bottom of that screaming, squealing melee of rosy cheeks, kicking legs, and flying snow. More noticeable still, he took what seemed to Joe an unnecessarily long time to wrestle his way to the surface. Watching from above, Joe decided that instead of "jobbing" Armstrong, Armstrong had "jobbed" him.

Despite all this rollicking horseplay, Armstrong worried about his future. Naturally ambitious, he did not want to grow up to be a blacksmith like his father and his father's father. To improve his education he attended McNeely Normal School at Hopedale, eight miles from Cadiz. Here, according to popular remembrance, he took part in a spelling bee. One of his fellow students tried to discomfit him by grimacing outside a closed window. Custer never hesitated a moment. He had a fist as square as his father's and it struck through the glass, hitting the wry face in the nose. This schoolmate, like Joe Dickenson, recalled that it was futile to impose on Armstrong Custer. His popularity grew with every prank.

In the summer of 1856 Custer taught in the little one-room schoolhouse at Locust Grove, earning twenty-eight dollars per month. With considerable pride, he took his first month's pay to his mother and dropped it all in her apron. That winter, beginning in November, he taught at Beech Point in nearby Athens, Ohio. Here he earned an extra two dollars a month by chopping wood for the school stove. His students recalled later that he was a likable teacher who tussled with the boys on the playground, washed the girls' faces in the snow, and played an accordion for opening exercises. Sara McFarland, who sat at a desk before him at Beech Point, said he liked to argue with the antislavery students, denouncing Black Republicans, but he was always good-natured about it. Once he assigned her the theme topic: "James Buchanan, Our Honored President." She wrote one on "Ten-cent Jimmie" and was not punished for her impudence. She also remembered Armstrong's dancing blue eyes, his curly red-gold hair which he brushed back over his ears as his father did. She thought, as she watched him, "what a pretty girl he would have made." [7]

Threats of impending war grew louder daily, but schoolteacher Custer laughed at them. He blamed Northern fanatics for the civil war raging in Kansas. He believed hotheaded politicians to be augmenting that trouble by carrying pistols to their seats in the Capitol. The North had no business depriving the South of its just rights,[8] and Senator Sumner deserved the caning he got from an irate South Carolina congressman. In case abolitionists forced war on the country, Armstrong certainly did not plan to fight for the North. What he wanted was a good education, and at West Point an education could be had free.

Armstrong's first problem was to get an appointment to the Military Academy. His case seemed hopeless because local congressmen made the recommendations and the Honorable John A. Bingham prided himself on his avowed hatred of Democrats, such as the Custers. He had been elected after making fiery speeches favoring free soil, freemen, and a high tariff on wool. The Custers owned no sheep on the Cadiz hills, did not want any Whig tariffs, and believed that slavery kept the Negro in his place. Armstrong Custer appeared to have no chance against such overwhelming odds, but — a true Custer — he threw caution to the winds and wrote Congressman Bingham, requesting an interview when he next returned to Cadiz from Washington.

An exchange of correspondence followed. The details of what happened are conjectural. Bingham, in his autobiography, said that he was impressed by the frank originality of the boy's letter and recommended him for the Academy. But that was hindsight. Certainly, when Custer became famous, Bingham urged his advancement and pointed with pride to his own early recognition of the young man's talents. Other things, however, seem to have earned Armstrong the Academy appointment. One of them was a girl. Autie had fallen in love.

As a teacher at Beech Point, Armstrong boarded in the home of a well-to-do farmer. There he became enamored with the farmer's daughter. Mary Holland's part in the appointment of Armstrong Custer has never been chronicled. She saved much of her correspondence with Autie, although she clipped out some passages, probably intimate ones. Among the mementoes she kept is the following poem, which contains the phrases a sentimental seventeen-year-old might be expected to remember from his reading and then try to incorporate in a composition of his own:

TO MARY
I've seen and kissed that crimson lip
With honied smiles o'erflowing.
Enchanted watched the opening rose,
Upon thy soft cheek glowing.

Dear Mary, thy eyes may prove less blue,
Thy beauty fade tomorrow,
But Oh, my heart can ne'er forget
Thy parting look of sorrow.

The future military terror of the Plains was certainly clumsily sentimental as a youth — an attribute, perhaps, of budding gallantry. But Mary gave him her picture and he, in turn, had a picture taken of himself admiring hers. He begrudged every moment of separation. Sitting at his desk after school and on Saturdays, he wrote letters to her. Boy and man, Custer preferred to express himself on paper rather than orally. He discussed a quick marriage with Mary before going to West Point ("if I ever go"). He told her, also, that he expected to study law for two or three years after finishing at the Academy, "but I will talk with you about it when I see you next at the trundle bed" — whatever he meant by that. Thus with plans for seven or eight years of study ahead, he seemed more anxious to get married than to begin keeping house — a usual youthful predicament. Custer ended his letter with: "Farewell my only love until we meet again from your true & faithful Lover, 'Bachelor Boy.'" [9]

Two days later, having seen Mary almost constantly, he wrote again: "You occupy the first place in my affections and the only place as far as love is concerned. . . . If any power which I possess or control can aid in or in any way hasten our marriage it shall be exerted for that object."

Mary Holland's father did not favor taking into his family the limber, laughing, poet-schoolteacher whose notorious father preached reactionary slaveholding politics contrary to the best progressive interests of wool-growing Ohio. Mr. Holland knew that West Point students could not marry. A capital idea! He would use his influence with Congressman Bingham.

The appointment came — an exciting day for the Custer clan, but two things marred Armstrong's jubilation. Acceptance meant postponing the wedding at least five years, and one statement in the official letter was frightening. To delay the marriage of a seventeen-year-old seemed sensible, but the grim warning in that official letter might have discouraged almost any boy except Armstrong Custer. He knew very well that he was no scholar, and the letter warned him that the West Point course was difficult, especially in mathematics. More than half the candidates would probably fail. He might, therefore, save himself and his family future humiliation by declining the appointment. This form letter was signed by Secretary of War Jefferson Davis.[10]

Armstrong handed the letter to his father to read. Members of the close-knit Custer clan habitually consulted one another before acting. Emanuel read the letter carefully, his lips pronouncing each word separately as was his habit. No, Autie should not be discouraged. Let him take that chance, pass if he could!

Mother Custer listened as the communication was read again. In family affairs she usually voiced an opinion and, if voted down, acquiesced philosophically. She did not want her boy to be a soldier, and the constant threats of civil war sounded ominous. Like her husband, she disapproved of this new "abolition" party which was growing in Ohio, and if it brought on a war she wanted her son well out of it. However, if the family voted for him to go to West Point, that would be God's will.

Half-brother David Kirkpatrick was consulted next. He voted for West Point. The final decision rested with the Reeds in Monroe, for Armstrong's half-sister, Lydia Reed, was as dear to him as his own mother.

The Reeds approved, so at the end of the school term Armstrong prepared for his trip East. Emanuel sold his little farm, getting a two-hundred-dollar down-payment for his son's expenses. (Generosity within the family was another Custer characteristic.) Twelve-year-old Tom watched his older brother pack his bag. He wanted to go to West Point, too, when he grew up.

During all the preparations nothing seems to have been said about Armstrong's following the Custer family's military inheritance. There was no reference to his descent from Revolutionary soldiers — a tradition that would come later.* Certainly Armstrong Custer started for West Point with no visions of hereditary heroes. He was just a country boy who still considered studying for the law and marrying Mary Holland.

The trip across New York state differed little from Armstrong's travels in the Midwest, until he reached Albany. The boat ride down the Hudson to West Point was a new experience. From the steamboat rail he watched the dark slopes of the Catskills, steeper, more precipitous than any bluffs he had ever seen in Ohio or Michigan. Other steamboats, sailboats, barges, great tows of canalboats glided past him. People kept house on some of them. He saw garbage thrown over the sides, and clotheslines stretched between masts. Varicolored shirts, towels, and underwear fluttered in the river breeze.

Other teen-age boys were on Custer's boat and, being a sociable chap, he must have spoken to them. All boys bound for West Point had much in common. They could joke about joining the army as war clouds blackened daily.

"We may all end under generals' epaulets," was a common boast.

"Yes, or under six feet of ground," cynics replied, usually evoking a laugh.

The boys were sure to spy any man in uniform on board, and if the buttons on his coat were marked CADET it seems reasonable to assume that the recruits would accost him, asking about life at the Academy.

* In due time the Milo Custer genealogy would disclose an Emanuel Custer, born in 1754, who served with five brothers and his father under Washington. Armstrong's great-grandfather was named Emanuel Custer, and he, like this Revolutionary War veteran, had been born about 1754. The two Emanuel Custers may have been the same man, but Armstrong's great-grandfather died only three years before Armstrong received his West Point assignment. Had this Emanuel been the Revolutionary War veteran, the Custers, with their strong family loyalty, would surely have known of the old man's background and have referred to him as they prepared Autie for a military career. (Milo Custer, *Custer Genealogies;* Milo M. Quaife's introduction, p. xix, in G. A. Custer, *My Life on the Plains.*)

A cadet was apt to be friendly off the post. He could explain that the Hudson was narrow at West Point and made two sharp turns. In the old days, sailing ships had to change their tack to get through. This made them a good mark for batteries on shore. To protect these batteries during the Revolution, Forts Putnam and Arnold — the latter's name soon changed to Fort Clinton — had been built on overlooking terraces. The passage had been made even more difficult by stretching a giant chain across the river. It was on exhibition now at the Academy.

As the steamboat approached the Narrows, bare rock walls loomed ahead. Through the chasm Custer saw a sloping mountainside. On this incline, he noticed a shelf — the famous Academy Plain. Surrounding buildings were hidden behind trees, but the red and white stripes of an American flag glowed above them like a living coal on the somber forest background.

The steamboat swung sharply to the left, then to the right, following the channel. "Like a dog's hind leg," Custer must have thought, as the rocky walls passed the ship's rail. Ahead he could see a wharf. Passengers moved their baggage toward the gangway.

The steamboat's paddle wheels began to churn the water as the vessel stopped and drifted in. Custer looked down on the dock, where straw-hatted wharfingers were scampering for the cables and looping them around pilings. He could hear the ropes strain, taut as fiddlestrings, as the ship grated against the landing. A gangplank swung out and the ship's bell rang. Passengers swarmed down the sagging, cleated planks.

Custer followed the crowd to the dock platform. Here he could look back at the steamboat, and ahead to the tree-covered bluff. An omnibus waited at the foot of the pier.

"Get in, boys," a voice said.

Everybody clambered into the swaying vehicle. The driver released his brake and the bus jolted away, plodding up a circuitous route. On one side, the Hudson slipped past them. The other side of the road was shored with stone masonry, between granite outcroppings. Here and there Custer saw dells with tinkling streams shaded by magnificent tulip, elm, and chestnut trees. The leaves overhead were light green, the

Maytime color. In the woodland, white flower-clusters glowed on honey locusts. This dripping forest with its lichened boulders was as inviting for play as any meadow near New Rumley. Yes, West Point would be a wonderful place if there were girls here and a fellow did not have to work too hard!

The road switched back for half a mile, climbing one hundred and sixty feet to an old hotel of stone and brick, with wide verandas overlooking the Narrows. Storm King Mountain and the Crow Nest appeared even more impressive here than they had from the deck of the steamboat. A tall hedge separated the hotel from the Academy's Plain. According to tradition, Robert E. Lee's horse had bolted with him when Lee was a cadet, and had jumped that hedge. Lee was a big man in the army now, a lieutenant colonel of cavalry. He had been superintendent here at West Point only year before last.

At the hotel steps, the West Point passengers alighted from the omnibus. The new boys seemed uncertain and a little self-conscious. On the veranda above them Custer noticed gaily-dressed cadets watching him and his uncomfortable companions. He had never seen such resplendent uniforms. Rows of brass buttons down the men's breasts and up their sleeves! Even the tails of their claw-hammer coats were studded with brass. No peacock ever held the plume on his head more erect than the pompons on the cadets' shakos.

In later years Custer could not recall any of the faces in that crowd — too many to remember. But, as they were mostly second-year men come to criticize, inspect, and later haze the incoming crop of candidates, it seems probable that among them stood the slim and beaming Virginian, John Pelham, a blond "personality boy." Tall, slender Wesley Merritt from Illinois, dignified even in youth, may have been standing beside Pelham. Sandy-haired, imp-faced Judson Kilpatrick from New Jersey was sure to have been there: always talking about girls, he could be counted on for every exciting event.[11] It also seems probable that an older, more serious classman stood among the cadets. Lieutenant Marcus A. Reno had recently graduated, and was waiting for his first assignment. Personal antagonisms may start at first sight. Certainly squareheaded, short-necked, stocky Reno, with his straight hair, steady eyes and determined jaw, was very different from lean, limber, curly-topped Custer, the country boy who stood in the road below him, laughing — always laughing, as his father did, even at jokes on himself.

On the veranda among the resplendent cadets Custer could see women, sure enough: apple-cheeked young ladies in crinolines, more magnificent than he ever beheld in Monroe or New Rumley. But to make matters really embarrassing, almost nobody paid any attention to the shabby newcomers with their dusty boots and carpetbags. The ladies and their escorts who did look at them seemed to enjoy the boys' discomfort. A cadet who had been friendly on the boat would be aloof and haughty here, staring through the new arrivals as though they did not exist.

So this was the army! Perhaps a fellow might be better off studying for the law.

2 Fanny's Probation

THE DISCONSOLATE GROUP OF BOYS STANDING IN THE ROAD WITH THEIR baggage heard a voice which seemed to have authority. It told them to report to the adjutant in the library, over yonder across "the Plain." The boys trudged away. They saw, over the green parade, a border of elms, and above the treetops a line of stone barracks, castellated walls, turreted towers. At the west end of the Plain, at the foot of a wooded mountain slope, stood the officers' and teachers' homes, small two-story houses with steep-pitched roofs shading narrow porches, called "stoops" by the Hudson River Dutch.

The gawky youths, lugging their baggage, timidly climbed the library steps and entered the big front door. "Is the adjutant at home?"

An officious gray-clad sentry ordered them to come in and stand at attention until called for. "Get your papers ready and hold your hat in your hand when you go in the adjutant's door there," he growled. The boys waited silently. Custer heard his name called. He stepped into the adjutant's room and stood before a seated officer and clerk. The clerk pointed to a registry book and said, "Sign."

Custer always wrote with a pen between the first and second fingers of his thick square hand. In the open book he signed: GEORGE A. CUSTER. He followed this, as requested, with his father's name and address: EMANUEL H. CUSTER, SCIO, OHIO.[1]

The clerk compared the names with Custer's appointment, wrote a ledger entry, and handed Armstrong a slip of paper. Then the adjutant turned to the next in line. When all had their names transcribed, a voice commanded an orderly to take the recruits to "quarters" — whatever that meant.

"Follow me," barked a young man in blue-gray swallowtail coat. They all staggered after him with their baggage — out the heavy doors, down the steps, and along the walk under the elms. They hurried past the Ionian pillars of a little chapel, crossed a thoroughfare, and stood by Academic Hall. Beyond stood the long barracks' façades. Halfway down the line their guide led them through a "sally port." Emerging in a courtyard, called "the Area," Custer looked up at four stories of surrounding windows. Like a real city!

The guide crossed the Area, and bounded up iron steps into a hallway. The boys stumbled after him. At a door marked ORDERLY ROOM, they stopped. The guide knocked.

"Come in," snarled a voice. Strange how mean and threatening those simple words could be!

The orderly opened the door and the recruits filed in. Cadet officers, almost as young as the candidates, sat at a table. They glared at the "animals" — the newcomers.

"Take off those hats; stand at attention," one of the seated figures barked. The recruits understood only the first of the two commands, and removed their hats. Custer must have become red-faced under his yellow curls as he suppressed a laugh at his own awkward attempt to stand stiffly erect.

"Let's see your papers," said another surly voice.

Each appointee now handed over the paper he had brought from the adjutant. The boy officer in charge wrote the number of a room opposite each name. Then the guide led the new boys upstairs to the fourth floor and down a long hall. Stopping in front of a door, he flung it open and called the names of Custer and Parker. The two boys toted in their bags. The guide pointed to two blue sheets of printed instructions on the wall over the fireplace.*

"Rules," he said. "Learn 'em." Then he stalked from the room. Custer must have gasped with amused relief, as he turned to his roommate.

"My name's George Armstrong Custer, from New Rumley, Ohio."

"Mine's Pahkah, Jim Pahkah, from Missouri. Glad to meet you-all. The family's from Kaintuckey, suh." Jim Parker was a rough-and-ready fellow, heavy-bodied for his age. His handclasp gripped like a vise.

"Missouri's near Kansas," Custer may have rejoined as he looked at his new roommate's serious face, noting that the grim wrinkles between his eyes melted away when he smiled. "Troublesome Republicans seem to be giving you fellows plenty hell out there. Think it'll bring on a war?"

The two boys had much in common. Armstrong's father came from Maryland and his forebears on the distaff side were Virginians. Southern traditions dominated both lads. Together they explored their room. Each had an iron bed, flat-topped desk, a washstand with pitcher, basin, and slop jar. One mirror hung over the fireplace, and there were two Windsor chairs.[2]

Formal examinations for admission to the Academy would be held in less than a month. Until then, newcomers must wear civilian clothes: the straw hats with ribbons, the stovepipe beavers, and the cowhide boots, oxfords, or pumps which they had worn from home. In the

---

* The above is recreated from the experience related by Morris Schaff, who entered West Point in 1858. Presumably conditions had changed little.

mess hall, Custer was assigned a seat beside LeRoy Elbert, a lad two years his senior.* Elbert had a prim, old-maidish expression with a disapproving scowl between his solemn eyes. He was called "Deacon" by his comrades. Custer's seatmate on the right was Morris Schaff, a little, bright-eyed chap destined for a distinguished career both as soldier and writer. While Custer appraised his seatmates, Morris Schaff formed a conclusion of his own about Custer: he liked him but thought he showed less soldier promise than any boy in school.

In size Custer was average in height, a little below average in weight. His body was lithe, his actions quick, eyes turning from side to side above a long, pointed nose. He enjoyed athletic stunts, like twisting his legs behind his head or bounding to his feet from a prone position. Easygoing and friendly, he got in no fights of record at the Academy, although plenty of cadet fights failed to get in the conduct books. However, Custer seems to have been more intent on making his companions laugh than on watching for affronts which must be settled with his fists. The first day in chapel a boy with fiery red hair sat in the pew ahead of him. Custer put his fingers in the hair, then, making a bellows of his cheeks, blew the glowing locks. Next, while the sermon droned monotonously along and the boys beside him suppressed their laughter, Custer withdrew his fingers, presumably sputtering hot, and began pounding them on an imaginary anvil.[3] He never worried about dignified conduct, even during the critical days of trial before formal admission to the Academy.

Second-year men were supposed to coach the candidates for entrance examinations. Often they made a mockery of this instruction, misleading instead of helping newcomers.[4] Indeed, John M. Schofield had been expelled from the Academy for such "breach of trust." He had been reinstated by what seemed to be political influence and now held a minor post on the faculty.

Upperclassmen also taught the candidates to drill, showed them how to stand at attention when spoken to — head up, chest (not stomach)

* The records are incomplete, but they show that Custer was assigned a seat beside Elbert in 1860.

out, little finger opposite the seams of the trousers with the palms awkwardly to the front. . . . "Wipe that smile off your face. Yes, you with the curly hair." . . .

The candidates marched in formation to meals and to classes. Every boy in each file was instructed to point his toes as he took each step, and at the same time to keep his eyes fixed on the collar of the boy ahead of him. An upperclassman shouted, "Hep—hep!" And if any boy trod on the heels of the fellow ahead, the sergeant halted the squad. A corporal pointed out the erring lad and shouted, "What's your name, Animal? Did you say Fanny? I thought so, Fanny!"

Custer's curly blond hair won him the name of "Fanny." He said later that he tried to become less conspicuous by clipping his hair. Slick as a peeled onion, he became more conspicuous than before, so he bought a toupee. By this time all the squad was watching to see what funny prank "that Custer fella" would do next.

Entrance examinations began on June 20, 1857. The ordeal lasted several days, because each candidate was examined individually. The prospect was a grim one: half the boys would fail. Every morning the nervous applicants watched the Examining Board walk from their residences to Academic Hall. The weather was sweltering hot, but Custer noticed that the professors all wore their blue dress uniforms and fringed epaulets. The most important man on the faculty — and the most feared — was Albert E. Church, LL.D., head of the Mathematics Department. Cadets said with awe that Church, as a student at the Academy, had roomed with Jefferson Davis. The professor was a small, stocky man with side and chin whiskers showing below his gold-laced marshal's hat. He walked with his head down as though watching the ground, his hands clasped under the tails of his brass-buttoned coat. "But don't think for a moment he doesn't see all that goes on," a cadet warned. "You'll find out."

Also in the Mathematics Department was First Lieutenant O. O. Howard, a kindly, considerate young man who was quite religious. "Be sure to attend his prayer meetings — especially before exams," another cadet said.[5]

All day long, Custer and his fellows waylaid the candidates who had gone through the inquisition ahead of them. Some reported the experience an easy one; others said not. Armstrong's turn came at last. He walked down to Academic Hall and into the examining room. Before him in a semicircle behind little desks, he saw the Examining Board, brilliant in blue and gold. He shambled in his habitually slouchy manner to the hub of the crescent, where candidates stood to be examined. His gangling, somewhat stooped, immature figure and ill-fitting country clothes seemed hopelessly unmilitary. Members of the board did not look up from the papers at their desks. Custer recognized the top of Superintendent Delafield's curly pate, his sandy protruding eyebrows, his big nose, like a ship's keel below his bowed head. Who would believe that old touslehead to be from a wealthy New York family? To the superintendent's right and left, the bald craniums of his staff shone between hunched epaulets. Custer looked along the line: two dozen at least. There was Church, head of "math." On the other side of the superintendent sat Chaplain John W. French, professor of geography, history and ethics; over yonder, Patrice de Janon, professor of Spanish and sword instruction.

On the horns of the crescent of little desks Custer noticed the assistant professors. These small fry were the ones who sometimes asked the hardest questions. Beside Lieutenant Howard's kindly face, he saw John Gibbon's thin sharp features. His bronzed cheeks under a white forehead gave him an outdoorsman's look, very different from the plump, pouting countenance of John M. Schofield. Beyond them, solemn as only young officers can be, sat Lieutenants Stephen Vincent Benét and John T. Grebel.

Professor Church began the inquisition. He never looked a candidate in the eye. Instead he turned his broad placid face to one side and spoke in a detached, complaining voice. A candidate who faltered saw the semicircle of heads rise. Dozens of eyes focused on Custer.[6] Some watched him sharply through little eyeglasses as through the peep sights of a gun. Others peered over their lenses.

George A. Custer, more widely-traveled than many boys, stood the test; but of the 108 examined, only 68 passed. On July 1, 1857, they were accredited for a six months' trial — two in camp and four in the classroom — before being formally recognized as cadets. Then, in the new five-year course initiated by Jefferson Davis, the survivors might hope to graduate in 1862. Long before that, they thought, the war which politicians now were talking so much about would probably be forgotten.

For this period of probation, the government paid Custer $30.00 a month. Out of this he must buy his uniform, bedding, books and paper. Shoes cost him $2.88 per pair, his blue-gray, swallowtail dress coat, $11.25.[7] White cross-straps from shoulder to belt made his youthful shoulders appear broader. Tight-fitting white pantaloons added apparent length to his already long legs. The heavy, short-visored shako ($3.52), with its pompon in front, made him hold his back as straight as a poker if he wanted to see anything. Even this cast-iron costume failed to give him a military appearance. Always there was something slouchy, limber, and laughing about this Ohio boy. He said later that he dared not sit in a chair to study lest he rumple his freshly-pressed white pantaloons. To save them he lay on the floor or bed.[8] It did no good. His clothes always looked untidy.

With the first hurdle behind him, careless Custer began to know his classmates. Among them were William W. Dunlap from Kentucky, John ("Gimlet") Lea from Mississippi, and George O. Watts, a sturdy fellow like Jim Parker, upright, hard as a rock and always ready for a lark. Then there was Patrick O'Rourke. He looked Irish and spoke the brogue. Older than most of the boys, he had performed well in his examinations. A solemn chap was named Alonzo H. Cushing. His dark, straight, greasy hair hung over his ears like a weeping willow. His nose was long and his full lips pouted above a weak chin. He was as smart as any of the boys, but something stubbornly tenacious in his character made him dull company. Undoubtedly, he would break his heart rather than flunk the ordeal ahead.

In July, all the cadets were ordered out of barracks into summer camp on the Plain — within half a mile of their rooms but much cooler nevertheless. Here Custer first learned how to pitch camp. Bundled tents were rolled out of wagons driven across the greensward. Cadets, under the direction of noncoms, smoothed out the canvas. Then, at the tap of a drum, the four corner stakes of each tent were driven. At the next drum tap ridgepoles were thrust under the outstretched tents. With another tap the front pole was inserted and the field became an anthill of white pyramids. A final drumbeat signaled the insertion of the rear pole. The tents were all up now. Intermediate guy lines required but a few moments to stake. A canvas city with eight streets, officers' quarters at one end, guard tents at the other, stood gleaming white on the green Plain.

Military life began in earnest here, and boys unsuited for it would be dropped. A gruff sergeant told every "animal" — or "plebe," the lowest order of humanity in Rome — to remember, "No soldier ever opens his mouth except to bite a cartridge." At dawn the morning gun convulsed the tent city. Cadets ran to roll call. They were drummed to breakfast, drummed to sick call, drummed to "assembly."

The drums — like all music — set Custer's pulse to beating. The cumulative alarm of the "long roll" always keyed him to ecstasy.

Drums also called cadets to drill, twice a day. The commandant, William J. Hardee, had written a drill manual and he insisted on perfection. His commands, shouted in a broad Southern accent, rang above the staccato throb of the drums.[9]

After supper, the cadets were drummed to quarters. Drums even tapped them to sleep — or were supposed to. But not candidate Custer. The six months' probation before he could be accepted in the Academy did not deter him from making careful plans for carefree evenings with equally adventurous companions. On the night selected they would all steal away after "lights out." The favorite rendezvous was Benny Havens's at Buttermilk Falls, a mile below the post. Benny

Havens had been expelled from the reservation for selling hot rum flips instead of coffee and ginger cakes to cadets. His tavern, now out of bounds, had become an institution. He liked to tell how Jefferson Davis, as a cadet, had almost been killed when he fell over a cliff while escaping from a raid.[10]

Custer admitted later that he spent more time at Benny Havens's than he should have, but he enjoyed conviviality and never could resist the charm of music. After a hot day's drill it was good to sit, glass in hand, on Benny's stoop. A night breeze always blew in from the lisping Hudson.

Some upperclassman would begin:

> *Come fellows, fill your glasses and —*

Boys seated along the dark veranda would follow with:

> *Stand up in a row.*
> *For sentimental drinking, we're going for to go.*
> *In the army there's sobriety, promotion's very slow.*
> *So we'll cheer our hearts with choruses at*
> *Benny Havens', oh!*

Dozens of other stanzas were sung to this melody, and Custer had not learned them all by the time camp broke up in August. Back in barracks, he and Jim Parker were assigned to a tower room in the 8th Division. From their window they looked north, across the Plain, to Pollopell's Island at the head of the Narrows. The bare rock faces on both sides of the gorge appeared as red as dried blood on the hides Custer had seen in the Cadiz tannery. Maybe neglected battle wounds would look like that! On clear evenings, as the sun set, a shadow crept up the eastern wall, erasing the suggestive colors.

The first frosty nights set the forest trees ablaze with autumn brilliance. Gloomy cedars on the ridges painted zebra stripes on the dazzling foliage — russet, yellow, or red-gold like Autie's hair. The smell of burning leaves was in the air, and supply sergeants issued winter uniforms. White drill pantaloons were replaced by blue woolen trousers with black velvet stripes down the outer seams. Serious schoolwork began now — the four months' test of academic ability. Armstrong wrote home, exulting in the mental hardships. Think of courses in mathematics, spherical astronomy, chemistry, drawing, geography, geology, French, Spanish, civil and military engineering, philosophy, ethics, and more mathematics [11] — all difficult subjects, and Armstrong ill prepared! Of course he would not have to master all these subjects at once, but letters home about them — especially about spherical astronomy — made interesting reading, he hoped.

Hazing was no longer intense now that they had moved back in barracks. Custer became acquainted with some upperclassmen: Alexander C. McW. Pennington from New Jersey; Horace Porter, the Pennsylvanian with a boyish pout on his face; from Illinois, handsome, upright Wesley Merritt; dark-eyed Stephen D. Ramseur, the North Carolinian who scowled in public as though imitating John C. Calhoun. Armstrong's closest friend, next to Jim Parker, was Thomas Jefferson Rosser, a tall, handsome, brown-eyed Texan who roomed next door with Virginia's blond and beaming John Pelham. Rosser was swarthy as a mulatto. His Southern drawl seemed full of humor. His bob-tailed coat and turned-down white collar looked too youthful for such a mannish frame.[12] He was twenty-one, and seventeen-year-old Custer watched him with admiring eyes, precisely as his own brother, Tom, watched Armstrong.

Students were organized into sections according to the quality of their work. New England boys made the best grades. Perhaps their schools prepared them better. Western and Southern boys found themselves in the lower sections. Two thirds of Custer's section mates — his best friends — came from slaveholding states, but Custer's classmates were not all Southerners. In mathematics he was placed with Alonzo Cushing of the weeping-willow hair. Alonzo was an odd chap. That pouting upper lip, which made his jaw appear weak, may have been stretched out consciously to hide his buck teeth. He was an inveterate reader, bookworm of the class.

In addition to grades, the cadets were rated by a system of demerits, black marks for being late to class, late to drill, failing to recognize drum calls, failing to salute an officer, wearing an untidy uniform or unblacked boots. One hundred demerits in six months automatically expelled a cadet. Custer acquired one hundred and twenty-nine during his first half year, but, fortunately for the history of the United States cavalry, the rule for demerits was changed on August 14, 1857. By the new definition he was charged with only sixty-nine, so the laughing cadet remained at the Academy.

If Custer proved weak in academic grades and in deportment, he showed unusual leadership in punishable pranks. Food at the Academy was notoriously bad and Custer became adept at providing midnight feasts. He even kept a stewpan hidden up the chimney in his room. From his tower window he could look down on the roofs and back yards of the officers' residences, which stood at a right angle along the west edge of the Plain. Several of the officers kept chickens, and the night-long crowing of a conspicuous buff rooster disturbed some cadets. Instead of annoying Custer, the gallant fowl made his mouth water. After taps one night he slipped downstairs, stealthily crossed the Area, and darted out the "sally port" into the shadows cast by the bare elms along the parade. Watching constantly for sentries, he made his way across the fallen leaves, sly as an Indian. At the first officer's house he slunk into the back yard and snatched Mr. Chanticleer from his roost.

Late that night, Custer and his cronies boiled the fowl in their fireplace, and devoured the delicacy. Then one of them was delegated to wrap the feathers in newspaper and dispose of them while his companions tiptoed to their rooms.

At reveille, cadets bounding downstairs for roll call saw a trail of buff feathers on the steps and across the Area to the trash heap.[13] The conversation at breakfast, for once, omitted complaints about the food, outrages in Kansas, and President Pierce's latest blunder. Fortunately for Custer the authorities could not backtrack the feathers to his room. Suppressed laughter over Custer's prank was followed by eager plans for the first Academy hop. Custer loved to dance and dancing was part of the training of an officer and a gentleman. The dancing instructor was Edward Ferrero, an Italian. His lessons were important, for West Point hops were social affairs of distinction. The military band was famous, even in New York.[14] Armstrong sent a formal engraved invitation to Mary Holland, but it is doubtful if he expected her to accept. At this ball he mingled for the first time in his life with the socially elect. His uniform erased all stigma which a blacksmith father might have given him in Cadiz or Monroe. These girls took a cadet at his face value, and Custer's dancing blue eyes and golden curls were conspicuous in any group.

The sight of a girl dressed in crinoline for the ball was sure to set George Armstrong Custer's heart pounding. His classmates have recorded how the rustle of starched dresses as the girls swept into the ballroom was the most exciting event at West Point, and Custer did not differ from the rest. Most tantalizing of all was Flirtation Walk, in the woods below the Plain. From a tinkling spring in a dell called Kosciusko's Garden, the famous path led under great trees to what was known as "the danger point."[15] A cadet soon learned that it was romantic to snip a "bullet button" from his dress coat and present it to his lady fair. Next day it was harder than usual to study, or even drill, in spite of the fact that the coming examinations might end a candidate's military career. The throb of the music still pulsed in a fellow's blood, and he could not forget a certain little hug from sleeveless arms during "The West Point Dream Waltz" — a gallant melody dedicated by the composer to "Mrs. General Scott."

A cadet was sometimes disconcerted, later, to see the girl of his dreams wearing an entire bracelet of bullet buttons; but every young gentleman could, and must, on all occasions say that the worst woman was better than the best of men. This was the code.

Snow came early in the fall of 1857, and the ground was covered by Thanksgiving. Cadets stamped the white flakes from their varnished boots as they came in after roll call. Only a little more than a month remained before final examinations in January — the first big screening. Not until plebes passed those were they given cadet warrants. Thus the first Christmas was a season of anxiety, with the hopefuls dragging themselves unwillingly to their rooms for study. Custer had as much to worry about as any of them. He said later that he was deeply concerned, though none of his schoolmates detected it. To them he seemed as carefree as could be.

Early in January a grim notice appeared on the bulletin board. It warned all plebes "not proficient" in the coming examinations to settle their accounts and prepare to go home.[16]

There was finality — and despair — in those few words.

3 West Point

ON FEBRUARY 6, 1858, ARMSTRONG CUSTER AND THE OTHER PLEBES WHO had passed their examinations marched, blue overcoats swinging, along the trail opened by a snowplow from barracks to chapel. Inside the little Ionic temple they stood before the altar, took oaths of allegiance to the United States, and each received his cadet warrant.

Custer was a plebe no longer! Moreover, he had been appointed "squad marcher" — not much of a job with snow on the ground, and he soon lost it for failing to take his rank seriously. In short, he still liked to make other boys laugh.

By March, the snow melted. Although the Plain was still soggy, outdoor drilling had now begun — infantry, cavalry, and artillery. Armstrong enjoyed watching the mortar batteries fire. He wrote a friend describing how a shell could be seen from the time it left the piece until it reached the target. "And when we drill at night," he continued, "firing red-hot shot, the sight is magnificent." After the explosion an echo answered from Storm King and the Crow Nest. Most exciting of all was practice with flying artillery. Like most boys writing home, Custer enjoyed describing the dangers of his new life. Galloping artillery horses often became unmanageable, he wrote, and caissons upset, spilling the gunners, "one or more cadets being seriously hurt and not infrequently killed." [1] (An inaccuracy! No one was killed at this exercise while Custer was at the Point.)

Custer, as a full-fledged cadet in the spring of 1858, drew his first book from the library. Perhaps he was stimulated by the example of the class's outstanding student, Patrick O'Rourke, who seemed to delight in Dickens, Cooper, and William Gilmore Simms. The other bookworm in the class, Al Cushing, studied naval history when not engrossed in the Waverley novels. His brother, Will Cushing, was down at Annapolis. Custer's best friend, Texan Tom Rosser, read Prescott's *Philip II* and no other library book for months. Custer tried John Pendleton Kennedy's *Swallow Barn,* and from its pages learned his first lesson about the South — a friendly, hospitable South of overgrown Virginia plantations with swamps and sandy roads. The slavery described by Kennedy was a kindly institution, the Negroes all gross, comical fellows, old house servants often bossing their masters. The book's hero, Ned Hazard, was always followed by a pack of hounds. He had a natty way of popping his riding whip against his boot. At Princeton, Ned had trouble with his studies. He liked to slip away for buckwheat cakes and juleps at Mother Priestley's (not Benny Havens's). In short, Ned Hazard was a model for the future Custer, even to being popular with girls. After *Swallow Barn,* Custer read Cooper's Leatherstocking Tales, learning about the Deerslayer and the Last of the Mohicans and men in fringed buckskin shirts who fought Indians.

The parade ground became greener under the sunshine and showers of April. Leaf buds unrolled on the trees. In May the tulip trees and honey locusts blossomed. Cadets felt the first touches of spring fever.

A few always climbed out on barracks roofs to sleep in the sun — sweet but dangerous relaxation, for examinations were due in June. To audit them and report on the instructors as well as the students, a special board came up from Washington. At this time, too, a new crop of animals arrived.

Examinations or no examinations, Custer must have his fun. Let the most important things in life come first! It was his turn now to stand on the hotel veranda and watch the newcomers. An animal from Indiana, one Jasper Myers, came wearing a full, albeit silky, beard. Custer, with mock courtesy, told him that he should go home and send his son. There must be some mistake in the appointment.

An animal from Maine also attracted Cadet Custer. The fellow's face appeared serious and timid. He carried a gigantic double-cased silver watch. Custer and his fellow tormentors asked continually to see the timepiece. On all occasions they insisted that he take out his key and wind the ponderous machine. They made him check the watch's time against the sundial and warned him that in case his watch did not keep sun time, he would be reported to the authorities as possessing a watch which reflected discredit on officers of the United States Army.

A favorite accomplice of Custer's for hazing pranks was the Kentuckian George Owen Watts. One night George went with him to call on two newcomers. Impersonating officers, they ordered the animals to get up and perform some useless fatigue duty. Tricks like this were common practice. Once an officer had returned to his quarters and found two animals moving everything out of it. They claimed to be acting under orders, but they could not identify the upperclassmen who had set them to work.

Two plebes, Kenelm Robbins and Reuben Higgason, determined to turn the joke on Custer and his kind if they came to disturb their sleep — a boast which New Rumley boys had found futile. The plebes fixed a washbasin on a chair in such a way that opening the door would upset the contraption. Custer and Watts walked into the trap. They were both surprised by the crash of tinware, but not dismayed. Custer said later that he was sure the noise would bring an officer, but no one came, so he and Watts strode into the dark room pretending to be officers, themselves.

"Who lives in here?" Watts bellowed as he entered.

A meek voice replied in a Massachusetts twang, "Kenelm Robbins." Another meek voice in the other bed said in a blurred Mississippi drawl, "Reuben Higgason."

"Mr. Robb*ins*," Watts repeated. He put authority and scorn in the last syllable. "Good God! Mr. Robb*ins,* come out of this!" He grabbed Robbins by the ankle, dragged him to the floor, out the door and along the hall. Behind him Custer hauled Higgason. At the head of the stairs both hazers dropped the men and bounded down out of sight, hurrying to their own rooms while the confused candidates picked themselves up and returned to their disheveled beds.[2]

In June, just before going to summer camp, Custer learned that he had passed his latest examinations. Eight other boys in his class were dropped. Of the 60 who remained Custer stood among the lowest 10. In all probability 20 or 30 more might flunk out before graduation, but Custer's spirits were high. From camp he wrote his sister exultantly, never hinting how low his grades had been. "I would not leave this place for any amount of money," he said, "because I would rather have a good education and no money than have a fortune and be ignorant."[3]

Lydia Reed wrote back announcing the birth of his first nephew. Her older children had been girls. She named the baby Henry Armstrong Reed and called him "Autie," she said.[4] Almost a year would elapse before Armstrong could hope for a furlough to see his namesake, but he began to make plans. In addition to seeing the baby, was he still thinking about marrying Mary Holland? Who can say? But he did send her a formal invitation to the 1858 West Point ball.

During the fall of 1858, Custer's second year, he was assigned a new roommate, Lafayette Lane, son of the Democratic territorial delegate to Congress — a Southern sympathizer from Oregon. This year Custer began his first mounted drill. Mastering academic equitation came easily to him, even riding bareback or with stirrups crossed on as rough a mount as Old Wellington. Custer could not remember when he did not ride. His father had sat him on a horse before his fat little legs could circle the animal. At West Point he soon demonstrated how to jump a three-foot hurdle and slash with his saber at a leather head stuffed with tanbark. Tradition says that he made the highest jump at West Point, excepting only U. S. Grant's on York. Perhaps! But in the study of cavalry tactics Custer received poor grades. On practice marches he distinguished himself only for originality. When riding at the rear of the column he had a habit of dropping out if a tavern was passed, then catching up before dismissal.[5]

Custer also received poor grades in English, although he always liked to write. He deemed one of his West Point essays sufficiently merito-rious to send home. It was entitled — of all subjects — "The Red Man," for whom he expressed great sympathy.[6]

On November 28, 1858, Custer drew his last book from the West Point library. This time he sampled William Gilmore Simms. In the pages of *Eutaw,* Custer read again about Southern life. Simms de-scribed the dismal swamps, croaking frogs, the whippoorwill's mourn-ful call. The slaves in his story, like those in Kennedy's, were happy folk, respected in their place. *Eutaw* was more dramatic than *Swallow Barn* — more fighting, more waving of sabers, heroes shouting defiance before superior numbers, men of courage dashing in recklessly and al-ways winning. Custer must have enjoyed this book, because he re-newed it a week later.

Custer's longed-for midterm furlough was granted in the summer of 1859, but it came very near being a discharge. He had received 98 and 94 demerits respectively in the two previous six-month periods.[7] The temptation to talk in ranks, play forbidden games of cards, or throw snowballs at a passing column was still more than he could resist. Moreover, discovery of the cooking utensils hidden in his chimney had cost him dearly.

The details of his trip home are obscure except that he wore civilian

clothes in preference to his cadet uniform. Possibly he had not completely given up Mary Holland and the prospect of a legal career. He
seems to have gone first to Scio, Ohio, where his parents resided.
Brother Tom was a big boy now, full of pranks and laughter. Tom
liked music, was always humming a tune or thrumming a jew's-harp
the way Armstrong used to do. Autie went next to see his "second
mother," Lydia Reed, in Monroe, Michigan. Little Autie was learning
to walk.

On August 28, 1859, Custer returned to West Point. Cadet James
Barroll Washington, a great-great-grandnephew of George Washington, entered that year. He remembered hearing the crowd shout, "Here
comes Custer!" The name meant nothing to him, but he turned, and
saw a slim, immature lad with unmilitary figure, slightly rounded
shoulders, and gangling walk.

Custer checked in at the adjutant's office, went to his room, and
emerged in uniform. He was glad to be back. The Plain, the barracks,
the drums all seemed good to him. Nothing had changed except the
flag. It carried two more stars — added for the admission of Minnesota
and Oregon, his old roommate "Lafe" Lane's state.

Hearing the explosive laughter of a bright-eyed plebe in the Area,
Custer asked the boy his name.

"Peter Michie, from Ohio, sir," the plebe replied in a Scotch brogue.

"Fellows," Custer shouted, slapping him on the back, "come here and
hear my fellow Buckeye laugh." [8]

Custer had changed little during his furlough, but his companions
called him "Cinnamon" now, from the spice in his favorite hair oil. His
affair with Mary Holland seems to have ended, although the scar may
not have healed. Certainly he had dropped his plan to study law. He
wanted to be a soldier now. But he still enjoyed exchanging sentimental poems with friends, male and female. In letters home the
messages he sent his little nieces were suitable for young ladies. No
wonder Emma and Maria, or "Riley" as the family called her, idolized
him! Custer also urged his parents to move to Monroe. His sister

Margaret would soon grow up, Autie said, and she could get a better education there.

Finances worried him for a time after his return. Some of his old friends had quit school and were now making big wages and profits. Their success disturbed him, and he wrote Lydia that he wished his schooling were completed so that he could help his parents. He feared they were working too hard. His mother seemed especially delicate. He was glad to hear, in May, 1860, that they had moved to Wood County, Ohio, near Tontogany, where his half-brother David lived, only forty miles below Monroe. Custers must always keep close together!

In all his letters Armstrong asked repeatedly for the latest developments at home. Was little "Aut" growing? Could he whip Emma? Then, lest he incite the tot, he added: "Tell him he must not fight his sister." Armstrong also asked his father to sign a permit which would allow him to buy tobacco. Emanuel refused. Custer complained in his next letter: he did not smoke or chew himself, he said, and only wanted the permit to buy tobacco for friends who in turn might help him.[9]

In January, 1860, Custer suffered from a corn — probably infected — and was hospitalized for a day. The weather outside was cold and snowy. He left the infirmary without permission and was arrested for violation of orders. Yes, three years at the Point had failed to discipline him. A fellow student remembered that Armstrong once stood unabashed before his professor and admitted that his lesson was unprepared. To talk so frankly before a class which usually tried to cover lack of preparation by bluff and bumble caused great glee. The boys admired Custer's daring. Once, in Spanish class, he asked the instructor (Patrice de Janon?) how a Spaniard would say: "Class is dismissed." The teacher complied and Custer led his mates out of the room.[10]

It was hard to dislike such a boy, but the professors kept disapproving eyes on him always. Whenever the adjutant appeared in the Area, Custer slipped away, feeling sure that the officer had come to arrest him for some offense. Custer himself said later that he spent sixty-six of his Saturdays marching post to pay for transgressions.[11] When he wrote to family and friends he told them about his hardships — walking post in full equipment, back and forth, turning every thirty yards, without speaking to anyone for four hours. He did not say that this extra marching was inflicted on him as punishment, and after describing the discomforts in detail he frequently ended: "Everything is fine. It's just the way I like it."

In April, 1860, the cadets received exciting news — especially important to Custer. A bill had been introduced in Congress to reduce their school term from five to four years. Threats of war were getting uglier. Young officers might be needed. Under the new plan Custer would have only one more year at the Point. Would the authorities crowd more work on the students and flunk out more of them or would the requirements be less rigorous? Of the 57 who had passed in 1859 only 35 remained now. Whose turn was it to go next?

Isolated as the cadets were, they watched the political pot bubble in the outside world. Every steamboat brought letters from home with news and opinions. Cadets discussed the proposed presidential nominations to be made in conventions this spring of 1860. Custer was as outspoken as his father against Republicans. He said he expected to see Seward nominated in Chicago, come May; and if so, that old Whig would be defeated along with other instigators of John Brown raids and circulators of Hinton Helper's book.

Obviously Custer was repeating the political clichés of his Southern friends and not thinking deeply. The Republican Party, from Lincoln down, had repudiated Brown's raid. The Helper book showed slavery to be uneconomical and the cause of Southern backwardness. To object to its publication repudiated the country's traditional freedom of the press. Armstrong's dislike of John Brown must have been intensified when he learned that Brown had captured the father of his friend, James Washington, at Harper's Ferry, and might well have killed him.[12]

The crucial conventions, both Republican and Democratic, met while the cadets were preparing for examinations. Custer repeatedly neglected his studies to argue politics. After taps, when all lights should be out, he would stealthily light his gas jet or a candle and sit late into the night writing letters to family and friends — another Custer characteristic which would grow with the years. In an eight-page letter to a boyhood companion, dated May 5, 1860, he told about the joys of West Point life, the good music, the dancing, the thrill of impressive reviews. But before ending he concluded: "I will change the subject by saying a few words on politics." Those "few words" occupied two and a half sheets of closely written paper, excoriating the "Black-Brown-Republicans," who "will either deprive a portion of our fellow citizens of their just rights or produce a dissolution of the Union." Southerners, he wrote, have had insult after insult heaped upon them until "they determine no longer to submit to such aggression." Custer said that he opposed Stephen A. Douglas for the nomination and hoped that the Democrats would choose Daniel Stevens Dickinson of New York, Joseph Lane of Oregon, or Robert M. T. Hunter of Virginia — all conservative supporters of slavery. Certainly the writer of these sentiments could not be expected to fight his Southern friends.

Lincoln's nomination on May 18, 1860, distressed Custer, because the Democratic Party, in its conventions, had split hopelessly on the question of slavery and the Republicans seemed sure to win the next election. This political quarrel had reached a toppling height of bitterness as Custer marched to chapel for Commencement exercises. Boys two years ahead of him — Horace Porter, Stephen D. Ramseur, Alex Pennington, Wesley Merritt, and others — were graduated.

Preparations for summer camp began at once. As the cadets moved out of barracks and spread their blankets under dazzling white canvas on the green Plain, they continued to discuss politics. Custer still favored the proslavery Democrats, felt certain that Lincoln's election meant war, and war meant death for many of his friends, high promotion for a few. Rumor, gossip, speculation buzzed about the camp. Custer received no demerits for three whole months. Perhaps uncertainty and excitement diverted his busy brain from pranks. Perhaps ambition made him toe the mark. Armstrong always worked hard when he saw a goal but never merely to discipline himself.

During this period of growing tension, Commandant Hardee went South on leave. Cadets whispered that he was seeking higher rank in the new army to be formed down there. His place was filled by John F. Reynolds, a bronzed veteran of the Mexican War. Lieutenant John T. Grebel, a known sympathizer with the North, also asked to be transferred back to his company on the line. In case of war, he wanted active service. Grebel was a dramatic fellow. In addition to teaching geography and history, he taught a class in public speaking and coached shrill-voiced Judson Kilpatrick in elocution and dramatics for the Academy's Dialectic Society.[13] "Little Kil," who had one more year of study, would miss him.

The cadets were back in barracks in November as election day approached. Most of them had lined up politically with their native states. Custer's sympathies pulled him in two directions. Would allegiance to Ohio or to his best friends prove stronger? A Democratic victory seemed the only solution to his problem.

On election night he, with many friends, stayed awake long after "lights out," waiting for the final returns. By midnight they learned that Lincoln had won. Disgruntled "Southrons" hanged the Rail Splitter in effigy from one of the elms in front of the barracks. Northern boys cut it down before dawn.[14]

Old friendships strained now to the breaking point, and Custer was still undecided. What should he do? As letters arrived for cadets from south of the Potomac, they resigned and went home. Lafayette Lane left for the South, not for Oregon. Charles P. Ball of Alabama and Gimlet Lea of Mississippi resigned. Admiring fellow students carried Ball on their shoulders across the Plain toward the wharf. It was Saturday, and Custer was paying the usual penalty for his pranks by "walking extra." As the departing Southerners passed, Custer could see no officer watching him, so he halted, clicked his heels together, and presented arms.[15]

By Christmas, 1860, peace on earth seemed hopeless. The cadets crunched through the snow to attend services in the Academy chapel. The mural painting of Mars over the altar had a new meaning now for all of them.

Then, on January 7, 1861, Lieutenant Griffin was released from the teaching of tactics, so that he could organize the regular army dragoons who had been stationed at West Point into a light battery of four guns, to be drawn by horses from the Academy riding stables. No more play-soldiering for them! Three weeks later, Custer was awakened at 4 A.M. Slipping on an overcoat in his cold room, he went to the window and peered down. Through the bare tops of the elm trees he could see on the snowy road four cannon being hauled by six horses each — Lieutenant Griffin's artillery. It was following the route across the mountain to the Erie Railroad, twelve miles away. A train there would take it to Washington, where General Scott was preparing for Lincoln's inauguration.

Arguments between cadets about politics often ended now with blows. Little Kilpatrick, always quarrelsome although undersized, got into a fight with William W. Dunlap, Custer's Kentucky friend. The two boys began slugging outside the mess-hall door. As the cadets came to dinner, some walked dutifully by to their tables. Others hesitated, wavering between missing a fight and gaining extra demerits for being late to mess.[16] The fight promised to be good, the dinner bad. Southerners hated that little, sandy-headed "Kil," who was always making trouble. They hated him doubly when he used the oratorical lessons he had learned from Lieutenant Grebel to malign their Southern institutions. They had to admit, though, that the little scamp could act, as well as fight.

On Washington's Birthday a holiday was declared. Cadets were free until tattoo, when they must all be in quarters. The evening was warm for February, with lowering clouds. Darkness fell early. Far out across the Plain, where the morning gun was always fired, Custer heard music — the Academy band. He opened a window into the Area and listened. He noticed other windows being raised. Black figures stood silhouetted against the oblongs of yellow light. There was Tom Rosser. Custer would know that gigantic body anywhere. He still liked him, but twenty-one-year-old Armstrong no longer followed his older friend as he had at seventeen. In other windows Custer recognized other Southern friends — good fellows all!

The music became steadily louder and louder. The band was marching toward the barracks. As it approached the elms out front, its tune changed: "The Star-Spangled Banner." Suddenly the music hushed. The band had swung into the "sally port," and the inspiring notes became very soft. Then, as the marchers emerged from the granite arch, it burst out, swelling up through the Area.

Armstrong, at his window, cheered — the shrill cavalry yell, soon to become famous. Such a display was against regulations, but boys at other windows took up the cry, shouting with him. This was Custer at his best, a leader always.

The band halted, then played "Dixie." Now Rosser led the Southerners at their windows, with a rebel yell, the Texas cowboy shout.

From opposite windows these best of friends' cheers vied with each other [17] — a dramatic incident during which Custer's indecision may have ended. Henceforth, he always lined up loyally with the North. He said, at this time and later, that he felt bound by his West Point oath to uphold the government which had educated him. His Southern friends, equally sincere, justified themselves in breaking that same oath. With blunt courage Custer dared tell them all that this was treason. Yet he did so with the same good nature which his Beech Point students had admired.

The study routine continued, regardless of impending war. Between classes the cadets met in the Area to smoke and discuss the latest rumors. Custer recalled later that at mess one day a Georgia cadet, Pierce Manning Butler Young, said to him: "We're going to have war. It's no use talking; I see it coming. All the Crittenden compromises that can be patched up won't avert it. Now let me prophesy what will happen to you and me. You will go home, and your abolition Governor will probably make you a colonel of a cavalry regiment. I will go down to Georgia and ask Governor Brown to give me a cavalry regiment. And who knows but we may move against each other during the war?" [18]

Newspapers delivered at West Point on March 5, 1861, announced that Lincoln had been inaugurated without violence. Old General Scott had seen to that! But there was no easing of tension. Custer was walking from class toward the Area with "Deacon" Elbert when he heard that Cadet Schaff had been bullied by a Southerner for daring to defend Ohio's Senator Benjamin F. Wade. The bully, bigger than Morris Schaff, had clenched his fist to hit him. A call to class saved Schaff from the blow, but not from a threat that he would get it when next they met. Custer did not like Ben Wade, though he knew him only as a blustering Buckeye who had once brought a squirrel rifle to his Senate desk to insure attention. But today, as Armstrong and Elbert walked toward the Area, they decided that no Southron could insult their Senator or punish a Buckeye cadet for praising him. They overtook Schaff coming from class and Custer slapped him on the shoulder. "If he lays a hand on you, Morris," Custer said, "we'll maul the earth with him." [19]

This, according to the record, was as close as Custer ever came to having a fight at West Point. It also shows how completely he had changed his attitude toward the South. Loyalty to his state and to the North was Custer's controlling allegiance now. On April 10, 1861, he wrote his sister, "In case of war, I shall serve my country according to the oath I took here." He closed the letter by saying that he expected war within a week. For once he was conservative. Only three days later, news of the firing on Fort Sumter reached the Academy. The cadets were in classes — all but Custer. At the end of each recitation, as the students headed for the Area, he met them with the news. These boys had been expecting war for months, but the realization that shooting had actually begun shocked most of them.

The next two weeks were feverish. Lincoln called for seventy-five thousand volunteers. Professors and instructors neglected their classes while they sought commands. Jovial Lieutenant Fitzhugh Lee, son of the Revolution's Light-Horse Harry Lee, and nephew of Colonel Robert E. Lee, resigned as assistant instructor of tactics to join the Confederacy. So, too, did Lieutenant Colonel Hardee, already on leave. Lieutenant Grebel, lucky to be down in Virginia with his company, could distinguish himself fighting for the Union in the first clash of arms. Also on the Federal side, Superintendent Delafield was planning more active service for himself. Even the dark-eyed dancing instructor, Edward Ferrero, had applied for a Northern command.

The class ahead of Custer would normally graduate in June, but now they were ordered to prepare for examinations on May 2. Kilpatrick delivered their valedictory address at Commencement. His beaming bride-to-be sat in the chapel watching him, and listened to his shrill nasal voice. Immediately after the services they were married; then impish "Little Kil," with a bride on his arm, set off for war. In Washington he hoped to get an assignment with Lieutenant Grebel at the front.

Custer's class was to be examined and graduated a month later. With his classmates he prepared the usual yearbook. Photographs of each member were pasted in. He sent a copy to his sister and asked her to keep it for him. He would write her as the war progressed, he said, and tell her more about these classmen and what became of them. Their adventures should be more real to her if she turned the pages to their pictures. Custer also helped select a class ring set with a flat oval stone of smoky blue. He wore it on the little finger of his sword hand. Inside was engraved: THRU TRIALS TO TRIUMPH.[21]

With final examinations scheduled for June, Custer worked as he had never worked before, but he usually wrote home before retiring. Long after "lights out," when other weary students were in bed, he would put away his books and hunch around a shaded candle as he penned a letter to his sister. He told Lydia that he was sleeping only four hours a night. He had already lost five pounds. At least 20 per cent of the class would probably flunk, and he did not intend to be among them. He closed this letter by saying that he might be killed in the war; but if so, "so be it." [22]

Custer was still studying desperately when news came of the war's opening battle, a fight at Big Bethel down in Virginia on May 10. Kilpatrick had got into action four days after leaving West Point, and he was now severely wounded. Lieutenant Grebel had been killed.

Final examination grades put Custer and Jim Parker at the foot of the class. "Deacon" Elbert's marks were almost as bad, except in deportment. Custer, on the other hand, had accumulated 97 demerits during his last half year — only three short of dismissal. Jim had 102, so he was dropped.

Graduation exercises were held on June 24, 1861, a week earlier than usual. When Custer stepped up in line for his diploma, Superintendent Delafield looked at him steadily for a moment, then handed him the document. Custer bowed very solemnly for once in his life. His comrades cheered.[23]

Six days later, the second class of '61 was on its way to Washington — all but Custer. He had got into trouble again. Under arrest, he smiled wanly as Patrick O'Rourke, Alonzo Cushing, Charles Parsons, George Watts, "Deacon" Elbert and his other friends — all officers now — marched away for great adventures. "Promotions or a coffin!" they worded it.

4 Bull Run

ARMSTRONG CUSTER, LANGUISHING UNDER ARREST, HEARD RUMORS ABOUT an impending battle in Virginia. Confederates were reported to be within a day's march of Washington. The opening — possibly the closing — battle of the war was sure to be fought any day now, and Custer's classmates down there would get all the first promotions, while he awaited court-martial. His crime seemed trivial to him. He had been serving as Officer of the Guard at the summer encampment. On the evening of June 29, 1861, two newly arrived candidates got in a fight over their respective places before a water faucet. Instead of stopping the fisticuffs, Custer had stopped intervention, saying, "Let there be a fair fight." He himself became so engrossed in the contest that he did not notice the circle of onlookers melting away; they had spied Lieutenant William B. Hazen, Officer of the Day, coming from the guard tent. Custer was placed under arrest and charges were preferred.

Lieutenant Stephen Vincent Benét presided at the trial as judge advocate general. Armstrong pleaded guilty. He said later that he never knew his sentence. He thought it was pigeonholed in Washington. Influential schoolmates, he said, interceded in his behalf, and the War Department, engulfed in battle preparations, telegraphed for him to report immediately in Washington. Custer embarked on the first down-river steamboat.

Perhaps it was unfortunate that Armstrong never knew the court-martial's decision. He was only reprimanded, and his sentence stated: "The Court is thus lenient in the sentence owing to the peculiar situation of Cadet Custer represented in his defense, and in consideration of his general good conduct as testified to by Lieutenant Hazen, his immediate commander." [1]

The records do not reveal "the peculiar situation of Cadet Custer," but had he known that Hazen was his friend at this time, future relations between the two officers might have been different. Hazen as he grew older became opinionated and fond of controversy. An able man, he was a dangerous enemy. He and Marcus Reno, who had entered the Academy together, would be Custer's marplots always.

Custer, at last on his way to Washington, stopped in New York only long enough to purchase his lieutenant's outfit at Horstmanns' — a sword, a Colt's side-hammer pocket pistol, and spurs, the three dearest possessions for a boy of that generation. For Lydia he had his picture taken — a hot, tired boy in a mussed uniform with wilted white collar.

Holding his new pistol in his left hand, he tried to look the big camera lens sternly in the eye.

This last gesture of family devotion completed, Armstrong boarded a night train for Washington. The coaches were packed with soldiers and civilians, all talking, boasting, drinking, scheming. Men in uniform looked at one another with a new curiosity. Privates had not yet learned to show respect for officers, and officers appeared embarrassed in the presence of enlisted men. At every station a crowd of matrons and girls stood under flickering torches offering trays of refreshments. Custer noticed that some emotional young ladies in their hoops and bonnets kissed uniformed boys whom they had obviously never seen before.

Early the next morning the cars rolled in under the domed train-shed at the capital, and Armstrong, alone in Washington for the first time, went to the Ebbit House where his former roommate, Jim Parker, was staying. Jim had failed to graduate, but he had been breveted a second lieutenant and resigned. Armstrong considered Jim his best friend and wanted him to reconsider his act. The desk clerk, sleepy from a night's vigil, offered to take Custer's card up to Parker's room and announce his arrival, but Armstrong strode up the stairs alone and knocked at Jim's door.

Parker, still in bed, was very unhappy. He had been offered a commission in the Confederate Army and had accepted it. Custer tried to dissuade him, but Jim was obdurate and did not weaken when reminded of his oath.* That could always be explained away. But not to Custer's satisfaction. For the rest of his life he would refer to it. He cared nothing about freeing the slaves or about the constitutional niceties of state sovereignty. Abstractions were foreign to his mind. He said later that the most meaningless subjects he studied at West Point were philosophy and ethics, but he had taken an oath and would live up to it.

---

* Custer, in his account, does not say that Jim had been dismissed from the Academy but the records show that he had more than the permissible number of demerits. Perhaps there is something in this incident that has not yet been unearthed.

After leaving Jim, Custer headed for the War Department to report to the adjutant general. On the street everyone was talking about the impending battle. Carriages filled with congressmen, gay ladies and lunch hampers jogged along the cobbled streets toward the Long Bridge which led to the settlement of Fairfax Court House in Virginia. There had been a skirmish out there two days ago, but nothing decisive. The real battle was to be fought tomorrow.

Custer found the adjutant general's office crowded. He waited until two in the afternoon before he had an opportunity to hand his papers to an officer. The man glanced over them, then looked up and, in an abrupt, military manner, said: "You have been assigned to Company G, 2d Cavalry. Major Innes Palmer, with General McDowell out at Centerville. Perhaps you would like to be presented to General Scott, Mr. Custer?"

Young Armstrong stood dumfounded. He had glimpsed the grand figure of Winfield Scott when that dignitary visited the Academy for reviews, but the general had been as untouchable as the upper social set back in Monroe. Custer could not have been more taken aback if he had been asked to meet Napoleon or Washington. He stammered assent, and the officer led the slim, long-nosed boy into an adjacent room, where sat a mountainous man in blue uniform with haughty head perched on a magnificent gilt-embroidered collar. Two rows of brass buttons — or maybe gold — dotted his bulging barrel-stomach. A group of gentlemen from the Congress sat around him. All were studying a map of the Bull Run country — Fairfax Court House and Centerville — spread on the table.

General Scott looked up — a grim face with bags under the eyes and side whiskers, between fringed epaulets.

"General, this is Lieutenant Custer of the 2d Cavalry; he has just reported from West Point, and I did not know but that you might have some special orders to give him."

General Scott, when sitting, could look down on a man. With cordial but unapproachable dignity he reached out his giant hand, which was big even for Custer's blacksmith grasp.

"We have had the assistance of quite a number of you young men from the Academy, drilling volunteers, and so on," the general said, watching Custer through rheumy eyes. "Now, what can I do for you? Would you prefer to be ordered to report to General Mansfield to aid in this work, or is your desire for something more active?"

Custer stammered that he preferred being assigned to the line with General McDowell.

"A very commendable resolution, young man," Scott replied. Then he turned to the adjutant general and told him to prepare the papers. Looking again at Custer, the aged general continued, "Go and provide yourself with a horse, if possible" (Scott realized that most of the horses in Washington had been requisitioned), "and call here at seven o'clock this evening. I desire to send some dispatches to General Mc-Dowell at Centerville, and you can be the bearer of them. You are not afraid of a night ride, are you?"

"No, sir." Custer smiled as he saluted and turned on his heels to depart. He could hardly believe his good luck. He was to carry messages from the Commander in Chief to the leading general in the field on the day of battle, and all this distinction because he had been court-martialed for neglect of duty, while his more dutiful classmates were rewarded with disciplined obscurity.*

There was only one flaw in Custer's happiness. Suppose he could not get a horse and deliver these messages? He spent the afternoon visiting livery stables, and became more discouraged at each one. Not a horse was available. The opportunity of a lifetime might wither in the bud. How could he face General Scott with a report of failure?

In this frame of mind, his kepi pushed dejectedly frontward on his uncombed red hair, his uniform mussed, he strode down Pennsylvania Avenue. Watching the crowd from the corners of his eyes — a habit

* F. S. Dellenbaugh, *George Armstrong Custer*, p. 14; F. Whittaker, *Complete Life of . . . Custer . . .* , pp. 51–52. Slight changes have been made to reconcile these two accounts. G. W. Cullum, *Biographical Register*, usually a good author-ity, shows Custer to be drilling recruits in Washington in June and July, 1861. In view of his court-martial, this seems impossible.

with him always — he spied a familiar figure. That man was one of the regular army dragoons from West Point whom Lieutenant Charles Griffin had organized into the flying battery that went to Washington for Lincoln's inauguration.

"Hello," Custer called. "What are you doing here?"

The fellow saluted, said *Captain* Griffin had sent him in from Centerville to fetch Old Wellington, a spare horse they had left in Washington. It was twenty-five miles out to the battery. Fighting might start in the morning, so he must leave at once. Custer persuaded him to wait until after seven o'clock.

That night Custer, on Wellington, rode with the dragoon across the Long Bridge. Jogging under the stars for five hours, they talked about West Point, life in Washington, and the forthcoming battle. When talked out, Armstrong hummed or whistled, gleefully anticipating the excitement to come. How like O'Malley and Mickey Free in the book he had read as a child!

Finally the riders saw fires ahead. They came to men bivouacked along the road. Many were singing instead of resting for tomorrow's fight. At the village of Fairfax Court House, bonfires lighted the main street. Horses stood at hitching racks in front of buildings. Officers hurried in and out of open doors. Custer and the dragoon did not stop. Centerville was still seven miles away.

Along the highway beyond the town they found more soldiers. Regiments stood leaning on their muskets. Others sat by the roadside. Still others, almost out of sight in the dark, rested in the tall weeds and fence corners. Custer admired his guide's ability to find the route.

"That's headquarters, sir." The dragoon pointed to a brilliant campfire and abruptly reined his horse away, leaving Custer to report alone.

The fire illuminated a group of tents. Custer rode toward them. As he entered the lighted area he saw a white-haired major. Custer told him proudly that he brought dispatches from General Scott to General McDowell. The officer held out his hand for the papers. He would deliver them to General McDowell.

Armstrong hesitated. The great moment he had counted on was being taken from him.

"I am Major Wadsworth of McDowell's staff," the officer said.[2]

Custer felt that he must give up the dispatches. He watched the major carry them to an open tent flap and hand them to a large man wearing a twin row of gilt buttons down his portly front. Custer believed that to be General McDowell — and he had missed his chance to meet him.

Major James Samuel Wadsworth came back from the general's tent and chatted with the boy lieutenant — asked what time he had left Washington; said he must be tired and hungry. Would he like some breakfast? The army was marching out to battle and it might be a long time before he could eat again.

Armstrong, still hoping to make the most of his opportunity among the top command, felt sure that a soldier should never be either tired or hungry — an opinion he kept always. He thanked the major for his consideration, said he did not care about himself but would accept feed for his horse, thank you — a gallant attitude, appropriate for Mickey Free.

Major Wadsworth ignored his gallantry and again Custer lost hope of recognition from high command. He got the grain for his horse, and left the animal munching it while he strolled around headquarters in the dark. He met one of his Academy schoolmates on the staff. The youth offered him a second invitation to breakfast. Custer accepted this time, and sat on the ground in the firelight, washing down steak and corn bread with black coffee. Nine years and many battles later he remembered how he enjoyed that meal. Only three days ago he had been a schoolboy in disgrace up at West Point. Another world!

After breakfast Custer put the bridle back on his horse, asked the way to the 2d Cavalry, and rode off in the predawn blackness. Some fifty regiments choked the roads around Centerville, and it might be difficult to find Company G. However, in the multitude of men there were just seven troops of cavalry.[3] Custer soon came to a column of horse standing in the road.

"Can you tell me where Company G, 2d Cavalry, is?" Custer asked. A voice in the dark replied, "At the head of the column."

Custer rode forward, his eyes still unused to the blackness. At the column's head he discerned five or six men sitting at ease on their horses. Custer could see no insignia of rank in the dark, and asked for the commanding officer.

"Here he is," a man said, as he reined his horse toward him.

"I am Lieutenant Custer, and in accordance with orders from the War Department, I report for duty with my company, sir." Armstrong knew the proper military language.

"Ah, glad to meet you, Mr. Custer. We have been expecting you, as we saw in the list of assignments of the graduating class from West Point that you had been marked down to us. I am Lieutenant Drummond. Allow me to introduce you to some of your brother officers." The commander turned in his saddle. "Gentlemen," he continued, nodding toward figures in the gloom, "permit me to introduce to you Lieutenant Custer, who has just reported for duty with his company." [4]

Custer bowed his cinnamon-scented head to the figures in the darkness — among them Second Lieutenant Leicester Walker, an appointee from civil life who ranked him by a few days. All sat their horses waiting for orders to march.

Custer now learned about the battle plans. The Confederates were supposedly commanded by General Beauregard. His army was known to be deployed on the far side of Bull Run, a few miles ahead. The steep-banked creek was difficult for troops to cross in formation. A few bridges spanned it, and there were several fords. The enemy held these crossings for some twelve miles, but surely did not have sufficient men to form a solid line between them. McDowell's plan was to trick the enemy by striking with one division under Israel B. ("Fighting Dick") Richardson at Blackburn's Ford down at the far end of the line. Then Brigadier General Daniel Tyler was to feint with another division farther up the Run at the stone bridge on the Alexandria–Warrenton

Turnpike. Presumably, Beauregard would concentrate to repel these two thrusts along the creek; and while the enemy was doing so, McDowell's remaining two divisions, under Generals David Hunter and Samuel P. Heintzelman, were to cross Bull Run above them, circle the enemy's left and attack his weakened flank. The plan seemed easy enough to remember.

Custer knew that his troop was in Hunter's division. This meant that Company G might spearhead the knockout blow. Good! Hunter was a regular; he had graduated from West Point in 1822 and fought in the Mexican War. Younger men said he was getting old, wore a wig and dyed his mustache. What of it? In battle he should be dependable.

At dawn the waiting cavalrymen heard firing down where "Fighting Dick" was to open the engagement. Custer saw the officers look at one another and smile.

"A fine Sunday morning, gentlemen," one of them said, nodding toward the milk-pale eastern sky.

The dawn light promised a clear, hot day. Six miles away the bombardment thundered persistently. Custer wondered how soon the vast army around Centerville would move. Daylight brought color to the trees, the fields, a distant farmhouse he had not seen earlier. With sunrise, a fresh breeze cooled the men's faces. They turned in their saddles to watch a marching column of Federal soldiers and realized that the army had started on its way. Custer noticed that these volunteer soldiers did not step along like West Pointers. They also lacked regulation uniforms: some dressed in flaming scarlet, others in green, black, or brown; only a few wore blue.

No order had come yet for the 2d Cavalry to move. Custer noticed Lieutenant Walker's hands tremble as he fixed a bridle buckle. The fellow was nervous, although obviously trying to be brave. Custer was nervous, too. He knew nothing about war — and, like Lieutenant Walker, did not intend to confess it. The two boys chatted together, each hiding his own fear.

Their conversation stopped when the column was ordered to march. The horses started at a walk along the Warrenton pike, crossed a bridge over Cub Run, went up a hill between fenced fields. This road led straight to the stone bridge over Bull Run, where Tyler was to attack the enemy. But before the column came to the bridge it wheeled to the right, through an open gate, and followed a private road towards a woods, thus beginning the encircling movement to cross Bull Run above the enemy and surprise him with a flank attack — surely as much fun as evading the guard to visit Benny Havens's.

Custer watched the column enter the woods and disappear like a snake going under a mat. Soon his own company rode into the trees, and for the next two miles he saw only the dark green July foliage overhead and last year's brown leaves on the brushy ground. The horses' hoofs were peculiarly silent and he could hear the clank of artillery caissons rumbling along behind.

At 9:30, Company G came out of the woods a mile from Sudley Springs. The sun shone hot in the fields now.

For half an hour the troop halted, watering horses, watching infantry splash across Bull Run and wind up the hill beyond. The 2d Rhode Island led the way. A section of artillery followed. Among the officers, Custer recognized Captain Griffin's drooping mustache and sunken cheeks. That cadaverous-looking man now commanded eleven guns,[5] more than twice the number he had taken from West Point that dark morning last January. Promotions came quickly in wartime.

Among other artillery officers who rode past, Armstrong thought he saw the thin, active figure of Lieutenant John Gibbon, the former teacher of artillery tactics at West Point. His sharp, bronzed profile with its pointed goatee was hard to forget. Gibbon had become chief of McDowell's artillery and must be a major, perhaps even a lieutenant colonel, by this time.

Heavy firing shook the earth before the end of the column disappeared over the hill. An aide galloped back down the road. Custer heard him tell Lieutenant Drummond that Company G must guard the artillery unlimbering along the ridge. Drummond waved his arm.

Sergeants barked sharp orders. The troop swung into column, forded Bull Run and trotted along behind the aide, horses' necks arching eagerly as they started up the slope.

On top, Custer saw galloping teams placing caissons and guns. This was like drill at West Point. Above them, little cottony clouds appeared suddenly in the blue sky. They looked harmless, but the shrapnel in them stripped trees of their leaves. Custer noticed, too, that solid shot hissed viciously as it passed overhead — very different from the dull boom of practice firing at the Academy.

When the guns were all in position along the open ridge, the cavalry retired out of range in a hollow. Here it deployed in column of companies, ready to sweep back over the ridge in case the enemy charged for the guns. Custer reined his horse in the proper position before his platoon. Beside him, in front of the next platoon, he saw tyro Lieutenant Walker. The two boy lieutenants were too far apart to talk without being overheard, but Custer realized that veteran officers behind the companies were watching: no one must see his nervousness.

As the troopers waited, an order was given to advance in formation toward the foot of the hill. Evidently the enemy was forming on the other side to rush the guns. The platoons started at a walk. Novice Lieutenant Walker called across, "Custer, what weapon are you going to use in the charge?"

Custer had enjoyed telling this fellow about West Point, never admitting that he himself knew little more than the civilian about a real charge; but West Point had taught Custer to answer promptly and with authority.

"The saber," Custer replied, drawing his blade.

Lieutenant Walker drew his. The line moved forward slowly, dressing on the guidons. Custer changed his mind about the saber. Perhaps a revolver would be a better weapon. He sheathed his sword and unbuttoned the holster he had purchased in New York. From the corner of his eyes he saw Lieutenant Walker do the same. Full of pranks always, Custer put back his pistol and redrew his saber. He repeated this several times as the horses walked up the hill, and Lieutenant Walker invariably copied him. Custer said later that he was really not sure which weapon to use but he had so much fun watching the green lieutenant imitate him that he forgot his own fright.

At the crest of the ridge the cavalry halted. Federal artillerymen were plying their guns, but no Confederates had charged. Company G withdrew to the sheltered hollow and waited again while shells crashed along the ridge, close to them but out of sight. Battle routine for cavalry seemed to be inactivity, standing by hour after hour. Occasionally the guns moved forward and the cavalry advanced a safe distance in the rear, to be posted in a new sheltered position.

Custer recognized the Warrenton pike as they crossed its hard surface. Evidently the battle was progressing satisfactorily. They had made a U-turn at least seven miles long, and were pushing against the enemy's flank as planned. Custer heard, by word of mouth passed down the line, that General Hunter had been wounded and carried from the field. A soldier at the front seldom saw such things. General Heintzelman, another veteran, now commanded both divisions, and victory still seemed assured — a victory with Custer firing no shot, seeing no enemy, just waiting, endlessly waiting.

Custer would learn that waiting was a big element in every battle, a major element in army life; but he was always an impatient waiter. Even now, in his first battle, he displayed a characteristic which would infuriate his critics later. He spied a classmate and cantered away, deserting his troop to talk with him. The two young men rode to a ridge where the battlefield lay before them. The stone bridge, where the Warrenton pike crossed Bull Run, was now behind them and safe in Union hands. Fresh troops streamed into the fields ahead, long lines flowing down the roads, standing in neat oblongs and squares in meadows and on hillsides. The young lieutenants watched eagerly. This was evidently the final concentration for the grand advance which would curl back the enemy flank.

As Armstrong watched, another column of soldiers emerged from a block of woodland. "Look," Custer's companion said, "more reinforcements."

The column halted, changed front in a strange maneuver.

"What's going on there?" Custer had hardly finished the sentence before he saw the glint of hundreds of gun barrels pointed with military precision. A strange flag unfurled above them, and white smoke puffed from the line.

"We're flanked! We're flanked!" The unmistakable cry came back to the watching lieutenants. The Union lines sagged, wavered for a moment; then the neat geometric squares of soldiers dissolved into a mob of fleeing, frightened creatures, some racing toward Bull Run, some back to the Warrenton pike. Cannon stood abandoned on hilltops. Artillery horses, carrying two and even three riders, galloped to the rear. The deserted battlefield was littered with muskets, flags, band instruments, cast-off clothing. At the stone bridge fugitives struggled frantically to get across. Where Bull Run cut the meadows, knots of frantic men could be seen splashing through the creek.

Custer galloped back to the place where he had left his troop. The G Company regulars still sat their horses stoically, waiting for orders. Another troop stood near by. These and a section of artillery seemed to be the only units of the two divisions that remained in formation. Could it really be so bad? In the confusion General Heintzelman rode up, his round face blurred by a close-cropped beard. His slanting eyes and sallow, sun-burned skin gave him an odd Mongolian appearance. He was wounded, but sat his horse with Oriental calm.

"Lieutenant," Custer heard him tell Drummond, "march your men back along the pike to Centerville." The general then turned and galloped away toward some batteries.

The cavalry formed in column of fours and trotted along the pike, scattering frightened footmen who clogged the way. Behind them Heintzelman followed with the artillery he had saved. On hillsides, many broken companies of men could still be seen. Custer thought the general might be planning to get ahead of the retreat, stop it, reorganize, and renew the battle. He was not sure, and a soldier's duty was to keep his mouth shut, except to bite a cartridge.

Company G crossed the stone bridge. Following the pike over the hills beyond, Custer recognized the gateway where they had turned off in the morning. The cavalry clattered by. From the crest of the next ridge, Custer sighted the Cub Run bridge. A crowd of men stood uncertainly in front of it. An overturned ambulance, wheels in the air, and a crushed carriage blocked their passage. Company G rode closer. Custer heard explosions in the débris. He saw spokes and splintered boards hurtle into the air. A Confederate cannon was placing well-aimed shells along the causeway. No one could cross that bridge, now! How did the enemy slip in here so quickly?

The column halted. Heintzelman ordered the cannon to be left on the road. Let the gunners save themselves! Armstrong Custer never referred to his next act in either letter or memoir. The war might develop certain flaws in the character of this boy soldier; enemies would call him a boaster; but in this instance all he said, later, was that he galloped up Cub Run with the cavalry until they found a place where the steep bank had caved in. Slipping down this decline to the creek, the horsemen forded and circled back to the pike. Two miles beyond, at Centerville, they halted. Here, hour after hour passed waiting again for orders. Heintzelman had disappeared somewhere in town among the press of disorganized men and wagons. He was evidently hunting for McDowell. The records are silent concerning the actions of Lieutenants Drummond and Walker but presumably they acted satisfactorily.

Darkness came early for July. The sky had clouded during the afternoon and was very black in the northeast now. Finally an order came. Company G must return to the Potomac. Too many regiments had already fled toward Washington to re-form here and make a stand. Custer mounted his tired horse and swung into the road at the head of G troop for the twenty-five-mile ride. In the inky blackness rain began to pelt his face, rivulets ran down his neck. A soldier's cap gave little protection. Bridle reins became slimy in the riders' hands. The tired horses stumbled. Men nodded in their saddles. By daylight, the company was still far from the familiar Potomac. As the horsemen approached Washington the roads became packed once more with disorganized soldiers plodding north. The cavalry halted repeatedly and stood, wet and weary, waiting for the road to clear.

By midmorning Company G reached Arlington Heights and turned into its old encampment. Custer, overcome after thirty hours' duty with little to eat, slid from his horse, lay down under a tree in the rain and fell asleep.[6]

He awoke stiff, sore, and wet; but with remarkable vitality he reported for duty. The Battle of Bull Run, he learned, had provided active service to twenty-two of his schoolmates — including little Kilpatrick, who, despite his recent wound, had commanded a regiment of New York volunteers. That little scrapper a captain commanding a regiment! All Custer could show for his three-day grueling service was a very slight acquaintance with two high-ranking officers, Scott and Heintzelman, a failure to meet McDowell, and a bit of heroics at the Cub Run bridge which he did not mention and apparently no one else had noticed. Armstrong certainly had failed to take even a first step toward the general's stars dreamed about by all West Point boys.

In days of discouragement Custer always appeared optimistic — self-defense perhaps! But he did have some things to be grateful for. Hadn't he graduated from West Point and got the education he coveted? For that favor he was indebted to Representative Bingham. Custer decided to call on the Congressman and thank him in person.

Bingham recorded the interview as follows:

I had never seen him, and was so engrossed with political cares in Washington that I almost forgot him. . . .

I heard of him first after the First Battle of Bull Run. In the report of that miserable fiasco he was mentioned for bravery. A leader was needed to re-form the troops, and take them over a bridge. Like Napoleon at Lodi young Custer sprang to the front — and was a hero.

I heard of his exploit with pride, and hunted several times for my boy, but unsuccessfully. Then one day a young soldier came to my room without the formality of sending in a card.

Beautiful as Absalom with his yellow curls, he was out of breath, or had lost it in embarrassment. And he spoke with hesitation: "Mr. Bingham, I've been in my first battle. I tried hard to do my best. I felt I ought to report to you, for it's through you I got to West Point. I'm . . ."

I took his hand. "I know, you're my boy Custer!" [7]

5 On to Richmond — and Monroe

SECOND LIEUTENANT CUSTER STOOPED AS HE ENTERED COMPANY G'S ORDERLY tent. Inside, seated at a table, First Lieutenant Drummond looked up from his papers.

"Here's an order from the new commander of this brigade." Drummond handed Custer a paper. "The general has selected you to serve on his staff. Not much of an appointment. See! He asks for the junior officer who can best be spared."

Young officers often talked with brutal frankness. Custer took the paper in his stubby fingers * and read it. General Phil Kearny had been assigned command of four regiments of New Jersey volunteers shortly after the Bull Run battle, and Company G of the 2d Cavalry was brigaded with them. He had no staff and wanted an officer, preferably a West Pointer, with sufficient knowledge of military routine to whip his volunteers into a fighting unit.

Custer knew Kearny by reputation as a wealthy professional soldier of fortune, a hard taskmaster but a superb fighter who had served with distinction in the Mexican War, and in the French Army in Italy. An assignment to his staff might be an opportunity for a young lieutenant. On the other hand, it might lead to a damaging blot on his record. Certainly Kearny had not selected him with any idea of promotion in

---

* Apparently Libbie Custer was much impressed by the peculiarities of Armstrong's hands. (Note p. 413 of her *Tenting on the Plains*.) In the above incident, direct quotations have been made from Custer's account given in F. Whittaker, *Complete Life of . . . Custer . . .* , p. 82.

mind — for, as Lieutenant Drummond said, he specified the junior officer who could *best be spared*. The risk did not seem to worry Lieutenant Custer. He accepted it, as he did most hazards in life, as non-
chalantly as he accepted the appointment to the Military Academy
after being notified that he might fail and disgrace himself.

Lieutenant Custer walked over to brigade headquarters. He found
General Kearny haughty and aloof, more distant and domineering,
even, than Academy teachers. The grizzled old veteran had to be
helped on his horse, but he wore an empty sleeve as badge of invinci-
bility in battle. He was quick-tempered and profane, especially with
officers who neglected the slightest duty. However, Custer noticed that
he seemed lenient with men in the ranks, blaming all their transgressions on their immediate superiors. Perhaps that was the way great
commanders ruled. Years later, Custer wrote: "Of the many officers of
high rank with whom I have served [and he served with the best],
Kearny was the strictest disciplinarian." [1] Evidently Kearny made an
impression on the twenty-two-year-old boy who hoped to be a general
some day.

In addition to Kearny's hauteur and rigid discipline, Custer noticed
another characteristic. The general's one great interest was training his
men. His first act after Custer joined his staff was to organize an un-
authorized raid against an enemy picket stationed five miles away. The
job was given to a lieutenant colonel and three hundred men. Somebody might get killed. Sure! But the survivors would get good battle
training. This is the way, sir, to make a brigade. Custer was sent along
to represent headquarters.

The detail marched off on a moonlight night. Custer admitted to
himself that he felt frightened. This battalion had never been under
fire, and he considered himself as green as any of them. He had been in
the army almost nine months, but his battle experience was limited to
being a spectator at the Bull Run retreat. Always, when he remembered those early days, Custer told about his fears — a remarkable admission, for within a few more months his worst detractors would
admit that he was absolutely fearless.

The raid failed completely, except for training the men. The detail learned to make a night march without asking their destination. Clouds covered the moon and orders were finally whispered in the dark, close to the enemy. Here the force was divided, to creep from several positions toward the picket post. But the moon came out unexpectedly. Enemy sentries spied the approaching soldiers and fired — vicious red streaks blazing from the trees.[2]

The Union force turned and fled. Bull Run all over again! Young Custer remembered this second spectacle for the rest of his life, as vividly as he did the first one. Always he told about it as a great joke, for he was one of those bubbling boys who loved movement, action, excitement, a fight or a foot race, and he could laugh with equal abandon whether he or the other fellow furnished the legs. But he remembered more than the humor of the incident. It impressed him, as Bull Run had, with the importance of discipline — something his instructors had failed to teach him in four years of study at West Point.

This ended Lieutenant Custer's assignment with Phil Kearny. The general sent him back to his company, not because he had run away from a fight, but because an order from Washington now prohibited regular army officers from serving under volunteer commanders.

Custer returned to his troop and with it, in the summer of 1861, was ordered to Cliffburn, two miles from Washington. No chance for action here! In August he was transferred to the 5th Cavalry, along with other young men — all speculating on promotions, and gossiping endlessly about McClellan's quarrels with the administration. In the newspapers now they read constant complaints: A great army and a timid commander, who would not lead it "on to Richmond." The squabbling was bad for army morale — no active duty, no chance for advancement — and the capital's fleshpots almost ruined Lieutenant Custer. Along with other youthful officers, he began to carouse. He met his schoolmate, Deacon Elbert of Iowa, who also fretted about promotions. A summer's military service had been a complete failure for both of them. Custer had been lucky in meeting top-ranking generals —

Scott, Phil Kearny, McDowell (almost!) — but all his best efforts had proved futile.

Please, waiter, another sherry cobbler.

The young lieutenants, talking over their drinks, complained that promotions came faster in the Confederacy than in the North. "Look at the men we knew at the Academy! Those who went South are high-ranking officers, now. And look at us!"

Custer's best friend, Tom Rosser, had distinguished himself at Bull Run and was a captain; so was likable John Pelham, and so was dark-eyed, dramatic Stephen Ramseur. And gossip said that Jim Parker, least likely of them all to succeed, had become a lieutenant colonel — only two ranks below God!

Make mine a smash, this round, waiter.

In October Custer became ill. His application for sick leave was approved and he left Washington to go home. "Home," of course, meant Monroe and the house of his half-sister, Lydia Reed.

October in Monroe was harvest time. Corn stood in tepee shocks in frosty fields. The village streets were fragrant with burning leaves. Overhead, wild ducks flying south etched the sky with long wavering lines of skirmishers. Second Lieutenant Custer's illnesses were always acute, prostrating, but short-lived. In no time his blue uniform, with its bright row of brass buttons, cut a conspicuous figure on the sidewalks, in front of stores, along front-yard picket fences. The village could boast few officers of the United States Army. Ambitious young men who had not volunteered moved to Detroit where opportunities beckoned them to the growing city. Thus the Custer boy was welcomed as a hero. Designing matrons gave parties for him. He was asked to sit on the platform at Union meetings and at patriotic rallies.

Aristocratic Judge Daniel Stanton Bacon pointed to him with pride as a true patriot, shook hands with him publicly on the streets where everyone could see — but did not invite him to his home. Public and private life were entirely different fields in the judge's mind. After all, the Custers and Reeds were respectable working people, but they had none of his intellectual interests,[3] weren't even Presbyterians. Moreover, his daughter Elizabeth was nineteen now. She would graduate from the seminary next spring, and girls of that age might be impulsive.

Libbie, as she was called, was not introduced to the young hero, whom she had known by sight most of her life. She admitted, later, that something about his nervous, excitable character irritated her — the first sign of personal interest in him, perhaps. Then one day, as she stood behind her curtained window, she saw him coming down Monroe Street with a rowdy companion. Both walked like sailors in a gale, and they seemed much amused by their own antics, clutching at imaginary ropes, roaring with thick-tongued laughter at the maple trees in their whitewashed boxes. The sidewalk ended across the street from the Bacon house. This amused them inordinately. As they passed, Libbie noticed that Armstrong's brilliant blue eyes seemed unable to focus. His mouth grinned senselessly. Monroe's glamorous boy hero was drunk. For the rest of her life Libbie remembered "that terrible day." To make matters worse, her father saw the same spectacle.[4]

The two boys staggered away toward Lydia Reed's house, half a mile south. What happened after they arrived there is conjectural. It was an age of dramatic temperance lectures and the signing of pledges. Armstrong's companion came out of the house alone, and when the lieutenant next appeared he was a chastened boy who had promised his half-sister never to touch liquor again — a pledge he kept even when his wife served champagne at table in later years. Clever women could usually influence Armstrong, and Sister Lydia was always as important to him as his mother. Moreover, her little "Autie" was four years old now, running and chattering. A man felt dignified and on his best behavior with a child named after him.

Early in February, 1862, Lieutenant Custer returned to Washington. The city seemed very different from the one he had left almost four months ago. Although the Capitol dome was still unfinished and lumber piles still littered the wintry lawn, soldiers no longer loafed under the trees along Pennsylvania Avenue. Perhaps it was too cold, or perhaps they were kept too busy in their camps. Certainly last summer's disorganized fuss and bustle had disappeared. Mule-drawn commissary wagons, with trembling canvas covers, rattled diligently over the cobblestoned streets and became suddenly silent on the dirt side roads. Now and again, on prancing steed, a resplendent officer in blue and gold rode by with his mounted staff.

Custer met friend Deacon Elbert again and learned that he was engaged to be married. Lucky pup! Custer and Elbert serenaded the happy girl with a military band. Then they played before the houses of other "fair ladies." Some of them had retired, but they got up, dressed, and invited the boys in for a glass of wine. Armstrong wrote his sister, with seeming pride, that he had refused the proffered drinks.[5]

At troop headquarters Custer noticed an air of expectancy. The officers were eager for spring and the opening of a campaign. All winter they had kept their men busy building fortifications to ward off an enemy whose own earthworks stood only twenty miles away. Trees had been cut down to open avenues for artillery fire. Redoubts cluttered the once peaceful countryside.

Custer found his company housed in canvas-roofed huts — dugouts with two-foot-high log walls, mud and stick chimneys, and stone slab stoves. The men were as restless as their officers, anxious to be off. General McClellan had made himself extremely popular. Soldiers liked him better than they did President Lincoln. They approved "Little Mac's" plan to advance on Richmond by floating down the Potomac and then march up the Peninsula — the tongue of land between the York and James rivers. That seemed better than forcing their way a hundred miles across Virginia. By Lincoln's proposed land route, the Union Army's communications would be long and easily cut off. By McClellan's water route, the Navy could bring it supplies.

Custer was surprised and shocked when, on March 9, 1862, the 5th Cavalry was ordered to join a column marching "on to Richmond" overland, instead of by water. He did not know that this movement was a feint to attract attention while transports were prepared for the circuitous river trip down to the Peninsula. He thoroughly disapproved of the overland march, but, as always when forced to toe the line, he obeyed cheerfully.

The roads south were dry enough for good marching, springy underfoot, and not yet dusty. Custer enjoyed being on a horse again. The rolling Virginia hills were still dank and muddy. Rain and sometimes hail pelted the column, but the sun shone between showers [6] and Armstrong's long nose smelled spring in the air. Most of the field officers had been detached for other duties. The regiment was commanded by Major Charles J. Whiting, and Second Lieutenant Custer was the only commissioned officer with his company. Thus for the first time in his life he commanded a troop of cavalry. Several reporters, eager for news, came along.

The 5th Cavalry marched at the head of the column. Custer took turns with other company commanders, each deploying his troop as advance guard — one platoon far ahead on the road, others trotting across the fields on both flanks.

The first night out they bivouacked halfway to Centerville. The men made brush shelters and rested beside fires. At reveille, their blue uniforms were daubed with mud and the white crossbelts on their cavalry jackets needed pipe clay, but morale was high and the horses seemed to be in good shape.

As the column approached Bull Run, the advance guard reported bristling fortifications ahead. This information was sent back to General George Stoneman, the top commander. He ordered a halt. Lieutenant Custer rode out to see for himself. He found a line of cannon frowning from empty works, but saw no sentries, no soldiers' heads, no enemy.

Had the fortifications been abandoned?

Lieutenant Custer and a few fellow officers rode up to a cannon's mouth and looked in the embrasure. That threatening weapon was a blackened log — a "Quaker gun." What would the politicians say when they learned that McClellan had stood back all winter, afraid of wooden guns? Such a statement, of course, would be unfair — but politicians usually were. Custer rode on. Other parts of the fortifications indicated that the enemy had left recently and in haste. Tell that to the politicians and newsmen! Certainly the litter in the abandoned camps was fresh, and black greasy smudges on the ground told where supply depots had crackled up in flames. The air still stank with the heavy odor of burned bacon.

Trumpets called the soldiers back to their colors. General Stoneman had ordered the cavalry to follow and, if possible, to overtake the enemy. The 5th Cavalry started down the road beside the Alexandria & Orange railway, Custer's company at the rear of the regiment.

Fifteen miles below Manassas Junction, two couriers came racing back along the column. They evidently brought news for Major Whiting, the regimental commander.

Custer beckoned to his first sergeant to take the company; Custer followed the couriers. They stopped, as he had expected, in front of the major. He heard them report that enemy pickets had been seen on the hill beyond the next railroad station — Catlett it was called.

Major Whiting held up his hand to halt the column. He sent a fresh courier back to General Stoneman for instructions.

Custer sat with the waiting officers, laughing and joking. Curious reporters came up, listening for news. The column, standing along the road, dismounted, troop after troop, and waited endlessly — the hated characteristic of army life. Men adjusted their saddles. Others sprawled along the railroad embankment. A few card games started.

When the courier returned, Major Whiting read the order aloud: "*Drive in the pickets.*"

Lieutenant Custer spoke at once: Could his troop have the honor? . . . Major Whiting nodded assent, and Custer spurred back to his men. The company remounted, and in two files jogged up the side of the resting column until it passed the lead troop. Then Custer formed column of fours and trotted gaily down the road.[7] This time he was not going to be left behind a hill while others fought and won distinction, as they had at Bull Run.

Custer stopped his troop when he saw the enemy pickets, and for a moment watched them with his quick dancing eyes. The Confederate horsemen ahead were dressed like farmers — no uniforms — but they held guns in their hands. They did not seem excited but stood, waiting for a fight. Custer's men tore down the fences on both sides of the road, deployed in the fields and started forward at a walk. To charge up the hill might wind the company's horses. Custer cautioned his men to hold their line, dress on the guidon.

The company reached the foot of the hill below the pickets who were now out of sight above them. Bullets twanged overhead, humming like strings on a gigantic guitar. They must come from the enemy on the hilltop ahead. To shoot at an invisible foe seemed futile. Hours could be wasted in such a bombardment. Custer decided to charge with sabers. He ordered his men to fire their pistols into the air. They must depend on cold steel alone; no halting to take aim and thus break the fury of a charge.

With every pistol back in its holster, Custer led the line forward at a walk. The troop rode up the hill slowly, bullets still buzzing around it. Close to the summit, where Armstrong thought one bound would carry his men at full speed into the enemy, he ordered: "Draw sabers!"

"Charge!" he shouted, whipping out his own blade.

Lieutenant Custer always remembered with pride the first time he gave that command, and how his men dashed forward with him, all as one. Over the crest they breezed. No enemy there! The troop swept down the other side, sloshing across a wet meadow. Ahead of the horsemen a fringe of hazel bushes skirted Cedar Run. Already spring buds and tender new leaves tinted the undergrowth a misty green. From the brushy fringe across the creek, a volley roared. Armstrong saw long jets of blue-white smoke spit from the guns. He wheeled his troop toward the road, where a bridge crossed Cedar Run, but smoke and crackling flames told him that the passage was blocked. He halted.

Dismounting, the troopers fired a few shots at the invisible enemy in the hazel bushes. Then Custer called them back. Safely out of range, he inspected his line. A bullet had scratched the head of one soldier. A horse was wounded.

Jubilantly the troop returned to the column. All felt like veterans, lucky members of a company which had charged the enemy. Newspaper reporters met them at the column's head. Casualties were still news, so they interviewed the wounded man. Custer, flushed with victory, told himself that a rain of bullets was not necessarily deadly. He also noted that cold steel chilled the courage of Confederate soldiers more than hot lead. That was something to keep in mind. But best of all, he remembered the fun of making rebels retreat.

This little sortie helped convince General Stoneman that the Confederates did not have sufficient numbers here to threaten Washington. Moreover, the transports for Richmond were ready now, back at Alexandria. The Army of the Potomac had begun to move "on to Richmond" by the water route. Stoneman called in the cavalry.

Custer, waiting his turn to embark, shaved, bathed, and changed clothes — the first time he had undressed for a week.[8]

6 "The Young Man I've Been Looking For"

W E ARE EMBARKING ON STEAMERS AND TRANSPORTS," CUSTER WROTE HIS sister on March 26, 1862. Then he looked up at the regiments standing around him on the Alexandria dock. He had learned to take advantage of long waits by writing letters even when he had to stand. Today, as Custer wrote, General McClellan stood farther along the Potomac wharf, watching with the trained eye of an engineer the hundreds of vessels loading troops, horses, and cargo. The great man had not noticed Lieutenant Custer when the 5th Cavalry marched out to await its turn for embarking, but the lieutenant had noticed McClellan, and now wrote: "The greatest expedition ever fitted out is going south un-

der the greatest and best of men. . . . The utmost secrecy is observed.
We have been shipping troops at the rate of 20,000 a day."

As usual, the enthusiastic Custer exaggerated. Troops had been embarking for nine days and many more were yet to go, so "20,000 a day" could not be correct. However, the movement was truly gigantic. Over one hundred thousand men, fourteen thousand five hundred horses and mules, forty-four batteries, countless wagons, ambulances, and pontoons were packed aboard four hundred vessels — steamboats, schooners, barges — shuttling up and down the Potomac for two hundred miles each way.

As soon as Custer took his place on a transport he wrote another letter, this one full of the apprehensions of a boy on shipboard setting off for war. It ended: "Good-bye my darling Sister. Good-bye all of you." *

Packed on deck like sardines, the troops watched Virginia's hills slip past the starboard bow. There was Mount Vernon, and, farther down the river, Stratford, where Robert E. Lee was born. Out in Chesapeake Bay, the soldiers crowded the ship's rail to stare at a monitor. That battered ironclad, they were told, had kept the *Merrimac* from coming out and sinking all transports. The flotilla anchored at Fortress Monroe, on the tip of the Peninsula, between the York and James rivers. The whole area had become an anthill of activity, a tent city of a hundred thousand men — parks of covered wagons, suburbs of puptents, steaming hot when the sun struck them.

On April 4, 1862, Custer's regiment was ordered to march up the James River in a column under General Erasmus Darwin Keyes. The sandy roads were soft under the horses' hoofs. Spring came earlier here than in Washington, and leaves were burgeoning on the bushes. Custer knew that another column, under General Heintzelman, was

---

* In his letter to Lydia Reed, March 26, 1862, Custer says he is embarking. The gigantic movement took from March 17 to April 6, 1862. Excellent summaries are in W. Swinton, *Campaigns of the Army of the Potomac*, p. 100, L. P. Paris, *History of the Civil War*, II, p. 5, and F. Whittaker, *Complete Life of . . . Custer . . .* , p. 98.

marching parallel to them along the York River toward Yorktown via Big Bethel — where Grebel had been killed and Kilpatrick wounded last year. The flat, swampy country seemed peaceful now. Sunbeams, warm and brilliant, sparkled between April showers, but company officers were cautioned to keep their men's powder dry.

Custer noticed the soggy pastures, the great brackish inlets fringed by tangled scrub forest. This was the Tidewater Virginia he had read about in *Swallow Barn* -- so different from the rolling hills above the "fall-line" out from Washington. Here were the croaking frogs, the wind-ruffled water-lily pads, the big shabby houses with gangs of hounds and smiling pickaninnies — all part of a way of life Custer relished. Probably at this time he began slapping his boot-top with his riding whip, just like the dashing Ned Hazard in the book. Certainly this habit of Armstrong's was soon noticeable.

On the second day's march, only twenty miles from camp, Custer's regiment stopped at a little stream, the Warwick, which ran south into the James. A series of dams converted this creek into a moat. Enemy redoubts stood in a threatening line on the far side. The Union column, as it arrived, fanned out along this line and waited for orders from McClellan. Sharpshooters crept forward and pecked away at the fortifications. The enemy fired back. Custer wrote about it to Lydia:

> Scarcely a ten minutes' interval during the day that the rebels and our men do not fire at each other. Both parties keep hidden as well as possible, but as soon as either shows itself it is fired at. At night, when it is too dark to shoot or be shot at, both come out of hiding-places, holler at each other, calling names and bragging what they intend to do. Then, when daylight appears, the party which sees the other first, fires, and that puts a stop till night comes, when the same thing is repeated. But we will soon decide the question. The great battle will probably come off before this reaches you. General McClellan is here to lead us, so we are certain of victory.[1]

This bluff and bluster lasted for ten days as the vast army marched up to the line. Officers established headquarters in tents. On sunny afternoons, they rolled up the canvas walls to enjoy every spring breeze. Tent flies were stretched over tables in the open.

Custer now received an order for detached service. West Pointers were presumably proficient in military engineering, and McClellan had ordered the building of a line of fortifications parallel to the enemy's. The work was to begin opposite Yorktown — famous as the place where Cornwallis surrendered to Washington in the Revolution. Custer, following orders, left his company and rode north for this assignment, chuckling over his own academic record, especially in engineering.

Lieutenant Custer reported for duty with Lieutenant Nicholas Bowen of the Topographical Engineers, and was billeted with General William F. ("Baldy") Smith's staff. His first job was unpleasant. A lot of dead soldiers must be buried. These men had been killed trying to do the job now assigned to Custer. He'd have to be more careful than they were when clearing the way for counter-fortifications. The gruesome sight of so many dead men was new to Custer, and he wrote his sister:

> Day before yesterday we buried our dead slain in the skirmish, in the clothes they wore when they were killed, each wrapped in his blanket. No coffin. It seemed hard, but it could not be helped. Some were quite young and boyish, and, looking at their faces, I could not but think of my younger brother.[2]

Tom Custer had enlisted in the 21st Ohio Infantry last September. The casualties did not seem to perturb General Smith. He explained to Custer a new plan for finishing his fortifications. Tonight the lieutenant, with a special detail, must dig rifle pits close to the enemy's line. Tomorrow, sharpshooters in those holes could knock down any artilleryman who dared fire at Union construction crews.

After dark, Custer led his little party out along the dams. He instructed them to dig close to the water's edge, as close as possible without flooding. He also warned them to dig silently. Sound carried along the surface, and a few rounds of shrapnel would mow them all down, dead as the poor fellows they had just buried. With these directions, the men dug silently. Custer, watching them, could hear the "rebs" talking in their works. He also heard the mournful call of whippoor-wills and croaking frogs, as in the *Swallow Barn* book.

Next day Union sharpshooters in the rifle pits prevented enemy artillerymen from manning their guns. The Federal fortifications were completed, and McClellan's entire line settled down for a siege. The roads back to Fortress Monroe were corduroyed to bring up the big guns. At General Baldy Smith's headquarters, a mile from the front, balloonists were sent up to spy behind the enemy line. Smith was dis-satisfied with the reports brought down by these aerial professionals. To get more reliable information, he next sent up a military man, General Fitz-John Porter. An unexpected east wind blew this general over the enemy line, and it seemed likely that he would be made a prisoner; however, enemy cannon could not be elevated sufficiently to shoot him down, and a change in the wind floated him back to safety.[3] But the perilous job must now be given to a more expendable man. Why not Lieutenant Custer?

Armstrong was pleased by the recognition, but he was also scared. He had schooled himself to meet death from a falling horse or a flying bullet, but going up in a basket under a fragile bladder of vapor un-nerved him. He said later that he tried to appear indifferent when he walked up and climbed in beside the operator. The anchor ropes were cast off, and the land sank rapidly. Custer saw many upturned faces, like daisies, watching them. Soon the faces became too small to recog-nize. Up in space the basket seemed very fragile. He noticed that he could look between the withes and see, far below, treetops and white tents. He asked if the basket was safe for the weight of two men, and his companion frightened him by jumping up and down on the frame to demonstrate its strength.

Custer soon learned that he must not look down. Instead he must look out at the horizon. Using his map as a guide, he located the York and James rivers, the housetops of Yorktown, and the trees near the old ruined church at Jamestown. White tents dotted the land between, like plant lice on a rose leaf. With his field glasses he could see tiny figures on the roads.

In the days that followed Custer went aloft many times, often at night, to count the enemy's campfires. On May 4, 1862, he was up among the stars at 2 A.M. when a large number of big fires flared suddenly in the darkness around Yorktown. He suspected that the Confederates might be withdrawing, and at reveille he noticed that there were no breakfast fires along their lines. Custer signaled to come down. On the ground again, he vaulted out of the basket and strode over to General Smith's tent. The general met him at the tent-flap. Two escaped slaves had aroused him to say that the enemy was evacuating. Custer's report corroborated the information.[4] General Smith telegraphed McClellan. Then, turning to an aristocratic brigadier general, Winfield Scott Hancock, Smith told him to call for volunteers to cross the Warwick and investigate.

Lieutenant Custer and Captain Theodore Read, from the adjutant general's staff, stepped up to the handsome, bearded brigadier and asked permission to go alone — and away they went, across the dam and into the earthworks beyond. The 5th Vermont was soon rallied and it followed, taking over from the two officers at 5:30 that morning. Bugles assembled other regiments, and the column started up the Peninsula again, marching slowly, watching for the enemy.[5]

McClellan gave this new advance to his second in command, the veteran soldier "Old Bull" Sumner (a nickname given him because he had lost his upper teeth and bellowed when leading a charge). Lieutenant Custer rode with Baldy Smith's aides. The next obstruction to be encountered was the narrow neck of land just below Williamsburg. Undoubtedly, the enemy would make another stand there.

At four in the afternoon of this same day, May 4, Custer heard heavy firing over at the left. The column marching up the south side of the Peninsula had evidently struck the enemy and was having trouble. No orders came from General Sumner, and Custer noticed that General Smith seemed unconcerned, riding doggedly ahead. Rain began to fall, drowning out the sound of the distant battle. At dark the men bivouacked. Fires were hard to start, but there was an abundance of dead wood. The army soon huddled around thousands of sputtering flames.

A courier splashed into headquarters with the report that Stoneman's cavalry, including Custer's 5th Regiment, had suffered heavy losses in the afternoon fighting — something for Armstrong to think about! Had he not been given this detached service, he might be a dead man now.

May 5, 1862, dawned cold and dreary. The men formed column with rain spattering on their guns. They shouldered arms and sloshed off up the road. Heavy firing began again to the south of them, as it had yesterday, but again Baldy Smith paid no attention and rode grimly ahead. Custer, riding with his aides, surmised that the general planned to flank or cut off the enemy. If so, the prospect was becoming worse hourly, because the rain had turned the country into a quagmire, and the cannon were bogging down in the roads. To find solid detours, Lieutenant Custer trotted ahead of the column. Dangerous work! Snipers lurked in the shabby colonial houses along the way. As he approached the bridge over Skiff Creek, a shot whistled past him. Custer swung from the saddle and fired back at an invisible enemy. This was like fighting at Catlett's Station again. Leading his horse, and shooting, he strode toward the bridge, found it on fire, stamped out the flames and scattered the kindling, but burned his hands. However, he saved the bridge for the column to cross, and Baldy Smith cited him for gallantry — the first in a long series of citations.[6]

The sound of firing continued all morning. Custer heard Baldy Smith order Brigadier General Hancock to take his brigade and investigate. Perhaps the time had come to flank the Confederates! Custer, with no authorization, decided to go along.[7]

Hancock's brigade turned off on a swampy road. Within a few miles, they saw a line of redoubts beyond a series of dams — the familiar Peninsular fortification. Hancock deployed and captured three small works without a fight. He crossed a narrow dam toward a fourth, but stopped when he saw it heavily manned and apparently impregnable.

That last redoubt seemed to be the key to the battlefield. If Hancock had reinforcements, he could take it and thus flank the Confederates who had made so much trouble for Keyes's column yesterday afternoon and this morning. Hancock sent off an aide seeking Smith's permission to do this, but before he had received a reply a messenger galloped in from Old Bull Sumner. Custer noticed Hancock's nervousness as he read Sumner's order. The brigadier general muttered something about Sumner's not realizing that this brigade held a position which could turn the tide of the battle. Hancock scribbled a note and sent it back to Sumner. Then he took out his watch and said, "It is now two o'clock; I shall wait till four: if no reply reaches me from headquarters, I will then withdraw."

Dark clouds threatened more rain as the soldiers settled themselves in a line beyond the narrow dam. Some lighted pipes while others napped. Only a few pickets stood guard against the enemy in the last redoubt ahead of them. Those Confederates over there must be in small numbers, for, although they stood their ground, they did not counterattack.

A half-hour dragged slowly by, and no answer came from Old Bull Sumner. Custer saw Hancock send a second message with the same request. Obviously the brigadier general was becoming more certain that this battle could be won by attacking yonder redoubt instead of obeying Sumner's order to withdraw. Here was a lesson in command on the general's level, and Custer watched Hancock's bearded face, his delicate nose, and solemn, worried eyes. It was bad to disobey an order, but it was worse to be denied the opportunity of winning a battle.

At the end of the first hour, Hancock sent a third message, and a half-hour later he sent a fourth. Custer understood the dilemma. Finally a fifth aide galloped away. Hancock and Custer were the only mounted officers left with the brigade. The hands on the general's watch approached four o'clock. What would he do?

The deadline came. Hancock turned and looked down the road toward Sumner's headquarters. "I will wait a half-hour longer," he said. "If no orders reach me by that time, I *must* retire."

A movement in the enemy redoubts now attracted him. Reinforcements had arrived over there, and they were preparing to attack. The enemy must have sensed the importance of Hancock's position, and now planned to kick him out. Already it was too late for the Union brigade to retreat rapidly across the narrow dam. A last stand would have to be made to hold back the enemy, while the brigade, in narrow column, made its escape.

To hold the enemy, Hancock formed his line. Custer, beside him, heard for the first time the rebel yell, a terrifying din from hundreds of human throats, as the enemy came forward. He realized that the brigadier's plight was desperate. Defeat now meant disgrace for disobeying orders. Custer, himself, having no authority for being there, could still easily escape — but that would have been unlike Custer. As he sat his horse he noticed that Hancock spoke to his men as quietly as though inviting them to dinner.

"*Gentlemen,*" the general said, "charge with the bayonet." *

Custer was impressed with this man's courtesy. He saw him take off his hat and gallop along the line, his fine face composed but resolute, his forehead white above bronzed cheeks.

The men started forward, hesitantly. They believed themselves outnumbered and trapped. Then, from their wavering ranks, rode an unkempt figure. At first they thought he was a threadbare newspaper correspondent, in a discarded military jacket, who had ventured out on the firing line for a story. The fellow's long yellow hair hung over his collar. He waved a tattered hat, shouted gleefully, and urged them all forward. Cowards felt brave when they saw Armstrong's laughing, freckled face. If bullets failed to hit him up there on a horse, men on the ground should be safe. They all began to cheer and run forward.

The enemy hesitated before the blue infantry wave with its tossing foam of bayonets. For a moment the gray line stood, then broke and retreated, abandoning the bastion and leaving a battle flag behind, the first captured by the Army of the Potomac. The victory — gained by

---

* Hancock's quiet manner is noted by Custer in his "War Memoirs," p. 689. For others who considered Hancock boisterous and profane, see Catton, *Mr. Lincoln's Army,* p. 9.

disobeying that order — assured Hancock due recognition. From now on, he would rise constantly until Gettysburg. He rewarded Custer with another citation, the second in a single day. McClellan's aide — the Duc d'Orléans, Custer called him — arrived in time to carry the captured flag to headquarters. (Undoubtedly this aide was one of the Orléans princes, probably the Duke of Chartres.)

The remarkable thing about Custer's spectacular charge is that he did not mention leading it in his next letter to Lydia, except to say, "I was glad to aid Genl. Hancock on that day, and was in the thick of the fight." * Again, as at Bull Run, Custer seems unnaturally modest. Were his critics unfair later when they called him a boaster, or did his personality change? It should be noted, too, that Custer in his letter said that the enemy came ten paces closer before breaking than he stated in his memoirs — a typical, happy-go-lucky Custer disregard for numbers, be they miles, income dollars, or advancing enemies.

Hancock's seizure of the flanking bastion ended the battle for Williamsburg. The enemy retreated up the Peninsula, and the Union Army marched into the picturesque town of ten to twelve thousand inhabitants with its several churches, city hall, insane asylum, and the beautiful colonial buildings belonging to William and Mary College. Along shady streets stood pleasant residences surrounded by gardens, but the soldiers noticed that the curtains were drawn, although here and there a face peered out. On galleries and at gates, Negroes watched the column; but no whites appeared.

Custer had plenty of time now to see his second battlefield. At Bull Run he had hurried past the broken carriages, dead horses, and abandoned guns left by his own retreating army. This time, as victor, he rode leisurely through the aftermath of destruction. In addition to the swollen carcasses of horses, he saw dead and wounded men, both blue

---

* R. de Trobriand, *Four Years with the Army of the Potomac*, p. 200, and J. M. Favill, *Diary of a Young Officer*, p. 90, describe the action and make no mention of Custer. The incident might well be dismissed as a journalist's story except for the official report, *O. R.*, I, XI, pt. 1, pp. 536, 543. Custer described it in his "War Memoirs," p. 689.

and gray, lying in fields and ditches. Over twenty-two hundred Federals alone were reported killed, wounded, or missing. The Confederates must have lost more. Foragers and scouts rode in constantly, reporting new corpses found in thickets and weed-grown fence corners.[8]

Among the wounded prisoners in a barn Custer saw Gimlet Lea and bent over him. Tears welled in his schoolmate's eyes as he raised his arms to "Fanny." Custer brought him a meal and the boys ate together, talking about the battle. Two athletes could not have discussed a recent game with more mutual respect. Custer learned that Tom Rosser had been wounded, but escaped. Stephen Ramseur and John Pelham were in the fight, too. Pelham's grandfather had played the organ in the Williamsburg church for fifty years. A man by the name of Early, General Jubal Early, had led that charge against Hancock at the redoubt.

When Custer left, he gave Gimlet some clothes and money. Gimlet, on his part, wrote his thanks in Custer's notebook, hoping that this might serve Armstrong in case of capture sometime. Bystanders who watched the two boys asked if they were brothers.[9]

For two weeks the Union Army moved cautiously forward out of the tainted Williamsburg air into the clean Virginia farmlands. Each day's march was easy. Rations came regularly. Foragers added delicacies to the menu — chicken, lamb, oysters.[10] The boys frolicked, played cards, bet their meager pay on cockfights, and adopted runaway Negroes who joined the camps. Custer was having as much fun as he did playing his way through West Point, but he liked action, too. Copies of Monroe newspapers brought news from home. Custer read complaints about McClellan's slowness. He disagreed. Maybe if the editor were risking his neck he would not be in such a hurry.

Finally, the Union Army came to White House Landing on the Pamunkey. Supplies were delivered here by boats on the York River. From this landing a railroad ran almost straight west across the fields to Richmond.

"There she is, boys: Richmond, only twenty miles away!"

Custer and a dozen others scouted ahead of the army, learning the country. Usually they rode in twos, and occasionally skirmished with enemy scouts. Custer reported that he got close enough to Richmond to hear locomotives whistle in the station. On each ride he sketched a map of the roads in his notebook. Behind the army scouts came engineers; the infantry followed.

On May 20, McClellan's van reached the Chickahominy, and four days later his line extended ten miles along that stream. His right wing had reached Mechanicsville, near enough to Richmond to hear the church bells on Sunday mornings. The enemy must be somewhere beyond that broad swampy stream.

McClellan established headquarters near the center of his line at the Widow Gaines's house, about a mile from the Chickahominy. Topographical engineers busied themselves preparing maps of all the crossings on the way to Richmond. Thus information gathered in part by Custer was used for the first military map of the region.[11]

One day the chief engineer, Brigadier General John G. Barnard, saw unkempt Lieutenant Custer loafing around headquarters. He nodded for him to follow, and the two rode toward the Chickahominy.

"What's your name, Lieutenant?" might have been the general's first question.

They followed a path for half a mile up a low hill, then down the other side to the swampy river bottom. A Federal picket presented arms as they passed. Beyond, in no man's land, the trees stood less dense along this part of the Chickahominy. The two men rode under towering white oaks with sprawling roots buried in the ooze. An enemy might be sighted any moment here, so the general and the lieutenant remained silent and alert. Quietly they came to the deep water of the Chickahominy, swirling through marshy banks. A movement on the far side attracted them.

"Look out!"

It was nothing. Only a limb from an overhanging bush being "sawed" by the current. No one was in sight.

General Barnard turned to the lieutenant. "Jump in," he commanded.

If the general expected the young man to be dismayed by this order, it was his turn to be taken aback. Custer slid from his horse, shed his jacket, pulled out his pistol and dropped into the stream. His feet sank in soft black mud. He stepped forward. Water swirled around his waist. Soon he was submerged to his armpits, but he kept going, his pistol held above his head.

What an excellent mark he made out in that stream! And to fall wounded in such water meant drowning. But Custer pushed quietly ahead, watching.

On the far bank he crawled out. Now General Barnard beckoned for him to come back, but Custer slithered away in the bushes. He never liked to obey orders blindly. Let the general sit his horse and be a fine mark for an enemy sentry! Custer enjoyed this kind of practical joke.

Back in the underbrush the boy lieutenant spied a Confederate sentry walking up and down a path. Armstrong also noticed smoke, farther on in the thicket, and decided to investigate. He waited until the picket turned his back, then crept forward, just as he used to do on the way to Benny Havens's at West Point.

Custer learned that the smoke came from a picket post where the guard rested between tours of duty. He also discovered that a bend in the river above his post might help a Federal raiding party to cut off and capture it. With this information, he crept back and waded across to impatient General Barnard.

Riding toward McClellan's headquarters, Custer explained what he had found [12] and the general seemed less provoked with the irrepressible lieutenant. After all, the fellow had accomplished his mission, and in addition had brought back information which might help Mc-Clellan decide where to pierce the enemy line. Passing over the low ridge, they came in sight of the Widow Gaines's house. The commanding general and his staff were riding away from it on an inspection tour. General Barnard trotted after them, and Custer followed. As they caught up with the resplendent blue staff, trailing its odor of saddle soap along the country road, Custer dropped to the rear among the orderlies. Bedraggled as he was, in his wet uniform, he felt embarrassed among the polished officers.

From an inconspicuous place in the rear, he saw General Barnard draw rein beside McClellan. The dapper little commanding general turned his head. Custer could see his visored soldier cap, his mustache and short goatee. Custer could also see the bearded face of General Barnard talking to him, as the regal staff swept along the soft dirt road, horses' hoofs twinkling spiritedly.

A few minutes later one of the aides dropped back, his mount fretting under the curb bit. He stopped beside the soiled and sopping Custer.

"General McClellan wants to see the officer who was down on the river with General Barnard," the trim aide said.

Lieutenant Custer flushed. Now he'd catch it, sure. McClellan was famous for the neatness of his appearance and the tidiness of his staff. What would he think of Custer's dirty boots and mud-caked uniform? Even the blue color had long since faded to purple. The lieutenant's tangled blond hair had not been cut since he left Monroe. A worse-looking scarecrow could not be ordered before the general. Custer spurred ahead, his tawny locks accentuating the blushes of embarrassment.

McClellan turned his jaunty head to greet him.

"Ride alongside," the commanding general said, "and tell me about this crossing of the river below the destroyed New Bridge, and what you saw on the other side."

The great man's manner set Custer at ease, and he replied without constraint, explaining the feasibility of surrounding and cutting off the picket post. McClellan asked for more details. The general was a good listener. Custer liked him.

"Do you know," McClellan said, "you're just the young man I've been looking for, Mr. Custer. How would you like to come on my staff?"

Custer was overcome. He probably never forgot the view of the road ahead, the deserted pasture fringed with woods, the rhythmic throb of prancing hoofs, as he heard those fateful words.

"You don't — really — mean it — General?" was all he could stammer.

"I do," McClellan replied. "How say you? Will you accept?"

The incident would smack too much of Horatio Alger to be credited were it not vouched for by McClellan as well as Custer, although McClellan placed the interview a day later.[13]

An even more dramatic account became current in the army. According to this version, McClellan and his staff came to the Chickahominy crossing. The general looked at the dark seeping water and said, "I wish I knew how deep it is." His staff exchanged glances but offered no replies. From the rear Custer was said to have spurred up muttering, "I'll damn soon show him!" and floundered in. Crossing over and back he called out, "That's how deep it is, General" [14] — a good enough story, true in spirit if not in fact.

This incident began a lifelong devotion between McClellan and Custer, although the two men were as different as could be — one neat, cautious, thorough, always hesitant to attack, and the other reckless in dress and deed, always ordering a charge. Perhaps this difference was the bond between them.

Secretary of War Stanton confirmed Custer's appointment to McClellan's staff as of June 5, 1862, and gave Custer the brevet rank of captain. Armstrong sent the cherished manuscript to his sister in Monroe for safekeeping.

7 Seven Days' Battles — and a Best Man

McClellan's version of the appointment of Custer as his aide differs from both the other stories. He said that by the time his army reached the Chickahominy Lincoln had withdrawn so many troops to defend Washington that there were not enough left to attack Richmond. Yet the newspapers in the North blamed McClellan instead of Lincoln. Why, the irate editors asked, had Little Mac taken almost two months to march seventy-five miles?

Thoroughly upset by these criticisms, the natty little general heard Barnard's report of Custer's crossing of the Chickahominy. The name Custer meant nothing to him. Other young lieutenants had already been cited for feats equally gallant during the march up the Peninsula. Also, three others had been scouting for Chickahominy crossings when Custer was with Barnard. The only difference, so far as McClellan knew, was that this chap Custer had a plan for cutting off a sentry post. Certainly capturing a few sentries would not affect the outcome of the war, but it might divert the newsmen and convince some Northern editors that the Army of the Potomac was not asleep.

McClellan turned to Colonel D. A. Woodbury of the 4th Michigan and asked him if he would like the honor of leading this little offensive. A squadron of the 2d Cavalry would accompany him and, as guides, he could have Lieutenants Bowen, Churchill, Humphreys, and Custer. These young men had been out yesterday, May 23d, wading up and down the river. They knew all the best crossings.[1]

Woodbury was delighted and returned to his regiment. He selected Company A — thirty men — to march farthest up the stream, cross, come down and, if possible, cut off the sentry post. The balance of the regiment was to wait on the east side, where it could flank any Confederates who tried to prevent the maneuver.

Company A had been recruited in Monroe, Michigan. It stood at the ford as Lieutenant Custer rode up to point out the crossing. He heard a voice in the ranks say, "Why, that's Armstrong Custer!"

"Hello, Autie!" said another.

Custer looked down from his horse. He saw a line of familiar faces and leaned over to shake hands. Then, straightening up in the saddle, he shouted, "Come on Monroe." [2]

The company splashed across the muddy stream and crawled out dripping wet. Their captain ordered them into line and they started downstream through the river-bottom brush, marching with guns ready, like rabbit hunters. Company A walked for about a hundred yards before the enemy opened fire with a blast out of the thickets. The Union men flopped down behind trees and hummocks and fired back at the lines of hats they saw along fallen logs ahead. Lieutenant Custer, laughing gaily, rode toward the river and shouted for reinforcements. Then he spurred into the stream and splashed across to let the new-comers see that the water was not deep.

He came back with three companies and a major, wading armpit deep, holding cartridge boxes over their heads. This battalion ex-tended the Union line along an old fence where a ditch had been cut to drain the field. The men stood in muck but they felt safe there.[3] The firing was continuous now, and Custer rode back to Colonel Woodbury. He explained the situation and suggested marching the reserves down the river a mile. Then, let them cross and come up-stream in the enemy's rear. Colonel Woodbury agreed to try it.

Down at the wreck of New Bridge the last five companies of the Michigan 4th crossed and started north.

"Go in, Wolverines!" Custer shouted. "Give them hell."

The fight lasted four hours. Then the shattered Confederate detach-ment surrendered. The Michigan boys shared their raincoats with wounded Southerners and helped them to Federal ambulances. The Union soldiers had lost only one man. Another lay dying, and five or six suffered from severe wounds. Of all the engineer lieutenants who knew the fords, Custer alone had distinguished himself for fearlessly crossing and recrossing the Chickahominy. He was first to get into the fight and last to leave the field.

McClellan reported to the Secretary of War that the victory had driven the enemy south of the Chickahominy; that fifty prisoners had been taken and many more killed.[4] In his memoirs he said that the reports of Custer's gallantry in this skirmish had first directed his attention to the lieutenant—not his daredevil crossing a day or two before, as usually believed. McClellan remembered later that he sent for the young man to congratulate him. He found Custer to be a slim, long-haired boy, carelessly dressed. "I thanked him for his gallantry," McClellan said, "and asked what I could do for him. He replied very modestly that he had nothing to ask, and evidently did not suppose that he had done anything to deserve extraordinary reward." When asked if he'd like to be aide-de-camp he brightened, flushed, seemed delighted. "Custer was simply a reckless, gallant boy, undeterred by fatigue, unconscious of fear," McClellan wrote in his memoirs. "His head was always clear in danger and he always brought me clear and intelligible reports. . . . I became much attached to him."

This story of McClellan's, told eleven years later, may be closest of the three to the truth, but it should be noted that the records show McClellan tried him out for five days after the fight before making the appointment.[5] During this time Custer guided engineering parties along the swamp roads he knew, helped map the country, cultivated side whiskers which he must have considered suitable to his new estate, and became acquainted with the three French princes who had come to America as observers and served on McClellan's staff.

The Union Army did not cross the Chickahominy in force at the place where Custer led the sortie. Instead, a third of the men found bridges far down the stream, while two thirds remained on the north side, protecting the army's supply line to White House Landing. Thus the army was dangerously separated on May 30 when heavy rains raised the Chickahominy above its banks, flooding the grassy meadows on both sides. McClellan realized that an alert enemy could now catch him badly split and defeat each portion separately. Next day his fears were confirmed by the capture of an enemy courier. Armstrong recognized the fellow at once — James Barroll Washington, West Point, class of '59. The young man would say nothing more than that he was on General Joseph E. Johnston's staff, but that was enough. The enemy must be very close and an attack imminent.[6]

Within hours the Confederates struck the Union forces isolated south of the stream. At Gaines's Mill on the north bank, McClellan could follow the battle's progress by the smoke above the treetops. If he sent

Custer across the morass as an observer, his new aide must have reported both sides to be fighting at many places in water to their knees, bullets ricocheting along the surface like the fins of striking sharks. Wounded men's heads were propped up to prevent drowning. Only on some elevated roads and on the railroad embankment could soldiers find dry ground. Old Bull Sumner rushed to the rescue with reinforcements, crossing the few bridges still above the flood. That night the rising Chickahominy covered the bridges. Engineers worked desperately to build new ones, but the rising tide flowed over the passageways as soon as constructed. To send more men became very difficult. Fortunately, the enemy had been checked.

This indecisive Battle of Fair Oaks, or Seven Pines, accomplished little except to give both sides confidence. McClellan spent the next month fortifying the ground he held, fighting mosquitoes, and promising the Northern press an offensive "tomorrow." Custer, with time on his hands, visited prisoner of war James Washington and arranged good treatment for him. The two schoolmates had their picture taken together.

Immediately after the battle, Robert E. Lee was assigned command of the Army of Northern Virginia. He decided to encircle McClellan's right and cut him off from his supplies at White House Landing. McClellan had already planned to change his base from the White House to the James River, twenty miles below his present location. He had barely started this movement when Lee hit his scattered forces at Mechanicsville on June 26.

Next day, Custer was helping the general prepare for a renewed attack from Lee when a bombardment five miles down the river surprised them. "Stonewall" Jackson had made an unexpected march from the Shenandoah Valley and struck Fitz-John Porter's corps, which had been left to guard the northern crossings. Porter was in serious trouble. McClellan asked Custer if he knew of any way to send reinforcements across the river and, if necessary, bring Porter's army back to safety.

"Yes," Custer said, "the grapevine bridge." [7]

McClellan gave him two brigades to guide across. The commanders were odd-appearing fellows. William H. French sat stiffly erect on his horse, his face flushed as though his collar were too tight. The other brigade commander, Thomas Francis Meagher, rode up under a green banner embroidered with a golden harp. He had recently escaped from an Australian penal colony where he had been jailed for plotting Irish independence. In America his countrymen enlisted under this foreign flag and insisted on carrying it into battle.

The crossing was precarious, and the two brigades did not get to the north bank until five o'clock in the afternoon. The confusion in the hills above the river reminded Custer of Bull Run. Frightened farmers, by hundreds, packed the roads. Among them stood deserters, skulkers, and dazed soldiers who would fight if they could find their regiments. The relief column, caught in the jam, could not pass. Yet constant firing from Fitz-John Porter's men told of his desperate predicament. General French deployed his men as skirmishers, cleared the roads, and both brigades got through to Porter. Spreading out as a shield, these fresh troops held back the Confederates until dark.

Next morning at reveille Custer reported that the right wing of the Army of the Potomac had been saved. The job of crossing the Chickahominy had taken all night, but Porter's men were safe at last on the south side. Good, yes, but also bad! The Confederates now held the Union Army's supply line to White House Landing. McClellan would have to establish the new one to the James River much faster than he had anticipated. Already Lee's army stood on two sides of him. The Chickahominy fenced his left. The only way of escape was through White Oak Swamp — a vast, densely wooded morass covered by an inch or two of water seeping away through invisible channels.[8] Captain Custer and the other scouts who had mapped the country would be invaluable now.

McClellan started moving his army at once. There was no time to rest. The weather turned steamy hot, breathless in the woods. Soldiers threw away their knapsacks, fell exhausted from the column, revived and stumbled along with strange regiments. The enemy tried desperately to get ahead of them, and cut in on their flanks at every wood road. Part of the line had to deploy constantly and fight while the rest moved on. Custer rode between the columns, carrying messages, keeping McClellan informed. His old chief, Hancock, brought up the rear behind five thousand wagons and twenty-five hundred beef cattle. Severely wounded men were left behind, surgeons staying with them; all thus became prisoners of war. For four days and four nights, Custer survived on one meal a day, if he could snatch it. When he slept, if at all, it was in wet clothes with his head on a log.[9]

On July 1, 1862, McClellan stopped at Malvern Hill to give battle to Lee. Already the Union van had reached the James River gunboats. The Confederate forces did not attack until mid-afternoon — a long wait for the expectant Federals. According to unconfirmed gossip, Custer and Lieutenant Bowen entertained the waiting line by daring enemy riders to venture out for fox and goose chases.[10] These stories cannot be verified, but Custer and Bowen had become inseparable, a friendship almost as close as Custer's and Tom Rosser's at West Point.

That night, after the battle, it rained, and McClellan marched his army on to Harrison's Landing, where it encamped safely in the mud near Federal gunboats. The soldiers rested for a month, happy to be alive, proud of an orderly retreat, and contemptuous of Northern newspapers which still howled "on to Richmond." Custer and Bowen enjoyed the rest. Both acquired "servants" from among the hundreds of fugitive blacks who flocked into the encampment. Runaway slaves eagerly tended horses or shined shoes for their keep. Custer also secured a dog, Rose, the first of many pets to accompany him through the war.

On August 2, McClellan sent Custer with a detachment under Colonel William Woods Averell on an expedition south of the James. They came back to Harrison's Landing within a week, but instead of getting time to bathe and relax they were ordered to march at 2 A.M.

next morning up into the White Oak Swamp country which Custer knew. He stopped at headquarters, got a fresh horse — his favorite black — and a letter from Lydia.

The little expedition consisted of three or four hundred horse and four cannon. Flying artillery had become a part of most cavalry columns. An Irishman, Lieutenant Richard Byrnes of the regular army, led the van and Custer rode with him. At 10:30 that morning they spied an enemy cavalry encampment. Colonel Averell ordered an immediate charge and they all thundered in, pistols booming. The unsuspecting Confederates surrendered or fled.

Colonel Averell began tallying prisoners and captured equipment. Byrnes and Custer, with ten men, trotted off to hunt stragglers. A short way up the swamp road, they met a detail of ten or fifteen gray-clad riders spurring toward the encampment. These Confederates had evidently heard the bombardment and were hurrying in to investigate. When they discovered the Union detail they wheeled out into the ragged fields as though to ride around it. Lieutenant Byrnes shouted, "Custer, you take the right. I'll take the left" — a common rule-of-thumb for quail shooters.

The Union horsemen fanned out after the Confederates, hoofs pounding the soft earth. Custer saw that he was riding straight for the officer at the head of the scurrying line. The fellow rode a splendid bay with black saddle and morocco breast-strap. Custer noted, with a marksman's eye, the enemy's fine equipment and urged his black charger to do his best. Armstrong knew he could not outrun the fine bay horse, but he hoped to head him off. A fence at the field's edge might force the man to turn and fight, or he might be thrown if he tried to jump it.

Custer watched through blurred eyes as his own black raced forward. The bay gathered for the jump and sailed over gallantly. Armstrong grinned grimly as he realized that it was his turn now to hazard a fall. A moment later his black skimmed the rails like a bird. In mid-air, Custer saw the Confederate turn his head to see if he was making the jump. On the far side, the race continued, but the enemy's bay soon slowed down in a spot of marshy ground. Custer shouted for the officer to surrender.

The man paid no attention. Custer raised his pistol and shot from the saddle. If the bullet hit, the rider did not flinch. Armstrong called again for surrender, then took more deliberate aim and fired again. The man teetered a moment in his saddle, reeled and slipped to the ground. His bay horse shied and ran off, bridle reins trailing. Custer's mettled black bounded off, too, carrying him away. In the brush on every side Armstrong heard shots and shouts as other members of his detail caught up with the enemy. He joined the fray, and helped capture a rebel who had jumped from his horse to hide.

Resting after the excitement, Custer saw five riderless horses huddled together in fright. One of them wore the red morocco breast-band he remembered. A distant bugle sounded "assembly." Evidently Colonel Averell believed his men had better come in and get out of the enemy's country while they could. The detail remounted and rode over to the loose horses.[11] Custer claimed the bay. He wanted that handsome black saddle and the ornamental silver studs. On the saddle hung a magnificent straight sword. This may have been what was later known as Custer's famous "Toledo blade," inscribed with the conventional sentiment:

DRAW ME NOT WITHOUT PROVOCATION.
SHEATHE ME NOT WITHOUT HONOR.

According to another account, the famous sword was given Custer by Major George A. Drew of the 6th Michigan because Armstrong was the only man strong enough to arch the blade above his head [12] — a story too much like the legends of King Arthur's Excalibur to be credible. Custer's future wife was never sure which of these accounts was correct. Maybe neither! The war was fought in an age when Tennyson's heroic poems were on everybody's tongue, and exact fact seemed inconsequential. Had there been no counterfeit chivalry in the mid-nineteenth century there might have been no Civil War. Certainly the war would have been very different.

Back on the James River, Armstrong answered Lydia's letter, writing on August 8 to "Dear Brother and Sister." He described the fight and the handsome saddle he had acquired, saying he intended to keep the horse. (Captured horses had to be appraised and bought from the government. Equipment was the property of the captor.) Armstrong also wrote his family that he had secured a double-barreled shotgun which he would send to "Bos" — his younger brother, Boston. He related the gruesome details of his victim's death:

> Owing to the confusion and excitement I was not able to see the officer after he fell from his horse, but Lieutenant Byrnes told me that he saw the officer after he fell, and that he rose to his feet, turned around, threw up his hands and fell to the ground with a stream of blood gushing from his mouth. I had either shot him in the neck or body. In either case the wound must have been mortal. It was his own fault; I told him twice to surrender, but he compelled me to shoot him.

A youthful big-game hunter might write like this after his first kill. The letter also shows Custer to have been a lad with limited battle experience. In spite of a summer's campaign, he was not yet inured to the grim details of violent death.

Loafing around headquarters at Harrison's Landing, Custer read in the newspapers that a new general was diverting popular attention from McClellan. Up near Washington, General John Pope had become a favorite and was now reported to be marching "on to Richmond" by the overland route Little Mac had feared to take. To make this bad news doubly distasteful, an order from Lincoln commanded McClellan to withdraw down the Peninsula.

Custer rode with the general's staff at the head of the army, to Williamsburg. Here he got permission to visit his wounded friend, Gimlet

Lea. The battle-torn fields were green now after a summer's growth. Farmers in the surrounding country were cutting hay. Rural life proceeded much as it had before the invasion, but the old colonial buildings looked neglected. Weeds grew around William and Mary College, and the ancient tower.

Armstrong learned that Gimlet was on parole, staying at a nearby house, and he cantered over to see him. Gimlet would be interested in the latest news from prisoner-of-war James Washington and he would know about their other friends. Armstrong had heard that John Pelham distinguished himself as an artillerist at Seven Pines, and that Stephen Ramseur, Pierce Butler Young, and Tom Rosser were all colonels. Was it really so? It sure paid to be in the Confederate Army! Still, Armstrong had done pretty well, himself, and would not be ashamed to face Lea. Although only a captain he was on McClellan's staff and, like a Southern gentleman, he had his own black servant to hold his horse.

At the house where Lea was living, Armstrong tossed the reins to his "boy" and mounted the steps. He found his schoolmate happy and almost recovered from his wound. Gimlet invited him to come in and meet the family with whom he was staying. In the parlor Lea introduced Custer to two attractive young ladies. The young people chatted for an hour. Custer replied with his nasal twang to the liquid Southern speech. His new friends insisted that he come back and spend the night — sleep in a bed after a summer in camp.

Custer agreed to do so if General McClellan would permit it. With a gay farewell, he popped his whip on his boot-top and cantered away, followed by his "servant" and dog.

In camp Custer scrubbed his face and hands, wrung the water out of his golden curls, perhaps even anointed them with cinnamon. Then he put on a fresh uniform and returned. That evening, after a bountiful country supper, the family gathered in the parlor. Custer beamed at the two young beauties sitting on the sofa, their broad skirts spread out before them like fans. Someone suggested music — Custer's favorite diversion. One of the girls played, and they all sang "For Southern Rights, Hurrah!" Armstrong bowed over the piano as he turned the pages.*

During the evening Gimlet Lea whispered in Custer's ear, "What do you think of the girls?"

"Beautiful, both of them. Beautiful," Custer replied.

"I'm glad you like them, for I'm engaged to marry the elder next week," Lea confided. "She came heah to nurse the wounded and I met her. You-all must stay for the wedden."

"I'm sorry. But there *is* a war."

"I'll get married tomorrow, if you'll be best man?"

"I'll ask the general for permission. But tell me: who is the other beauty? Is she your sweetheart's sister?"

"No. She's her cousin, down from Richmond for the ceremony."

Custer returned to camp in the morning and got permission to stay for the wedding. He was back at the bride's house in full dress regalia long before the appointed time. Lea awaited him in a newly tailored gray uniform, properly trimmed with gold lace. The minister came, a deferential man in rusty black, with clerical vest and collar. Neighbors dropped in. Finally, someone struck appropriate notes on the piano and the two girls came down the stairs, both dressed in white, wreaths of white flowers on their heads.

"I never saw two prettier girls," Custer remembered, and he qualified as an experienced judge, or thought so.

The ceremony was performed according to Episcopalian ritual — a reminder of West Point days. Lea responded in a clear, dignified voice. The bride answered the first question only. Custer thought the sweet thing confused and excited. After the ceremony, she laughingly admitted that she had neglected to respond purposely so as to be free from the obligations.

* This account is recorded in three copies of a letter written by Custer to Lydia Reed, September 21, 1862 (MS, West Point), in F. Whittaker, *Complete Life of . . . Custer . . .* , pp. 125–129, and in M. Merington, *Custer Story*, p. 35. See also M. Schaff, *Spirit of Old West Point*, p. 180. The account of the wedding is from these four sources.

Custer made a point of calling the bride "Mrs. Lea." Her pretty companion kissed her, then sat down sobbing.

"Why, Cousin Maggie," Gimlet said, "What are you crying for? Oh, I know. You are crying because you are not married; well, here is the minister and here is Captain Custer, who I know would be glad to carry off such a pretty bride from the Southern Confederacy."

The girl looked up through her tears. "Captain Lea," she sobbed, "you are just as mean as you can be."

Supper was announced. The bride took her husband's arm. Custer presented his to "Cousin Maggie." Walking in with her, he bowed his curly head to whisper, "I don't see how such a strong Secessionist can take the arm of a Union officer."

"You *ought* to be in *our* army," she replied.

Custer, the flirt, asked what she would give him if he resigned and joined the Confederacy.

"You are not in earnest, are you?" she countered as they all sat down around the glowing candles.

Next morning the sun shone high in the sky when Captain Custer cantered back to camp, the moist Virginia air fanning his cheeks. At McClellan's headquarters, he found that the general had moved to Yorktown. Custer's servant, not knowing what to do, had remained with Rose and the horses.

Armstrong's mind was too concerned with memories of little dancing slippers and coquettish side-glances to be much disturbed by McClellan's disappearance. Instead of catching up with the general, he rode back to his friends' home in Williamsburg, taking along his servant and dog. At the telegraph station he wired for permission to remain a few days. McClellan was now hurrying to Washington with troubles of his own. There is no record of his reply.

For almost two weeks Custer dallied with his Southern friends, listening to "Cousin Maggie" sing "Maryland, My Maryland," "Dixie," and "The Bonnie Blue Flag." Between songs they all played cards — euchre or independence. Occasionally they played to see if the North or the South would win the war. Invariably Gimlet Lea beat Custer, to the great merriment of them all, Armstrong said later.

Custer was still enjoying life at Williamsburg when he learned that McClellan had arrived in Alexandria and his army was following as fast as transports could be provided.

This probably meant that Custer was already alone in enemy territory. The Confederate Army, or even the local constabulary, might arrest him any moment. He waited indoors until dark. Then, with his servant and dog at his heels, he rode to Yorktown. Arriving at 1 A.M., he was told that the last transport had gone, but he booked passage on a steamboat bound for Fortress Monroe. Here he discovered that McClellan had been relieved of command. Aide-de-camp Custer had no chief! He must get back to Washington, if he could.

Fortunately Armstrong found a vessel headed north. In due time he landed in Baltimore and learned that McClellan's successor, John Pope, had been badly beaten in the Second Battle of Bull Run. The North seemed much discouraged. In the gloom and confusion, Armstrong got transportation to Washington, where he was told to report to Chief of Cavalry Alfred Pleasonton.

Custer found Pleasonton a sarcastic and exacting regular of the old school, a bachelor notoriously hard to please. The fellow lacked McClellan's cordial personality, ruled his men through fear instead of loyalty. Habitually he wore a whip on his wrist, symbol of what he expected of the new cavalry. Already his staff carried whips on their wrists as proud badges of the service. Captain Custer was awaiting what he felt would be an unpleasant assignment when the encampment was shocked by startling news.

"Robert E. Lee is invading Maryland!"

Pope's shattered and discouraged army was in no condition to oppose the Army of Northern Virginia. What could be done? In this emergency, Lincoln restored McClellan to command. The exhausted troops immediately revived. Regiment after regiment forgot its recent defeat and cheered for joy. No commander in all American history ever inspired such response from an army. And among all the happy, whooping men, none was happier than Captain Custer. To ride again with his adored general and drive back the invader was music to his melody-loving ears. How soon do we start?

8 Antietam

CUSTER RODE TO McCLELLAN'S HEADQUARTERS AT ROCKVILLE, TWELVE miles from Washington, on September 8, 1862. With him were Lieutenants James Harrison Wilson and James P. Martin.[1] The three boys were reporting for duty on McClellan's staff. They had known each other at West Point. Wilson had been appointed to the Academy from Illinois, Martin from Kentucky — one of the thousands of Kentuckians who remained loyal to the Union. Staff duty was new to Wilson and he admitted being nervous. "Cinnamon" had served in few other capacities.

When the aides arrived at headquarters, the Army of the Potomac was already on the march, long dusty columns winding westward seeking the invader. According to reports, Lee had crossed the Potomac some forty or fifty miles above Washington and by this time might be in Pennsylvania. McClellan would soon take the road in person.

For Armstrong this was a holiday. What more could he wish than the joy of marching across Maryland behind his beloved chief in the bracing September weather! It was good to feel a horse between his knees once more, to hear the tinkle of curb-chains, the rhythmic pounding of spirited hoofs, and to joke with other aides. He enjoyed matching the mettle of his mount with theirs and as they marched along, the young men dared one another to jump roadside ditches and barriers.

The marching soldiers seemed as gay as the officers, every man happy to be back under McClellan — the hero who had made this army. Moreover, Maryland farmers cheered as they passed. In every village matrons stood at picket gates with trays of goodies, pitchers of water beaded with cold sweat. Girls in freshly starched dresses waved flags from upstairs windows. Custer, his kepi over one eye, his cinnamon-scented curls on his shoulders, waved back, and no doubt spurred his horse furtively to make him prance.

Moving eighty-seven thousand men took time. McClellan's van reached Frederick, Maryland, on September 12. Next day Custer rode in with the commanding general, his band, the brilliant flags, and the smartly dressed officers. Confederates had evacuated the town only a day or two ago.[2] Ahead, in plain sight, Custer saw a long broken ridge — the Catoctin Range. Pleasonton's cavalry had already been across it, to Middletown in the next valley, but had failed to find Lee there. On the second ridge, five miles farther west, Union patrols had been stopped at Turner's Gap where the National Road crossed South Mountain. Perhaps Lee planned to fight over there.

At headquarters in Frederick the aides sat on camp chairs unloaded from the baggage wagons. As they talked, a rider galloped in, swung to the ground, and disappeared into McClellan's tent with a bulky envelope in his hand. The aides looked at one another. Something important, you bet!

McClellan called for an officer who knew the handwriting of General Lee's adjutant, who was formerly a Federal soldier. Several officers volunteered and examined the documents. They pronounced them genuine. Here in McClellan's hands were Lee's private orders, disclosing the position of all his troops and the directions he wanted them to march! Some Confederate general must have lost them. The orders showed that Lee's army was well across South Mountain and divided into at least three units. What an opportunity! McClellan might defeat each one separately — if he got there in time.

Two main roads crossed South Mountain, one at Turner's, the other at Crampton's Gap. At the former, Pleasonton's scouts had already been stopped, but the resistance had been slight. McClellan must capture both gaps at once. Then he could pour his men across in two columns, thus getting them on the west side in half the time, and in a good position to prevent Lee from uniting his forces.

McClellan ordered Lieutenant Wilson to go as his representative with the column bound for Crampton's Gap, southernmost of the two passes. Custer and Martin were told to report to Pleasonton for the attack on Turner's Gap, where some resistance had already been met and the hardest fighting might be expected. Both columns must start forward in the morning. Lieutenant Wilson remembered, later, that he wondered why McClellan told the columns to wait until morning when an all-night march might have put the Union Army between Lee's units. A twelve-hour delay could ruin McClellan's opportunity. . . . But Wilson obeyed silently and trotted away to join the left-hand column.

Lieutenants Custer and Martin rode off to join Pleasonton on the National Road with the right-hand column. Darkness had fallen when they found the tart but handsome middle-aged general at Middletown. He read the order to start in the morning, and before dawn was in the saddle, his men and horses all fed and ready to go. The old-maid cavalryman was a fighter, all right — thin, tough as whalebone and contemptuous of any man who could not keep up with him. No wonder his staff carried whips on wrists, like their chief, and were proud of the symbol!

By daylight, September 14, 1862, Pleasonton's column of horse had reached Turner's Gap, a four-hundred-foot depression in a thousand-foot ridge. The sound of a rifle shot halted them. This was the place where the enemy had stopped Union scouts yesterday. The thin-faced, immaculately uniformed commander snapped a few orders and advance patrols trotted off along the wood roads ahead. Custer saw that the geography was more complicated than it appeared from Middletown. A little valley cut into the gap from the north. Byroads meandered into the broken country on both sides.

Custer enjoyed spanking along, spying for Confederate outposts, galloping back with reports to Pleasonton. The enemy seemed to have moved into this country in considerable force during the night. Could Lee have learned about the lost orders and be doing his best now to hold back McClellan at this pass until the Confederate Army consolidated?

From the slope of South Mountain, Custer looked back toward Middletown. The road was blue with approaching soldiers. He saw advance corps swing from the road, cross the fields and disappear in the trees south of the gap. That was Reno's corps — not the Reno he had known at West Point, but General Jesse Lee Reno. Other blue columns, under "Fighting Joe" Hooker, streamed north of the pike to climb the ridge there. The plan was to force the heights on both sides of the gap. Custer could also see the reserves standing along the National Road, a long blue-black line — Gibbon's "Black Hats." The thin, active instructor in artillery tactics who had taught Armstrong at West Point was a brigadier general now. His men were to sweep up the highway when the enemy was flanked from the heights.

Custer noticed that the country ahead of these advancing troops was rough and densely wooded with scrub oaks and thickets of mountain laurel. Here and there small clearings with stone fences made natural fortifications. The battle would be many little skirmishes because no continuous line could be advanced. As Custer watched, he heard the rattling fire of muskets in various places along the bushy slopes. The fight had begun.

By nine o'clock most of the Union Army had reached the crest south of the gap; but north of it, in the rough country, Hooker was having trouble.

The cavalry could not function in the narrow gulches, among the stone fences, and on brushy hillsides. It remained on the slope of South Mountain below the firing line. Waiting here, Custer and Pleasonton watched the main army cross the valley from the Catoctin Range to reinforce the divisions already fighting along the summit of South Mountain. The Army of the Potomac in battle formation flowed across the fields, an undulating blue tide of men, vast, steady, inexorable as the ocean. Even veteran Pleasonton paused to watch with admiration.

At 4 P.M. the blue line had spread along the base of South Mountain. Soon it began climbing up to the sputtering rifles on the summit, the slow steady grinding movement of a great army going into battle. Back on the Middletown road, McClellan's tiny flag could be seen among more waiting legions. From where Custer sat his horse, neither the blue nor the gray line seemed to be flinching. Absorbed in the spectacle, he failed to notice that the sun had set behind the tree-tufted ridge and darkness was settling down. In the twilight, the shots from distant guns which had been firing all afternoon suddenly appeared like fireflies on the black mountain side. By nine o'clock the shooting stopped except for flurries from nervous pickets. In the dark Custer and Martin dismounted beside Pleasonton's campfire. McClellan sent word that Gibbon had pushed his Black Hats up the road, fighting after dark in the gap. On the ridge to the south, Reno had been killed. Burnside now commanded that corps. Reports had not yet come in from Hooker, north of the gap.

The staff crouched around the blaze, Pleasonton silent and always aloof. Nobody seemed to know whether the battle had been lost or won. During the night a strange thing happened. Somebody noticed that they all sat under a cone of gray light — a cone like the inside of an Indian teepee. Fog had crept over them and the campfire caused a strange optical illusion.

Before dawn, on September 15, Pleasonton strode around restlessly in his Wellington boots, his uniform still neat as though on parade. Who had won yesterday's battle? Pleasonton determined to find out in his own aggressive way. Let this fog hide Union movements as well as the Confederates'. He spoke quickly, dealing out orders as a professional gambler does cards. Vedettes mounted and disappeared in the fog, groping their way along the ghostly roads — a grisly business. The acrid smell of yesterday's burnt powder still clung to the wet leaves underfoot. Dark tree trunks emerged ominously in the mists. Enemies behind logs could see movement without being observed themselves.

At sunup, fog still blanketed the woods. No enemy had been found, and Pleasonton learned the advance dispositions of the Union troops. He told aides Custer and Martin to join Colonel Elon J. Farnsworth's 8th Illinois Cavalry. That regiment must spearhead a pursuit of the retreating enemy. Hooker's I Corps would follow the horsemen down the road. Behind Hooker would come the II Corps under Bull Sumner. The IX Corps would follow — plenty of support, surely! All that he, Pleasonton, expected of Custer, Martin, and Farnsworth was for them to stop and hold the Confederate Army with one regiment until these corps arrived.

This sarcastic request — typical of Pleasonton — brought no complaint from Custer. He wanted action and was beginning to admire this dashing cavalry commander. Why shouldn't a regiment be big enough to charge into the Army of Northern Virginia? Battles were sometimes won by that kind of audacity.

Custer and Martin clattered away with Farnsworth's 8th Illinois. West of the mountain they emerged from the fog. The sun beat down sultry hot, making the horses sweat, but their riders spurred ahead, trotting on the downgrades, galloping when the road curved up. They entered the first town, Boonsboro, as the enemy was leaving, but the Confederates were not running away. Instead, they retreated in good order with a rear guard of skirmishers.

Custer knew only one way to fight such a formation, so he circled across the fields with a detachment, galloped as far along the retreating column as he dared, then fired at it from behind fences. When the terrain permitted, the horsemen swept out of little depressions with wild yells, shot at the gray column, then dashed away, but these diversions failed to interrupt the enemy's march. Two miles past Boonsboro, Custer received an order from Pleasonton to come back.

Returning, he picked up two abandoned cannon and several hundred Confederate stragglers — barefoot, ragged fellows in remnants of all kinds of uniforms, but prisoners of war, nonetheless.³ From them Custer learned that he had been fighting his West Point commandant, Fitzhugh Lee. Tom Rosser had been in the battle at the gap and Pierce Manning Butler Young had been wounded there. The Georgian's prophecy that they would meet in battle had come true, and in all probability they would meet again.

Pleasonton cited both Custer and Martin for their heroism and McClellan reported the captured guns and prisoners to Lincoln. McClellan described the Battle of South Mountain as a great victory, but he seemed in no haste to go ahead and destroy Lee. On the afternoon of September 16 he established headquarters on the highlands east of sluggish Antietam Creek. Lee had been hurrying his separated units into the open country beyond. The big battle would undoubtedly be fought here.

McClellan moved into a large two-story brick mansion, the Pry House, where he could view the surrounding country. Orderlies pitched tents on the lawn and drove stakes for the telescopes through which troop movements could be observed. Custer, with his own field glasses, studied the ground ahead. Far to the left Antietam Creek joined the Potomac, forming an acute angle. The pie-shaped area between the two streams was a checkerboard of farms. Sharpsburg stood back from the Potomac at the narrow end. On the distant roads and along the fences, Armstrong could see thousands of little men marching with fluttering banners, the varicolored state flags peculiar to the Confederate Army. On hill crests, cannon were already planted. Lee had certainly got his army together again and planned a decisive battle.

Turning from the distant field, Custer watched his general prepare for the conflict. Like McClellan, he realized the importance of this battle. If Little Mac won it decisively, he would go down in history as the great general of the Civil War. If he lost, he would never command again. Under this strain McClellan did not seem disturbed. Custer admired his composure. The General moved slowly, methodically, checking all details. He called for his horse and rode out around the battlefield, examining the terrain and pointing out stations to be occupied by troops still coming in. After dark he sent his aides back along the line to see that all divisions had found their proper places.

The plan of battle seemed a good one. Lee, with his back to the Potomac, had concentrated on the pie-shaped piece of land. The Antietam, in front of him, had a few bridges and could be forded at places, but large bodies of men would find it difficult to cross. The obvious way to attack him would be from the north, between the Potomac and Antietam Creek, down the upper end of the triangle. Surely Lee would prepare to meet the assault troops there, and McClellan planned to fool him. He deployed his men in a six-mile crescent along the north and east sides of the Confederate Army. First he would feint on the north front. When Lee sent his reserves up there, McClellan would drive in with Burnside from the southern horn of the crescent, striking near Sharpsburg. Then, as the two Confederate flanks crumbled, he would attack in the center and demoralize Lee's entire army. A good plan, surely, provided it deceived Lee. To Custer, McClellan never planned wrong.

Next morning, September 16, 1862, dawned very hot. The Union soldiers dragged their feet in the dust. Bull Sumner's II Corps had been marching all night and it stopped near headquarters to erect puptents — the hottest kind of shelter. The old general came over to headquarters, champing his false teeth. Custer had not seen him since the Peninsular campaign.

By eleven o'clock dark clouds threatened rain. McClellan ate dinner with his staff and the afternoon dragged by. Sumner's men folded their tents and trudged leisurely away. Custer showed no impatience with McClellan's slowness. At four o'clock an observer at the telescope reported that Hooker, far to the right, had begun the encircling feint. The waiting aides heard the firing two miles away, but could see little. The setting sun shone in their eyes. Finally, when darkness inked out the landscape, red arches from cannons' mouths told them that Lee had brought up his artillery and was firing back. This indicated that he was being deceived as planned.

Early in the night, rain drizzled across the dreary fields and drenched the headquarters tents. Custer lay down, without undressing, as raindrops pattered on the canvas. Distant cannon fire throbbed in the murky mist. At midnight McClellan's candle went out. Custer dozed, confident that his beau ideal had reviewed all the details for the battle of his life.

At dawn on September 17 McClellan's aides stepped out of their tents, brushing their slept-in uniforms, trying to appear neat and ready for orders. Sipping coffee in the morning twilight, they watched the lowering sky. The sound of distant shooting increased with the light. At 6 A.M. nearby cannon began blasting away at miniature figures across Antietam Creek. Custer, standing beside his horse, could see, far to the right, long wavy lines of men advancing across the fields. They would disappear at some wood lot or fence, then reappear.

For an hour the distant troops moved about with no apparent purpose discernible from where Custer stood. Finally he saw other thin lines with flags pointed forward. Tiny geysers of dirt blossomed in the fields where shells exploded. Sometimes an advancing line dissolved. One moment a whole corps resembled a rectilinear design and the next it had melted into little irregular blotches.

"Sumner's met something ugly," an aide would say as he studied the terrain through a telescope. "His men are huddled like sheep in a hollow, out of range yonder."

McClellan, always composed, slow, and thoughtful, turned to Lieutenant Wilson and ordered him to ride along the north line and find out the trouble. Custer waited to be sent south to tell Burnside to go in when the Confederates' north line began to waver.

Lieutenant Wilson came back an hour later. He had ridden the entire north line and was discouraged. The men and their commanders, Hooker, Sumner, and Gibbon, showed no aggressiveness, no will to fight. Meagher's Irish Brigade, with their green and gold banner, were eager to charge, but many other soldiers had quit firing to boil coffee. Oh, for a reckless front-line leader who could stir enthusiasm and cheer all the men to victory! If Lee realized the condition up there he might rout the Union Army.

Reports from the other end of the line were only slightly better. Burnside started his attempt to cross Antietam Creek at nine in the morning, but it was three o'clock, after several regiments had failed, when Colonel Ferrero established his New Yorkers on the west side. Custer's dapper West Point dancing instructor was making good, and today he won a brigadier's star. Other regiments followed his lead and with hard fighting pushed almost to Sharpsburg before Confederate reinforcements, streaming in from Harper's Ferry, drove them back.

Custer, watching the battle beside McClellan, may have noticed a time or two when his chief could have turned the tide of battle by throwing his reserves in where Lee's army seemed weak. But this would have left his own line vulnerable and without reinforcements — a chance McClellan was unwilling to take. Yet, remarkably enough, Custer always maintained that McClellan used good judgment — a statement revealing the blindness of his loyalty, for Custer, when he became a general, usually threw in everything he had against what often seemed to be hopeless odds, and profited from the hazard.

But at Antietam, on the second day, McClellan had won only a stalemate. As the bombardment stilled, a new sound came from the battlefield — the moaning of thousands of wounded men left alone in the dark. Almost twelve thousand Federals had been killed and wounded.[4] Custer had never seen anything as bad as this.

Next day the two armies watched one another. Both sides expected an attack, but neither dared start one. Stretcher-bearers ventured out for survivors, while other details buried the dead. During the second night Lee retreated, crossing the Potomac in the dark and marching up the Shenandoah Valley. McClellan moved his headquarters leisurely across the creek to Sharpsburg; and here, on September 21, Armstrong wrote a long letter to "My dearest Sister." He began by saying: "You are perhaps in doubt whether I am still among the living or numbered with the dead. These few lines will show you that I belong to the former." [5]

"These few lines" consisted of four tightly-written pages telling not a word about his current duties or the recent fighting. Instead he described in detail his adventures at Gimlet Lea's wedding a month ago.

McClellan had many Confederate prisoners on his hands. Cautiously he moved his own headquarters down the Harper's Ferry road while he sent aides Custer and Wilson ahead with paroled men who wanted to go home. The little party, with their white flag, crossed the Potomac, passed Confederate pickets and rode to Lee's rear guard, in a Virginia village. Here the paroled Confederates were given their liberty while Custer and Wilson exchanged cards with their erstwhile enemies. Custer asked about West Point friends. He wrote a letter to Gimlet Lea and sent greetings to several others — old friends like Tom Rosser and the wounded Pierce Butler Young. To John Pelham, the handsome young artilleryman who was making a name for himself, Custer wrote: "I rejoice, dear Pelham, in your success." *

On the street Custer and Wilson recognized the familiar figure of a girl they had known. She came tripping along the walk in ballooning skirts.

"Why, I know you," she exclaimed as they passed.

The two aides turned and smiled. "Why, of course you do," Wilson replied, extending his hand. "How do you do?"

"Excuse me, Mr. Wilson, but I cannot do it." The girl blushed scarlet and buried her hands in the folds of her crinoline.

The Union officers felt embarrassed, and as they strode on, Custer heard Wilson mutter, "She made the first advance and I expected to meet with Virginia hospitality on this side of the river, but must confess I was mistaken." [6]

---

* This quotation (from M. Schaff, *Spirit of Old West Point,* p. 133) must be considered with caution. It is typical of Schaff and also of Custer, but it could hardly have happened during the truce at Fredericksburg, as Schaff says, because Custer was in Monroe, Michigan, in December, 1862.

Custer chuckled. What an experience! He'd write Sister Lydia all about it in his next letter. She'd laugh.

The visit ended all too soon and the two aides rode back across the Potomac to their own lines. Here Custer wrote to Lydia as planned, describing the trip. He also said the army would go into winter quarters next month and he hoped to get a furlough. "I intend to make myself as troublesome as possible," he said, "and I would not be surprised if I still have an engagement down town." [7]

Which girl was Armstrong thinking about? He continued the letter by saying that he looked forward to sleigh rides and trusted that his brother-in-law had three or four good horses and warm buffalo robes. Also his mouth watered for food better than army hard bread, salt pork, and *"coffee without milk."* He closed the letter by asking his sister to "kiss all the girls for me and tell them I am sorry I cannot be there to perform that duty myself."

Before sending the letter Custer took a silk rag from his pocket and folded it in the envelope explaining with a postscript that he had torn it from a rebel flag captured "at Sharpsburg, or the battle of *Antietam* as it will be known in history." He explained further: "It is pronounced by the inhabitants of this country An-tee tum, an indian name. The flag from which the strip was taken was a beautiful *state* flag, edged with gold fringe."

During the first week of October Custer seems to have been in McClellan's headquarters at Harper's Ferry. The maples, gums, and oaks were brilliant now with the reds and yellows of autumn. A tingle of coming winter spiced the air, great weather for riding but too late in the season, perhaps, for a new campaign. Besides, the Army of the Potomac was badly mangled and needed rest.

Then, to the North's consternation, the Confederate cavalryman, James Edward Brown ("Jeb") Stuart, swept into Pennsylvania on October 9, raiding completely around McClellan's army. Jeb had made a similar circle of the Union forces on the Peninsula just before Little Mac retreated to the James. This second exploit prompted Lincoln to say that he was reminded of a game called "Three times around and out." If Jeb Stuart ever went around the Union Army a third time, Lincoln said, McClellan would be out.

Custer disliked such aspersions against his hero. Like some other cavalrymen, he believed that the President failed to appreciate McClellan's problem. With only 800 serviceable mounts, how could the cavalry defeat Jeb's force of twice that number? Why had the worn-out Union horses not been replaced?* And worse still, why had Lincoln followed the Battle of Antietam with that Emancipation Proclamation? Custer and other good Democrats, including McClellan himself, were not fighting this war to free slaves.

Then Lieutenant Wilson went to Washington on leave and came back with news which dismayed Armstrong. Popular pressure, Wilson said, to remove McClellan was tremendous in the capital. The general's aides greeted the idea furiously. They began drinking, and swaggering around the headquarters tents. Slapping their holsters, they advocated resistance. Whisky voices threatened to "change front" on Washington and set McClellan up as dictator rather than see him deposed. Lieutenant Wilson remembered one thick-tongued braggart — and it may well have been Custer, although he didn't drink — who shouted, "Dismiss McClellan and I'll serve Lincoln's government no longer. I'll resign and go home."

Other thick tongues took up the cry. Hotheads congregated around Custer. Lieutenant Martin, who had been watching silently, became angry. He got up from his camp chair, drew out his wallet, and exclaimed in his Kentucky drawl, "I'm tired of such talk." He slapped the pocketbook, "I'll bet fifty dollars, and here's the money, that not a d——d one of you ever resigns so long as Uncle Abraham's greenback mill keeps grinding. Now put up or shut up." [8]

That ended the fulminations. If Custer had made the threat, he

* The adequacy of McClellan's horses is open to much argument. McClellan claimed to have only 1,000. The quartermaster's records showed he had received 10,000 in the last six weeks, *O. R.,* I, XIX, pt. 1, p. 15; pt. 2, pp. 421–423. C. D. Rhodes, *History of the Cavalry of the Army of the Potomac,* p. 164.

backed down. No one could ever question his bravery in battle; but his entire record, in and out of school, was free from personal combat.* In short, this warrior incarnate disliked personal fights.

9 Boy Meets Girl — and Chancellorsville

ARMSTRONG CUSTER WAS SICK AT HEART AS HE RODE THE TRAIN WEST across the drab wintry mountains in November, 1862. Every bang of the car bumpers, every jerk of the slack couplings added to his unhappiness. He had lost his job along with his adored general. McClellan's recall automatically reduced Custer from a captain to a lieutenant. The whole catastrophe seemed impossible to him. Armstrong was sure that Lincoln was making a mistake by dismissing Little Mac. His successor, Ambrose Burnside, would fail to inspire soldiers. Custer had watched him at Antietam, so he ought to know — or thought so.

The memory of the night McClellan was dismissed near Warrenton, Virginia, stuck in the boy's mind. Snow was falling when the fatal order came. The general had stepped from his tent and told the obstreperous aides to accept the verdict. Orders were orders.

Custer's train lurched out of the Alleghenies and chuffed across the flat Ohio cornlands toward Monroe. Near Lake Erie a cold wind blew into the coaches whenever the doors opened. Passengers huddled around the stoves in every car. North of Toledo the train skirted those familiar marshes, russet reeds and cattails stretching drearily as far as

* This statement should be qualified by placing emphasis on "the record." As noted previously, Custer may have engaged in fights at West Point but they are not of record. In a letter from Custer to Lydia Reed, September 21, 1862, he said he would horsewhip the editor of the Monroe paper for slandering McClellan. (F. Whittaker, *Complete Life of . . . Custer*, p. 129.) His threatened horsewhipping of Captain Benteen will be described later. I have also found references to a fight Custer is said to have had in Louisville when he was stationed in Elizabethtown after the war, and another in Washington, D.C., in the spring of 1876, but, so far, have been unable to verify either of them.

Custer could see. Winter was coming and with it the sodden prospect of being assigned back to his company in some cluster of muddy huts down in Virginia. Humiliation surely, for a young man accustomed to staff service with commanding generals!

Custer's periods of depression were always short-lived, however, and by the time his train jolted to a stop in Monroe his sunburned face sparkled with its usual smile. Let winter come! He'd enjoy a few days sleighing with the girls. After all, McClellan was right: orders *were* orders. Custer always buckled down with terrier cheerfulness when disagreeable duties must be performed, but seldom before.

In Monroe the patriotic citizens turned out to fete young "Captain" Custer, who had served on McClellan's staff and hobnobbed with three French princes. The title "Captain," which he had just lost, stung his sensitive ears, but he smiled bravely among the dignitaries in banquet halls and on platforms at public meetings. As an orator on these patriotic occasions he proved awkward and embarrassed. He was only twenty-one years old and frankly preferred more lively parties with people his own age, preferably girls. However, he was ambitious, and when he learned that a volunteer regiment was being raised in Michigan he pulled political strings to get the command. One company was to be recruited in Monroe. Judge Isaac Peckham Christiancy, associate judge on the Michigan Supreme Court, founder of the Republican Party in the state, and a Monroe booster, offered to help him. Armstrong would be young for a colonel, surely, but he had been closer to high command and knew much more about battle than many political officers who were taking regiments to the front.

Custer did not let his ambition prevent him from having fun. Monroe was a good town for officers on leave — more pretty girls than elsewhere, people said. The cold, moist atmosphere from the lake gave them temptingly rosy cheeks. Armstrong found himself a social lion. All the girls wanted to stitch Havelock cap-covers for him.

Late in November, at a party in Boyd's Seminary, he met Elizabeth Clift Bacon, the daughter whom Judge Bacon had preferred to keep away from the young hero. Libbie Bacon always remembered the meeting date as Thanksgiving, although Lincoln did not proclaim the last Thursday in November a legal holiday until a year later. Libbie's features were regular and delicately cut. She wore her luxuriant, wavy, chestnut-brown hair parted, pulled back over her ears and knotted on her neck. She had laughing eyes and liked dresses with low necks. Her shoulders would make any man hungry. She said later, when thirty-four years old, that she first knew Armstrong when she was seventeen. Still later, as an old lady in her nineties, she changed the age to twenty-one — which is correct, and twenty-one was a bit old to be unmarried in Monroe.*

Libbie Bacon may have been a spoiled girl. She was the only one of the judge's four children who had survived. He married first at the advanced age of forty and when Libbie was twelve her mother died, leaving only father and daughter in the big house. Libbie was a tender-hearted, romantic-minded child, already developing a gift for literary expression. Of her mother's funeral she wrote: "Oh, why did they put her in that black coffin, and screw the lid down so tight?" [1]

After the funeral, Libbie went to live at the Reverend Mr. Boyd's Seminary in Monroe. Her father was one of the school's trustees, so she became a favored pupil. She also learned to take advantage of sympathetic elders who referred to "poor motherless Libbie Bacon." Later she remembered: "How shamelessly I traded on this. What an excuse I made of it for not doing anything I didn't want to do! And what excuses were made for me on that score."

When Libbie was seventeen, her father married Rhoda Pitts, a widow from Tecumseh, Michigan. She owned property and was "not objectionably intellectual." Judge Bacon refurnished the house for his elderly bride and put a furnace in the cellar. Libbie moved from school back

---

* Elizabeth's birth date, April 8, 1842, has been taken from the Bacon family Bible. If she supervised the writing of F. Whittaker, *Complete Life of . . . Custer . . .* , as she says, she permitted him to say, p. 136, that she was seventeen in November, 1862.

into her old home. A young lady now, she was prone to satirize her associates, including her father and stepmother; yet she did it with a loving affection which soothed hurt feelings. She liked to tell how the new Mrs. Bacon would admonish the judge with, "As my former husband Mr. Pitts used to say . . ." [2]

Libbie and her father got even by keeping a picture of the first Mrs. Bacon on the living room wall. Libbie could say with the best of good humor that five, instead of three, individuals lived together in the big house — two of them deceased spouses — and all in happy adjustment.

Libbie became very fond of her new mother, but the girl's life was in school rather than in the home. She "detested" arithmetic but "simply adored" George Eliot, Tennyson, and even Shakespeare. [3] As she matured she worried about the slimness of her figure. Little Libbie had been plump as a butterball, but in her early teens she began to shoot up — all wobbly legs and knees. With hoop skirts, she hoped, the boys would imagine her legs as fat as older women's, perhaps even with dimples on her knees.

During her senior year at the academy Libbie reached the age when she realized that she must soon choose the man she would live with the rest of her life. Every day she and her classmates walked home from school in little groups confiding plans and discussing eligible boys. None of them ever mentioned George Armstrong Custer. He lived in a separate world. The most talked-about young man in town was a Southerner — tall, slim, with dark eyes and romantic tongue. The girls "simply adored" his liquid accent and the charming sentimental stanzas he wrote in their memory books. They were entranced by tales of his ancestral plantation in Louisiana. [4] But with the outbreak of war he went to the South, leaving the schoolgirls desolate. Of course they were all properly patriotic. They believed in freeing the slaves and maintaining the Union, but when these sentiments meant taking from their lives the eligible men, it was not fair!

In June, 1862, Libbie graduated from Boyd's Seminary, valedictorian of her class. Dressed in a high-necked white Swiss muslin, she curtsied formally to the teachers; to the trustees, including her father; to "about fifty white-neck-clothed ministers" — she wrote later — and then to the audience. At the close of her valedictory address "there was scarce a dry eye," a visiting cousin remembered.[5] Poor motherless Libbie Bacon!

After graduation, "in the interval between one security and another," she amused herself by painting with water colors. Judge Bacon did not permit dancing in the house, but young people — many of them married now — enjoyed themselves by singing, playing games, and promenading on the piazza.

Libbie must have known Armstrong by sight since the days when he was a youngster living with his half-sister, Lydia Reed. According to some accounts, Autie did chores in the Bacon stable and kitchen but never came in the parlor except to lay the fire — a possible story but improbable. The Reeds lived a half-mile from the Bacons, and other available choreboys surely lived closer. Libbie's account of their first meeting in November, 1862, is more credible.

Armstrong seems to have fallen in love immediately. He followed the introduction by coming to call, debonairly leaving the front gate open and whistling up the front steps. The big prim residence differed greatly from the topsy-turvy, yelling, romping households, with chairs askew and toys on the floor, which Autie Custer had always associated with "home." Judge Bacon's childless mansion was a model of neatness. His official dignity permeated everything.

Waiting in the cathedral silence of the Bacon parlor, "Captain" Custer thought he could hear Libbie in the room above. He looked at the sedate furnishings. A large, icy picture of General Scott on a frozen steed decorated one wall. On another he saw militant Sam Houston, the Texan who opposed secession. Judge Bacon liked history. He considered himself an authority on the Battle of the Raisin, fought at Monroe in the War of 1812. The judge also believed that everything in his home must be in its proper place, even to a bowl of apples on the dining room table.[6]

Judge Bacon had been cordial with "Captain" Custer until he noticed his growing interest in Libbie. That shocked him. Old Emanuel Custer was already known as a character in town, a harmless eccentric who talked nothing but Democratic politics. Even the local train-conductor knew Emanuel's failing and shouted political maxims at him from the brakeman's platform as the cars rattled through Monroe. Certainly an alliance between the Bacon and Custer families was unthinkable. The Custers belonged to the wrong church and, moreover, that drinking spree was hard to forget.

Judge Bacon decided to end the romance. He ordered his daughter to see the young man no more. They must even agree not to write.

Dutiful Libbie obeyed, but with reservations. Custer replied to the ultimatum with his usual impetuosity. He proposed marriage. Libbie turned him down, but she exchanged daguerreotypes with him, and on Sunday when she went to church she saw his golden curls in a neighboring pew. She also noticed that after singing class he escorted another girl, Fanny Fifield, home. The flirt!

Armstrong may have hoped to make Libbie jealous. He succeeded only in giving the judge an opportunity to show his daughter that the young man was no proper person for a husband.[7] However, Libbie did not seem convinced; so the judge decided to send her to Toledo until young Custer left town. A friend, Annie Cotton, had been visiting her in Monroe, and a return visit was convenient.

On the day of the girls' departure Custer turned up at the railroad station, smiling, laughing, striding around on his long, uniformed legs. He gallantly touched Libbie's elbow to help her onto the car. Judge Bacon watched, aghast. He had not dreamed that their intimacy had gone so far. When the train steamed away with smiling faces and waving handkerchiefs at the windows, Judge Bacon returned home and wrote his daughter a stern, fatherly letter criticizing the young man's obvious familiarity with her when he helped her mount the car steps.

In the big city Libbie enjoyed shopping. She was thrilled by a concert where Adelina Patti sang, and she was properly upset emotionally by John B. Gough at a temperance lecture. What had Captain Custer ever seen in Demon Drink? Then her father's letter arrived. Arranging her hoops so she could sit down to write, she answered him, saying:

Father, I told Mother to tell you of my interview with Captain Custer. I never had a trial that made me feel so badly. I did it *all for you*. I like him very well, and it is pleasant always to have an escort to depend on. But I am sorry I have been with him so much, and you will never see me in the street with him again, and never at the house except to say Good-bye. I told him never to meet me, and he has the sense to understand. But I did not promise *never* to see him again. But I will not cause you any more trouble, be sure.

This was a good start. She continued:

You have never been a girl, Father, and you cannot tell how hard a trial this was for me. At the depot he assisted Annie Cotton just as much as he did me.[8]

In December, while Libbie was still in Toledo, news came of the great battle at Fredericksburg. Losses equaled those at Antietam, and much less had been gained. Custer always had said that Burnside could not supplant his idealized McClellan, and he hoped this defeat would open the politicians' eyes in Washington. With the news came an order for Custer to report to McClellan in Trenton. The general was preparing an official account of his campaign, and requested Custer's aid. Little Mac seemed really impressed by the gallant young man's ability.

In Trenton, under his beloved chief, Custer learned that a military report always exalts the author. No commander admits defeat. When whipped, he always "withdraws before superior numbers," sometimes "with severe losses" but never more than to be "expected under the circumstances." Custer must also have noticed that his general stretched the truth in other respects. For instance, when McClellan reported that he met 30,000 of Lee's troops at South Mountain and defeated them, Custer must have realized that McClellan knew better.[9] Yes, the boy aide was learning about high command.

Working with McClellan, Custer read in the papers that Burnside's failure at Fredericksburg had cost him the command of the Army of the Potomac. Burnside's greatest rival, Fighting Joe Hooker, had been given the post. Hooker talked confidently about what he was going to do to the enemy: "God have mercy on Gen'l Lee for I will have none." Armstrong had his doubts. He had heard the wind blow before, and believed that only McClellan was capable of defeating Lee.

Foremost in Custer's mind, however, were memories of Libbie. He obtained a leave from kindly McClellan and sped back for a surprise visit. Custer also hoped to get command of that Michigan regiment as well as Libbie. She had returned home from Toledo shortly after he left, but on seeing him again she refused to disobey her father's instructions to neither entertain nor to write "Captain" Custer. However, she did consent to a plan for limited communication. Armstrong would write to a mutual friend, Annette (Nettie) Humphrey, daughter of the hotelkeeper. Nettie was big,* accommodating, and had a love interest of her own named Jacob Greene. As a matchmaker she agreed to show Custer's letters to Libbie, writing him the young lady's responses.

Custer's short visit terminated with an order to report to Washington, then to New York, where McClellan had moved. The general's admirers had presented him with a fine house there. In it Custer met and was charmed with Mrs. McClellan. That night, back at the hotel, he wrote sister Lydia that he had never before been in such a palatial residence. Then, writing page after page, as he liked to do, Custer asked Lydia to tell him all about the children. He did wish Emma could see the dolls for sale in New York. Some of them could be wound up like a clock and put on the sidewalk, where they walked around without anybody touching them. In their dolls' dresses, he said, they looked exactly like little girls.

Custer found less war enthusiasm in New York than in Washington. The streets were full of deserters, insolent fellows who sometimes dared the provost guard to arrest them. Living costs were annoyingly high. Custer had to pay $2.75 per day for room and board, and if he stayed here long he might have to purchase civilian clothes. Men in uniform were unpopular in the city. The people Armstrong met seemed to have

---

* As Mrs. Jacob Greene, Nettie weighed 165 in 1865. E. Custer, *Tenting on the Plains,* p. 189.

little faith in this new man Hooker. Then, to cap the discouraging prospect, Armstrong was ordered, on April 16, 1863,[10] to report to his company in Washington. Evidently Hooker was preparing for a battle, just as Burnside had; and, like Burnside, he would probably get whipped. Thousands more Northern boys would be killed, including Custer himself, perhaps.

The young officer bade farewell to McClellan, the only general in whom he had confidence, and boarded a southbound train. At Washington he was given an office job instead of being sent to the front. Custer called this duty "idleness and theatregoing." The only advantage he could see in such annoying leisure was that it gave him time to write Annette Humphrey the letters he knew she would show to Libbie. In the first one of these, he told Nettie that if "a certain party" thought that absence would change his feelings toward her, that "party" was mistaken.[11]

Custer's indoor assignment was cut short by an order to report at Falmouth, Virginia, just across the Rappahannock from Fredericksburg. Was Hooker going to fight that battle over again? Custer went dutifully, but full of misgivings. The Army of the Potomac belonged to McClellan, and Armstrong resented seeing anyone else in command. He felt better on arrival when told that Hooker was reorganizing the army, making a Cavalry Corps with three divisions. This might give men with Custer's talents an opportunity. He'd see. General Stoneman commanded the new corps. Generals Alfred Pleasonton, David McMurtrie Gregg, and William W. Averell headed the three divisions. Custer was again assigned to ride with Pleasonton, that bronze-faced, ironhearted cavalryman.

The Army of the Potomac, one hundred and twenty thousand veterans, was clamoring for action. The men were eager to make amends for Fredericksburg. Lincoln came down to review them. Then Hooker initiated his first offensive, feinting before Fredericksburg while he circled to get behind Lee. But Lee foresaw the maneuver and caught Hooker in his own trap at Chancellorsville by having Stonewall Jackson outflank the Union troops with a bold night march across their entire front. The records do not tell Custer's part in this gigantic movement, but the battle might well have turned into another Bull Run except for Pleasonton, whose cavalry discovered Jackson's march just in time. In his official report Pleasonton also credited himself with stopping Jackson's advance by commandeering artillery and thus turning the battle tide. Colonel Pennock Huey would claim later that he and his 8th Pennsylvania Cavalry, not Pleasonton, were responsible for the checkmate.[12] Thus Custer learned again that a successful general must strike first with the most, and report first with the best possible account of his own action. This seemed to be part of military success. He had helped McClellan make such a report. Now he saw Pleasonton send in a similar one; and Hooker, retreating northwards across the Rapidan and the Rappahannock, sent in a third, blaming his defeat on the absence of Stoneman who, with two divisions, had raided south to the outskirts of Richmond.

Hooker relieved Stoneman and gave the Cavalry Corps to Pleasonton — a fine promotion, and with it Custer moved up as aide to a corps commander. He wrote home jubilantly on May 6, 1863, and in the same letter the big boy told about another bit of good luck: he had acquired a new dog, a hound pup two months old. He said, too, that he called the handsomest of his horses, the big black, "Harry" — for his namesake, little Henry Armstrong Reed.

Custer also told the folks about his food. He ate with General Pleasonton, and the general sent to Baltimore daily for vegetables and other delicacies. "We have onions, radishes, and *ripe tomatoes,* asparagus, fresh fish, mackeral, beef, mutton, veal, *Bacon* [Was he thinking of Libbie when he capitalized that word?], pound cake, oranges, ginger snaps, candies, *peas,* warm biscuits (instead of hard bread), fresh milk, butter, cheese, & everything." *

Before closing the letter Armstrong added that the general had a

---

* This is another of the many Custer letters which have been preserved in two or more copies. The copy at West Point has been used here. Another may be found in M. Merington, *Custer Story,* p. 53.

Negro man and wife to cook and wait on table The woman, he said, was not much to look at. She tied her hair up in a handkerchief and did not wear hoops. The general called her Aunt Hanna, and so did Armstrong. That made the Negress a relative of them all. Little "Em" should see her aunt. Ha! . . . Evidently Custer was one of those chaps who liked to tease the girls and hear them squeal. Many big boys outgrow this habit. Some never do. Would Armstrong?

Custer reveled in his new position, especially the band music at headquarters and daily rides through the command with his chief.[13] On May 19 Pleasonton called Custer to the general's tent. General Pleasonton had a peculiarly daring adventure to discuss. He pointed to a map of Tidewater Virginia on the table. Spies, he said, reported that a party of Southern civilians were bound from Richmond to Urbanna, and thence by boat down the Rappahannock with important mail and a large amount of Confederate money. To intercept them behind the Confederate lines seemed next to impossible, Pleasonton said, but Hooker wished it and an attempt must be made.

Custer bent over the map, his cinnamon curls hanging around his face. Urbanna was almost as far south as Richmond, and only about fifty miles east of that city.

The scene in Pleasonton's tent which followed is easy to imagine. The immaculate whalebone commander, with whip on wrist, pointing a bronze finger at the map, saying in his precise military manner: "A boat might float a cavalry detachment down the Potomac to the Northern Neck just above Chesapeake Bay. From there it is only forty miles across to Urbanna — not too far for good horses to raid. Notice Yeocomico Inlet? It's over ten miles long, with no settlements on either side except a few fishermen's huts and oyster-diggers' shacks. The big plantations of the Washingtons, Custises, Lees, and Marshalls are above. The Yeocomico has a hundred branches where vessels could hide until the raiders return."

"Does anybody here know that country?" Custer must have asked.

"That's the trouble. No one does, but we've detailed seventy-five troopers under Captain George H. Thompson, 3d Indiana Cavalry. Lieutenant Shannon will accompany him. They're loading the horses in two steamboats on Aquia Creek now. I want you, as my aide, to go along. Take this map. You may need it." Pleasonton turned in his brisk way to the next business on his table.

Custer folded the map and stuffed it in his pocket. This was like accompanying the raiding party when he served under Kearny.

After dark that night the horse-laden steamboats floated down the Potomac with lights dimmed. Several times they stranded on sand bars. By midnight, Custer could see only an occasional light on the distant southern shore. The boats began to pitch as they approached the broad, open waters of Chesapeake Bay. At dawn, no land was in sight except a thin line of marshes and the tips of dark pines against the gray starboard sky. Custer's map was of no use here, but the pilot claimed to know the coast and signaled for the boats to turn south. As they neared the shore the soldiers saw nobody, not even a boat. A cove opened before them, and they steamed into Yeocomico Inlet. The water was calm behind the first bar and the little steamboats idled along for five miles between walls of rushes. No landmarks distinguished one promontory from the next, and Armstrong's map was still useless.

Finally Custer and Thompson agreed on a good hiding place for the boats and decided to land. By 11:30 they were off in column of twos following wagon-ruts which served as a road through the flat, tidewater woodlands. Custer led, setting the pace, the map in the stubby fingers of his right hand, the dank smell of fish and turpentine in his nose. He tried to locate something on the sea-level landscape to correspond with his chart, but could see only sand and pines. However, the wheel-ruts led south — the right direction. So he followed them at a fast trot. Behind him came the troopers with saddles squeaking, canteens thumping and saber chains tinkling. The road led past a marshy field and dilapidated fence. In the distance stood an old brick house. A few minutes later the column passed back into the pines, out of sight.

Shortly after noon the road led into more weed-grown fields. Custer spied houses ahead, one a two-story brick building with mansard roof. That must be the Heathsville on his map. The road was wider here and the squadron formed column of fours. Without halting, they swept up the lane and through the hamlet, scattering chickens and leaving loungers on the store-galleries gaping open-mouthed. It was Heathsville all right, and from here on the map served Custer's purpose.

Fifteen miles below, the column swung through Lancaster Court House, the horses' hoofs throwing sand against unpainted buildings. So far, the squadron had ridden faster than word of their coming could travel. Yet they had stopped several times long enough to impress the best horses they saw along the way, often leaving surprised and outraged drivers by the roadside with nothing but their buggies and harness. Custer marveled at the quality of the horses down here — trotting stock of the best breed.

South of Lancaster Court House, the riders turned off the road which led to the Urbanna ferry. Darkness was falling, and they halted in a clump of thick pines on the north bank of the Rappahannock.

They had ridden at least thirty-seven miles and were tired. The soldiers unsaddled their horses and fed them, but lighted no fires. Instead they rested, dozing on pine needles. Little waves lapped through the sedge and cattails. The smell of rotting vegetation pervaded everything. Armstrong Custer would write all about this experience in his next letter home, if he survived. Lydia, Libbie, and all the other girls in their comfortable houses seemed a long way from the quaking sands of the lower Rappahannock.

Before dawn the men were up, prowling along the marshy shore. They found two leaky boats. Captain Thompson put his men to work calking the slimy boards. As soon as both vessels were seaworthy he detailed two crews of ten men each to man them. The rest of his troop was ordered to stay around the horses — allow no one to approach.

Custer and Lieutenant Shannon boarded one boat, Captain Thompson the other. Crossing the sound, they saw a sailboat. Nine or ten persons appeared to be on board. Perhaps this was the party they had been sent to intercept. Custer's boat gave chase. The sailboat promptly tacked for the southern shore. Evidently the crew had noticed the blue Union uniforms and bristling guns.

The Federal soldiers bent to their oars and followed the sailboat into tall grass where, three hundred yards from shore, three Negroes jumped overboard and waded off. Six passengers in the boat were captured. They carried a considerable amount of Confederate money. All claimed to be refugees from the Confederacy trying to escape. Two of them, Custer reported later, were attractive young Jewish ladies. He surmised that all were members of the party he had been sent to arrest, so he detached a guard to take them in the sailboat to the bivouac as prisoners. He'd see them there later!

The remaining soldiers rowed Custer west along the south shore of Rappahannock Inlet toward Captain Thompson's boat. On the way, Armstrong glimpsed a prosperous plantation. He landed with four soldiers and walked toward the house. A man in Confederate artillery captain's uniform sat on the gallery, engrossed in a book. Custer turned to his followers and waved them to halt. He would go on alone.

Unnoticed, Armstrong walked across the lawn. At the foot of the steps he drew his pistol and called to the captain, telling him that he was a prisoner of war. The surprised Confederate surrendered and his captor, with a typical Custerish gesture, called for the ladies on the plantation. When they appeared he apologized for taking away the man of the house, thus interrupting his reading and his furlough. Flashing on them his Custer smile, he hoped to be forgiven, then marched his prisoner back to the boat. Armstrong found the fellow congenial, as he did most Southerners, but he dutifully sent him to the bivouac.

The remaining raiders entered Urbanna shortly before noon. Startled citizens stayed quietly indoors and no shot was fired. These Federals learned that the party they had come to capture, together with the important mail, had passed through town yesterday. The people Custer and Thompson had captured may or may not have been the ones the Federals sought. In any event the best thing for Thompson, Custer, and their men to do now was to get back in a hurry if they wanted to get back at all. News of the raid must be spreading fast. Moreover, the fishermen down here all owned double-barreled duck-guns and knew how to use them.

Hurriedly the Federals burned the bridge south of town, destroyed the boats along the wharf, confiscated several cases of boots which might be serviceable for Confederate soldiers. This consumed all afternoon, and night was falling when they climbed into their boats and shoved off. Fortunately they could not be followed in the dark, and no one knew their destination.

In spite of the inky blackness they found the bivouac. The soldiers remaining here had not been idle. They had captured three extra prisoners — men who had stumbled into camp and, after being caught, claimed to be Confederate deserters. Carriages had also been "requisitioned" for the prisoners, now totaling twelve.

At midnight the roll was called, and the column started north. Custer hoped that he could now follow, at night, the road which they had traversed in daylight. They whipped back through the same towns, finding them dark, everybody asleep. Horses which failed to stand the pace were abandoned. Riders swung their saddles on remounts picked up along the way. At 2 A.M. on May 23, the column stopped to feed the animals. Some of the men nodded drowsily, but not Custer. On raids he often went thirty or more hours without sleeping a wink.

Dawn found the column trotting along the road once more, every man in place, watching the white crossbelts on the rider ahead of him. By noon they drew rein at the hidden steamboats. The horses were loaded as quickly as possible, and the raiders chugged down the inlet and out into the Potomac. All afternoon and all night they throbbed up the broad river. Next day at noon they unloaded at Aquia Creek.

The troop had not lost a man. Counting out abandoned horses, it was ahead fifteen remounts. Custer had captured two animals he prized highly. One was a black stallion his owner claimed was worth nine hundred dollars. Custer named him Roanoke, and said he was much too beautiful to ride into battle. He would be saved for parades. The other fine animal he sent with his compliments to Pleasonton.

This raid was an unimportant war incident, but it is very important to an understanding of young Armstrong. Compare the revealing accounts written by Captains Thompson and Custer. Allowance should be made for the fact that Thompson had almost reached the age of twenty-nine and was writing for the official record, while twenty-three-year-old Custer was writing a letter to Annette Humphrey to impress his best girl.* But the difference is characteristic. In Custer's account the raiders rode a little farther, a little faster, burned bigger vessels, and captured a few more prisoners. Custer also claimed to be the commander of the expedition. He said that he captured the artillery captain. Thompson credited this to Lieutenant Shannan. Most Custerlike of all was Armstrong's description of the female captives as "young ladies." Thompson called them "children." As one of Autie's friends said later, Custer never purposely exaggerated. He just saw things bigger than other people.

It should be noted, too, that by this time Armstrong may have learned a lesson from the McClellan and Pleasonton reports. At any rate, when the war ended Custer was a major general of volunteers, while meticulous Captain Thompson had advanced only one rank.

10 Beverly Ford and a Brigadier's Star

GENERAL PLEASONTON USUALLY SPOKE WITH CAUSTIC AND TOLERANT irony, but he seemed genuinely pleased with the horse which Custer brought him from the Northern Neck. Army tensions had slacked in May, 1863, and the taciturn commander took time to chat. Hundreds of enlistments had terminated; many of his men were going home. Pleas-

---

* O. R., I, XXV, pt. 1, p. 1116. The personal account appears in at least three copies of what may be the same letter, all dated May 27, 1863. One is in the library at West Point, another is printed in Whittaker, Complete Life of . . . Custer, pp. 149–151, and another in M. Merington, Custer Story, pp. 53–54. Like most of the copies of Custer letters, the three are not identical but the differences seem due to carelessness in copying.

onton ordered those who remained to build floors under their tents, and to construct arbors over them, to break the sun's rays.[1] Did this mean that no troop advance was planned, or was Pleasonton following the old army maxim, "Busy soldiers never desert"?

In either case, Custer made the most of his chief's leisure. The curly-head even dared show the general a full-length picture of Fanny Fifield. The austere bachelor admired her, said he wanted a copy and would send the lady his picture in exchange. Thus reassured by the successful progress of his interview, Custer asked next if his Monroe friend, George Yates, might be appointed to the general's staff.[2] Yates had enlisted in the 4th Michigan at the age of sixteen and in two years had worked up to first lieutenant. Pleasonton consented. Was he influenced by Custer's magnetic personality or was it gratefulness for the gift horse? Perhaps neither! In any event, the relationship between master and aide seemed really intimate now, and Custer made the request closest to his heart: Would the general recommend him to Governor Austin Blair for command of that Michigan regiment?[3] To this Pleasonton agreed, also. More West Pointers with fighting spirit should command these huge volunteer organizations.

Custer strode back to the aides' tent in high spirits. The twenty-three-year-old had made a good horse trade with the thirty-nine-year-old veteran. At the foot of his bunk Custer opened his trunk, took out pen and paper and wrote at once to Judge Christiancy, saying that his application for the Michigan regiment was to be endorsed by five generals. If disapproved it would not be for lack of military recommendations. Custer finished the letter, folded it with his strong square hands, and began another to his sister. To her he confessed haunting fear. Politicians might never forget that he was a "McClellan man." Father Custer's politics, and his own, might disqualify him.[4]

The first week in June dragged in the big Falmouth cantonment. Two new aides had joined Pleasonton's staff — Wesley Merritt, Custer's dignified upperclassman at the Point, and Elon Farnsworth, the slim and dashing young man who had helped Armstrong chase rebels from South Mountain. He and Custer made a picturesque pair riding in the general's suite, one dark-eyed and brown-haired, the other blue-eyed and golden-locked — a black and tan couple. Both wore broad-brimmed hats like their chief.

In periods of inactivity Custer was always bored. He did not dream that the most important month of his career had commenced. With other aides he watched Pleasonton, listened to grapevine rumors, and speculated on the next military maneuver. The young men heard that Hooker was reading Richmond newspapers. Confederates seemed to forget their near-defeat at Antietam last fall, and remembered only the victories on their own soil at Fredericksburg and Chancellorsville. Richmond editors were clamoring for another invasion of the North. Lee might try to do it by slipping, unseen, up the west side of the Blue Ridge. Certainly he knew that Hooker's Army of the Potomac was reduced to 80,000 men. Lee's 68,000, together with James Edward Brown ("Jeb") Stuart's 10,000 horse, should be a match for the Northerners. Besides, military supplies, hard to find in Virginia, could be captured easily in the North. Pennsylvania's granaries were bulging with last year's crops.

Hooker's next act stopped the aides' speculations. He ordered Pleasonton to march his whole Cavalry Corps up the Rappahannock, cross on both sides of the Orange & Alexandria Railroad, and find out whether Lee was marching around the Union Army's right to invade Pennsylvania. This was the first time that Union cavalry had gone into action as a unit, and the result would be important.

Pleasonton divided his corps, to cross the river above and below the railroad bridge by Beverly Ford and Kelly's Ford, respectively. The advance was ordered for June 9.

On the night before, Custer was officer of the day. After supper Pleasonton and his staff retired to their tents for a night's rest. Custer made the rounds of the encampment, then sat by a fire to write his sister a long letter describing, as he always did, every detail of his duties. "I will wake the general at 2 A.M.," he wrote, "and at 4 we cross the Rappahannock to strike at Culpeper." He told his sister that his health was excellent, that he never felt better in his life, but the chance of being killed tomorrow was great. "In case anything happens to me," he wrote, "my trunk is to go to you. Burn all my letters. I received a long one from Fanny." [5] Evidently the reckless Custer was cautiously keeping two strings on his cupid's bow.

At the appointed time he roused the general. No trumpet sounded reveille because enemies might be only a mile away and Pleasonton intended to surprise them. Colonel Benjamin F. Davis, with the 8th New York Cavalry, had been ordered to lead the advance of Pleasonton's right wing. Last night he had bivouacked within half a mile of Beverly Ford, and was to cross at dawn. Pleasonton sent aide Custer to join him. The young man was delighted with this opportunity to ride into battle with "Grimes" Davis, as the colonel had been called at West Point. Grimes had been graduated before Armstrong entered, so they were not acquainted, but Armstrong knew him by reputation. Davis had made himself a famous cavalryman last fall. Just before Antietam he had escaped from Harper's Ferry during the night when other Union forces were surrendered. He had not only escaped the encircling enemy, but on his way out captured a Confederate wagon train. Yes, it was a real honor to ride into battle with such a leader.

Before daylight, Custer and Davis started down the dark road through the trees with the 8th New York. The 8th Illinois and 3d Indiana Cavalry followed. Close to the Rappahannock, they entered a thick fog. Custer dropped behind to see that the files were closed and to warn the riders that unnecessary noise might bring sudden death to all of them. While he sat his horse by the roadside, the ghostly blue-gray column passed. Each rank could barely see the crossbelts of the men ahead, but all rode in close formation.

Custer cantered back to Colonel Davis and reported everything in order. The column came to the ford. Surely the enemy must have a sentry on the south bank, but perhaps a nearby waterwheel splashing and thumping was loud enough to muffle the sound of the approaching cavalry. Davis ordered the front ranks, if challenged in midstream, to charge, sweep away the pickets, scatter any support behind the pickets, and find out if Lee's infantry was marching toward Pennsylvania. With these instructions the first rank entered the stream. The regiment followed. Emerging in the shallows on the south bank, they heard a sharp cry in the fog ahead:

"Halt! Who goes there?"

Custer and Davis fired their pistols and charged with the lead companies. Out of the Rappahannock and up the bank they went, in a cataract of splashing water. They surged around the helpless sentinel, thundered past him through the woods to his camp, captured it, and pounded on to the fields beyond. Here the sight before them was enough to make most cavalrymen draw rein — but not Davis or Custer. They saw scattered before them a thousand Confederate horsemen just getting up. Many still huddled beside little fires, cooking breakfast. Armstrong heard the startled shouts of officers: *"To Horse!"* But most troops were hopelessly separated from their mounts. The 8th New York Cavalry clattered through this disorganized mass; whole regiments of Confederates surrendered to Union battalions.[6]

Custer and Davis smiled at the surrounding bedlam as their officers took the prisoners in hand. However, the victory turned out to be not so complete as they had imagined. Along the stone wall at the next woodland they saw soldiers' heads — hundreds of them. Those heads evidently did not belong to the infantrymen they were seeking, because many horses stood in the woods behind them. Furthermore, the enemy cavalry over there might well be preparing for a countercharge to retake the prisoners and wipe out the 8th New York.

Davis called a halt, ordered an about-face, and the regiment herded its prisoners back toward the Rappahannock. At the edge of the trees, they met the 8th Illinois and 3d Indiana. Here were enough men to test the mettle of the Confederates behind that stone wall!

The three regiments formed for a charge, while Davis and Custer questioned the prisoners. The fellows confessed that they were part of Jeb Stuart's ten thousand "invincibles." They had never dreamed of being attacked here. Jeb had assembled them for a grand review by

Robert E. Lee. No one thought Union troops were within miles of them. Those men behind the fence yonder were only the outer echelon of Jeb's force.

The three Union regiments had formed now and stood ready to charge. If Jeb Stuart's entire force waited over there the Yankees were outnumbered six or eight to one. Davis and Custer pointed their swords toward the string of heads along that stone fence. "Come on, boys." With the brigade behind them, they thundered across the field, broke the line, tore down and jumped the wall, crashed through the woods beyond. On a side road, they detected a battery of flying artillery whipping to the rear and made a rush for it. What a feather in their caps if they could capture some of Jeb Stuart's guns! [7]

Racing across a field and down the road, Armstrong saw a body of horse forming on his flank to pinch off his squadron. He looked for Davis, but the dashing colonel had been shot down. The immediate command devolved on Custer. He ordered a halt and turned around. The road back to the Union lines was packed with Confederate horsemen.

"CHARGE!" Armstrong shouted. Hacking and slashing with sabers, the Union men cut their way through. Some unhorsed soldiers came out of the *mêlée* riding double. Armstrong was convinced, more than ever, that sabers beat pistols in a close fight.

The wind was blowing from the north, but in spite of it Armstrong now could hear shooting in the south — cannon as well as rifles. The Pleasonton divisions that had crossed at Kelly's and some smaller fords down there must be engaged hotly. In addition, those that had crossed the Beverly Ford behind Custer and Davis were now making the woods tremble with bombardments. In the tumult Custer noticed that the enemy line opposing him was becoming thinner. Stuart must be drawing off men to send elsewhere. If so, good! Custer, never one to wait, ordered the entire brigade to feel out the enemy line in a dozen places all at once, probe for a weak spot, keep the shrinking line worried.

Squadrons ventured across the fields and along roads toward the enemy. Now and again Confederate horsemen rushed out with flashing sabers — like splendid cavalry exercise; beautiful — except for the crippled and struggling horses left behind and the bodies of men sprawled in ditches and along fences.

Before noon Custer saw Pleasonton riding along under his resplendent general's flag, the sparkling silk colors he carried in battle. Caustic Pleasonton seemed pleased by his aide's ability to take over in a crisis and fight with ceaseless tenacity against overwhelming odds. In his grim, undemonstrative way the slim, handsome general reported what prisoners had already told Custer: the enemy was Jeb Stuart's entire cavalry force, including the commands of Fitzhugh Lee and Wade Hampton — the best in the Confederate Army. Moreover, the Union forces had held their own all along the line. Never again need the name of Jeb Stuart daunt Northern cavalrymen!

This alone was worth the battle, but Pleasonton had come to find out if Lee's infantry was marching north. With his jubilant horsemen he pushed down the railroad track for six miles to Brandy Station — a few houses and a warehouse. Here he found several trains of cars unloading regiment after regiment of soldiers. They had been run up from Culpeper, packed in the coaches, on the car-tops, on the brakeman's platforms. Lee had sent these infantry divisions to reinforce Stuart's cavalry.

That was all Pleasonton wanted to know. The Confederate Army must have moved out of Fredericksburg, else so many soldiers would not be available here, forty miles west. This information should be sent to Hooker at once.[8]

Pleasonton now ordered his troops to retreat north across the Rappahannock. The Confederates called it a victory, because they held the field. The Yankee horsemen disagreed.

Armstrong was sent to Hooker's headquarters with a captured flag and a list of prisoners. He had been cited for "gallantry throughout the fight." Many of his acquaintances had also received recognition. Pleasonton's new aide, George Yates, had distinguished himself. That justified Armstrong's recommendation of him. Custer also noticed that his upperclassman, Alexander Pennington, had been cited. So had Leicester Walker, the timid civilian appointee who had ridden with Autie at Bull Run three years ago.[9] Marcus Reno had been wounded and would undoubtedly get a major's rank. He was advancing, not rapidly, to be sure, but steadily, and was now well ahead of Custer. Armstrong had promised to keep Lydia posted on the fates of his schoolmates and this battle gave him much to tell her. On the Confederate side his friend John Pelham, the artillery genius, had been killed at Kelly's Ford. Pierce Manning Butler Young had been wounded again but was carried away before being captured.

On June 15, six days after the Beverly Ford fight, the cavalry encampment was set agog by a disturbing bit of information. Lee's troops were in Winchester, sixty-five miles northwest. Had he moved his Brandy Station infantry up there? Yet Hooker maintained that enemy soldiers were still in Fredericksburg and might attack Washington from the south. Something seemed wrong! Up in the capital Lincoln looked at the map in the War Department and decided that Lee's army was spread out in a great crescent with its head over a hundred miles from its tail. He wrote Hooker pointedly: "The animal must be very slim somewhere. Could you not break him?" That would indeed be the surest way to prevent an invasion of the North.

Pleasonton set off with his cavalry to find the place to break. His horsemen spanked along, a blue stream flowing over and around the green Virginia hills. Roadside fields waved with clover, knee-high and ready to cut. Orchards glowed with rich, red cherries. Soldiers broke off branches and ate the fruit as they rode along. On hilltops shaded by trees, the cavalrymen saw stately, pillared façades embellishing great country houses. The gateway to one was marked BERKELEY MANSION. Foragers who entered these plantation residences found them to be barnlike structures, with bare floors, and pictures and wallpaper out of style in the North a generation ago.

"These people have made their money by planting, I suppose?" a war correspondent asked a Negro servant.

"Yes, sir," he was told, "and raising colored people to sell." [10]

Judson Kilpatrick, who now commanded a brigade, led the cavalry van. West of the cultivated fields the soldiers saw a long, low ridge, the southern extension of the Catoctin Range. On June 17 Little Kil was watering horses in a brook crossed by the Winchester-Washington pike near where it cut through the ridge. A few shots were fired at him from the cluster of houses known as Aldie.[11] Kilpatrick's shrill metallic voice ordered an immediate attack. He found Jeb Stuart's horsemen in town and drove them back. Evidently Jeb had circled to keep the Union cavalry from reaching the Blue Ridge, where they could look down and see whether Lee was marching north on the other side.

In the rock-bound fields beyond Aldie, the Confederate horse dismounted for battle, with artillery placed to sweep the main road from the east. A series of gallant Union charges drove them back. One account of that battle states that it was won at a crucial moment with a charge led personally by Kilpatrick, Colonel Calvin S. Douty of the Maine 1st, and Aide-de-Camp Custer. According to this report, Douty was killed as the line rushed forward, Kilpatrick's horse was shot under him, and only Custer, on black Harry, reached the enemy line — indeed pierced it and raced on to the open country beyond. In this version, the exploit is said to have earned him a brigadier's star.

The preceding account has been accepted by some Custer biographers, but the records fail to substantiate it. Instead they reveal that Douty was killed in one part of the field, Kilpatrick's horse was shot in the neck in another area, and Custer spent the time carrying messages for Pleasonton. The only basis for the spectacular charge is in the accounts printed in Michigan newspapers, perhaps to help Armstrong secure command of that Michigan regiment. There is, also, a letter Armstrong wrote home telling how black Harry stampeded and carried him unwillingly across the enemy line. Safely in the Confederate rear, Armstrong said, he noticed that his tattered straw hat caused Southern stragglers to mistake him for a Confederate cavalryman. This disguise permitted him to get safely back to the firing line.

Then, clapping spurs into black Harry, he sped through the uproar of battle to his own side.

These incidents seem to have been woven into the spectacular story of the charge. Years later, War Correspondent A. R. Waud drew a dramatic picture showing Douty killed, Kilpatrick unhorsed, and Custer charging on. Waud was with the column during the fight, but his picture is certainly apocryphal. An artist is not a historian, and no man can see a whole battlefield. At the time of the action, Waud drew another sketch showing Custer as a wild, slouchy figure, with unkempt locks, battered straw hat, and boots too big for him.[12] Ill-fitting boots, allegedly captured from the enemy, had become Custer's latest whim. Soldiers sitting their horses in line had learned to listen for the exultant smack of Custer's whip on his rebel boots. This helped morale. Fighting men determined to get some outlandish boots of their own on the next charge.

Kilpatrick followed the fight at Aldie with other cavalry battles on June 19 and again on June 21 at Middleburg and Upperville, respectively. Each encounter was important, for it put the Union cavalry closer to the Blue Ridge. Armstrong must have realized that Little Kil's achievements would undoubtedly earn him a major general's stars. Kilpatrick was going up, up, up; while he, Custer, had reached only a captaincy last year, and lost that when McClellan was relieved. Perhaps he would get it back again when Pleasonton's promotion presumably elevated his aides; but such a minor gain in rank seemed poor compensation for a year's dangerous service. Armstrong felt the same ambitions as other officers, and at every mess the popular toast was: "To promotion — or death."

In fits of depression, as of elation, Custer always blurted out whatever was in his mind. So in the camp at Upperville he said, thoughtlessly, that he intended to be a general someday. He was saved from being teased about the boast by the arrival of exciting news. Pleasonton's signalmen had climbed to the top of the Blue Ridge. Up there they looked across the broad Shenandoah Valley to distant Winchester, and north to the hazy blue Bolivar Heights, near Harper's Ferry. They had trained their telescopes on all the roads leading to the Potomac, and they had seen what Hooker and Pleasonton had feared — endless columns of men, of horses, of wagons, worming their way northward. The whole Army of Northern Virginia was on the march. The threatened invasion was a fact.

No need, now, to guard the left wing of the Union Army. Hooker must march, and march fast, if he wanted to keep the enemy from either overrunning Pennsylvania or getting between him and Washington.

The race began: On June 25 Custer, riding beside Pleasonton, crossed the Potomac. Rain peppered the muddy waters, trickled from the broad brims of their hats. The Maryland shore was barely visible through the slanting downpour. On the north side, a report stated that Lee was already nearing the Pennsylvania line. Pleasonton's cavalrymen stopped only long enough to tie up their horses' tails to keep the mud from weighing them down, then sloshed up the shining roads to overtake him. Next day the drenched column arrived at Frederick, in central Maryland. Custer recognized the town. He had been here last fall on that glorious march with McClellan which ended at Antietam.

Now, in the rain, the tired riders heard astonishing news. General Hooker had been replaced by George Gordon Meade. The Cavalry Corps was being reorganized on the march. Divisions were given to John Buford, Douglas McMurtrie Gregg, and Kilpatrick. Custer was right: the lucky hero of Aldie got a major general's command — the 3d Division — and the exalted rank would surely follow.

That afternoon Custer was assigned the menial task of inspecting pickets. He floundered off in the rain, hurt by lack of recognition. His job was disagreeable. The Army of the Potomac began celebrating its return north of the Potomac with a wild drunken spree. Irresponsible soldiers straggled everywhere. At the edge of town two spies who had been convicted were left hanging as a warning to other wrongdoers.[13] He was glad to get back to headquarters.

Tired and wet, he dismounted, tramped through the mud to the aides' tent and threw back the flap.

In the smoke-filled tent a facetiously pompous voice greeted him, "Gentlemen, General Custer!"

Why had Armstrong ever made that slip of the tongue about getting a star?

"How are you, General Custer?" another voice taunted.

"Hello, General," a third shouted derisively from behind the blue-gray veil of smoke.

"You're looking well, General."

Custer flushed at this brutal, youthful mirth. "You may laugh, boys," he stammered. "Laugh as long as you please, but I *will* be a general yet, for all your chaff. You see if I don't, that's all."

The aides roared with glee, making the smoke skeins whirl. Custer's blue eyes flashed, fighting mad. Lieutenant Yates came to his rescue.

"*Look on the table,*" he said.

Custer saw a large official envelope addressed to BRIGADIER GENERAL GEORGE A. CUSTER, U.S. VOLS. He could not speak. The mortification, the chagrin, the emotional change from rage to supreme happiness overpowered him. He sank down in a chair and feared that he was going to cry.[14]

On June 29, 1863, Custer wrote Secretary of War Stanton accepting the commission, adding the boyish irrelevancy that he was only twenty-three years old.[15] He made no reference to Stanton's former residence in Cadiz and the possibility that he may have known his father there when both were outspoken Democrats.

Custer was assigned the 2d Brigade in Kilpatrick's 3d Division.[16] This gave him command of the 1st, 5th, 6th, and 7th Michigan Cavalry, together with Battery M, 2d U.S. Artillery. The 5th Michigan was the cavalry regiment to which Custer had once hoped to be assigned as colonel. What would Governor Blair think now? Battery M consisted of six three-inch rifled guns commanded by Brevet Captain Alexander C. McW. Pennington. Custer remembered the day in 1860 when he watched Alex graduate from West Point along with Horace Porter, Stephen Ramseur, and Wesley Merritt. Why was Pennington only a brevet captain? General Custer would remedy that if the fellow showed merit, for Armstrong lavished rewards on deserving subordinates.

Wesley Merritt and Elon Farnsworth both received brigades at this time. Pleasonton recommended all three promotions, so his definition of the qualifications of a cavalry leader seems pertinent. An officer, he said, is always like an actor on the stage before a watchful audience. In a crisis one leader may cause confusion, panic even, by the way he shouts orders. Another, with the dramatist's gift, can hold the attention of his men, make every soldier feel himself hero of the play, forget his fears and charge recklessly.[17] This gift, of course, was Custer's to a marked degree, and Pleasonton, the first general to make cavalry an important service in the Civil War, had already been the first to stop Jeb Stuart. Custer would lead the charge that killed the great Confederate.

During the excitement of his sudden promotion, Armstrong, for once in his life, found no time to write home. Later he told Lydia that Pleasonton was like a father to him. Hitherto, only McClellan had received such affection.

Custer's new brigade had already gone ahead and was encamped forty-five miles away. Muddy as the roads were, Custer made a night ride to assume command. He knew that many of the older officers in the brigade would resent his appointment. On arrival he concealed his embarrassment by being abrupt and unfriendly with the commanders who greeted him. He admitted, years later, that he was copying Kearney and Pleasonton, especially when he inspected the encampment next morning and complained about everything. Why was no officer at stable call? Why was a sergeant alone at reveille? Why did those enlisted men fail to salute?

Custer had no time to get a new uniform, so he discarded his lieutenant's jacket with its single row of brass buttons for a velveteen jumper covered on both sleeves with loops of gold braid. He stitched a star on the tips of his broad shirt-collar. Around his neck he tied a bright red tie. "The Boy General with his flowing yellow curls," a *New York Herald* correspondent called him.[18] In this costume, and with jealous fellow officers, General Custer led his brigade north to overtake Lee somewhere in the neighborhood of a German settlement called Gettysburg.

Some officers resented Custer's sudden rise. None had more cause than stolid, thick-necked Marcus Reno. He had served creditably with the 1st Cavalry on the Peninsula last year, earning a captain's bars. He had fought at Beverly Ford and Upperville but was now only a brevet major, while that laughing, limber, irrepressible underclassman was a brigadier general. What right did Pleasonton have to make a pet of Custer? His critics had not seen Armstrong take over a brigade at Beverly Ford, or encourage faltering lines at Aldie and Upperville. To them promotion from lieutenant to brigadier was unprecedented, but so was Pleasonton, and what he planned doing to the United States Cavalry was unprecedented, too.

11 Custer at Gettysburg

BRIGADIER GENERAL CUSTER HAD NO TIME TO MEET ALL THE OFFICERS IN his brigade until after its first fight. On June 29, 1863, he crossed the Pennsylvania state line, his brigade spearheading Meade's army. The route assigned him lay north-northeast. Evidently Meade intended to stay between Lee and Washington.

Along the road, Custer noticed farmers mowing hay — no thought of battle in their minds. Golden grain, ready for the sickle, waved on the rolling hills. Indeed, a beautiful country! Custer kept vedettes ahead, hunting for the enemy. After dark these men rode in reporting a few skirmishes with gray horsemen — enemy foragers perhaps, but not an army.[1]

On the second day's march, at ten o'clock in the morning, Custer's column reached Hanover. The men rode proudly down the main street carrying red and white swallow-tailed cavalry flags, bullet-riddled relics of Aldie and Upperville. Girls in the windows of neat brick houses waved at them. Old men at open doorways capered and cheered. At front gates women in hoops and bonnets held out trays of white bread spread with apple butter, delicious fare for horsemen fresh from cornpone country. This was like last September's march to Antietam, except that Armstrong was a brigadier general now, with gold braid on his velveteen jacket and a gold star pinning up the right side of his dashing black hat.[2]

Moving beyond town into the lush farmlands, he relaxed. Fields, orchards, spacious Pennsylvania-Dutch barns drifted by his marching column. An hour and a half out of Hanover, Armstrong saw, among treetops ahead, the roofs of Abbottstown on the Gettysburg–Lancaster pike. To impress the girls there, the twenty-three-year-old general probably pushed his black hat over one eye in the gay cavalier fashion he enjoyed. Oh, if Fanny and Libbie could see him now!

Before reaching the village Custer heard shooting behind his long, dusty column. He reined in his horse and looked back. The brigade behind his, still out of sight, was Farnsworth's 1st. It must be fighting.

Custer ordered an about-face. With a quick nervous gesture he pressed his rakish hat solidly on his curls * and led the way back at a spanking trot, back along the winding country road, past the orchards, white farmhouses, sultry summer fields. Every mile he rode, the firing sounded louder.

An aide from division commander Kilpatrick galloped out to meet him. Breathlessly the man explained, "Farnsworth's brigade was halfway through Hanover when the rebs — Jeb Stuart or Wade Hampton — charged in from the side streets almost cutting him in half." The aide pointed to the east. The Confederates had retreated that way. Their rear guard still stood in yonder fields.[3]

Custer deployed the brigade, his first time to fight with his own

* Libbie always remarked about the peculiarly rakish manner in which Armstrong put on his hat.

troops. The seasoned veterans rode to their places promptly. Pennington's battery unlimbered where it could prevent the Confederates from concentrating for a countercharge on the town. Then Custer cantered ahead of his men into Hanover.

Citizens had thrown up barricades — wagons, carts, bales of hay. With shotguns, old muskets, pistols, and hay forks, they stood ready to repulse another attack. Custer glanced up at the windows where the girls had waved — no little flags there this afternoon, only frightened tear-shellacked faces of women and children. Hysterical cheers followed his gaily dressed figure as he rode along.

In the fight Farnsworth had lost fifty men and a flag — heavy casualties in such a short time, but the Confederates had retreated,[4] frightened no doubt by the host of reinforcements tramping in along the Frederick road. Certainly the "rebs" had not expected to meet the van of Meade's whole army. Oddly enough, they had ridden east towards York and the Susquehanna River. Surely Lee was not in that direction.

By noon, or shortly thereafter, Kilpatrick's entire 3d Division assembled near the Hanover railroad station. Many men in the 2d Brigade saw now for the first time their "Boy General." Captain J. H. Kidd of the 6th Michigan Cavalry Regiment was surprised by his general's extreme youth, his blue eyes, girlish complexion, and the curls on his shoulders. He noticed Custer's magnificent black hat, brilliant red tie, and gold spurs on high-topped boots. Kidd thought the youth must be a courier or aide, surely not a commanding general. But he noticed that the young general spoke with assurance as the officers discussed the situation.

They all concluded that the enemy must be Jeb Stuart on another of his spectacular rampages, this time trying to ride around Meade's entire army as he had ridden twice around McClellan's in 1862. Perhaps by turning northeast he would be late in joining Lee's column. Let him do so! Without cavalry, Lee would be blind and an easier mark for Meade.

Custer's 2d ("Michigan") Brigade camped at the edge of Hanover. That afternoon Meade's infantry streamed in — hot, tired, beards clotted with dust, eyes red with it. They bivouacked in the fields for miles around. West of them, only thirteen miles away, stood Gettysburg — an important little market town where many roads converged.

Next day, July 1, 1863, Custer resumed his march to Abbottstown, crossed the pike there and traversed the rolling hills beyond, until he came to the Harrisburg pike. As he rode along, he kept details trotting ahead, and on both sides, to guard against a surprise attack. That Jeb Stuart was a foxy fellow who might turn and strike suddenly.[5] About ten o'clock in the morning Custer heard shooting over toward Gettysburg, nine miles from his present position. General Buford's 1st Cavalry Division was scouting in that direction. Perhaps he had flushed the game. Certainly the shooting lasted all day and it seemed to come closer to Custer's column as evening approached.

At dark his detachments assembled at brigade headquarters near Heidlersburg.* During the night a detail which had ridden to the west clattered in with bad news. Buford had found the Confederate column beyond Gettysburg, no mistake. He had fought it half the morning and all afternoon — his dismounted cavalry against Lee's infantry. The XI Corps had come to his support, fought doggedly, and prevented a rout, but Lee had cut it into ribbons — ten thousand casualties! The survivors were camped tonight on the high ground — Cemetery Ridge and Culp's Hill — south and southeast of Gettysburg. Darkness had saved them. With a few more hours of daylight Lee might have crushed Meade's army, defeating each corps in detail as it came at him.

Custer watched his men sleeping restlessly that night. The air was hot and a full moon illuminated the pike, surrounding farmlands, and wood lots. Very peaceful — but not for the men, lying like mounds in a graveyard.

* Kilpatrick, following Custer, spent the night of July 1 at Abbottstown. (J. Moore, *Kilpatrick and Our Cavalry,* p. 88.)

At dawn, July 2, Custer strode through the milky half-light. The moon was setting behind a dark strip of woods, so romantic! He must write to that girl in Monroe—perhaps both of them—if he lived through this battle. Overhead he heard crows caw as they flew to their feeding grounds. A robin bobbed across the greensward. No shot disturbed these wild creatures—not yet—but Custer knew that Meade's men had marched all night in this ghostly moonlight. The biggest armies ever assembled in America were now maneuvering near here for a death grapple which would determine the course of history in America and in the world.

The Michigan brigade breakfasted early, then stood to horse. Hour after hour they waited for orders. Custer had long since learned that watchful waiting was a part of war. At midmorning a courier raced up with an order for the brigade to ride, double-quick, to Gettysburg, nine miles away. Some top commander must have remembered that this part of his cavalry was not being used!

Down the Harrisburg road they went, belts, bandoleers, and canteens slapping riders' backs like harness on trotting horses." At two o'clock they came to Rock Creek and were ordered to halt. Again they stood waiting. Beyond them a terrible bombardment shook the earth, and clouds of white smoke billowed up from the ridge ahead of them. "That bald-headed rebel, Dick Ewell, is knocking hell out of Howard's XI Corps," Custer was told. "Losing a leg at Bull Run last summer hasn't crimped Dick's style!"

"Howard's loss of an arm at Fair Oaks hasn't crimped him either," was the obvious reply. Lieutenant O. O. Howard, who had taught Armstrong "math" at the Point, had certainly gone up in the world. A brigadier in September, 1861, next a major general, now Howard commanded a corps—and tonight might be a corpse. How the cadets used to laugh about being under epaulets or six feet of sod!

For more endless hours, Custer's brigade listened to the nerve-shattering din. The noise indicated that the battle line was moving south. Howard seemed to be holding onto Culp's Hill, but Ewell was apparently encircling him. If the Confederates took that timbered knob, the

Union Army — on Cemetery Ridge, below — would be flanked. Half a dozen times during the afternoon, Custer moved his brigade across the fields, keeping abreast of the fighting beyond the trees, but he never fired a shot. His orders were to watch for enemy cavalry which might swing around the Union right wing and cut off supplies. At each stop, the Michigan troopers dismounted and sat with bridle reins looped over their arms while the horses nibbled grass. At about five o'clock, with the bombardment still roaring and the sun still high in the sky, Custer received an order to cut Ewell's communications. Stop him from pressing so hard on Howard! [7]

Custer led the way north, crossed the York turnpike and the railroad beyond, horses' shoes tinkling over the iron rails. Before reaching the Harrisburg turnpike, down which he had ridden this morning, he came to the Weigelstown road and turned south along it toward Gettysburg. This was a soft dirt road, and the column moved noiselessly except for the clank of their weapons.

As they approached Hunterstown, five miles from Gettysburg, Custer saw, on the road ahead, standing between the rail fences, a solid mass of Confederate cavalry. In the fields on each side of them men stood deployed as skirmishers on foot. Had Jeb Stuart got back from his raid and joined Lee's army? If so, Custer's job of flanking Baldy Ewell had become a hard one.

Custer halted. His sharp, nervous eyes looked right and left. The enemy force did not seem big. If part of Jeb Stuart's, it must be only advance squadrons, possibly a regiment. (It was, in fact, Wade Hampton's division.) In any event Custer had seen practically no action since becoming a brigadier, so he prepared to attack at once. With quick commands he dismounted three companies and deployed them in the fields opposite the enemy skirmish line. He planted Pennington's artillery behind a fence at a turn in the road where, in case of a repulse, it could sweep the road behind his retreating men. Then he told Lieutenant Colonel Henry Elmer Thompson of the Michigan 6th to charge down the road with one squadron.

The horsemen formed in the road. Armstrong drew his straight

"Toledo blade" and, waving back his staff, rode up beside Thompson. "I'll lead you this time, boys," Custer said. "Come on!" *

The charge failed utterly and only part of the attacking squadron returned safely to the division. Thompson was badly wounded. Custer had his horse shot, and came out of the *mêlée* riding behind one of his privates. Thirty-two men were lost — a serious defeat, considering the number engaged. Pennington's battery probably saved the command. Certainly Wade Hampton was no man to be attacked recklessly, and Ewell's communications had not been disturbed. Meade reported the action "indecisive" — a courteous military apology for failing to accomplish the mission. Nevertheless, Kilpatrick cited Custer for gallantry.

After that fight Custer's battered command bivouacked by the roadside. They had scarcely finished coffee at 11 P.M. when Kilpatrick's entire division, including Custer's brigade, was ordered to march to the south end of Meade's line, which had been fighting along Cemetery Ridge all day and was still insecure. In fact, it had barely been saved by Chief Engineer Warren — Armstrong's onetime teacher — who commandeered troops which did not belong to him and ordered them on to Little Round Top, an unoccupied knob overlooking the Union position.

In the morning Lee might try to take Little Round Top and from there roll up the Union line. To prevent this, Kilpatrick was now ordered south.[8]

The moonlight ride behind the Federal line was a horror for Armstrong. Refugees blocked the road. Wounded men and stragglers, frightened after a two-day battle, said that the North had been badly

---

* O. R., I, XXVII, pt. 1, pp. 992, 998; pt. 2, p. 724; G. Meade, *Life and Letters*, II, p. 94. Custer's part in this charge sounded too romanticized to be accepted by this writer when he read about it in the laudatory biography by Whittaker, p. 173. Captain J. H. Kidd, of the 6th Michigan, though a Custer admirer, does not mention it in his *Personal Recollections . . .*, p. 134. However, the story of Custer's being unhorsed appeared contemporarily in the *New York Times*, quoted in J. Robertson, *Michigan in the War*, p. 587, so it cannot be ignored.

whipped. Why fight on to certain death? Custer spent four hours in riding the six miles to Kilpatrick's headquarters at Two Taverns on the Baltimore pike. His tired men unsaddled there at 3 A.M. on July 3. West of them along the pike lay Farnsworth's 1st Brigade, about three miles from Little Round Top, where the fight was expected this morning.

Before dawn an aide came down the highway from Kilpatrick with an order for Custer to rouse his men and form the 2d Brigade in column. Custer handed the order to his adjutant and pulled his own mussed uniform together. He could hear sleepy men slap saddles on their horses, then shuffle into line. Sergeant after sergeant down the road barked the command to mount. In the half-light he saw dozens of legs swing over the saddles. The men sat upright on their horses, ready to go. Ahead of them, on the pike, a ripple of shod hoofs indicated that Farnsworth's 1st Brigade was marching. Custer's line turned by fours into column and followed.

A courier from the rear overtook Custer. It was light now, and Armstrong recognized the man as an aide from General David McMurtrie Gregg, commander of the 2d Cavalry Division, which had replaced Kilpatrick's 3d above Culp's Hill when Custer left there last night. The aide handed Custer an order to return now, at once, to his last night's position.[9]

To withdraw his brigade from the division while on the march was unusual procedure, but Custer cared little about technicalities. An emergency must have arisen at the other end of the line. If he could help there, he would. Custer reversed the march of his brigade and trotted north, his cavalry a thin blue column worming its way through the country at Meade's rear. Now, in daylight, the roads were still clogged with disorganized skulkers, ambulances, ammunition trains. Every farmhouse had become a hospital filled with wounded soldiers.

Passing Culp's Hill, Custer heard heavy cannonading. Was old Baldy Ewell still pounding Howard over there? If so it would be his third day trying to take that timbered knob.

Custer trotted on. When he arrived at the Hanover (or Bonaugh-town) road,[10] Gregg's adjutant assigned him a place along Low Dutch Road at the extreme right of the line. Here Custer deployed, facing Gettysburg.

At 10 A.M. the bombardment on Culp's Hill stopped suddenly. What did that mean? Custer saw troopers look at each other questioningly. The entire battle line down Cemetery Ridge had become quiet, too. Fields, woodlands, orchards which for two days shook with constant bombardments simmered now in the sultry sun.[11] Custer's brigade dismounted. Men edged into the shade of trees, or crouched drowsily by their mounts. Flies buzzed and horses stamped, making sleep dangerous. The hot, dusty hours dragged along. Custer had time to think of his home folks, of Lydia, his parents, of Fanny and of Libbie. Old Judge Bacon should not be too stuck-up to have Brigadier General Custer for a son-in-law.

At noon Custer learned that an assault (Pickett's charge) was expected on the Union center, three miles away. Lookouts also reported a large column of rebel cavalry riding toward Gregg's position, probably Jeb Stuart's horse. Evidently it planned to wreak havoc on the Union rear, cut communications, capture ammunition depots at the time Pickett struck his all-out blow in front. Gregg realized the supreme importance of checking this movement.

Soon a terrific bombardment commenced over on Cemetery Ridge — rebels softening the line for their assault. Enemy horsemen also appeared at the right of Custer's line — the other prong of the Confederate pincers. A little cloud of smoke puffed from under a grove of trees. Seconds later, Custer heard the cannon's boom. With field glasses he studied the terrain. Broad pastures were cross-hatched with stone fences. On the horizon the ground rose slightly to Cress's Ridge, scarcely a mile away. In front of trees on that ridge he saw a farmhouse — Rummel's — and a big Dutch barn with loft jutting over a cowyard. A nearby patch of woods might hide cannon or screen assembling cavalry. As Custer watched, tiny horsemen rode into the field beside the farmhouse. Armstrong deployed the 5th Michigan as dismounted skirmishers. He held the veteran 1st in column of squadrons as a mounted reserve. The Boy General moved his men with confidence.

An aide from Pleasonton now galloped up on a foam-spattered horse.[12] The general had missed Custer on the march from Two Taverns. He wanted Custer's brigade back with Kilpatrick on the other end of Meade's battle line.

Custer was sure that his brigade was needed right where it stood if all those rebels yonder belonged to Jeb Stuart. Cannon were pounding the Union center and a sudden attack on the rear might lose the Battle of Gettysburg. However, orders were orders — unless it seemed more sensible to evade them. Custer saw General Gregg's battle flag approaching and he decided to explain the situation to him. General Hancock had defied an order at Williamsburg. Gregg might do so, here.

General Gregg was a tall, regular army officer with a biblike beard covering the upper buttons on his coat. He was self-effacing even when surrounded by aides under his billowing general's flag, but he had dogged courage and understood the problems of battle. The terrific cannonading, the vicious whistle of exploding shells, did not disturb him. He had been studying those distant horsemen and had decided that they belonged to Jeb Stuart. If so, Jeb's four crack brigades, under Fitzhugh Lee, Wade Hampton, J. R. Chambliss, and A. G. Jenkins, totaling five thousand sabers, outnumbered Gregg's three — unless Gregg kept Custer. Gregg believed, too, that the Battle of Gettysburg might be lost right here, if Stuart got through to Meade's rear. He ordered Custer, for the second time that day, to serve in his command regardless of other orders. Jeb Stuart must be stopped! *

* *O. R.,* I, XXVII, pt. 1, pp. 956, 993; pt. 2, pp. 290–291; J. M. Hanson, "Civil War Custer," p. 27; H. J. Hunt, "Third Day at Gettysburg," p. 378; W. E. Miller, "Cavalry Battle near Gettysburg," pp. 403–404; C. D. Rhodes, *History of the Cavalry of the Army of the Potomac,* p. 63. W. Brooke Rawle, "Right Flank at Gettysburg," p. 478, states that Custer was marching away when stopped.

The earth-shattering bombardment subsided at about three o'clock. Perhaps Pickett had begun his charge. Certainly Jeb Stuart's horsemen showed renewed activity. The Confederates must be closing in, front and rear. Custer, never willing to wait for an enemy to strike first, now asked Gregg's permission to open the ball. The general nodded assent. Armstrong turned to Colonel Alger and told him to advance with the dismounted 5th Michigan.* The 6th Michigan Regiment, and McIntosh's brigade from Gregg's division, would cover his flanks.

Custer, on his horse, watched the opening maneuver. The whole battlefield lay before him. His men advanced to the first fence, climbed over, and realigned. Out ahead of them he saw an enemy line emerge from the woods and come toward his men. He felt confident that his troopers with their eight-shot Spencers could outshoot and stop them.

Soon puffs of white smoke and the rattle of carbine fire told him that the lines were within range. Little geysers of dirt and smoke jumped from the green fields ahead of the advancing Union men. Evidently enemy cannon were shelling them.

"Tell Pennington to silence those guns. Two can play that game."

Battery "M's" guns began to fire in rapid succession. The Confederate line stopped, then drew back slowly. White puffs of rifle smoke showed that they were fighting as they went.

General Gregg rode up beside Custer. The two generals were a study in contrasts: Gregg slow, thoughtful, his head bent, beard on his breast; Custer erect, nervous, tossing his red-gold locks, his blue eyes racing. They watched the Michigan 5th follow the enemy, fence by fence, to a combination post-rail and stone barrier below the Rummel farm. There the Union regiment stopped, then came back, leaving men sprawled on the field.

"Could they have run out of ammunition?"

"Repeating rifles always make men squander their shots!"

As the Union line retreated, the enemy jumped from behind the

---

* W. Brooke Rawle, "Right Flank at Gettysburg," p. 477, says McIntosh opened the fight; but Col. J. H. Kidd of the Michigan 6th was sure that this was erroneous. His version has been accepted.

wall and came after them — a long wavering flight of little figures with running legs, like wild fowl winging south. Dirt spurted up from the fields in front of them as Pennington threw out shells to stop their advance, but the gray soldiers came on, field by field.

Custer looked at Gregg's solemn, bowed head for the next command. The general ordered the Michigan 7th to draw sabers and sweep in from the right.

The 7th was Custer's newest regiment, still unseasoned. Armstrong watched it move forward in column of squadrons, leather squeaking, colors waving, the fear in raw troopers' hearts masked by grim pride. Then Custer cantered to the regiment's front. Green troops must not go into battle without him. Besides, Custer was always happier charging with his men than maneuvering them from the rear.[13]

"Come on, you Wolverines!"

Shells screamed overhead. Bullets whistled between soldiers riding stirrup to stirrup. Explosions blew up dirt, gravel, bits of broken men. Ebullient Custer waved his sword, and the riders bounded ahead; but the charge failed. These rebs were a match for any man.

Custer cantered back, unhurt, to General Gregg's side. Together they watched the fighting in other fields — charges and countercharges, squadrons sweeping out from woodlands, cutting off enemy detachments, only to be cut off themselves — a grand game of tag, except for riderless horses and the dead men dotting the fields. Then suddenly the gamboling horsemen disappeared. Something was moving out from the distant trees. Custer dismounted to study it better through his glasses because his field of vision wavered when he watched from the back of a restless horse. Moreover, the light was uncertain. Clouds had been gathering all afternoon, and the sun was setting now.*

Over on Cress's Ridge, regiment after regiment of gray horsemen was taking position in solid formation — more than a brigade surely, perhaps more than a division. They were, in fact, Stuart's two choicest brigades — Wade Hampton's and Fitzhugh Lee's — massed for the

---

* W. Brooke Rawle, "Right Flank at Gettysburg," p. 480, states that this was at 3 P.M. — just as Pickett struck. Late afternoon seems more probable.

final thrust around Meade's right wing. Pierce Manning Butler Young, Tom Rosser, and Stephen Ramseur were probably in that oncoming column. At the van Custer could see a general's flag.[14]

Shattered remnants of the 5th and 7th Michigan drew back from this ominous cloud as it advanced across the meadows. Now Pennington elevated his guns and set his men to bombarding the great wall of Confederate horsemen. Custer and Gregg saw holes cut in the gray ranks, but the Southerners' battalions held their shape and crept forward — slowly, confidently, the general's flag in front. Evidently the horses were being rested for a final dash.

Gregg determined to stop the enemy's advance. He ordered McIntosh to prepare to strike with his feeble force from the woods on the right. Remnants of the Michigan 5th and 7th would strike from the left. Pennington was ordered to double-shot his guns with canister — and if the enemy did not stop, triple-shot them. Then Gregg, with Custer beside him, rode over to the commander of the Michigan 1st, the veteran regiment which had stood in reserve all day.

"Colonel Town," Gregg said, "put those people out of there."

Custer turned to Gregg, saluted, and rode over beside Colonel Town. The Michigan 1st was confronted with a supreme test of courage. It must charge into three or four times its number; but Custer could always be relied on to lead, and lead gaily, into desperate actions far beyond the strict call of duty.

"Come on, you Wolverines!" [15]

The Michigan 1st, heartened by Custer's example, started at a trot straight for the solid column. The horde was already well down the slope of Cress's Ridge, with a front rank fanned out, banner waving.

In the twilight, distances became deceptive. The head of the advancing column disappeared in a shallow depression. Custer beckoned for his men to jog-trot but be ready. At each side he could see small Union detachments — his 5th and 7th, and McIntosh's brigade — slipping stealthily on the enemy's flanks. Next moment the general's flag reappeared. It belonged to Wade Hampton, a name second only to Jeb Stuart. To his right and left, guidons fluttered over his still invisible ranks. Soon the heads of the leading horsemen rose above the ground level. Custer could hear an officer call, "Keep to your sabers, men, keep to your sabers!" At Brandy Station and at Aldie the rebels had used pistols to their disadvantage.

The grim confidence of this ominous wall of oncoming horsemen was enough to make the front rank of the Michigan 1st hesitate. Wade Hampton had mauled the 6th Regiment badly at Hunterstown. He must not do so again. Past defeats never shattered Custer's courage. His voice rang out, clear and defiant as a bugle:

"Come on, you Wolverines!"

All soldiers who ever heard that cry attest its magic, its power over fighting men in a crisis. Armstrong spurred out four lengths ahead of the regiment and charged. His men followed with wild yells. The separate Union battalions at the right and left struck with him. Captain William E. Miller of the 3d Pennsylvania Cavalry, who was far to one side, heard the two lines meet. The sound reminded him of the roaring crash when woodsmen fell a great tree.*

Riders on each side penetrated deep into their enemy's ranks, steel clashing on steel, sparks flying in the darkness, men swearing, the sickening thud of bodies falling to the ground under churning hoofs. Horses reared, pawed the air, squealed in fright. Hampton was wounded — a saber cut on his head — and Federals seized his flag. In the gloom and tumult all formation dissolved. Some Confederates surrounded Union horsemen and took them prisoners, but most of the gray riders straggled away in the darkness, confused and baffled, lost from their regiments. The Southerners' charge had been broken into bits.

As the Confederate cavalrymen groped their way back to safety, Pickett's men, three miles west, were limping down the slopes of

---

* H. J. Hunt, "Third Day at Gettysburg," p. 378; W. E. Miller, "Cavalry Battle near Gettysburg," p. 404; W. Brooke Rawle, "Second Cavalry Division," p. 279. This article contains a detailed map of the cavalry positions. See also *O. R.,* I, XXVII, pt. 1, p. 761. The importance of the cavalry in this battle varies with the analyst's prejudices.

Cemetery Ridge, also repulsed. The Battle of Gettysburg had been won by the North, thus determining the war's final outcome. Had Stuart encircled Meade's right, as planned,[16] and cracked down on his rear, the outcome might have been different. Gregg, as top cavalry commander on the right wing, deserves the credit for stopping the maneuver, but a study of the casualties shows who did the fighting that turned the battle tide. Gregg's two brigades lost thirty-five men. Custer's single brigade lost 257.*

The Boy General, in his first official report as a brigade commander, said of this final assault: "I challenge the annals of warfare to produce a more brilliant or successful charge of cavalry." [17] Extravagant as this sounds, it was a common Civil War expression. Note that Custer was bragging about the brigade, with no mention of himself. He would write like this many times in the years ahead, and by so doing build up tremendous morale — and much jealousy. Of course, he was really flattering himself for, in his mind, he and the 2d (Michigan) Brigade were one. But there is no gainsaying that General Custer had made an auspicious start. Moreover, he could hardly forget that he had successfully evaded a superior's order and, by doing so, became a gallant — perhaps a key — figure in winning the greatest battle of the war.

12 Engaged to be Married

ON JULY 4, 1863, MEADE'S EXHAUSTED INFANTRY RESTED ALL DAY. HOWever, the day was not one of rest for Armstrong Custer. He returned to Kilpatrick's headquarters in a pouring rain, riding past makeshift shelters where grim but triumphant soldiers clustered around their

---

* The estimated losses vary according to the source. Those given above are Meade's for the period July 1 to 4, 1863 (*O. R.,* I, XXVII, pt. 1, p. 186). Burke Davis, editor of McClellan, *I Rode with Stonewall,* p. 346, quotes Col. Robert N. Scott, of the War Records Office, Washington, as stating that he has proof that Gregg's total division loss in the July 3 fight was 33, and Custer's 219. Custer reported in *O. R.,* I, XXVII, pt. 1, p. 998, that he lost 86 in the saber charge alone.

mess fires. Casualty lists had not yet come in but they were known to be staggering. Generals Gibbon and Hancock had both been seriously wounded. Armstrong had lost five schoolmates from the West Point classes of 1860 and 1861. Another, Malbone Watson, had lost a leg, and amputations were often fatal. Among the dead were Patrick O'Rourke, the honor student, and Al Cushing, the bucktoothed introvert and bookworm.[1] Allie had died with great heroism during Pickett's charge. Wounded first by an exploding shell, he held himself erect and continued to command his battery. A bullet in the shoulder knocked him down but he staggered to his feet with the grim determination which he had displayed at West Point. Facing the enemy in a rain of exploding missiles, he stood firm, as gun after gun in his battery toppled over. A second bullet hit him in the stomach. He refused to give up and ordered his only remaining cannon triple-shotted with canister. A third bullet killed him instantly. No man had shown more bulldog courage.

To Custer the most distressing of all the casualties was Farnsworth's death. Only a short time after Armstrong left him, yesterday morning, Kilpatrick had assigned him a perilous task, a two-mile advance with both flanks exposed — as futile as the charge of the Light Brigade at Balaklava. Farnsworth had pointed out its hopelessness.

"If you are afraid to lead this charge," Kilpatrick told him, "I will lead it." [2]

Lashed by these insulting words, Farnsworth straightened in the saddle and saluted. Kilpatrick watched him go. Part of the brigade survived, but Farnsworth's body was found later in a roadside ditch. He had been struck by five bullets.

Other ugly stories were being told by men in the dripping shelters, but Armstrong had little time to hear them. Lee was retreating, and the Union cavalry must stop him if it could.

Custer led his brigade eleven miles southwest to Emmitsburg, Maryland, by noon. Rain continued splashing across the landscape and torrents of muddy water streamed down the roads. Gray lakes appeared in the fields. The battle-weary horsemen became soaked to the skin despite their rubber coats. Riding west to get ahead of Lee, Custer's brigade crossed the Catoctin Mountains into the valley beyond. No enemy yet! South Mountain, ahead, was visible only between rainy gusts.

Darkness settled over the cavalry column and Custer halted at Fountaindale, where the road began to climb over South Mountain. He reined his horse under the branches of a tree and his aides built a fire. Out of the darkness rode Kilpatrick. He stopped and shook the water from his hat-brim. Two years of war had changed Little Kil from the youth Armstrong had known at West Point. His jaw, firm when he was a boy, appeared more pronounced now. Ginger-colored side-whiskers adorned his cheeks, probably to conceal his youth, and deep wrinkles had developed between his eyes. His straight mouth looked like a scar across his face, but the boyish grin was still there, or was it a perpetual grimace? Certainly he showed no sign of re-morse for ordering Farnsworth to his death. That was war! General Kil had stitched little American flags on the turned-down corners of his collar — just as Armstrong wore gold stars on his.

Kilpatrick said that the division must cross South Mountain during the night. He hoped to surprise Lee on the other side, at least cut off his wagon trains. Custer ordered the 5th Michigan to take the van. Pennington's flying artillery would go with them. The road up the mountain was narrow, a dugway along the slope. Brush whipped the stirrups of outside riders in the column of fours. Pennington sent back word that he could not unlimber into battery in case they met the enemy. Kilpatrick rode along unmoved, a grim smile on his in-scrutable mouth.

As the regiment toiled up the dark hill, the two young generals may have talked about old days at the Point, surely about girls. Little Kil always had an eye for accommodating women. Custer was still con-sidering marriage to Fanny Fifield or Libbie Bacon.

The young men's conversation must have stopped abruptly at ten o'clock when a red flash split the darkness ahead and a cannon roared.

Both spurred front along the edge of the column. Just below the summit they found the lead squadrons jammed confusedly in the narrow road, with no room to retreat. They had almost reached the open country on top when a cannon was fired at them.

Kilpatrick ordered Custer to prepare an attack at once: get the broken squadrons off the road so the first men in formation could gallop out. Then Kilpatrick disappeared down the dark road to make sure that all regiments came on promptly.

Custer rode ahead with the first rank. In the open country on the summit he saw, dimly in the gloom, a building — the Monterey House. Evidently there was a road which ran down the ridge-crest, crossing at right angles the one on which he had come. By watching gun flashes, Custer decided that the enemy must be only a small detail sent to protect the escaping Confederates' flank. He ordered his advance regiments deployed and, as he watched, Nathaniel Richmond, ranking colonel from the lamented Farnsworth's 1st Brigade, reported his outfit for duty. Kilpatrick had sent them up to help.

Custer ordered the new brigade forward in column to pierce the enemy line, while his deployed Michigan boys mopped up the resistance here. Joining the newcomers, he trotted down the road west of South Mountain. Within half a mile they came to a Confederate wagon train headed south. The teamsters had heard the shooting on the ridge, but thought it thunder. Their train, they said, belonged to Baldy Ewell's corps.

Custer divided his force, sending riders up and down the train to turn all wagons off the road. He accompanied the squadron that rode south seeking the train's head. They overtook it at dawn in Ringgold, Maryland, eight miles away. The entire train was in their hands — three hundred wagons, fifteen ambulances, and a guard of thirteen hundred men.[3]

This same day — July 5, 1863 — a reporter for the *New York Times,* Edward A. Paul, who had followed the cavalry since the Hanover fight, overtook the Union van here. It was Sunday and he reported finding Custer fast asleep under the dripping eaves of a chapel, his curls in the mud.[4] The Boy General had been riding and fighting in the rain for almost twenty-four hours. Awaiting disposal of his prisoners and wagons, he had toppled over, exhausted. Paul was attracted to the spectacular youth and would write about him later.

After two hours' rest, Armstrong was in the saddle once more, leading his brigade fifteen miles to Smithsburg. Here churchgoers met the mud-armored knights with patriotic songs and pyramids of bread and jelly. Horsemen reached for the delicacies from their saddles like merry-go-round riders reaching for rings. By dark the column rode into Boonsboro, only five miles from the Potomac. As yet they had failed to find Lee's army. Perhaps they were now ahead of it.[5]

Next morning, July 6, the cavalry rode northwest, fanning out along country roads paralleling the Potomac. A mile below Williamsport, Custer's brigade met enemy pickets and pushed them back. Armstrong became convinced that they were only an advance guard sent ahead by Lee to hold the river crossing. He determined to take the crossing himself, and thus prevent the Confederate Army from escaping into Virginia. He realized that his little brigade would have to hold back the entire Army of Northern Virginia — a last stand if there ever was one! — but Kilpatrick could reinforce him immediately and Buford's division could help until Meade arrived with the infantry.

Custer deployed and began fighting along a two-mile line. He was confident of victory, but Kilpatrick ordered him to withdraw. Armstrong learned that the order came from Meade. Meade was afraid to fight Lee again and wanted him to escape — or at least that is what Pleasonton, who was with Meade, would dare to say later.*

* *O. R.,* I, XXVII, pt. 1, pp. 995, 998; A. Pleasonton, "Campaign of Gettysburg," p. 455, and *Report.. ....on the Conduct of the War,* p. 365. The Union cavalry seems to have had more than double the Confederate force at Williamsport when Custer arrived. Imboden's "Lee at Gettysburg," p. 512, says he was in command with only a guard and a 17-mile wagon train of wounded. To defend the crossing he impressed teamsters as they arrived — some 500 of them. At sunset, Fitzhugh Lee clattered in with his cavalry — but that would have been too late. Jeb Stuart arrived during the night.

Custer withdrew reluctantly. A chance to end the war had been overlooked. However, his daring initiative which created that chance impressed Pleasonton as it always had. For the next week the cavalry worried the flank of Lee's army but failed to stop its leisurely march to the Potomac, which in due course it began to cross. Union cavalry harried Lee's rear guard constantly, capturing stragglers, retaking twelve thousand cattle and eight thousand sheep the Confederates had appropriated in Pennsylvania.[6] No wonder three generations of Pennsylvania farmers would say, "Lee did to us what Sherman did to Georgia, except for one difference. Lee got stopped quicker."

On July 12 Lee's rear guard left Hagerstown, Maryland. Custer fought it two days and two nights as it withdrew along the eight miles to Williamsport. He was still pounding it at 6 A.M. on the fourteenth, when the end of the Confederate column forded the Potomac. Townsmen told Custer that many of Lee's men had marched down-river four miles to Falling Waters and were crossing on a pontoon bridge there.[7]

Armstrong snapped a few short orders that set the bugles blowing. Deployed horsemen trotted into ranks, and the column swerved away, mud flying from galloping hoofs. The down-river road was still soggy from the recent flood. Within two miles shots halted them. Custer drove the enemy skirmishers back half a mile. Then he saw two bastions which Lee had constructed to command the road. Armstrong turned to Major Peter A. Weber and told him to dismount half the 6th Michigan and have them advance on foot, shooting to keep down any heads that appeared over yonder works. Let the other half charge mounted.

While this maneuver was being executed Kilpatrick rode up and changed part of it — with bad results, according to Captain Kidd, who was present. (Already Custer's admirers believed that he could do no wrong!)[8] The mounted men charged ten times their number, slashing with their sabers, but the assault proved costly. Thirty of the hundred horsemen, including Major Weber, were knocked out of their saddles. However, the rest of Kilpatrick's division brushed by, capturing fifteen hundred men — the last of Lee's army north of the Potomac. In his official report Kilpatrick said, "To General Custer and his brigade, Lieutenant Pennington and his battery . . . all praise is due." [9]

On July 15, Kilpatrick left on sick leave. Pleasonton gave Custer command of the division. He was ordered to march down the Potomac, and, on the seventeenth, he crossed into Virginia at Berlin, below Harper's Ferry, his long column of horsemen singing "Carry Me Back to Old Virginny" as their mounts plodded up the south bank. [10]

Armstrong knew that he would not command a division long, so he intended to make the most of Kilpatrick's absence. Also on his mind was a disconcerting message he had received from Nettie Humphrey. Libbie was angry with him, even threatened to terminate the "understanding." Perhaps it was only a woman's way of forcing a showdown in their romance. In any event, she expressed the suspicion that Armstrong had been too friendly with Fanny, who, it seems, had told her that Autie showed her that ambrotype which she had given him in secret.

With this letter in his pocket Armstrong led his division south along the eastern slope of the Blue Ridge, camping the first night at Purcellville. On July 19th, at the noonday rest, he replied to Nettie. "While my staff are reclining on the grass in front of a Secesh house I am inside, at a table, penning these few lines," he said. "I have but a few minutes, as I intend to march several miles before night and to attack the enemy cavalry in the morning."

With this detailed Custerish introduction, he defended himself against the charge of intimacy with Fanny. "Tell Libbie," he wrote, "that Fanny *has nothing in her power to bestow that wd induce me to show her that ambrotype.* I know nothing of what representations of our intimacy she has made to Libbie. It is no different from what I told her. I would write more, but must mount my good horse and away. Please call [on] my sister and tell her that I am well." [11]

Next day Custer skirmished at Ashby's Gap and took a few prisoners. Two days later he was at Upperville. On the following day,

July 23, he crossed the Rappahannock and rode to Amissville. Already he had penetrated over fifty miles into enemy country, meeting little resistance, but he knew Lee's army must be very close now. He captured two deserters from Fitzhugh's brigade. They were too drunk to talk coherently, so Custer pushed ahead. A Negro he met on the road told him that General A. P. Hill's Corps was racing for Culpeper. Custer, with only twelve hundred men, decided to be there first. If he could get between Hill and Longstreet, and if Meade would only follow up and fight them separately, Lee might be whipped right here.

Custer found Culpeper undefended and pushed ahead four more miles toward Orange Court House. Small bodies of skedaddling "Secesh" were all about him now. He captured the Negro servant of Jeb Stuart's medical director. Hill turned suddenly, pinched off the 5th and 6th Michigan and Pennington's battery. They cut their way back, and Custer realized that he must retreat now or lose his whole division — a fine way to demonstrate his ability in Kilpatrick's absence! From Amissville he notified Pleasonton that unless Meade sent support he would have to withdraw farther.[12]

While waiting for a reply Armstrong wrote his sister. As usual, he devoted most of the letter to telling about things which had long since happened. Did she know that he was a brigadier — "the youngest General in the U. S. Army by over two years, in itself something to be proud of." He told her, too, as though it were news, that he had fought in the Battle of Gettysburg, had three horses shot under him. One of them was Roanoke, the beautiful black captured down on the Northern Neck in the spring of '62. A minie ball had hit the stallion in the foreleg, but he would recover. Autie said that he was keeping the bullet for a relic. Armstrong also told Lydia about his love problems, said he had been so busy day and night on his push into Virginia that he had prevailed on a staff officer to write Fanny. He hoped to come home on furlough as soon as Kilpatrick returned. Pleasonton, Autie said, had promised him a leave on the condition that he would go home and marry Fanny Fifield. "Shall I come?" he asked his sister. Evidently the boy was still undecided. Perhaps he was trying to arouse Lydia's curiosity.

Custer's request for military support was denied by Meade. Thus for the second time Meade passed up an opportunity to fight Lee. In anger and disgust, Pleasonton reported this negligence to Congress along with an account of Meade's procrastination after Gettysburg. The rift between the cavalry commander and General Meade was growing ugly. Custer, also, was disgusted, but he drew back dutifully and camped in comparative safety at Warrenton Junction. Kilpatrick returned for duty on August 4, but he, too, was restrained from opening the way for another battle.[13] Meade's excuse now was lack of man power. Enlistments were expiring. He must wait until the draft filled his ranks.

Loitering in camp, Custer was annoyed by a new peril, John S. Mosby, former member of Jeb Stuart's staff, had started to operate an "underground." His men had no encampments and few uniforms. Their job was to cut Union communications, waylay supply trains and bushwhack work parties. Their pay consisted of a share of all loot, although Mosby, a minister's son, said that he, himself, never took any. They proved particularly dangerous when they donned Union blue, pretending to be soldiers, and rode with small Federal details, stealthily murdering their companions. Armstrong organized 300 picked men to hunt down these partisans, but when pursued they repeatedly escaped by scattering to farmhouses, where each assumed the role of a peaceful husbandman.[14]

Between pursuits, Custer wrote Nettie Humphrey — for Libbie Bacon's information — about their bountiful living here in camp. Always Armstrong accepted his misfortunes cheerfully. Country women, young and old, he said, came to their mess tents with baskets full of eggs and vegetables to trade for sugar, coffee, and salt — three things they could not get under Confederate rule. Armstrong also asked Nettie what Judge Bacon thought of his promotion to general — surely he had read about it in the papers? The high rank, Armstrong warned, was no bed of roses. Generals were more subject to censure and dismissal than captains. He knew, for he had seen McClellan, Burnside, and Hooker get the ax.

With time on his hands, Custer organized his staff. Pleasonton let him have George Yates, who had distinguished himself again at Gettysburg. For adjutant he got Nettie Humphrey's suitor, Jacob Greene. To cook for his mess, he hired a runaway slave named Eliza, who claimed that she "jined up with the Ginnel" to try "this freedom business." A cadaverous waif, Johnnie Cisco, attached himself to headquarters and waited on table, washed Armstrong's clothes, and slept with the general's dog.[15] Another boy, Joseph Fought, who had enlisted in one of the Michigan companies, deserted his outfit at every opportunity to be with Custer. Stray boys and dogs always congregated around the Boy General's tent, but when a stray white girl joined the throng trouble started.

Annie Jones was a teen-age terror. She said she wanted to serve as a nurse, but she brazenly admitted having lived intimately with various officers. Morals in the Army of the Potomac had become lax after McClellan's dismissal. Captain Charles Francis Adams of the 1st Massachusetts Cavalry, a son of the United States Minister to Great Britain, wrote in his autobiography: "During the winter (1862–63), when Hooker was in command, I can say from personal knowledge and experience, that the Headquarters of the Army of the Potomac was a place to which no self-respecting man liked to go, and no decent woman could go. It was a combination of barroom and brothel."

Annie Jones seems to have prospered in such surroundings, and now — in August, 1863 — she stayed several days at Kilpatrick's and Custer's headquarters. Acquiring a horse and a semimilitary costume with major's straps, she visited picket posts, delighted in showing off her bravery by exposing herself to enemy snipers, and once rode over to the enemy for a day or two, claiming, when she returned, that she had been with Mosby's men. After this, Kil and Custer sent her away.

Soon thereafter the division was ordered to establish a new line below Aquia Creek, some fifty miles southeast. Here Annie found them again, arriving at dusk one evening in an ambulance which, she said, had been assigned to her by General Warren, Armstrong's "math" instructor and the hero of Little Round Top. This time Armstrong turned the problem over to Adjutant Greene, Nettie Humphrey's admirer, with instructions to get her out of camp in the morning and send her back to Warren — with an escort if necessary, but get her out! Armstrong may have been somewhat perturbed at this time by a letter he had just received from Nettie. In it he learned that Libbie was playing "hard to get," or perhaps really worrying about Fanny. In any event, Nettie hinted — nothing definite, just a hint — that Libbie's romance with Autie might be ended.*

Armstrong replied with the schoolboy eloquence of the mid-nineteenth century: He said he could meet the reverses of life like a soldier. "My own mother may disown me," he wrote, "and turn me from my home; I may lose my position among men, and be thrown solitary and alone among strangers, without the sympathy of a single friend; and yet, with all this, there is a strange indescribable *something* in me, that would enable me to shape my course through life, cheerful, if not contented. . . . Now that you know this, you need not hesitate to tell me *all*." [16]

Apparently no reply to Custer's declaration of faith came before September 13, when Meade ordered an advance along the whole line.

---

* Reports, March 3, 22, 1864, on Annie Jones (National Archives); C. F. Adams, *Autobiography,* p. 161. The exact date of this letter and of Annie's return cannot be determined, but they were within a few days of each other. Custer and Kilpatrick were at Hartwood Church on August 26, 1863. (See Jones Report, March 14, 1864, and *O. R.,* I, XXIX, pt. 1, p. 78.) Custer replied to Nettie a week before he was wounded on September 13.

Was the General recovering at last from "the slows"? Lee's army stood below the Rapidan, Meade's above the Rappahannock. Between them lay no man's land except for Jeb Stuart's cavalry, with headquarters in the middle, at Culpeper. To lead the offensive, Meade sent his cavalry across a dozen Rappahannock fords and started them south in a broad line straddling the Orange & Alexandria Railroad.

Armstrong remembered this rolling, parklike country. He had distinguished himself here at Beverly Ford last June. Now in this September offensive Gregg's division rode to the right, Buford's in center, and Kilpatrick's on the left. Custer's brigade was assigned the left of Kil's left. Pleasonton, the first Union general to make cavalry an important branch, rode with his staff, watching his five-mile line — a magnificent display of mounted military might, with neighing stallions, the sun glittering on epaulets, brass ornaments, and dazzling white crossbelts. Skirmishers rode ahead; solid regiments followed. At regular intervals, two to the mile, brigadiers' flags could be seen.[17]

Confederate vedettes appeared on the distant hills but they always retreated out of range. At Brandy Station, some rebels made a short stand. Custer heard the boom of cannon and saw puffs of smoke — but that was all. In the rolling country beyond, Kilpatrick's 3d Division was sent ahead by a left-hand road. Gregg and Buford trotted along the railway. As they approached Culpeper, six miles below, both divisions deployed in a crescent around the town. Part of Kilpatrick's division joined them; but Custer, at the extreme left of the semicircle, had almost twice as far to go, and had not yet come in when Jeb Stuart started a counterattack by shelling the New York 2d Cavalry (the Harris Light), which stood precariously on the end of the line, where Custer was to join it. Captain Willard Glazier, of the Harris Light, told later about his fear that day. The regiment, he said, showed signs of worry, and the line might have broken had not Custer suddenly appeared at their left, racing toward the batteries which were making all the trouble. He was followed only by the Michigan 1st and the Vermont 1st, both a part of "the Michigan Brigade." The rest of Custer's men had been delayed by a swamp, so Custer had come without them

—just in time. The Harris Light immediately regained confidence as he passed, and they followed his charge.*

That charge was watched by Pleasonton and by an observer from Meade's staff, Colonel Theodore Lyman. A wealthy, sophisticated graduate of Harvard, Lyman could hardly be expected to admire a slouchy country boy like Custer, so his remarks in the first letter he wrote home after the battle are noteworthy. He said that he and Pleasonton were watching a train, in the Culpeper station, apparently getting up steam to run out of town. They also noticed the enemy batteries which held back the Union advance. Then, while they watched, they saw an independent body of horse charging magnificently, straight for the Confederate cannon, sabers sparkling in the sun. The cannoneers began limbering at once, and whipped into town. The charging Union horse followed like a field of fox hunters. What happened next Lyman was unable to see, but he soon learned that the spectacular charge had been led by the Boy General mentioned so often in newspapers. This day the Boy enhanced his reputation by acquiring more Confederate cannon, and also by taking Jeb Stuart's headquarters, including the general's dinner! In doing so, a horse had been shot under him and he was wounded, though not seriously. Shortly thereafter Custer came back to Pleasonton's flag. Lyman thought him the funniest-looking chap he had ever seen, "like a circus rider gone mad!" The fellow wore a hussar jacket and tight trousers of faded black velvet, trimmed with tarnished gold lace. On his head of short flaxen

---

* F. F. Van de Water, in *Glory Hunter*, p. 58, censures Custer for abandoning his troops in the swamp and commandeering regiments that did not belong to him for the glory of leading this charge. Van de Water overlooks the fact that the Vermont 1st was part of the Michigan Brigade, and that the New York 2d and 5th which followed the charge belonged to Custer's division and were commanded by a colonel. Thus Custer was the ranking officer in that area, and earned Pleasonton's reward. Had he waited to extricate his entire brigade before coming forward, the battle might have been lost. (F. Phisterer, *New York in the War*, I, p. 751; W. Glazier, *Three Years in the Federal Cavalry*, p. 313; G. G. Benedict, *Vermont in the Civil War*, II, p. 612; L. N. Boudrye, *Historic Records of the Fifth New York Cavalry*, p. 77; *O. R.*, I, XXIX, pt. 1, pp. 119, 121, 127, 129. F. Whittaker, *Complete Life of . . . Custer . . .* , p. 195.)

curls perched a little gray felt hat. Gilt spurs clamped the heels of high-topped boots. "His aspect though highly amusing," Lyman wrote, "is also pleasing, as he has a very merry blue eye, and a devil-may-care style. His first greeting to General Pleasonton, as he rode up, was: 'How are you, fifteen-days'-leave-of-absence? They have spoiled my boots but they didn't gain much there, for I stole 'em from a Reb.'" [18] Custer held out a foot admiringly. The boot leg was torn by the shell-scrap which killed his horse. His leg was torn, too.

Pleasonton certainly did not know how important this requested leave was to Custer's love affair. He did know that Custer had arrived on the battlefield at a critical moment, that he immediately sensed the vulnerable spot in the enemy's defense, and that he had displayed the military magnetism which made soldiers follow him into the breach. Already Custer's men were wearing red neckties as a badge of everything a cavalryman admired. Men with those red ties could rightfully swagger when they went home on leave. The army needed more such leaders. . . . Pleasonton gave Custer his fifteen days and added ten more.

In Monroe, Armstrong became a celebrity—enough to spoil any boy of twenty-three. He had put his home town on the nation's map. The October 3, 1863, issue of *Harper's Weekly* carried a picture of him charging enemy guns. The "best people" could be heard to remark, with studied casualness: "When Custer was at our house to dinner, he said . . ." Girls vied with one another to sit near him at parties. Some brazen ones even stood outside his sister Lydia's home, tapping parasols invitingly against the picket fence.

Mrs. Bacon was away. Libbie and her father were boarding at the Humphrey house. So Armstrong met Libbie at once, and in no time they agreed to marry. Custer said he would ask the judge properly for her hand, but each day he put it off. He felt no fear of most men, none of Pleasonton certainly, or of Jeb Stuart; but Judge Bacon awed him. He could not muster enough courage to ask the question, so Libbie, on the night before he left, told her father that they were engaged. Next day, October 5, father and daughter joined the farewell crowd at the station. When the train pulled in Custer shook the judge's hand, saying, "I had desired to speak to you, but was prevented from doing so. I shall write you later."

The judge looked solemnly at him and replied, "Very well." Not much encouragement, surely! Did the old fellow feel as he always had?

At Toledo, Custer boarded a lake steamboat. As the vessel splashed eastward across the inland sea, he wrote a long letter — not to the judge but to Nettie Humphrey. He told her that he felt sad and lonely. He discussed the philosophy of life, as he understood it, its dangers and duties; then ended by saying, "How I wish I could be with my little girl to-night, and yet I cannot complain."

Two days later, in Baltimore, Armstrong had to wait several hours between trains. Once more he wrote Nettie, knowing that his letter would be delivered to Libbie. In this one he said that he had spent the day considering the letter he must write the judge. "I cannot rid myself of the fear that I may suffer from some unfounded prejudice," he said. Again he ended with, "Tell my little girl I am lonely without her. Kiss her for me, and tell her I have been real good since I left her." [19]

That night in Washington he went to the theater, occupying a box. From a flower girl he purchased a bouquet. With typical Custer absent-mindedness, he forgot to put his purse, containing seventy dollars, back in his pocket, and did not miss it until next morning. Fortunately he had transportation to his brigade at Culpeper. Before boarding the train he visited a photographer's studio, and sat for a picture to be framed and colored at a cost of thirty dollars. This picture, four times larger than the one of him which Lydia kept on her sitting-room wall, was for Libbie — as soon as he dared write that letter to her father. [20]

Late in the afternoon he was back in camp, greeted by ragged Johnnie Cisco, black Eliza's beaming face, Adjutant Greene, and Aide-de-Camp Yates. Oh, if brother Tom could be added to his staff! * Always, Armstrong wanted his organization to be a big family. As evening darkened, Custer and his aides went in the headquarters tent to sit around a candle. Soon the band outside began to play "Hail to the Chief." When the heroic strains ended, soldiers in the darkness gave three cheers.

Custer stepped out of his tent. Silhouetted against the triangle of yellow light, he told the men that he was glad to be back, but sorry to see their camp no nearer Richmond than when he left. In the next thirty-six hours — forty-eight at the latest — he hoped to give them some action. "Come on, you Wolverines!"

13 Marriage

C USTER'S DESIRE TO SHOW HIS MEN ACTION WITHIN THIRTY-SIX HOURS sounds like idle talk. Presumably a brigadier general is subject to orders from above. However, Custer had learned that Lee was starting an offensive. Jeb Stuart's riders were already concentrating less than twenty miles away on Robertson's River, an upper tributary of the Rapidan, so Custer knew that sharp fighting was imminent. On the morning after his return he ordered the brigade to prepare for a march. All day long on October 9, 1863, he supervised the proper inspections and at the same time considered what to write Judge Bacon. After dark the first of his regiments started south and Armstrong planned to follow when he finished that letter. If he left camp at midnight he could reach the van by dawn. At eight o'clock in the evening he retired to his tent, tied the flap cords, trimmed a candle's wick, got out paper and ink, then settled down with a pen held firmly between the index and third fingers of his strong square hand. He had thought a lot about what he wanted to say to the judge but somehow could not start. Instead,

* In a letter to his sister, November 6, 1863, Custer says he is trying to get his brother a commission at West Point.

he wrote another letter to Nettie. He was very serious and the letter was very long. He told her about his responsibilities with so many lives in his care. "And to think that I am just leaving my boyhood," he said, "and yet I have no fears, nor do I think that this latter fact is due to any self-conceit or egotism on my part."

Having started this introspection, Custer found it hard to change his thoughts. He continued: "When deciding upon any course to pursue, I have asked myself, is it right? Satisfied that it is, I allow nothing to swerve me from my purpose. Few persons have disregarded public opinion so much as I. . . . To this simple rule, framed though it be in humble language, I can attribute, more than to any other, my success in life."

Custer philosophized in this manner to Nettie on two long pages, finally asking, "Why have I written all this? Surely I do not know." (Nor does a reader, three generations later, except that this was the way young people thought and wrote in the 1860's.) Then, coming back to the purpose of his letter, Armstrong concluded, "I would have written that letter to her father to-day, but that I know I should be interrupted, which I do not wish to be, when writing so important a document."

In a postscript he added: "Please give these flowers to L. They were plucked in front of my headquarters, not far from the Rapidan." [1]

With this letter posted Custer rode away into the night, relishing the prospect of campaign hardships. Always he liked dramatics, and the memory of Libbie's last passionate kiss contrasted vividly with the prospect of battle ahead. The morning star had faded and the rising sun illuminated the Blue Ridge when he joined his troops. Kilpatrick, with the rest of the division, was groping his way southward somewhere to the left. All moved forward cautiously hour after hour — a monotonous day. At three in the afternoon Custer met his first opposition as he approached Robertson's River. The gray horsemen appeared in such numbers that he sent for help from Kilpatrick, but that commander had met resistance all along his line, too. Moreover, the Confederates were reported to have infantry behind their cavalry. The

Union horsemen were obliged to retreat slowly toward Culpeper, hoping that Meade would send infantry support.

During the night Custer halted, still watching for relief, but none had arrived next morning and the Confederates renewed their attack. Once more Armstrong retreated, fighting every step.[2] At noon he finally reached Culpeper. Kilpatrick's other brigades were ahead of him, and had already gone through town. To everyone's surprise Meade had retreated north of the Rappahannock, leaving word for the horsemen to follow him. He suspected that the offensive against his cavalry was a feint to draw attention from a massive Confederate attack on his flank. The cavalry, thus left alone in enemy country, backed out as rapidly as they dared without breaking into flight. Their road north of Culpeper paralleled the railroad track. Custer's rear guard reported that the enemy was following closely — much too closely. Armstrong increased his speed, being careful to keep on Kilpatrick's heels, for with Meade's infantry gone, the cavalry divisions must guard against being pinched off.

Shortly before reaching Brandy Station, Kilpatrick sent back bad news. The enemy had got ahead of them. Custer galloped forward to inspect the field. A heavy oak woods stood on the right, open fields on the left. The railroad embankment made an impregnable fortification flanking the road. But the enemy surrounded them, no mistake. The Union troops must surrender or cut their way out. Neither Pleasonton, Kilpatrick, nor Custer knew the meaning of surrender. They organized a half-dozen spearheads of horsemen to thrust through — keep the enemy guessing where the main blow would strike.

Custer deployed the 5th Michigan in column of squadrons for his offensive. He had a broad green field ahead with a thin line of opponents along a broken fence on the far side. Riding ahead of the regiment, he stood up in his stirrups and shouted, "Boys of Michigan. There are some people between *us* and home; I'm going home, who else goes?" The band struck up "Yankee Doodle" and scores of bugles sounded the charge. Custer tossed his cap to an orderly. No matador could do so with more drama! Then he drew his straight sword and away he went, the regiment at his heels, mad with battle ecstasy.

Later, Custer remembered that just before this charge he took from his pocket a picture of Libbie Bacon and looked at it for what he knew might be the last time. Then, he gave the command.

The attack did not end in storybook fashion. Halfway across the field his men came to an unseen ditch where the horses piled up in confusion.[3] Custer's horse was shot under him. Remounted, he tried to assemble his troops but the second horse crumpled between his knees. On a third mount Custer got his men around the obstacle and with a series of charges cut through the enemy lines, reaching the Rappahannock at eight o'clock that night. Across the stream Custer could see the welcome fires of Meade's infantry — bivouacked comfortably, while the desperate cavalry had fought a half-day's retreating action without support. The last of the horsemen crossed the river by ten o'clock.

Next day the tired men rested and "doctored" their jaded horses. Kilpatrick cited Custer for the gallantry of his charges. Eliza prepared a special dinner for her chief, and Armstrong, in his own official report, gave due credit to the courage of his men. Custer also wrote to Libbie, still via Annette Humphrey. "Oh, could you but have seen some of the charges that were made!" he wrote. "While thinking of them I cannot but exclaim 'Glorious War.'" He told how he set the band playing and tossed aside his cap because it was so small. He ended the letter by saying: "Heavy cannonading is going on a few miles to my right. A general engagement is expected to-morrow or in a few days. Give my love to Libbie, and tell her I thought of her so often during the battle yesterday."[4]

Custer folded this letter and, while still flushed with battle excitement, he wrote that oft put off letter to his prospective father-in-law. At last he would "beard the lion in his den, the beardless Bacon in his hall," to misquote Sir Walter. But Armstrong proved a humble suitor. He acknowledged his unworthiness and former intemperance.

He told the judge he had promised his sister two years ago to stop drinking, and had kept the pledge. He admitted that his flirtations with other girls last winter, after he stopped seeing Libbie, may have appeared trifling. He said his object was to prevent gossip. Then, as a final apology for himself, he concluded, "I left home when but sixteen, and have been surrounded with temptation, but I have always had a purpose in life." [5]

Soon after mailing his two letters to Monroe, Armstrong received orders to march thirty miles back toward Washington. Meade still feared that Lee was marching around his flank and might attack the capital, but on October 18 he ordered the cavalry to march south again along the Warrenton pike. Meade had decided that Lee's advance was only a trick and he decided to strike back. The first night on the return march Custer bivouacked at Gainesville, twelve miles north of Warrenton. He knew the enemy was close, so his men slept with arms in hand. Next morning scouts reported only a few gray horsemen in sight. Good news! Custer skirmished down the pike for two miles, chasing them. Kilpatrick followed. At Buckland Mills, Custer's troopers reported capturing Jeb Stuart's headquarters again, this time devouring his unfinished breakfast.

Here Kilpatrick's 1st Brigade took the lead, and Custer's men stopped to boil coffee. Little Kil rode by with his aides, orderlies, and "dog-robbers," one of them leading his race horse, Lively. He congratulated Custer on his early morning dash. Custer maintained later that he warned his chief to be careful: the situation might not be so good as it seemed; that man Jeb Stuart must be watched. The Union cavalry column's rear was open, and could be cut off as it had been last week.

Custer recalled that he had hardly finished speaking when gunshots indicated that the enemy was doing exactly what he suspected. Kilpatrick and Custer rode toward the shooting to investigate. They found the enemy advancing against their flank with footmen. They called up Pennington, but his artillery failed to stop the oncoming line. Kilpatrick said the enemy must be infantry, not just Stuart's dismounted horsemen. Obviously the Union column had been led into a trap.

Soon Kilpatrick's entire force was struck in a dozen places. Formations broke. Excited horsemen pounded back along the roads, adding to the confusion. Pennington barely escaped with his guns. Kilpatrick lost his race horse. Custer's headquarters wagon, containing his tent, desk, and papers, was captured. Never before had the two generals suffered such a disastrous surprise. It happened so quickly that they were glad to escape with their lives. To Armstrong, the defeat was unusually disconcerting. He had been roughly handled in every fight since he and Libbie came to their "understanding" and this was the one time in his life when he wanted most to demonstrate military competence. He estimated a loss of 214 men since October 9, three quarters of them left dead or wounded in enemy hands, and he was short many hundreds of horses. To know that he had been whipped by his old teacher, Fitzhugh Lee, and the incomparable Jeb Stuart was little satisfaction. He must have felt still worse when he learned that another of the Confederate leaders in this fight was his West Point friend, Tom Rosser, now a brigadier general commanding the Laurel Brigade — an organization becoming as famous for the green foliage worn by its men as Custer's brigade was for its red ties.[6]

While tallying his losses and wondering what to use for headquarters, Custer was handed his mail. Perhaps the reply from Judge Bacon! Armstrong flipped through the letters with his short, strong fingers. Several from Monroe! Yes, there it was. He tore open the envelope.

The letter was long and wordy. The judge described his intense love for his daughter and his anxiety concerning her future. "The subject broached," Custer read, "calls for weeks — months, even, of deliberation." However, the judge said, Libbie "is at full liberty to communicate to you."

This did not satisfy Custer. He wanted to marry the girl — not just write to her. Armstrong could be as wordily stubborn as the judge and he replied with great courtesy and determination. Defeat in battle seemed to give the Boy General extra courage in love. He rejected the implied permission to correspond with Libbie. Instead he wanted a definite commitment on "the subject broached." [7]

Once more after mailing a letter Custer received an order to march down the pike. The victorious Confederates had withdrawn below the Rappahannock again, and Meade planned to follow them. Custer hoped the general would not stop short of Richmond. Let Judge Bacon reply to him there!

But Meade did not go on to Richmond. He stopped at Brandy Station, twenty miles below Warrenton, and put his men to work sawing boards for tent floors and building winter huts. Custer fretted at the prospect of "holing up" for the winter, but it gave him one consolation. He could write every day to Libbie. Sometimes he wrote twice a day, and he watched every mail delivery for word from Judge Bacon. Wistfully he noticed Pennington — newly married, the lucky fellow — writing to his bride.

Between letters to Libbie, Armstrong corresponded with Lydia, with his mother, and with her kinfolk back in Ohio, enclosing pictures. He wrote a special letter to his niece, Maggie, treating her as the young lady she was growing up to be — another example of his unending family devotion. He also sent a letter to Judge Christiancy, who had tried to get Armstrong that Michigan regiment. A few days later the judge's son returned with Adjutant Greene from a furlough in Monroe. Armstrong was eager for news from home. After taps the three young men spread their coats on the ground before a campfire and talked about old friends, boyhood pranks, and the girls. How was Libbie? Had they seen Judge Bacon? The boys were still talking at 5 A.M. when servants lighted fires for breakfast.

Sad news came to camp along with the gossip. Armstrong learned that LeRoy Elbert had died — "Deacon" Elbert, his West Point classmate who had stood shoulder to shoulder with him when Southern cadets had threatened Northern boys. Elbert and Custer had enjoyed serenading girls together in Washington only two years ago. That seemed like a lost world. Poor Elbert had not died from gunshot wounds like his other schoolmates, Allie Cushing, Patrick O'Rourke, and John Pelham. He had distinguished himself at Fredericksburg, but died with fever down on the Mississippi. Armstrong said that Elbert was one of his best and truest friends.[8]

Meade's army was settling down dutifully for a dreary winter in camp. Out along the picket lines blue-clad sentries traded salt and hardtack for Confederate tobacco. Jeb Stuart notified Custer that he held some mail for him, captured weeks ago. Well, one thing was certain: Jeb would not get Judge Bacon's reply to Armstrong's last. It was due any day now.

Custer's salary as a brigadier seemed princely, especially in camp. He urged his parents to buy a home in Monroe and sent them money for a down-payment. He offered to pay for Maggie's schooling at the Seminary — Libbie's school. He wanted her to go there, rather than to the Methodist academy. "You Methodists are too prejudiced against our school," he wrote Lydia. However, if Maggie had her heart set on the academy he would acquiesce.

Custer soon learned that a brigadier's income was less munificent than he had anticipated. Never having much money-sense, he found it difficult to make later payments on his parents' home, but he blamed himself, not them, and wrote Lydia contritely that he was extravagant in many ways. "I could live on the money I squander," he said. "I lost ten dollars today I bet on a horse race with Gen. Kilpatrick." Then Armstrong revealed a secret to his sister. He was going to get married, but he did not say to whom. (Did he plan to elope if Judge Bacon refused his consent, or was he still thinking about Fanny Fifield?)

Inactivity in camp gave officers and men time to gossip, speculate, and scheme for promotions. One evening fifty enlisted men came to Armstrong's tent requesting transfer to his command. The aspiration of many young blades to wear a red tie and fight under the Boy General pleased Custer. However, drilling without action bored him, and he asked for another leave to go home. Pleasonton said he might have a furlough if he would capture Jeb Stuart — a joke, of course, but not to Armstrong. He led several little cavalry chases across Stuart's baili-wick. Instead of getting either Stuart or a furlough, however, he got censured by Pleasonton for taking a detail from a regiment on outpost duty.[9] Hancock had done as much at Williamsburg; so had Gregg at Gettysburg; but when Custer tried it, he failed to achieve a victory; and victory, the Boy General must learn, was what counted in war.

On October 23, Meade ordered another general advance. His en-campments bustled with preparations. The weather was fine. Leaves were falling from the trees and rustling underfoot. Jeb Stuart could no longer hide his horsemen in the woods for surprise attacks. The Union cavalry would get him at last. Then it snowed, and Meade post-poned the advance until November 26 — a day Lincoln had set aside for Thanksgiving. This time Custer was to open the offensive with a demonstration on the upper Rapidan fords — Raccoon Crossing and Somerville — while Meade thrust his infantry across the river below, and thus got around Lee's flank. Pleasonton ordered Armstrong to cross as soon as he heard Meade fire a cannon.

Custer set off in the night of November 25. A mile from the Rapidan he established field headquarters in the bare winter woods. He ordered his men to build big bivouac fires for miles up and down the stream to give the impression that a vast army was preparing to cross at dawn. He also ordered the band to play at different places throughout the night.

Custer seldom slept before a battle — too nervous. Although re-putedly calm under fire, he was always excited, flushed and jumpy before an action began. He rode out in the dark toward the Rapidan. Across the stream he heard chopping and the crash of falling trees. Evidently the enemy was building earthworks to resist his advance.[10]

The cold, ash-gray dawn brought no sound of cannon from below. Custer's men huddled around their fires, drinking steaming cups of coffee. Then they fell in rank, each at the head of his frost-covered mount. Custer's charger felt frisky in the cold air. He pranced as the

General rode along studying the south bank of the Rapidan where enemy works showed plainly, now that daylight had come. A percentage of his Michigan boys, including himself perhaps, were going to die in a few hours for no reason except to draw attention from Meade's infantry down the stream. Michigan boys! Michigan! . . . Warm houses, good food this Thanksgiving Day, and "The Girl I Left Behind Me." Let the band play it. Oh, when was Judge Bacon going to make up his mind?

Back in Monroe on this same Thanksgiving Day, Libbie wrote her suitor a letter. The judge had replied to Custer, and Libbie was sending a letter of her own by the same post. "To-night is the anniversary of our first meeting," she wrote. "Just a year ago you and your little girl bowed heads in formal introduction. . . . And what we said I am dying to know for I remember nary a word."

Meade's offensive proved to be a failure. Lee refused to stand and fight on a field of Meade's choosing. Instead, he withdrew across Mine Run and fortified himself in "the Wilderness." There he would fight a Confederate Gettysburg if Meade dared storm his lines. Meade declined the opportunity and withdrew.

Custer returned from his futile feint at Raccoon Ford and received the all-important letter from Judge Bacon. The Boy General's hands might well have trembled as he opened it.

The judge consented to his daughter's marriage!

The same mail contained two letters from Libbie. Armstrong read them eagerly, replied that he wanted to get married at once, then bring his bride to camp for the winter.

This impetuous proposal prompted Libbie to be coy. "Ah, dear man," she replied. "If I am worth having am I not worth waiting for? The very thought of marriage makes me tremble. Girls have so much fun. . . ."

Custer tried threats on his little sweetheart. Now or never! He even wrote Nettie to use her influence. He said he could come home for the wedding during Christmas week or as soon thereafter as he got a leave.

General Pleasonton decided the date for Custer by giving him a furlough in February. The elated young man sent by express to Judge Bacon the large photo, in colors, which he had ordered in Washington last October. He wrote the judge to hang it in Libbie's room as a surprise. Then he wrote Lydia describing his little game. In this letter he said the picture cost forty-five dollars; last October he had told her thirty dollars. Always he was careless with figures — whether dollars or enemies. He also told Lydia about his wedding. He wanted to know what his mother and the rest of the family thought of the marriage. Ever playful with his father, he wrote: "Tell Pop I forgot to get his consent." Armstrong asked if his niece, little "Em," would like to live with her "*Aunt Libbie*." In his excitement, Custer lost the key to his trunk and had to send to Lydia for the duplicate.

The wedding was to be a grand affair. Most of Custer's staff would attend. He planned to wear a coat that cost a hundred dollars — a gift, he was careful to tell frugal Lydia. Armstrong cut his hair "quite short." A chilly change during cold weather! [11]

Libbie started making her preparations. She sent to New York for silks, went to Detroit to have dresses designed, and employed a seamstress to come to her home. She wrote her cousin, Rebecca Richmond, "I am having my underclothes made on the machine." She told Armstrong she had ordered a riding habit, then added: "Would you like a description of my wedding dress?" Without waiting for a reply, she described it.

During the last six weeks before the wedding, Libbie watched daily for her father to come home through the snow with the mail. On December 27 she wrote: "My Dearest Armstrong, I believe you would love me a little if you knew how I say, afternoons, 'Half-past four — Letter *please* arrive!' " Libbie went on to say, "I showed Father part of your last letter — that is, I handed him one sheet. After reading and re-reading it he looked at what I held . . . [and said] 'That isn't all!' To which I replied, 'It is all you can see!' So write me what you wish. Oh, I scarce know how to write a gentleman in so unconstrained a manner. Not that I am an entire novice in corresponding with gentlemen . . . but I have always been careful to give no indication of a warm feeling."

Libbie wrote her cousin, Rebecca Richmond, that Autie never touched liquor nor frequented the gambling table "and though not a professing Christian yet respects religion."

The church was Libbie's most important interest—next to boys. She regretted that Armstrong was not a member. For a soldier to fight or march or for a girl to write letters on Sunday had seemed sinful to her unless absolutely necessary, but she was beginning to change. She even concluded one letter to Armstrong with: "I seldom write letters on Sunday though I confess to spending much of the day in sleeping. But I can not think it really worse to be writing you than to be dreaming about you."

She was not so sure in her own mind about Autie's morals, for she wrote him: "And yet, love, there is a stain on your character. Mother told me Father told her someone told him that Gen. Kilpatrick used an oath with every sentence he uttered, and that General Custer was not much better. I know this is exaggerated. But . . . God cure you of it."

Then, having criticized her fiancé, she confessed her own shortcomings. Autie must not be disappointed. Always she was mortified because her legs were not fat like mature women's. She said, too, that she would not want a personal maid but, being a poor cook, would want Eliza. Among her other faults, she said, was vanity. "I am susceptible to admiration," she wrote him. "In church I saw a handsome young man looking at me, and I blushed furiously. Mother says I am the most sarcastic girl, and say the most *withering* things."

Class lines were strictly drawn in Monroe, and although the population was small, ladies were not acquainted out of their restricted circles. Libbie confessed to Armstrong, "I know your family by sight. I stood near them at the Lilliputian Bazaar. I think they knew me." Of course the women in both groups at the bazaar must have watched one another covertly, but it would have been socially improper to speak. However, now that a wedding date was set Libbie decided to call on the

Reeds. With Nettie Humphrey for companion, she drove down to their part of town in her father's sleigh, bells jingling merrily. Inside the warm house the young ladies removed their heavy wraps and sat in Lydia's formal parlor, where pictures of Pleasonton, Kilpatrick, and Armstrong dominated the walls and mantel. After returning, Libbie wrote Autie: "The little ones, aren't they cunning! The youngest [Henry Armstrong] so bashful, almost afraid to kiss me. In that respect so like his Uncle Autie!"

As Libbie wrote she looked out her window at the wintry street. Sleighs slipped by silently except for the bells. Pedestrians hurried in the cold. A bearded man rode past on a prancing horse, plumes of foggy breath spurting from the eager animal's nostrils. Libbie recognized the rider and added: "Your father just passed riding your horse. I am surprised, a man of his age, riding so well." [12]

In January, less than a month before the wedding, Armstrong began to worry about confirmation of his brigadier's commission. He did want to be an acknowledged general for the ceremony. A friend in Washington wrote him that Senators Howard and Chandler had questioned his Michigan citizenship. A vote for him, they said, might deprive some native son of the honor.

Custer knew that his father's politics and his own reputation as a "McClellan man" were always obstacles to his advancement. Secretary of War Stanton, a Democrat who had lived in Cadiz, Ohio, might help. On the other hand, his support might do more harm than good with a strong-minded Republican like Senator Zach Chandler. Custer decided to appeal to his friend Judge Christiancy, a staunch Republican and a power in Michigan politics. He wrote a letter to him, but the uncertainty still plagued Custer. That evening he wrote Christiancy a second letter, saying that Pleasonton had called him to his tent and advised him to use all the political influence he could muster. Opposition in the Senate was strong.

Judge Christiancy sent a reassuring reply, so Custer — although his commission was still unapproved — set off in high spirits, with his staff, for the Monroe wedding. The gay party in their brilliant uniforms en-livened the cars on the three-day trip across the wintry Midwest. It was a vacation for all of them. Aide-de-Camp George Yates could show the home folks his tailored uniform and well-earned lieutenant's bar. Adju-tant Greene could renew his courting of Nettie Humphrey, and in anticipation played love tunes on a flute he carried in his baggage. Armstrong read, and no doubt reread, the last letter he had received from Libbie. "You'll be here a week from Monday," she wrote. "If it takes you three days to travel you'll start on Friday. Soldiers have to travel on Sunday, I suppose, tho I hope Autie doesn't. Still if it brings you here a day sooner. . . ." [13]

Custer looked out the car window at the drab landscape with yellow tepees of shocked corn in the snow-covered fields. Yes, that girl would have to change her attitude about Sunday. This war was changing lots of people's points of view. At its beginning Jeb Stuart had objected to fighting on the Lord's Day, and look at him now!

Before the happy party reached Monroe, Private Tom Custer joined it. He had obtained a furlough from his Ohio regiment. Armstrong hardly recognized him. Four and a half years had made a big change. The boy had grown to manhood since Armstrong saw him last on his vacation from West Point in 1859. Tom was a Custer, every inch of him. He had the blondness, the laughter, the love of rhythm, the spar-kling, sapphire-blue eyes, and restless energy.

"Let's fool Pop," Autie said, looking at the strapping image of him-self. "I'll introduce you as Major Drew, my aide." [14]

A practical joke on the old man always delighted the boys.

The citizens of Monroe, bundled in fur coats and mufflers, met their distinguished fellow townsman and his staff at the railroad station. The brilliant officers attracted all eyes as they strode along the wintry streets.

At the Custer residence, which Armstrong had bought for his par-ents, the gay fellows stamped up the steps, kicking snow from their polished boots. Inside, Autie embraced his mother and whispered that "Major Drew" was really Tom but don't tell Pop. A futile precaution!

Maria Custer did not have to wipe her little glasses on her apron to recognize her own son. As for Pop, he was prepared for his boys' jokes and usually paid them back in their own coin.

The Custer homestead rang with laughter, babbling voices, back-slapping. A constant stream of callers swept in with cold, outside air on their clothes. People remembered that Armstrong Custer, as a boy, had shown much promise. Everybody knew that he was going to be a great soldier someday. The family told about the Mexican War excitement back in Ohio, when Autie was a little boy, and how he had mimicked the politicians by piping, "My voice is for war."

His mother remembered that she had made him a little soldier-suit to wear when he accompanied his father to militia muster. Libbie, dreaming of little ones of her own, wanted that tiny suit as a keepsake — and she still had it when she died sixty-nine years later. (However, in spite of the good story, it should be noted that the little shirt and trousers resembled nothing military.*)

From the Custer home the merrymakers went to the Bacon residence. The shortest route was out the back door, up the alley one block, and in through the judge's stable. However, Judge Bacon never welcomed guests by that entrance, so the jolly crowd walked around the square and entered by the picket gate in front.

In the spacious Bacon parlor Libbie's wedding presents were displayed — a silver dinner service from the 1st Vermont Cavalry, a silver tea set from the 7th Michigan. Other well-wishers had sent berry spoons, napkin rings with gold linings, a syrup cup, sugar spoons, two white silk fans, Mrs. Browning's poems lavishly bound, a knit breakfast shawl, a handsome Bible from Libbie's father, a white silk parasol covered with black lace from her stepmother. Autie gave her a gold watch in a hunting case, engraved E.B.C.

The wedding ceremony was performed in the First Presbyterian Church by Libbie's schoolmaster, the Reverend Dr. Boyd. Adjutant Greene served as Custer's best man, and Libbie floated down the aisle on her father's arm, his Websterian head towering above the admiring

---

* This little suit is in the Custer Battlefield National Monument.

congregation. The bride's hoop-skirted, mist-green wedding dress, trimmed with yellow cavalry braid, swayed and billowed above her gaiters — practical footwear for a frigid brick church in February. Long sleeves, wide at the wrists, narrow at the shoulders, and crossed with horizontal stripes, added to the fashionable pyramid effect of the day. At Libbie's throat a brooch, containing a lock of her mother's hair, fastened a small white collar. The bride wore her chestnut-brown hair parted, rolled over each ear, and coiled in a knot on her neck under a green silk wedding veil. A corsage of roses, red as Libbie's cheeks, completed the ensemble. Newspaper reporters, accustomed to feminine brilliance, did not exaggerate when they raved about her scintillating beauty.

After the ceremony the wedding party sped away in jingling sleighs to the Bacon home for a reception. The judge provided a bounteous buffet, including tubs of ice cream. Libbie changed to traveling clothes and bride and groom left Monroe on the midnight train. After they were gone Libbie's father was unable to sleep for fear burglars might steal the gifts. As soon as the bank opened in the morning he took them there for storage. His big, quiet house seemed lonely without Libbie, and he was not quite reconciled to her choice of a boisterous soldier. Someday, when he felt better satisfied, he must write Armstrong's name in the family Bible, but not now.

He never did.*

The honeymooners arrived in Cleveland at nine in the morning and drove through the cold, blustery streets to the Waddell House. In the afternoon, they were entertained at a reception and next day traveled east, stopping at Buffalo, Rochester, and Onondaga. They enjoyed a play, *Uncle Tom's Cabin,* and visited what the judge called "lineal descendants" — all Bacons, of course. At each home Libbie displayed her trousseau: nine dresses, an opera cloak, a "silk hood with rich tassels," a riding habit of dark green with brass buttons, and for inclement weather "a waterproof with armholes."

* The Bacon family Bible has been preserved in the Monroe County Historical Society's Museum.

Libbie wrote her father that admiring relatives at one stop "Ohed" and exclaimed "Exquisite" until the station porter called for their baggage — still unpacked — and said the train would soon arrive. Here was the bride's first test of poise in an emergency. She met it with gay laughter. Enlisting the youthful "lineal descendants" present, she set them to stuffing her trousseau into trunks and boxes. Armstrong helped and Libbie said later that he got entangled in a farthingale, delighting one of his new relatives, who shouted: "Surrender!" If this be war, no wonder men loved it! In high spirits the laughing party drove to the station, boarded the train, and, as they chuffed away, Libbie waved her husband's hat at the crowd — waved it until the hatband blew off.

The Custers stopped next to visit West Point. The Hudson was frozen, so they crossed on the ice. A husky man pulled Libbie on a sled while Armstrong pushed. At the Academy everybody greeted the distinguished alumnus cordially. Even the dogs seemed to remember Autie. Most dogs did. Back on the train, chugging around the granite cliffs east of the Hudson, Armstrong chided Libbie for letting a professor kiss her. This was her first taste of a husband's jealousy.

"He was a veritable Methuselah," Libbie told him tearfully, "and the cadets who showed me Lovers' Walk were like schoolboys with their shy ways and nice clean, friendly faces." [15]

Armstrong did not send her back to her parents, although she claimed later that she feared it. Instead he took her to the Metropolitan Hotel in New York — his favorite stopping place. He had stayed there when working for McClellan. The waiters remembered him, and called him by name — a courtesy important to both Armstrong and his bride.

The couple moved on to Washington, anticipating a gay fling in the capital — theaters, dinners, receptions for military and political leaders, and opportunity for Libbie to wear her nine dresses, that opera cloak, and the "silk hood with rich tassels." What fun it was going to be to read about herself and her clothes in the morning papers!

But this was not to be. A telegram ordered General Custer to the front. He wanted Libbie to stay in Washington. She objected. The newlyweds faced a real test of adjustment. Custer's word might be law for a brigade of the most reckless cavalry in the United States Army, but not for doe-eyed Libbie. She was sure that she could rough it! Why else had she bought that dark green riding habit?

General Custer surrendered. A bad way, it is said, for a husband to begin married life!

14 Battle of the Wilderness

Custer took Libbie to his headquarters at Stevensburg, a country town five miles south of Brandy Station, Virginia. Here for the first time she met the vagabond servants who followed her husband throughout the war — the fugitive slavegirl, Eliza, and the white waif, Johnnie Cisco, who waited on table and insisted on serving the general before his wife.[1]

Ten or twelve miles to the south, the enemy still held the Rapidan, so Libbie realized that she was in dangerous country. Moreover, she must remain here alone, for Armstrong had been recalled to lead a "secret" raid — one of those "secret" raids known to almost everybody in the Union Army. He was to march his 2d Brigade south along the Blue Ridge, slip around Lee's left flank, tear up the Gordonsville & Lynchburg Railroad bridge across the Rivanna River, and destroy Confederate supplies at Charlottesville. No doubt Lee would turn to destroy him, and when he did Kilpatrick was to sweep around the Confederate right with his division, capture Richmond, release the fifteen thousand prisoners held there, and distribute pamphlet reprints of Lincoln's offer to amnesty to all Southerners who returned to Union allegiance.

The plan was that of Kilpatrick, a rash man, always eager for notoriety. Custer was the pawn to be sacrificed just as Farnsworth had been at Gettysburg. Before leaving, Armstrong installed Libbie in a farmhouse where the owners appeared to be friendly. Eliza accompanied her as maidservant, and a small guard was detailed for their protection. Libbie had begged so hard to come to Virginia that she dared not complain now. Mustering all her courage, on Feburary 28, 1864, at two o'clock in the afternoon, she watched her husband ride south with his men. It was Sunday and she had learned another lesson in war's disrespect for the Sabbath.

Beside Custer at the head of the column rode many of the wedding party — Libbie noticed Aide-de-Camp George Yates, Adjutant Jacob Greene with his flute, and the artist and war correspondent, Al Waud, reporting for *Harper's Weekly*. As part of Custer's brigade, Alex Pennington commanded two guns of flying artillery which could keep up with cavalry. Johnnie Cisco followed with a spring wagon to transport delicacies, for Custer liked the drama of being Spartan one moment, epicurean the next. He could ride three days without eating, but after such an ordeal he relished roast piglets or turkey with cranberries.

Libbie had never before seen these Michigan cavalry regiments, their riders proudly wearing little red ties like her husband's. Four abreast, the men filled a mile of roadway. Libbie shivered as she watched them go, for the February wind across the wet fields cut to the bone. The big roll of blankets behind each saddle seemed scant comfort for a chilly night. Already many riders sat hunched in their capes and some had let down the flaps of their havelocks to warm their ears. But Autie did not even wear an overcoat.

Charlottesville was fifty miles away. A column of this size was sure to be detected soon, but Armstrong planned a night march which should put him deep into enemy country before he was stopped. To support Custer if driven back, General John Sedgwick was moving up with his VI Corps. As the two columns started, Custer called briefly at Sedgwick's headquarters to discuss their strategy. The two men examined a map of the country ahead. Armstrong pointed out the hopelessness of his chance for escape, and asked if the war council — dominated by Kilpatrick — which authorized this raid realized that Rosser had five thousand horse in the valley. Did they expect Custer, with only fifteen hundred horse, to cut his way through Rosser's forces while

Jeb Stuart might attack him from the other side? Sedgwick replied that that had been considered.

"Well, then," Custer told him, "the only way for me to get out may be to cut my way across Lee's entire rear to join Kilpatrick, or else start with all the men I can keep together and try to join Sherman in the Southwest."

Such an escape would have meant leading his brigade three hundred miles through the mountains without communications or supplies, but Custer would undoubtedly undertake it before surrendering.

The column bivouacked that night near Madison Court House. At 2 A.M. they were in the saddle again, edging toward the towering wall of the Blue Ridge. At Wolftown, where the road paralleled the Ridge, shots were fired at them by bushwhackers or vedettes from Rosser's force. Custer did not stop. He trotted on to the Rapidan, a small stream here near the mountains.

At dawn, the horsemen splashed across the icy water. The road led them through wintry woodlands. In clearings, farmers were plowing. The column's outriders took all good horses from the plowmen and sent the drivers in as prisoners. No men were left behind to bushwhack. Custer ordered his soldiers not to forage, but officers looked away when chickens squawked in barnyards.

At Stanardsville the townsfolk turned out, as for a circus, to see the invading cavalry. Custer ordered all the men arrested and taken along. Negroes followed willingly, whooping with glee. In the afternoon the column came to the Rivanna River. At a milldam where a long bridge with four piers spanned the stream, Custer led the way across.

Charlottesville was close now. He detached a regiment to scout while he waited with the rest of the brigade. Soon he heard firing as from a skirmish. The regiment came back with fifty prisoners. An enemy artillery outpost had been surprised. The prisoners said — falsely perhaps — that Fitzhugh Lee occupied Charlottesville, only two miles beyond their encampment.

Custer believed them. He could never destroy the railroad bridge there now, nor escape to Sherman. Besides, he did not want to go to Tennessee. He wanted to go back to Libbie. His mission had been accomplished — at least partially — and Kilpatrick had got through if he was going to. Custer ordered his men back across the Rivanna bridge and set it on fire to delay pursuit. He also burned the mill and all Confederate supplies in it. After dark, he started north up the road in a cold, drizzling rain. Four miles from the river the column halted for an hour and a half to feed horses and rest. Fires were difficult to kindle in the wet. The rain froze on tree limbs and crackled like breaking glass with every breeze. Men who had kept their saddles dry were glad to remount at midnight although very tired, sleepy, and cold.

One of the prisoners claimed he could lead the column north by a shorter route. Custer let him ride with the van. At dawn the Boy General noticed dazzling snow on the Blue Ridge above the ice-sheeted lower landscape. The first rays of the sun lighted myriads of diamonds on every limb and twig along the road. Vedettes, their uniforms stiff with ice, crackled in from the slippery roads with reports of Confederate cavalry concentrating all around them. Custer thought Jeb Stuart must be observing the Union cavalry's strength before consolidating for an attack. As he jogged along Armstrong also became suspicious of his guide. That fellow might be leading them into a trap between Jeb's cavalry and Lee's infantry. The Rapidan, Sedgwick's VI Corps, and safety were not far ahead now.

Custer decided to fool the guide. Let the van follow him. But he, himself, would drop back, divide the column and, with the main army, hurry to another ford. Then, at the last moment, the van could wheel and race away to join the army's rear, and thus escape if they were headed for a trap.

The ruse worked, for it turned out they barely escaped. With a long, running fight, Custer reached Sedgwick's infantry. Not a man had been lost, and only a few were wounded. At the Rapidan ford Custer released all civilians, holding as prisoners only the captured soldiers. A hundred Negroes stayed with him, too.

After dark Armstrong burst in on Libbie at Stevensburg. He bubbled with happiness — no indication that he had ridden more than a hundred miles in forty-eight hours, through freezing weather and with practically no sleep. He wore a new, broad-brimmed hat. Where did he get it? From a reb, of course! And he had outwitted Jeb Stuart. What more could a cavalryman ask? Armstrong wanted to talk, to tell about his experiences. Johnnie had almost been captured, with a wagonload of chickens and turkeys, but Custer had galloped back and ordered him to abandon the vehicle. . . .[2]

Next day Autie took his wife to dinner at General Webb's headquarters. They drove behind a splendid team garnished with the silver harness he had captured last summer. Everybody watched with admiration as they jogged by, so Libbie thought. Hadn't the Custer raid been successful, while Kilpatrick, who had selected Autie as the pawn, had failed? Little Kil had reached only the outskirts of Richmond and barely escaped down the Peninsula, leaving three thousand horses behind in the mud. His peace commissioner, Ulric Dahlgren, had been killed.

For the next week or two the Custers enjoyed their first true honeymoon. Armstrong was often on active duty but he spent many hours with his bride. She learned the little inconsequential things about a husband that interest and amuse a woman. She noticed that he brushed his teeth after every meal and seemed to be always washing his square, hard hands. Libbie noticed, too, that a tragic play or a sentimental poem seemed more genuine to him than situations in real life. Perhaps that was why he saw only glamour and gallantry in the dirtiest of civil wars. Libby was also fascinated by the social functions in camp, especially the luxurious table set by high command. She wrote her father that Pleasonton served six-course dinners and she was so proud when Autie refused wine.

Late in March, 1864, a rock was tossed into the Custer love nest. It came in the form of an inquiry from Meade's headquarters asking for details of Annie Jones's visit to the brigade last fall. Annie was in Old

Capitol prison and wanted to get out. She had been incarcerated shortly after Custer sent her away from camp in September, 1863. Released on parole, she was soon rearrested. In her present plea for pardon she admitted having lived intimately with army officers in their quarters during the last two and a half years. She also boasted about improper relations with the prison superintendent and the guard. Moreover, she claimed to have been "the friend and companion" of both Kilpatrick and Custer, living in their quarters. General Kilpatrick, she said, was very jealous of Custer's attentions to her, and went to Meade's headquarters, where he charged her with being a rebel spy.

The provost marshal's office was constantly looking for spies. Lieutenant Charles H. Shepard was given this case. He learned that Annie had come from Cambridge with the 135th Massachusetts Volunteers. She seemed to have lived, as she said, in many army camps, often with high-ranking officers — General Sigel for one — but he failed to find a complaint on file against her by General Kilpatrick. A letter mailed at Falls Church accused her of being a spy but it was signed "R. L. Birch," not Kilpatrick. Lieutenant Shepard could locate no "Birch" in Falls Church, but he suspected that the letter had been written by a jealous rival. He concluded cryptically: "It was a very amusing investigation on the whole."

Custer read these allegations. He had heard that Jeb Stuart kept a female aide on his staff, was even seen riding with a fair damsel in front of him on his horse, and he a married man! What better precedent could a cavalryman want? On March 22, 1864, Custer made his official reply. He admitted that Annie had come twice to his headquarters. The second time, he said, she arrived at dusk after driving thirty miles in an ambulance furnished her by Major General Warren — Armstrong's old teacher, "Warren of the Topogs." Custer said that he had ordered his adjutant, Captain Greene, to send Annie back to General Warren in the morning. He described her as a harum-scarum adolescent whose sole purpose seemed to be an insane desire to distinguish herself with acts of foolhardy daring. "Her statement in relation to Gen. Kilpatrick and myself," he concluded, "is simply untrue." [3]

With his report in military channels Armstrong decided that Libbie must go back to Washington. This area would be no place for her when spring campaigning began. He got sick leave to go to the capital with her and find a boardinghouse. They traveled north on a special train with Lieutenant General U. S. Grant, a man from the West who had just been appointed commander of all the armies. Grant's aide-de-camp was Horace Porter, a schoolmate of Armstrong's who had seemed much older when they were at the Point but who was only a lieutenant colonel now.

Libbie was disappointed in Grant's appearance, but she liked him very much. He was so unassuming, and a good talker, full of amusing stories. He said small men invariably rode tall horses. Fearing his cigar might offend her, he smoked on the car platform until Autie told him Libbie did not object.

In Washington the Custers enjoyed the theater. Rip Van Winkle, like Uncle Tom, made Armstrong weep a little. Congressman William Kellogg introduced the happy couple to President Lincoln. At a "hop," Senators Wade and Chandler both asked Libbie to dance. "I have to laugh when I think of these old men as being my beaux," Libbie wrote her father and mother. The biggest thrill of all in the big city was to read in the newspapers about Custer's spectacular Charlottesville raid. *Harper's Weekly* devoted its front cover to a picture of him leading a charge, and a week later the double-page spread in the center of the magazine contained Al Waud's drawings of incidents in the raid. [4] People recognized the couple on the streets. Libbie resolved to start a scrapbook of clippings about her husband. [5] Custer decided that he liked his hair short, and had it cut again. He also experimented once more with side whiskers. He and Libbie celebrated when his commission as brigadier general was approved by the Senate. They were not so gay when they learned that Grant had replaced Pleasonton with a new man, "Little Phil" Sheridan, a tough officer from the West. Custer would have to get acquainted with another superior and might not like him. It was some consolation, however, to learn that Kilpatrick was being transferred, too. Armstrong had been careful to say nothing publicly against his old schoolmate, but the antagonism between them was growing.[6] Annie Jones may have noticed this before making her statement. Perhaps she was part of it, as she said. In any event, things were happening in the Army of the Potomac, and Armstrong knew he had better get back to his brigade.

Custer reported first to Sheridan's headquarters, and found the new cavalry general to be a little jockey of a man with a bullet head, a flushed face, and a foul mouth. His bandy legs barely reached the ground when he was sitting on a chair. Sheridan spoke cordially but with abruptness. He told Custer to stay all night; said he wanted to know his seven brigadiers.

Waiting at headquarters, Armstrong learned that Sheridan had divided the cavalry into three divisions. Custer's Michigan Brigade and Tom Devin's would make up the 1st Division, under A. T. A. Torbert. The 2d Division was to be commanded by General Douglas McMurtrie Gregg, under whom Custer had fought at Gettysburg. The 3d was assigned to James H. Wilson, another man from the West, a Grant pet transferred to Sheridan. Custer had seen Wilson last when they were aides to McClellan at Antietam. So, bright young Wilson commanded a division already! Lucky army pet! [7]

Custer knew his new commander, Torbert, as an oldish infantryman whose waving mutton-chop whiskers would blow over his shoulders in a cavalry charge. But Armstrong, at this stage of his career, made it a point always to say he liked his superiors. He wrote Libbie how pleased he was with both Sheridan and Torbert.

On April 16, 1864, Custer rode over to Kilpatrick's headquarters. Little Kil was giving a farewell dinner. Fellow officers, jealous of his bravery, yet hating the brisk brutality with which he could order others to their deaths, drank to his health and sang his praises. This was the army Custer knew so well. Next day Armstrong joined his own Michigan Brigade and posed for pictures with Torbert. Then the Boy General shaved off his mustache, mailed it to Libbie, and finagled a forty-eight hour pass from Torbert and Sheridan to go back to Washington and see her.

Libbie heard him coming up the stairs as though the house were afire. Kissing him without his mustache seemed like kissing a girl. The lovers knew they would not meet again before Grant's spring campaign — sure to be the most deadly of the war — and Libbie had so much to tell! She had gone to a "hop" with Senator Chandler, and found him "an old goosey idiot." His wife was away and he was drunk all the time, she said, "and O, so silly." [8]

Armstrong rejoined his brigade as Meade, under Grant's immediate supervision, marched the Army of the Potomac south to find Lee. McClellan, Burnside, and Hooker had all failed in the last three years. Could Grant do better? Certainly he would lead many men to their deaths trying to prove his worth. Armstrong often felt the need of religion as a battle loomed. He wrote Libbie that, although a nonprofessing Christian, he was not an unbeliever and had absolute faith in the Almighty. "This belief . . . makes me brave and fearless as I am," he said. [9]

The order of march disappointed Custer. He and Devin covered the army's rear, guarding the wagon trains — a routine job. Sheridan would never learn Custer's talents if Armstrong had to stay back here with Eliza, her fancy cook-wagon, and his ragamuffin retainer.

On May 5, 1864, Custer led his brigade across the Rapidan by Ely's Ford. The main army under Meade and Grant had crossed farther up the river and was miles ahead of him. All afternoon Custer had heard firing. He knew that a great battle had begun — Grant's first opportunity to come to grips with Lee. Gregg and Wilson, at the army's head, must be in it. They would get the promotions.

At dusk, the brigade encamped on a slope of the plateau overlooking "the Wilderness" — a name with ugly memories for the Army of the Potomac. In May, a year ago, Hooker had suffered his great defeat in that brambly jungle of second-growth timber, and Grant might well suffer one, now. Custer watched the scene from his saddle as darkness settled over sinister swamp pines and scrub-oak thickets. The bombardment died out with the daylight and myriads of bivouac fires twinkled along invisible highways. Lee seemed to be coming in on side roads from the west to strike Grant's flank while it was stretched out hopelessly in the Wilderness. Those fires must belong to both friend and enemy.

At midnight an order came for Custer to move down to the junction of the Brock pike and the Furnaces road. Armstrong studied his map in the firelight. The Brock pike was a main thoroughfare, leading south across the Wilderness to open country in Virginia. The Furnaces road led to it from the east — opposite from the way Lee was coming. Custer learned that the Union Army was in trouble. Wilson's vedettes had failed to see the oncoming Confederates and had led General Warren's Corps into a trap. Gregg had been called to help him, but Torbert's division was needed, too.[10] However, Torbert was on the sick list. An abscess at the base of his spine made riding unbearable.[11] His division had been given to Custer's schoolmate, Wesley Merritt, who was not present, so Armstrong and the Michigan brigade started down the slope alone toward the dreaded Wilderness at 2 A.M.

His column entered the woods — like riding into a tunnel. Fog filled the road at every swamp, wet the men's faces and jackets. Arriving at the road junction where he was ordered to report, Armstrong found himself at the extreme southern tip of Grant's infantry — which was commanded by Hancock, already recovered from his Gettysburg wound. Custer dismounted his men and attached them to the left of a brigade that was under sandy-haired John Gibbon. Custer's West Point artillery instructor appeared more bony and wrinkled than ever, since recovering from his Gettysburg wound. Custer fought beside him for two sultry days, often charging on foot across the broom-grown fields or repelling countercharges.

At night Armstrong's dismounted cavalry bivouacked under moss-draped pines in an eerie country haunted by bats and whippoorwills. In the fog, nervous sentries sometimes challenged a blooming dogwood bush, thus arousing a whole regiment. Custer realized that he was fighting one of the great battles of the war, but he did not know who was winning. Documents found in the pockets of a dead Confederate officer disclosed him to be Rosser's adjutant. Interviews with deserters and prisoners revealed that they were members of either Rosser's or Pierce Manning Butler Young's commands. This meant that the officers Custer watched rallying their men for charges across the clearing were his old schoolmates, and yonder enemy must be Jeb Stuart's invincible cavalry.

On the afternoon of May 7 the enemy withdrew into the woods across the clearing. Custer decided to lead his men two miles down the pike to see how Gregg was faring at Todd's Tavern. As the column moved off, crippled horses which had been left behind neighed frantically. Some, with swinging broken legs, hobbled to their places in ranks. Sergeants ordered them shot.[12]

At Todd's Tavern, Custer found Sheridan with Gregg. Little Phil was in a towering rage, red-faced, teeth gritting. Meade had sent him an order forbidding him to advance down the road, which was clear all the way to Spotsylvania. By delaying, they would have to fight for every inch of it later. Only yesterday that damned slow, methodical Meade had countermanded an order, which meant Sheridan had to retake the Brock pike at great loss of life after he had already captured it. By God, Sheridan wasn't going to put up with such contradictory commands!

The profane little commander jogged off to see Meade — perhaps to go over his head to Grant. Cavalrymen were notoriously independent fellows! While Sheridan was gone, Custer and the division commanders ordered their men to rest, tend their horses. No one was sure yet who had won the last fight.

Sheridan came back next day sparkling with good humor. Grant had taken his side in the quarrel. The cavalry would be held no longer in the underbrush with the infantry. Sheridan could go out on his own, find and whip Jeb Stuart if able to do so. The Battle of the Wilderness had been a draw, but Grant was not going to retreat. Instead, he would march deeper into Virginia and fight Lee wherever the Confederate tried next to stop him.

15 The Charge on Stuart's Battery

ON THE MORNING OF MAY 9, 1864, SHERIDAN'S CAVALRY — TEN THOUsand horsemen — headed straight for Richmond, free at last from Meade's infantry. Surely that would bring Jeb Stuart from cover! The column moved at a walk, not the trot usual for raiding parties. Sheridan wanted his men and horses to be fresh when Jeb caught up with him. The Union column, with seven batteries and wagon train, occupied thirteen miles of road and took four hours to pass a given point. Custer's Michigan men led the way. Behind them rode Sheridan and his staff under his red and white flag with its two stars. "Little Phil" liked always to be near the front. Next came Tom Devin's brigades, then Wilson's 3d Division.

In the afternoon, Custer heard firing at the column's rear. Jeb had found them already! Lee's infantry was still too close to risk a fight, but Sheridan rode back to supervise the rear-guard engagement while the column marched ahead. In Sheridan's absence Custer decided on a little independent action of his own. With his brigade, he spurred down the road thirty miles to Beaver Dam Station on the Virginia Central Railroad, where he surprised the little settlement and captured two trains. One was bringing a million and a half rations from Richmond to Lee's army, the other taking to Libby Prison three hundred and seventy-five Union soldiers Lee had captured in the Wilderness. Custer destroyed the locomotives and supplies. The prisoners gladly joined the cavalry, even though on foot.[1]

Sheridan's horsemen trooped into Beaver Dam Station during the night and in the morning the column started down the road once more for Richmond, now only thirty miles away. Jeb Stuart rode into Beaver Dam as Sheridan's rear guard marched out. It was now plain to him that the Union cavalry was headed for the Confederate capital, not circling to hit Lee in the rear.

That night Custer unsaddled beside the South Anna, in a lush, peaceful agricultural country where the horses filled their paunches and rolled in the green meadows. All the soldiers knew that Jeb Stuart was racing around them by parallel roads to get ahead and fight a decisive battle.

May 11 dawned clear and balmy. The roads were becoming dusty. It was Devin's turn to lead the van, so Custer waited while the old fellow passed. Officers said that Devin had shaved off his graying beard last night to look younger.[2] After all, he was forty-two — "old for this man's army." Custer swung his brigade into the road behind him. Gregg's and Wilson's divisions followed. Men joked about being in Richmond by dark, unless stopped.

At Ashland, only fifteen miles from Richmond, Custer rode past the flaming wreckage of railroad cars and the depot. Devin's men, ahead of him, were doing their job. Out in the quiet country again, Custer heard the distant roar of battle far to the north across the green horizon. Lee and Grant must be fighting today somewhere around Spotsylvania. Lee was too far away now to help Jeb if Stuart struck Sheridan down here.

Seven miles ahead, at Yellow Tavern, the road on which the Union column was advancing joined Telegraph Road. From this point the two roads, now merged into one, became the Brook Turnpike which led to Richmond, only six miles beyond. This intersection was the place where Stuart might stop Sheridan. Custer could not see the Union van as it undulated along the road through Virginia's green fields, but he knew that Devin would be there soon.

Shortly before noon Armstrong heard a cannon shot ahead. At last!

The whole column shook as with a convulsion. Men drew together. Horses' heads tossed. Sheridan pounded ahead under his great flag, aides scampering behind, clods flying from their horses' hoofs. The general would inspect the field and place his brigades in battle line as they marched in.

Sheridan's first order sent Devin off the road, across country, to a position on the Brook Turnpike below Stuart's line. He deployed Custer at Devin's left. Next came Wilson, then Gregg. Each brigade, as it arrived, dismounted and took position at the left of its immediate predecessor. The battle line was not formed until three o'clock. Sheridan planned to have the whole line strike simultaneously, and thus give Jeb Stuart no opportunity to move reinforcements from one place to another.

By the time Sheridan was ready, Stuart had placed a battery at the south end of his line where it began killing Custer's held-horses. Armstrong examined the guns' position and decided that they were vulnerable. He galloped over to Wesley Merritt, his schoolmate, who was now commanding the 1st Division in Torbert's absence.

"Merritt," Custer said, "I'm going to charge that battery."

"Go in, General," Merritt told him. "I will give you all the support in my power."

The two generals saw Sheridan approaching, but Custer hurried off. When the major general rode up Merritt explained what Armstrong was doing.

"Bully for Custer," Sheridan said. "I'll wait and see it."

The whole line was advancing now, carbines crackling along the road. Custer ordered the dismounted 5th and 6th Michigan regiments to hold firm at the edge of the woods, where the battery was hidden. He galloped back to the 1st and 7th regiments, eighteen hundred horse. With them, he circled away to the right where the trees extended down the hillside. Custer cautioned his men to mind their alignments. Sheridan was watching.

The two regiments, in column of squadrons, moved forward as on parade, the 1st leading, the 7th in reserve. Red neckties sparkled along the ranks.* The Confederates spied them and turned the batteries in their direction, but the shells went high. The guns could not be depressed sufficiently. However, the fury of the explosions and the crackling canister overhead tried the nerves of horses and riders. Custer turned to his musicians and ordered "Yankee Doodle."

Five times the leaders dismounted to tear down fences, but the shrill music never stopped and the formation did not waver. At a deep ditch, spanned by a narrow bridge, musket fire joined the cannonading. Regiments had to progress in files of three to cross, then re-form in squadrons on the far side. Though under heavy fire none faltered. A few minutes later, Sheridan heard the distant bugle sound, Trot. The men leaned forward in their saddles and jogged ahead, red and white guidons pointed to the front. A moment more and the bugle call Charge came across the fields. Sheridan saw the squadrons dash away under a mist of waving sabers. No one but Custer could lead cavalrymen so lightheartedly. People said that even the horses caught the wild spirit of his onslaughts.

"General Merritt," Sheridan said as he turned to inspect the rest of the battlefield, "send a staff officer to General Custer and give him my compliments. The conduct of himself and his brigade deserves the most honorable mention." [3]

Custer's dismounted regiments swarmed forward through the woods, adding to the confusion wrought by his charging horsemen. The brigade captured two guns and a hundred prisoners. The Confederate line, flanked on the left and hard pressed from end to end, began to break and retreat. The victors heard that Jeb Stuart had been killed in Custer's charge. A captured staff officer, queried about the truth of the rumor, replied, "Yes, d——n you, and we ought to kill every one of

---

* The 1st Vermont also participated in this charge. It was said that Wilson gave it to Custer reluctantly, after an appeal to Sheridan. (G. G. Benedict, *Vermont in the Civil War*, II, p. 637; *O. R.*, I, XXXVI, pt. 1, pp. 813, 817; J. Robertson, *Michigan in the War*, p. 596.) The action is described in W. C. King, comp., *Camp-Fire Sketches and Battle-Field Echoes*, p. 408; P. H. Sheridan, *Personal Memoirs*, I, p. 378; S. H. Miller, "Yellow Tavern," p. 76.

you"[4] — a revealing remark. These soldiers had much in common with boys playing war in vacant lots.

After the battle General Wilson seemed very unhappy. He felt that his 3d Division, fighting beside Custer's brigade, deserved credit for breaking the Confederate line. His resentment against Sheridan for citing Custer would grow in days to come.[5] He was particularly annoyed by newspaper accounts which, he thought, gave Custer credit for the victory. Armstrong, in his official report, did not claim that Jeb Stuart was killed in his charge, although any cavalryman might have been proud of such distinction. Trophies, not dead men, were the things that interested Custer. He coveted enemy battle flags, enemy cannon, relics to decorate headquarters the way a boy decorates his room. Later, without taking any credit for himself, he cited a private who was reported to have fired the shot that killed Stuart.

The Battle of Yellow Tavern ended the menace of Jeb Stuart's cavalry. Sheridan had accomplished his mission. He probably could have captured Richmond, but knew he could not hold it. Instead, he hoped only to escape. His soldiers, having been on duty since three o'clock in the morning, were allowed two hours to rest, feed horses, and boil coffee. Untransportable wounded men were carried into farmhouses and left to the mercy of the enemy. Rain was falling, pelting the men's faces, when the column started south again. Soldiers remarked that the lightning which crackled across the sky seemed inconsequential after the roar of battle.

It was General Wilson's turn to lead the column tonight. He posted a bugler on a white horse with the guide. Custer rode far back in the column. Muffled explosions ahead revealed that Confederates had mined the road. Some horses were killed and men wounded. Sheridan sent for prisoners to come front and unmask the deathtraps.

The column turned off the road, padded through fields, and dipped into soft muddy places near a stream. Richmond must be very close now. A sudden red flash and a roar of cannon in the inky blackness swung horses around, bumped them together. The men dismounted and crouched behind any cover they could find. Custer, far back in the column, learned that a spy in Federal uniform had led the van, under Wilson, away from the road into the outer defenses of Richmond. Home guards had fired at a range of two hundred yards, overshooting the column. But the concussion made the strongest men tremble. Blinded and confused, the whole column could do nothing but "stay put" waiting for dawn. South of them Custer saw, on the clouds, reflections of the Richmond lights, and heard bells ringing alarm.

Daylight revealed Sheridan's army wedged between enemy earthworks and the Chickahominy, now swollen by last night's rain. Nearby, Meadow Bridge had been destroyed and the cavalry seemed trapped. Wilson remembered later that Sheridan became "as much excited as any man in the command." Sheridan's friends remembered it the other way around. From the little evidence available, this seems to have been a domestic squabble with each general begging the other to be calm.[6] The situation became worse when Confederate sharpshooters across the stream began to pick off Union horsemen. Sheridan turned to Custer, ordered him to disperse the rascals over there and repair the bridge.

Custer did both with dispatch; and as he moved his men among the humming bullets, he plucked a honeysuckle blossom for Libbie, pressing it in his order book. He felt happy. Certainly he was making good now with the new general. Capturing the trains at Beaver Dam Station and breaking the line at Yellow Tavern surely indicated more than common military initiative. In the meantime, Grant's pet, Wilson, had made an uncommonly poor showing.

While the army waited for Custer to restore the bridge, two newsboys came through the lines with Richmond papers for sale at "two bits" each. They did a thrifty business before the cavalry rode away, clattering across the makeshift bridge and trotting southward through the battlefields of '62. All that day thunderstorms drenched the riders. Spasms of lightning disturbed their night's rest at Mechanicsville, but Custer never heeded rain. He recognized Gaines's Mill, the grapevine bridge, and Malvern Hill. Next day, at Haxall's Landing on the James, the column joined General Ben Butler's army. The Navy brought supplies here regularly.

Sheridan's cavalry had been on the road five days and had lost 715 men. The casualties in the three days' fighting in the Wilderness had been even worse. Custer wrote at once to Libbie, "We have passed through days of carnage and have lost heavily," but he added, "The Michigan Brigade has covered itself with undying glory." In the letter, he enclosed the pressed honeysuckle blossom, picked where the force was trapped by the Chickahominy.[7]

At Haxall's Landing, Custer learned first about the terrible losses in the Wilderness — 18,000 casualties, almost as many as the 23,000 lost at Gettysburg. Among the Union generals killed was Corps Commander J. S. Wadsworth, the "Major Wadsworth" whom Custer had met that night before Bull Run. General Sedgwick had been killed at Spotsylvania. But more interesting to Armstrong was the news that Stephen Ramseur, his old schoolmate, had led a Confederate charge against Hancock's wing — perhaps against Custer's own men — so gallantly that he had won a major general's stars.

Sheridan rested two days. His wounded men and the Confederate prisoners embarked on transports to Washington. Then the cavalry was ordered to prepare for a return march across Virginia, skirting Lee's right wing, running the gantlet of Confederate cavalry until they found Grant and Meade. The night before leaving the James River, Armstrong wrote another letter to Libbie. Boylike, he said that he — not Sheridan — was sending the detail to Washington; that during the late battles he had guarded his tongue, sworn less than ever before "all owing to the influence of my beloved darling." Describing the Yellow Tavern fight, he enlarged the number of cannon he had captured from two to three. Jealousy of Wilson and friendship for Sheridan, in their bickering, appeared in Armstrong's remark to Libbie: "Wilson proved himself an imbecile and nearly ruined the corps by his blunders. Genl. Sheridan sent me to rescue him."[8]

Sheridan would probably have agreed with Custer's appraisal, but Wilson lived to have the last and most philosophical word. Years later, at the close of a distinguished military career, he wrote of these Civil War days: "The modest man is not always the best soldier. . . . Some of the best, while shamelessly sounding their own praises, were brave, dashing, and enterprising to an unusual degree." [9]

16 The Shenandoah

G RANT GAVE THE CAVALRY NO TIME TO REST AFTER SHERIDAN LED IT BACK from the Yellow Tavern victory. Torbert had recovered from the operation removing his abscess and had reassumed command of the 1st Division. He was ordered to guard engineers who were constructing a pontoon bridge across the Pamunkey so that Grant could penetrate deeper into the South. Custer's brigade was one of the first to cross and he fought gallantly at Haw's Shop, clearing the road to Cold Harbor for the infantry. His presence on any battlefield, his waving sword, always instilled enthusiasm. When his band played, men cheered and sang:

> *Yankee Doodle is a tune*
> *Americans delight in,*
> *Good to fiddle, dance or sing,*
> *And just the thing for fightin'.*

Meade's aide, Colonel Theodore Lyman, wrote his family back in Boston that most officers would go into any danger when it was their duty, "but fighting for fun is rare . . . [only] such men as . . . Custer and some others, attacked whenever they got a chance, and of their own accord." In eight days Armstrong suffered more casualties than he had in the Wilderness. Another horse was shot under him. Adjutant Greene was hit in the head by a spent bullet but not hurt seriously. Jim Christiancy was badly wounded, and had to be sent to Washington where Libbie could help nurse him.[1]

After every battle Grant sidled away — never retreating, just pushing around Lee's wing deeper into Virginia. Crossing the James he was stopped by elaborate fortifications below Petersburg, an extremely important railroad junction twenty-three miles south of Richmond. Grant set miners to work tunneling the fortifications and sent Sheridan back across the devastated country which Lee had just occupied. Sheridan was to circle Richmond and destroy the Virginia Central Railroad, Lee's supply line from the northwest.

The expedition was partially successful. Sheridan destroyed the railroad at Trevilian Station, but Lee sent cavalry after his raiders. Custer and Pennington, with one brigade, were caught between the divisions of Wade Hampton and Fitzhugh Lee. The surprise was worse than at Buckland Mills. Custer lost his headquarters wagon, bedding, field desk, all his clothes, a precious bundle of love letters from Libbie, and her ambrotype. Adjutant Greene and his flute were captured; so were Johnnie Cisco, with Custer's three spare horses, and Eliza, with her antique carriage and cooking outfit. In a desperate last stand the color bearer was shot down. Custer snatched the tottering flag, tore it from the staff and stowed it under his own jacket. He lost four hundred and sixteen men — more than at Haw's Shop and Cold Harbor combined — before Torbert cut a way to him. After dark Eliza and Johnnie Cisco escaped to the Union lines. Custer and Sheridan's other brigades were also badly mauled, and he ordered a general retreat. Some soldiers said that Custer's luck had changed since he cut off his curls.[2]

At the first halting place in the Federal lines — White House Landing on the Pamunkey — Custer wrote Libbie about the disaster, said that he had lost everything but his toothbrush and feared the rebels would laugh over her love letters. He, himself, laughed about the rebs' getting Adjutant Greene's ubiquitous flute.

Four days later the disabled column reached the James River across from where Grant was laying siege to Petersburg. Here Armstrong received a reply from his letter to Libbie. She seemed unconcerned about those love letters. "No Southerner," she wrote, "could say, if they are *gentlemen* that I lack refinement. There can be nothing low between man and wife if they love each other. What I wrote was holy and sacred. Only cruel people would not understand the spirit in which I wrote it." Libbie also told about her latest adventures in Washington. Congressman Bingham had called. She found him a charming man who still considered Autie his protégé. She said, too, that she had gone to a presidential reception and when the aide introduced her, Lincoln exclaimed, "So this is the young woman whose husband goes into a charge with a whoop and a shout."

Best news of all for Custer was that Congressman Kellogg had arranged to bring officers' wives to City Point on Lincoln's yacht, the *River Queen*. Libbie was determined to join the excursion and in another letter wrote Armstrong: "Mr K was here to-night. Very cordial. Too much so, for I avoided his attempt to kiss me by moving aside and offering him a chair. Any lady can get that man to do anything. But all I want is that he shall take me on that trip, to you."

The ladies' boatride was gay, especially after they met their husbands at City Point. Sheridan brought a band on board, and joined the dancing and laughter even while siege guns boomed like distant thunder against the Petersburg defenses. Slim and graceful, Libbie could fit herself perfectly into a dancing partner's arms, following his steps, reversing without the slightest jerk or hesitation. Taller than Sheridan, she smiled as he twirled her around with a peculiar hopping step. "It was too funny," she said later. "He had never danced until this summer and he enters into it with his whole soul." But Libbie liked him, she said, although she found him very different from quiet, connoisseur Pleasonton.

Armstrong accompanied his wife back to Washington, but stayed only one night. Thirty-six hours after bidding him good-by she heard the familiar sound of his feet racing up the stairs "with such a bounding step as no one else has."[3] But again he had come on borrowed time, tarried only a few hours, and was back in the saddle on July 30, 1864, when Grant exploded the Petersburg mine and cut a hole in Lee's elaborate defenses. However, the Union Army failed to enter the gap promptly and thousands of soldiers died needlessly. The blame fell on Edward Ferrero, Custer's dancing instructor who had distinguished himself so gallantly at Antietam. In war, bubble reputations burst in a twinkling.

Failure at "The Crater," as it was called, hurt Grant's reputation, too, and it seriously threatened Lincoln's re-election come fall. The possibility of a political upset did not disturb Armstrong, although he was already beginning to differ with his father's conservative Democratic principles. Perhaps the biggest stumbling block to Lincoln's re-election was his inability to drive Confederate armies out of the Shenandoah Valley. From those fertile farmlands enemy raiders constantly crossed the Potomac into Maryland and Pennsylvania. To many Northerners it seemed likely that Washington might fall before Richmond. Already Jubal Early had forced several towns to pay hundreds of thousands of dollars as tribute under threat of burning. He had even marched to the suburbs of Washington. Armstrong realized that something must be done before election and Lincoln's next move pleased him, albeit for purely personal reasons. The President ordered Grant to dispatch sufficient troops to Harper's Ferry, at the lower end of the Shenandoah Valley, to defend the capital and drive Early from the area. Grant sent Sheridan, and as his cavalry passed through Washington, Armstrong dropped out to visit his little Libbie. The couple stayed together at the Metropolitan Hotel until Sheridan, who had gone on to Harper's Ferry with the army, wired for the Boy General to report with his brigade immediately. This was war, not a honeymoon! [4]

Armstrong hurried to the gigantic encampment near Harper's Ferry. Sheridan had been assigned command of what was now known as the Middle Military Division. His forces included his own cavalry, General George Crook's cavalry from the Department of West Virginia, the XI Corps, and part of the XIX Corps — 30,000 or 40,000 men to defeat Early's 18,000 or 20,000.* However, victory was not assured. Early had rail connections with Lee, so reinforcements could be sent quickly. Already the Shenandoah Valley had ruined the reputations of Generals Banks, Sigel, and Hunter. Sheridan was a new man, comparatively unknown. Would he do better?

Little Phil's first act was to march up the Shenandoah. Torbert commanded all the cavalry now. Merritt had the 1st Division and Custer retained the Michigan Brigade. Brevet Major Marcus Reno was appointed Torbert's chief of staff. From this seat on the footstool of the mighty, Reno's influence could be tremendous, but if Custer felt any apprehensions he kept them to himself. The country was beautiful in August — rolling hills, shocked grain in the fields, orchard succeeding orchard, all heavy with reddening apples. The blue-clad horsemen saw, on hilltops, pillared mansions with majestic galleries. At one gate a servant asked Armstrong to call. His mistress, Mrs. Lewis W. Washington, appreciated the kindness Custer had shown her son, James, when captured on the Peninsula in '62, and wished to express her gratitude by presenting him with a button from George Washington's coat. However, such courtesies were exceptional. Instead, troops usually skirmished daily somewhere along the line.[5] The deeper the cavalry penetrated, the more severe became the opposition. Sheridan suspected that Lee was sending Early reinforcements. At the end of fifty miles he recalled his troops, fearing that their supply line might be cut. As they marched back Sheridan ordered the destruction of all crops useful to an enemy army. Planters professing loyalty to the Federal government were to be given receipts for confiscated property. Sheridan also told his men to hang all Mosby partisans without trial. These guerrillas had been the bane of earlier commanders and Grant had told Sheridan to end this nuisance. Little Phil began at once. He reported hanging one of them on August 16 and shooting six. Mosby declared that

* Accurate figures are difficult to obtain. The above estimate is from T. L. Livermore, *Numbers & Losses in the Civil War,* pp. 127, 129, 130. *O. R.,* I, XLIII, pt. 1, pp. 974–987, gives Sheridan 100,000 on paper. F. Whittaker, in his laudatory *Complete Life of . . . Custer . . . ,* p. 231, gives Sheridan only 21,500 to defeat Early's 30,000, and explains how he arrives at these numbers.

the executed men were not his, but it was, of course, impossible for a Federal officer to distinguish between a Mosby man and an independent freebooter.[6]

In spite of Sheridan's destructive policy, designed to check an enemy advance, Early almost beat him back to the Potomac and in a surprise attack cut off Merritt's Reserve Brigade. Custer went to its rescue. With the enthusiasm he usually incited in troops, he quelled a near-panic, got the Union soldiers across the river in a splashing fight, and Chief of Staff Reno sent him congratulations from Division Commander Merritt.[7]

The withdrawal set Northern newspapers howling derisively. They said Sheridan had failed in the Valley, just like his predecessors. To save Washington more troops must be drawn from the siege of Petersburg. In this crisis, Mosby's men redoubled their depredations, sniping sentinels, capturing couriers. And at the height of the excitement, Libbie arrived unexpectedly in Harper's Ferry. She was lonely; she wanted to see her Autie. Custer was in camp sixteen miles away. With two fellow officers who were willing to chance being bushwhacked, he trotted into town. The lovers, especially Libbie, had much to talk about: such gossip as the shocking way married folks carried on in Washington; Senator Chandler, more sober than usual, flirting now with "Major G's wife." Libbie also wanted to discuss her fall wardrobe. Everyone seemed to be buying plaids but she preferred plain colors. She wanted a black silk dress and asked Autie if she might spend sixty dollars for it. She had a new bonnet and said, "I look nearly good enough to kiss when it's on." She also wanted to know how Autie was going to vote. Senator Chandler made terribly bitter speeches cursing Copperheads, she said. On Washington streets, banners carried the names of Lincoln and McClellan. Soldiers expressed preferences by cheers or groans as they marched past. Libbie favored "Abraham," but way down in her heart she wanted peace at any price. When people asked her how her husband would vote she had to say she did not know. Between caresses, the couple laughed. Armstrong was so glad to see her, and to listen to her jokes, even silly stories like the one about the newly married man in Washington who laced his bride for a party. Her stays were a yard and a half long to the points. Just before he finished he found he had threaded them wrong, had to unlace and begin again.

Autic told Libbie a soldier should have no politics; he asked her if Jim Christiancy was recovering from his wound; and he wondered where in Harper's Ferry to find suitable lodgings for his "little Durl."

Libbie had brought only the clothes she carried in a satchel but was sure they would suffice for two weeks — almost. If she got desperate she could return to Washington. Armstrong found a place for her to board a mile out of town but safe enough, he hoped, from Mosby's gangs. Then he started back to camp. He always rode away from her nostalgically, moody, unable to laugh and joke with his companions. At camp, as soon as he dismounted, he wrote a note to "My dear little Army Crow."

Every few days Armstrong braved the guerrillas to see her. In his tent between times he caught up on his correspondence — always important to him. In a letter to his sister he said admiringly, "It is all I can do to keep her [Libbie] from coming right out to camp in the government wagons that come with forage and rations."

A letter which Armstrong wrote to Judge Christiancy was more serious. He described Jim's recovery from his wound, discussed the coming election, and professed to be a "peace man." But he said a just peace could be secured only by acknowledging one government supreme. "The peace commissioners I am in favor of sending," he continued, "are from the cannon's mouth. Let the people at the proper time support the soldiers. We are fighting for human rights, liberty, for the preservation of a free people." [8]

On September 16 Grant came up from City Point to see Sheridan. The two men walked together in a field where aides could not hear them — two small men puffing cigars, one silent, the other gesticulating. [9] Both were concerned with newspaper criticism of the do-nothing campaign in the Valley, especially as this was election year. After Grant left, Sheridan told his generals to prepare for a renewed offensive. He and Grant had decided that Early was sending troops down to Lee. As soon as they were too far away to be sent back quickly, the Union forces would strike at Winchester, principal town in the lower Valley. General Wilson's 3d Division was to take the lead, the infantry following. By other roads Merritt's 1st Division (with Custer's brigade) was to advance on the right wing. The first resistance to be expected was along Opequon Creek, ten miles from Winchester. Armstrong was assigned one of the fords.

On September 19, 1864, reveille sounded at 2 A.M. As Custer pulled on his boots he could hear, far to the east, bugle after bugle repeat the call. He ate a hasty breakfast — close by the fire, for there was a feel of autumn in the air. Then, mounting his horse, he led his Michigan Brigade and the 25th New York Cavalry away from the ruddy flames into the night. The soft country road lay black before him but as he approached the ford enemy pickets began to fire. He could see the red streaks from the gun muzzles. Custer halted, dismounted, and deployed. At dawn his line groped forward. The sun rose in crimson splendor, setting all the clouds aglow and illuminating brilliant autumnal foliage.[10] Under the dancing copper and gold leaves along Opequon Creek Custer saw fortifications. Clouds of smoke puffed from them sporadically. He ordered the 6th Michigan to open fire: keep those fellows' heads under cover until the 25th New York and 7th Michigan cross the stream and charge them.

The van waded into the water as shells screamed overhead and the water boiled with enemy bullets. Men collapsed, staining the foam red where they fell. The front line broke and churned in confusion. Custer's shrill, commanding voice called for the Michigan 1st — his favorite. Waving his sword with the radiant assurance which inspired men to follow him, even to certain death, he led them into the stream. The regiment reached the south bank, dug in, and the reorganized brigade followed.

The Confederates retreated before this display of courage. A few stragglers were captured in the abandoned earthworks. When questioned they named the companies in which they had served, said Major General Stephen Ramseur was in command. So that West Point friend, who had won renown with his gallant charges in the Wilderness last May, was in the Valley! The schoolmates might kill each other any day now.

Custer did not wait for orders. He seldom did. Instead, he followed the retreating enemy. But he rode cautiously, stopping his column often to watch his own vedettes prowl through fields of shocked corn on both sides of the road, tear down gates in stone fences, scout for wood-lot ambushes.

Sugar maples had turned pure gold. Poplar leaves were canary-yellow. Oaks and sweet gums glowed red as fire. In this dramatic countryside the vedettes found no lurking enemy, but Custer heard continual firing far to the left. A fierce battle must be raging where the infantry advanced. Half a mile from the ford Armstrong met his enemy again and pushed him back once more. At the end of another half mile Custer's men rode into blue-clad cavalrymen — General Averell's division, on foot — fighting stubbornly against a line of embattled Confederates. Here Armstrong learned bad news. The battle, over in the center, was not going well. Wilson's cavalry had failed to perform as Sheridan expected. Infantry divisions had tangled on a narrow road, some regiments breaking. Early was pushing his men into the gap. If he cut the Union line, both wings must save themselves as best they could.

Custer and Averell decided to hold their positions until more definite orders arrived. While waiting, Armstrong amused himself by leading little charges from hiding places beneath clumps of trees. They all failed, but the survivors seemed eager to try again. It was exciting to sweep like a flying-V of teal into the enemy's line, then out again — always with flashing sabers, no carbine or pistol shots.[11] Custer had convinced his men that bullets never demoralized an enemy like the sight of oncoming horsemen slashing right and left, crashing through fences and over ditches.

On the main battlefield a lull had come in the fighting. Every soldier knows this may mean the crisis when the next move breaks the courage of one side or the other — victory or defeat. In this instance Sheridan, insanely furious with the threat of defeat, God-damned his demoralized men back into the line which Early had severed. Then, with the impetuosity that made Little Phil famous, he ordered an immediate advance.

Custer, far on the right wing, saw the Union infantry appear on distant fields, brigade front, regiments in parallel columns of platoons, a great carpet enameling the russet hillsides with blue, while bands played, flags billowed in the autumn breeze, and the sun glinted on thousands of guns and sabers. Who but Sheridan — unless it were Custer — could instill such pomp and confidence in an army on the brink of demoralization? Early's Confederates were bound to break when they saw this tremendous host!

A messenger rode up to Custer with an order to charge the earthworks on the Confederate's extreme left where the rebel cavalry had dug in. Until they were dispersed, Sheridan could not hope to flank the enemy. All afternoon Custer had pecked at that fortification. He believed it suicide — and a lost battle — to assault it with horse at this time, so he sent back a request to use his own judgment as to the time of his charge. Amazing insubordination! Yet Sheridan, knowing the boy's reckless courage, seems to have acquiesced.[12]

Custer watched Sheridan's army creep closer to the waiting enemy as the sun sank in the west. He also watched the Confederate earthworks he had been ordered to attack. Men were being withdrawn from them to reinforce Early's line where Sheridan's massive infantry would hit. Good! Custer planned to strike as the line thinned. A rear guard seldom fights stubbornly and if it retreats, even though slowly, can often be made to run. Custer's brigade waited, horses pawing, switching, stamping. Band instruments and banners glowed in sunset radiance. The distant infantry was getting very close to the Confederate line. Custer waved to the band leader. The line started forward with troopers' hearts beating to "Yankee Doodle" and bass drums bobbing on the big horses as they trotted off.

"Steady!" "Dress on the guidons."

"Not too fast. Let them fire . . . then charge before they can reload." With a thunder of hoofs, Custer's cavalry bounded through blue smoke skeins and over the enemy earthworks. In the chaos of triumph, victors must always beware of a counterattack. Their success may be changed to disaster by a disciplined enemy. Custer's troopers swung from their saddles, wheeled around the captured cannon and pointed them down the enemy's flank. In the growing darkness red flames belched from the cannons' mouths. The crisis had passed. Custer had won! The gray line, barely visible in the dusk, melted away. Frantic Confederates streamed through Winchester and on up the dark roads to Strasburg and Front Royal.*

In Washington Libbie heard a hundred cannon boom the good news to cheering people. Sheridan had captured Winchester! After seven weeks of frustration and retreat, he had delivered a smashing victory, becoming a hero overnight. Moreover, Custer was lauded as one of the principal figures in the battle. With four hundred men he had taken seven hundred prisoners and seven battle standards. He was brevetted colonel in the regular army. Military theorists probably oversimplified the engagement when they pronounced this the first time a cavalry charge decided a battle.[13]

Sheridan moved his army south from Winchester along the main roads leading up the Valley, his men exulting in victory. Twenty miles above Winchester, Early made another stand at Fisher's Hill just beyond Strasburg. Sheridan resolved to defeat him again and this time prevent him from escaping. He massed his infantry for a frontal attack and ordered his cavalry on a forty-mile circle up the Luray Valley and back across the main pike at New Market, thus blocking Early's only way of escape. On September 22 the Union infantry struck and routed the Confederates, but the cavalry failed to stop the retreat. Early had foreseen Sheridan's plan and Rosser checked the Union horse at Mil-

* *O. R.*, I, XLII, pt. 1, pp. 377, 427, 458. Torbert credited the prisoners and battle flags to Custer's commander, Merritt. The action is analyzed by G. F. R. Henderson, *Science of War*, p. 275. Captain J. W. De Forest watched this charge and described it in *Volunteer's Adventures*, p. 189. He may have seen Custer at another time, p. 187, without recognizing him.

ford, east of the pike, and held them there until Early's retreating army had passed. When Rosser withdrew, Custer followed the Confederates for twenty miles, but captured only worn-out horses and a few stragglers.[14]

Sheridan censured Torbert for tardiness, but did not blame Custer. Quite the reverse! On September 30, Grant's pet, Wilson, whom both Sheridan and Custer disliked, was transferred to the West and Sheridan gave Custer his 3d Division — the beginning of a relationship which led almost to mutual dependence.* Armstrong's promotion meant parting with the "Michigan Brigade," which had made him famous and which he in turn had given national renown. It also meant that he would be a rival of his former commander, Merritt, and henceforth Marcus Reno might regard him with increasing jealousy. So be it! The Shenandoah Valley was open country, ideal for cavalry. Mountain passes permitted dashing flank movements and sudden surprises. Custer intended to make the most of it. He let his hair grow again and became his old self. Merritt would have to look after his own reputation.[15]

As a division commander Custer received his first important order on October 3, 1864. Sheridan wanted him to burn all residences within five miles of headquarters, then near Dayton, Virginia — a brutal order, but Sheridan was furious. His engineer officer, riding to camp with one companion, had been joined by three men in blue uniforms who turned out to be guerrillas. They had murdered the engineer, but his companion escaped.[16] To teach the neighborhood a lesson Sheridan ordered all houses burned.

Custer obeyed the order with his usual enthusiasm until Sheridan decided that five miles might be too large a radius and called him in — but not before several residences crackled up in flames. Three days later Sheridan ordered his army to march back down the Valley — another withdrawal, not a retreat, he was careful to say. Winter was coming and his ninety-mile communication and supply line seemed dangerously long.

* O. R., I, XLIII, pt. 2, p. 218. Prior to this, on September 26, Custer was given the 2d Division but he never assumed command.

The Valley opened out here almost thirty miles wide, so Sheridan spread out his men from the Appalachians to the Blue Ridge. Merritt was assigned the Strasburg pike, Custer the back road which skirted the Blue Ridge, still brilliant with russet-leaved oaks splotching the dark pine forests. The two roads were from three to six miles apart. Each division kept contact with the other across rolling fields. All harvested crops and barns caught in this great dragnet must be burned and the livestock driven north.

Every night, and sometimes in daylight, Custer's pickets were attacked. He learned that the snipers belonged to Rosser, and Armstrong disliked retreating from him without a fight. The two old friends both held independent commands today, each worthy of the other's steel. Daily Rosser became bolder, more challenging, nipping at any lagging party, pouncing on every tardy wagon. Torbert submitted to this but Sheridan lost his patience. He had said this was a *withdrawal,* not a *retreat;* he gave Torbert a famous order: Stop, and either whip the enemy or get whipped yourself.[17]

The cautious Torbert stopped to fight and on October 9 Custer and Merritt wheeled against the harassing foe. Armstrong sent Alexander Pennington with one brigade up the road to hunt for Rosser. Alex came back reporting their mutual schoolmate on the far side of Tom's Brook, waiting behind stone walls with his men, his cannon screened by timber on a ridge.

Custer had never led the 3d Division in battle. He was not sure how they would act, but he was very sure they must beat Tom Rosser and they must also perform better than Merritt's 1st Division — with Custer's own boys — who were going to fight, this same day, against General Lunsford Lomax's horse, over on the pike. Armstrong ordered his division to deploy along Tom's Brook opposite the enemy. As the regiments reached out right and left, Custer, with his staff and billowing flags, rode toward the enemy. He halted his aides in a prominent place and went forward alone. Tom Rosser must see him now! Armstrong reined in his charger, lifted his broad-brimmed hat and bowed. Let this be a fair fight!

Custer clapped the big hat on his curly head and turned back to his men. He ordered the 3d Division to advance. His line lay now across the sunny hills for three miles and it writhed forward like a side-winding rattlesnake, but soon broke into a dozen pieces. A strong breeze blew away smoke from carbine and cannon. Far to the west, Custer heard the opening shots of Merritt's attack on Lomax's horse. Let the best man win the best victory! [18]

The battle was strictly a cavalry engagement, all horse, no foot. Little details made surprise attacks, sallying from gaps in stone fences with the sudden "whoop and holler" and clash of arms which Custer loved. Tom Rosser tried to deceive his former schoolmate by retreating two miles, then setting a trap to catch Custer's division when it became disorganized in pursuit. The ruse failed. Armstrong sent a scouting detachment out through the hills to swoop down on Rosser's flank before the ambush was laid. The Confederates, surprised in the midst of this maneuver, broke and soon massed in flight along the dirt road up the Valley. Custer chased them for ten miles in what was called "the Woodstock Races." He overtook six cannon, Rosser's supply train, ambulances, and headquarters wagons, containing his official papers and trunk of clothes. Armstrong got back Libbie's ambrotype, and in addition, acquired Rosser's pet squirrel, a goat which he gave Eliza, and a pet raccoon that henceforth slept in Custer's bed, its little masked face on Armstrong's pillow. Next day Custer appeared before his men wearing the giant Rosser's uniform, grotesquely large for him. He wrote a note to Tom telling him to have his tailor make the tails shorter next time. Then he sent the coat to Libbie. In a pocket was a handkerchief taken from the effects of General T. T. Munford. A package of love letters to that General were returned "without reading," Armstrong was careful to say.*

In his official report Custer cited Pennington for exceptional gallantry and with characteristic grandiloquence said: "Never since the opening

* Armstrong wrote Libbie about this on October 10, 1864. She related the incident in *Boots and Saddles,* pp. 91–92, and gave the coat to the U.S. Military Academy, where it may be seen in the Museum.

of this war had there been witnessed such a complete and decisive over-
throw of the enemy's cavalry" which proved "deficient in confidence,
courage, and a just cause." Secretary of War Stanton telegraphed congratulations, and newspaper correspondents, delighting in colorful copy,
described the battle with Custerlike recklessness. Merritt did not like it,
for he had won an equally successful engagement that same day. But a
count of captured cannon showed six for Custer and only five for him.
Custer luck! But unfair all the same, in the eyes of some fellow officers.[19]

After this victory the Union Army continued its withdrawal. Custer
gloried in the sounds and smells of October, the flaring autumnal foliage so different from drab tidewater Virginia. His division passed Strasburg, splashed across Cedar Creek, and camped for an indefinite stay
on the north bank near Middletown. The valley had narrowed down to
twenty miles here and the Union Army encampment spread out over
five miles with Custer posted farthest west.[20] General Early was presumably vanquished, so Sheridan went to Washington to discuss his
next move: Should he go up the Valley again, take Lynchburg and cut
Richmond off from the West, or should he swing to the east and join
Grant at Petersburg?

With no specific duties, Custer rode to headquarters. Torbert, as well
as Sheridan, had gone away and the mice were having fun in the cats'
absence. Tony Forsyth sat in Torbert's tent being shaved. Armstrong
sat at Torbert's desk, using his ink and pen. Of course Autie wrote
first to Libbie. In her last letter she had told about being disturbed by
Senator Chandler "tight as usual, and disgusting when he has taken
too much." Old Zack, like Congressman Kellogg, had tried to kiss her
and Libbie enjoyed telling Autie about these escapes.[21]

When Armstrong finished the letter to Libbie he wrote next to his
father. Old Emanuel, a peace Democrat, had objected to the strong war
language in his son's last letter to Judge Christiancy. But Armstrong
stood his ground. "We entered this struggle determined to restore the
Union and reestablish the government," he wrote. "I have risked all
that I have, my life itself has been perilled on scores of battle fields" to

bring this about. "Shall the blood of those patriot heroes," he continued, "which has been poured out upon the altar of our country as a sacrifice to freedom and independence be shed in vain?" [22]

As the army rested, word came that Mosby had raided a B & O train inside the Union lines and made a great haul in greenbacks. But that was far in the rear. Rumors that Early was coming back to reattack their front seemed more important. However, scouts reported no sign of his army. The Valley above them had presumably been stripped of supplies until no troops could be supported there.

On October 19 at 1 A.M. Custer was aroused from bed by the sound of shooting at the far end of the encampment, five miles away. Probably a nervous sentry! The moon was just past full and objects appeared exceptionally clear. His head dropped back on the pillow, beside the pet raccoon, perhaps. By four o'clock, when Custer ate breakfast, the bombardment had become alarmingly persistent. He sent a courier for information and ordered his division under arms.

The messenger brought back news which shocked the brigade. General Early, after his supposed defeat, had come back and surprised the Union left. At this very moment he was fighting his way up the flank of Sheridan's encampment. Hundreds of Union soldiers had already been taken prisoners, thousands were milling down the road toward Winchester, some in formation, many thoroughly demoralized. Bull Run all over again! Crook's cavalry had been scattered. The VI Corps, two brigades of the XIX, plus Custer's and Merritt's cavalry were all that remained of Sheridan's army.

Custer, his men standing in formation, ordered a change in front — from south to east — no small maneuver, but he was ready when the first gray skirmishers appeared. Fortunately for Armstrong, many Confederate soldiers stopped on the way to loot and eat Union breakfasts, so Early's whole army did not strike him at once. Custer repulsed those who charged and watched them re-form for a second blow. Defensive fighting never appealed to him but he could do nothing now but make a last stand. Waiting for the charge that might well wipe him out, he heard a strange, shrill noise coming up the Winchester-Strasburg pike, growing louder constantly. The day was cloudless, quiet and smoky, with Indian summer haze misting autumnal foliage. The sound roared shriller, more intense. Soldiers were cheering some object coming in his direction. Armstrong galloped toward it. On the road ahead he saw a general's flag floating above a small party of horsemen. It was Sheridan, back from Washington, on big black Rienzi, gray now with caked sweat. The little General's ruddy face glowed. A rowel on one spur was broken and he waved a switch cut from a bush. Confidence radiated from him. "Turn back, boys!" he kept shouting. "We've got the Goddamnedest twist on them!" [23]

Of course Sheridan had no such twist, but when Little Phil spoke soldiers believed. Custer threw both arms around the General and kissed him on the cheek.[24] Sheridan had ridden less than eleven miles from Winchester — not twenty *to* that town as a popular poem would soon say — but he had come in time to save the day and Custer was one of the few who had held the line so he could save it. For several hours after he arrived Sheridan shifted troops to a new line. He found dead men so densely sprawled about the place where the Confederates had first struck that he had to order his soldiers to "march at will" and pick their way across ground sloppy with blood. Most of the corpses were stripped to underclothes: Confederate soldiers had needed their woolen uniforms.

At four in the afternoon, Sheridan ordered a general advance. Dry leaves in the wood lots rustled under thousands of marching feet. When Early saw the blue army coming he shifted his formation to strike Sheridan's flank. To change front with a two-mile line was difficult. Half must pivot forward, half back across rolling farmland. The line must not break, divide, or develop intervals. Sheridan watched Early's maneuver through his field glasses — and he spied a gap in the hinge. He pounded over to Custer and ordered him to strike that gap with his whole division. Infantry would follow him, and the enemy would be cut in half.

Custer's cavalry rumbled away, a torrent of blue riders making the earth tremble under their horses' hoofs. They split the Confederates as planned. Then, Custerlike, the Boy General, instead of resting on his laurels, rode on to Cedar Creek. It was now late afternoon and in the flush of sunset he splashed across, placing his division west of the road the Confederates would use in a retreat. Thus the army which had flanked Sheridan found itself flanked and outmaneuvered. In the gathering darkness the Confederates started an orderly retreat across the Cedar Creek bridge. Custer dashed into the middle of Early's column, broke the formations, sent men pellmell over the fences into the woods. The sudden appearance, here and there, of charging horsemen at all the fords soon broke Confederate morale. Early said later, "The Yankees got whipped and we got scared." [25]

Soon the pike south to Strasburg was choked with abandoned guns, wagons, ambulances. Custer sat his horse by the roadside directing his riders to gallop ahead, reach the van, and capture all equipment. A Confederate ambulance drove by. Two of Custer's men rode up, reaching for the team's bridles.

"Who have you got there?" one of the Union soldiers asked the driver.

"Do not tell them," came from within the curtains in a North Carolina drawl familiar to Armstrong. He knew and loved that voice.

"Is that you, Ramseur?" Autie called, riding alongside to peer through the curtains at his badly wounded schoolmate. Then he told the soldiers to conduct the ambulance at once to Sheridan's headquarters. Custer did not report there himself until nine o'clock at night. By this time he seems to have forgotten Ramseur, for he leaped joyfully from his horse shouting: "By Jesus, we've cleaned them out and got the guns." In his enthusiasm he hugged the flushed and beaming little Sheridan, then waltzed with him around the campfire. Next he embraced dignified Torbert, who pushed him back with an indulgent smile. "There, there, old fellow. Don't capture me." [26] Then someone remembered Ramseur. Pennington, Merritt, and Custer went to the wounded man's cot. He was dying, shot through and through. His three schoolmates did all they could to make him comfortable, took last messages to his wife and a lock of hair for the baby he had never seen. At ten o'clock next morning he died, as captured cannon, battle flags, caissons, and hundreds of wagons trundled into Sheridan's headquarters for a triumphal review.* Regiments of prisoners were herded down the pike. Federal soldiers noticed that the poor fellows were dressed in rags.[27] The South must be bled white. How much longer could war last?

Northern newspapers lauded Sheridan's unprecedented victories in the Valley. Sheridan, in his turn, recommended promotions for both Merritt and Custer,[28] but E. A. Paul, reporter for the *New York Times,* lavished most of his praise on Armstrong, saying: "Custer, young as he is, displayed judgment worthy of a Napoleon." Merritt objected, officially — even hinting that Custer may have supplied the correspondent with a false number of cannon captured by his division. Paul replied, in the press, that he got his information from officers in Merritt's own division. But Custer did not let the disagreement die there. He was a division commander himself now, intent on building morale in his new organization by seeing that it received due recognition. He asked for a board to determine who took the most guns.† In this dispute Marcus Reno, whose gallantry in the battle earned him a recommendation for promotion to lieutenant colonel, probably concurred with Merritt, and thus may have taken another step toward his implacable

* M. Schaff, *Spirit of Old West Point,* p. 57. H. A. DuPont, *Campaign of 1864,* pp. 174–175, tells a different story.

† *O. R.,* I, XLIII, pt. 1, pp. 33, 453, 480, 528; *New York Times,* October 27, 28, November 8, 1864. Custer's charge undoubtedly took the cannon which controlled the Strasburg pike. Then he sent the 1st Vermont and 5th New York up the pike to overtake the fleeing enemy. Dark having come, he and Merritt rode to headquarters. Devin, with a brigade from Merritt's division, also rode up the pike, taking abandoned guns. Devin asserted, and this is the crux of the dispute, that his troops were first to go up the road. Custer asked for a board to determine the case if Sheridan questioned his claim to priority. Evidently there was no question in Sheridan's mind. See A. C. Hamlin, "Who Recaptured the Guns at Cedar Creek?" p. 195 ff.

hatred of Custer. Both Reno and Merritt must also have resented the fact that an investigation showed Custer to be right, and Sheridan sent the Boy General with the captured flags to Washington for a formal presentation to the Secretary of War. Every enlisted man who had captured a color was to go along and carry it himself in the ceremony.

Election day was close now, and Sheridan's victories, after so many years of Lincoln's futile war effort, were politically important. Certainly the press would give the presentation ceremony wide publicity. Armstrong, never averse to riding out in front, made plans for another visit with Libbie. But when he arrived in Washington, Libbie was not at her boardinghouse. She had gone to New York to visit her father's relatives and buy winter clothes. Before leaving she had written Autie about her proposed trip and ended the letter: "I don't care if fifty rebels read this letter. I miss your kisses." [29]

She found the journey to New York more difficult than she expected. Traveling alone in one of those newfangled sleeping cars frightened her. She had to change stations in Philadelphia — another dismaying experience — but the polite conductor put her on a horsecar for the trip across town. At her relatives' home she was eating breakfast when someone brought in a copy of the *New York Times* announcing Sheridan's victory and Custer's proposed trip to Washington — and she would miss him!

Libbie fled to her room and fell sobbing on the bed. She was aroused by children's voices piping, "He's come. He's come!" Armstrong burst in the door, swept her up in his arms, dried her tears, and rushed her back to Washington. The celebration had been postponed. To get there in time, they rode in the cab of a locomotive for the last forty miles. On arrival they commandeered an omnibus and, with captured Confederate flags flying from the windows, drove up Pennsylvania Avenue amid a snowstorm of waving handkerchiefs. At Stanton's office a little speech was made about each flag and the soldier who captured it, including the two boys who took Steve Ramseur's standard. Secretary Stanton asked if Armstrong was related to the Ohio Custers, said he remembered Emanuel. They had both been good Democrats.

When did the family move to Michigan? Then the Secretary turned to the assembled veterans and, taking Custer's hand, continued: "General, a gallant officer always makes gallant soldiers." A boy in blue shouted: "The 3d Division wouldn't be worth a cent if it wasn't for him!" A kind press reported, "The embarrassed looks of General Custer, as he bowed his thanks, showed that his modesty was equal to his courage."

Back in camp after the hurly-burly, Armstrong wrote Libbie: "Dear little Durl . . . I am sending for you to visit camp. You must make up your mind to fewer comforts than you now enjoy. You will lead a real soldier's life. Do not come if you do not desire it. Retain your room. Bring riding-habit, one small trunk . . . Good-night and a kiss from your devoted Boy Autie."

Libbie replied: "I love luxury, dress, comfort. But, how gladly I will give them up. I can be ready in a day or two. I can hardly wait." *

17 Apotheosis

Petite Libbie Custer found the winter of 1864–1865 in Winchester gayer than Armstrong had pictured it. General Custer established his headquarters in a Southern mansion and she presented dozens of red "Custer ties" to her husband's men. Armstrong assigned Pennington to one of his brigades and recommended him for a promotion. Dinners, dances, parties at camp and in the little village enlivened military life. At the Michigan Brigade's ball each dance on the program was given a name. There was "Kilpatrick's Lancers," "Pennington's Quadrille,"

---

* In the Whittaker biography of Custer, p. 270, presumably written under Libbie Custer's supervision, she went to the War Department hunting Armstrong while he hunted for her at the boardinghouse. The account accepted for this text is from a letter Libbie wrote her father October 25, 1864 — certainly better evidence than anyone's memory twelve years later.

and a galop called "Custer's Charge."[1] Sheridan enjoyed the "hops," bobbing around the room holding his partner like a guitar. People gossiped about his interest in a certain young lady. Some also gossiped about the appearance in camp of Corporal Tom Custer with a lieutenant's commission and an assignment to his brother's staff. This was nepotism, yes, but it was also the army. Look at Sheridan's brother, Michael, on his staff and Lincoln's son on Grant's. . . .

In public the two boys treated each other with stiff-backed dignity, and Tom said, "If anyone thinks it is a soft thing to be a commanding officer's brother he misses his guess." * However, within the spacious mansion Autie and Tom tussled like the boys they were. And no matter how noisy and how rough, Libbie laughed at their antics — not with reluctant indulgence but with genuine enjoyment.

Why not be gay? The war was coming to an end. Sheridan had conquered the Shenandoah Valley, Sherman had taken Atlanta, and Will Cushing, brother of Armstrong's classmate Allie, had sunk the Confederate *Albemarle,* down in North Carolina. The war produced no greater heroes than those Cushing brothers, both of them grim and unhappy, yet in courage and reckless gallantry a perfect match for the gay and carefree Custers.

An odd request came from another of Custer's old acquaintances. General Wilson, the "imbecile" who had irritated Armstrong, now applied for his services in his new western command. This was not the last time officers who disliked Armstrong personally would ask to have him transferred to their commands. But Sheridan prized Custer's talents too much to let him go.[2]

Camp gossip took a new turn on November 7 when a 5th Michigan trooper came into the lines with a grim story. The fellow said that he had been captured by Mosby's men and had escaped. Some twenty-two

---

* Private Tom Custer became a corporal shortly before being assigned to Armstrong's staff as a lieutenant on November 8, 1864. He received a captain's commission, February 11, 1865. The quotation is from E. B. Custer, "Beau Sabreur," p. 298.

other prisoners, he said, had been forced to draw lots to determine which seven of them should be hanged in retaliation for the hanging, without trial, of Mosby men caught by General Custer.

Four days later Mosby confirmed this account by sending a letter to Sheridan in which he said that he had hanged seven Union men to pay for six of his men killed by Brigadier General Custer at Front Royal and one man killed by "Colonel Powell" on his Rappahannock raid.

This was an odd letter, strangely full of misstatements. The hanging at Front Royal had occurred immediately after the fight at Milford where Rosser held back the Union cavalry which had gone to cut off Early's retreat. At the end of the engagement Torbert sent an ambulance train of wounded northward in charge of Lieutenant Charles McMaster. This train was intercepted at Front Royal on September 23 by a gang of Mosby guerrillas. They had hardly begun looting when the Reserve Brigade — not Custer's — appeared. The freebooters fled but six of them were caught red-handed. Amidst the wreckage lay Lieutenant McMaster, mortally wounded. He said that he had surrendered, been robbed, then shot by his captors as they retreated.*

All Union soldiers were under orders from Sheridan to hang guerrillas without trial. Infuriated at the sight of the wrecked ambulance train, squads of soldiers led off the six prisoners. They shot four of them at the edge of town, and duly hanged the other two. A note was pinned on the coat of one of the hanged men. What it said is controversial. According to Mosby, who was not present, it said this would be "the fate of Mosby and all his men." Perhaps it did say this, but another pro-Confederate remembered its words later as: "Hung in retaliation for the death of a Federal major, killed in an ambulance this afternoon."

The reader may take his choice. The important thing is that Custer's brigade was not in Front Royal on September 23. Instead, it was fol-

---

* He died on October 15, Heitman, *Historical Register*, p. 442, *O. R.,* I, XLIII, pt. 1, pp. 105, 441, 519; pt. 2, pp. 566, 909–910, 920, 922. J. J. Williamson, *Mosby's Rangers*, pp. 292–293, and *Southern Historical Society Papers*, XXV, pp. 239–244, give details of both sides of the fight. There is nothing official to indicate that Custer was present, much as he may have wished to be.

lowing the retreating Confederates through New Market and on to Harrisonburg.* Thirty-three years later, after Mosby's letter was well known and tradition had made Custer a principal in the lynching, two old-timers in Front Royal claimed they had seen him there. One of them described his gold braid, resplendent "suit of silk velvet," and the long hair on his shoulders. Since Custer at this time wore neither long hair nor a braided uniform, it should be remembered that the memories of the best-intentioned men play tricks. It should be borne in mind, too, that Mosby was careless in his statements about hanging seven men, himself. He hanged only three. The rest bribed their executioners, were released because they were Freemasons, feigned death when shot, or escaped in the dark. Moreover, those executed were not hanged, as Mosby said, "on the Valley turnpike."

Another Mosby prisoner who escaped the hanging was Captain Charles Brewster of Custer's staff. When forced to draw lots for his life he told Mosby that he knew nothing about the Front Royal hangings, and was not there. Mosby cut him off with "That will do — it will not help your case." [3] Whatever the true facts may be, it should always be remembered that it was Grant and Sheridan who gave the order to hang guerrillas without trial. Had Custer hanged them he would have been obeying orders, and enhancing his own military record; yet he did not report killing any, while Colonel Powell, whom Mosby designated as a secondary antagonist, reported officially that he had killed four between October 3 and 13.[4] Custer's conspicuous activity un-

---

* Custer might possibly have ridden through Front Royal September 23 but if so he took a 10-mile detour on a 40-mile march. The Michigan 1st passed through Front Royal that day but it was commanded by Col. Peter Stagg, not Custer. (See *O. R.*, I, XLIII, pt. 1, pp. 99, 463.) J. S. Mosby in his *Memoirs*, pp. 300–302, admits getting the facts from a Richmond newspaper report, which said Generals Torbert, Merrill, and Custer were present. Notice that Mosby carelessly transcribes the date incorrectly. On p. 368 he says Custer hanged the men, not on account of his orders, but for revenge. This is psychology, not history, and Mosby's qualifications in the new profession may be questioned. Also note, p. 372. Pending the discovery of more tangible proof, Custer must be deemed innocent until proved guilty. See also R. B. Irwin, *History of the Nineteenth Army Corps*, pp. 400–401; G. N. Bliss, "Cavalry Service," p. 18.

doubtedly brought him undue blame from his enemies. Certainly he, with Tom at his side, was indefatigable in destroying all crops and food which might be used either by the guerrillas or by Lee's army. This was total war and Sherman, following the pattern in the deep South, boasted this same autumn that he was preparing "to make Georgia howl."

The scorching of the Shenandoah Valley lasted until after Thanksgiving, certainly one time of the year when Armstrong preferred to be with Libbie. Since they had met first at that Seminary party in late November, for the rest of their lives they celebrated Thanksgiving as their "anniversary." When unable to be together on that day they always wrote. Yet perhaps the greatest joy of their first Thanksgiving season came from a petition signed by three hundred and seventy soldiers in the 1st Michigan asking to be transferred to Custer's division. And as orders came for a midwinter expedition up the Valley, one hundred and two boys in the Michigan 7th also petitioned to join his outfit.[5]

The weather turned very cold in December, with rain, hail, snow, but Sheridan determined to find and destroy Early if men and horses could stand the exposure. He sent Torbert with two divisions, Merritt's and Powell's, east of the Blue Ridge toward Gordonsville and Charlottesville. Custer was glad to be sent on an independent expedition with his one division, for he always preferred to operate alone. He was to ride up the Valley and draw attention from the larger force.[*]

This was the first time Autie and Tom rode out together in the war. With them was Pennington, commanding a brigade. As they marched south into the trough between gloomy ridges at the upper end of the Valley, the wintry sun set early. Daily the snow drifted higher and the temperature lower. Even the houses in this upper country looked different. The area had been settled by Scotch-Irish and Pennsylvania Dutch. The folk here lived not in pillared mansions but in steep-roofed brick buildings with double chimneys on the end-walls. At Lacey Spring,

* Note contradiction, or change in the plan to have Custer go on to Lynchburg, in *O. R.*, I, XLIII, pt. 2, pp. 803, 810.

nine miles from Harrisonburg and seventy-five from Winchester, Custer bivouacked in the snow. He knew of no enemy within miles, and a strange silence settled over the encampment. Large moist flakes soon covered men and horses. Before daylight Armstrong called his sentries in from the snowstorm's trembling chaos, and prepared to resume the march.

Shots rang out from behind the black curtain of night. Armstrong heard wild cowboy yells from hundreds of throats. Almost four years had passed since Tom Rosser had shouted this same staccato challenge from a window at West Point. Custer replied with his shrillest cavalry commands. Pennington's brigade at the rear was already in the saddle, so they spurred front to meet the enemy.

The battle was short and indecisive, with charge and countercharge through snow-laden underbrush, red flashes in the blue-white air, dead men lying on their faces in wet leaves, hot blood melting splotches in the snow. Custer reported capturing two battle flags and thirty-three prisoners, but then he "skedaddled" down the Valley, many of his soldiers riding bareback. As in the Charlottesville raid last year, he believed that he had accomplished his mission by diverting attention.[6]

By the time his column got close to Winchester many of the men were badly frostbitten. Five miles from headquarters Armstrong left them. Eager to get home, he let his black horse go — wild hoofs throwing mud recklessly over staff members who tried to keep up. Libbie met him in the hall. His wool clothes and mustache smelled of the cold outdoors as she kissed him. Tom stamped in behind. Both boys brimmed with exciting stories. The funniest one was about a Dutchman who refused to let them use his house for headquarters because "the Old Lady" was "agin it." Armstrong, and Tom too, began calling Libbie their Old Lady, especially when she disapproved of anything they wanted to do.[7] Henceforth, for the rest of their lives, this was her nickname, and Libbie always enjoyed it.

During Armstrong's absence Libbie's father, stepmother, and a cousin had arrived for a visit. They were accompanied by the Reverend Dr. Matson, who had helped officiate in the Custer wedding. With these distinguished guests, Armstrong arranged a special religious service for his bedraggled column. Evangelistic revivals had become popular during the later war years. Armstrong, always sensitive to music and impassioned oratory, knelt at this service and "accepted Christ as his savior." [8]

As soon as men and horses were rested, Sheridan prepared them for another march. Important orders had arrived from Washington. The Middle Military District, no longer a danger area, had been given to General Hancock, a now famous and thoroughly dependable soldier, but one who seemed to have lost his old aggressiveness after being wounded at Gettysburg. Sheridan was to retain the cavalry corps and lead them to Lynchburg, one hundred and twenty-five miles west of Richmond. After destroying the railroads there, he was to go on into North Carolina and join Sherman, who had marched across Georgia to the sea and was now coming north. In case Sheridan found this infeasible, he was to return to Winchester.

Custer, as well as Sheridan's aides, saw that their chief did not like the order. They had learned to be quiet when the little bullethead gritted his teeth. [9] They all knew that the war was almost ended and that Lee could not survive the coming summer. Obviously Sheridan felt outraged at the prospect of trailing off behind "Sherman's bummers" instead of being with Grant at the kill. Custer had always been impressed by the manner in which some officers in high command evaded distasteful orders. What would his idol, Sheridan, do now?

The column was ordered to start on February 27, 1865. Before leaving, Custer attended another evangelistic service, explaining his conversion later by saying, "Years of reflexion and study had convinced me that I was not fulfilling the end of my Creator if I lived for this world alone. Life is at all times uncertain, but to one in my profession it is particularly so." [10]

The day of departure dawned warm and cloudy — one of the first mild days of the winter. The column contained nine thousand horse. Custer led the 3d Division. Adjutant Greene had been exchanged since his capture at Trevilian Station and was with him again,[11] still carrying the flute about which Armstrong liked to joke. Edward A. Paul, the *New York Times* correspondent, also accompanied the column. Custer began the march riding his favorite mount, Jack Rucker. The first day they advanced thirty miles up the pike, going through Strasburg and bivouacking at Woodstock, familiar to them all since Custer's triumph at the Woodstock Races. The ground was muddy. Melted snow gurgled in the brooks. Officers and men warmed their fingers around fires and speculated on their destination. Were they headed for Sherman's army or would they come back to Winchester? Many prophesied that Sheridan would find some way to circumvent the order and join Grant.*

Next day they marched twenty-nine miles — a blue ribbon of riders undulating along the turnpike. They passed through New Market and camped at Lacey Spring, where Custer could show Edward Paul the site of his narrow escape. The men were happy, singing as they rode, shod hoofs rippling along the hard pike. On muddy byroads they saw squads of lurking horsemen but the fellows did not attack. Sheridan called them his "provost guard." Soldiers would not stray from his lines with those cutthroats at large.

On the third day's march they came to Harrisonburg, a typical Pennsylvania Dutch town. The hard-surfaced pike ended here. The next twenty-six miles, to Staunton, were bottomless red Virginia clay, and from there on to Lynchburg lay another seventy-five miles of mud. Icy cold rain made the roads more impassable daily. The column slipped and sloshed along, Custer's 3d Division at the rear now. Word came back to Armstrong that the enemy had been in Staunton but was moving over to Waynesboro, just west of Rockfish Gap in the Blue Ridge Mountains. That night the cavalry camped in the Staunton streets, which were still tracked deep with the enemy's footprints. Tomorrow,

---

* Lieutenant S. M. Thompson, in his diary, p. 536, says the day was warm and cloudy. Major F. C. Newhall, Sheridan's aide-de-camp, in *With Sheridan in Lee's Last Campaign,* says it was cold and drizzly. Although the column presumably headed for Lynchburg, Thompson told his diary they were going to join Grant.

March 2, Custer would take the lead.* Rain still slanted down. The road was knee-deep in slime. Sheridan watched the column start, floundering along. He said that he could hardly recognize men he knew among the mud-caked soldiers. Horses lurched and wallowed, sometimes to their bellies. Armstrong worked constantly to keep intervals closed between his fifteen hundred men. He was determined to catch up with the enemy, and Sheridan promised to send Devin with a thousand reinforcements in case "Jube" Early stopped to fight. At noon, after struggling along for sixteen miles, Custer spied through the downpour the squalid buildings of Waynesboro. Already they had been fortified by the Confederates. Rockfish Gap must be two miles beyond, but it was invisible in the rain.

Custer immediately displayed the characteristic which made him both famous and despised. A cautious officer would have waited for his army to come up. Several hours would have been consumed studying through field glasses the enemy's positions and placing troops to advance properly against them. Not Custer! He attacked immediately with the first brigade that arrived, and while the enemy was busy repelling them he sent three regiments, under Pennington, to circle the village and occupy the road through the gap. Then, before the enemy had time to make countermoves, Custer deployed the next two brigades that trudged in, and renewed his frontal attack. Within three hours the Union soldiers occupied Waynesboro and Custer was leading a pursuit party after fugitives who had evaded Pennington's regiments at the gap. On the road, he stopped long enough to scratch off a note to Sheridan telling of his success, saying he had captured three pieces of artillery, three battle flags, a large train of wagons, ambulances, and four hundred prisoners. His men, in pursuit of the enemy, splashed past him while he wrote. Armstrong ended the note with: "Am in hopes of catching Early. I am pursuing him through the gap. My loss is slight." In a postscript he added: "Another handsome battle flag is just captured."

* F. Whittaker, *Complete Life of . . . Custer . . .* , p. 273, recounts this differently from the *O. R.*, I, XLVI, pt. 2, pp. 735, 778.

That evening Custer led his men through Rockfish Gap and camped on the edge of Virginia's piedmont, a rich agricultural country rolling some hundred miles toward Richmond. After dark Custer called Chaplain Holmes to his tent and with him knelt to thank God for the victory. He had failed to catch either Early or Rosser, and suspected that they must have stayed behind, hidden in some residence in Waynesboro, but he had captured seventeen battle flags, eleven guns, and sixteen hundred prisoners.[12] Tom Custer had shown exceptional gallantry — a chip from the Custer block — and received a promotion.

During the night Sheridan rode in. That man Custer had done it for him again! Little Phil inspected the bivouacs where the men rested. He congratulated them, and they made the night echo with cheers.

In the morning a drizzle of rain misted the encampment. The Blue Ridge wore a cap of new snow. South and east, beyond the curtain of rain, the sun shone on the piedmont hills, least touched of all Virginia by marching armies. Charlottesville stood only twenty miles away. Sheridan counted off fifteen hundred men to take the prisoners back to Winchester. He, with the rest of his horsemen, would march down into the sunny Virginia countryside, into the land of the Tuckahoes so rich in the romance of colonial America, a land where handsome gates stood guard on country roads and pillared mansions crowned the hills. To hell with that order to get back into the mud! It would ruin all his horses and put him helplessly afoot. Custer, riding proudly with his division, led the way toward Charlottesville. Once more he realized that commands were evaded by generals powerful enough to take the risk.

On the road, a mile from Charlottesville, the mayor met the column and handed Custer the keys to the buildings. The faculty of the University of Virginia stood on the campus under a white flag as the horsemen passed. Armstrong established his headquarters in a fine colonial mansion and sent a guard to protect Monticello. Sheridan arrived and selected another mansion for his headquarters. Pennington said later that he, Armstrong, and Tom with other aides were sitting on the gallery of their mansion when a civilian was brought to them — obviously a Confederate officer in disguise. The fellow insisted that he was not a spy — only a soldier come to see his kin. Custer let him visit the family without a guard and then, before sending him on to Sheridan, he noticed that the fellow was wearing pumps — certainly unsuitable footwear. Custer pulled off his own boots and gave them to him.[13] A small gift — forget it! He'd capture a new pair from a reb on his next successful charge.

Here in the comforts of Charlottesville Sheridan abandoned his last opportunity to go to Lynchburg. As he had anticipated, many of his horses were already unserviceable with "grease heel" caused by the mud. Moreover, the change from oats to corn scoured them badly. These circumstances made it impossible for him to go back into the mountains. All he could do now was strike east into familiar country, get supplies, and rest under the gunboat protection at White House Landing on the Pamunkey. The best horses were given to Merritt and Custer for side raids to destroy crops needed by Lee's embattled army. The raiders were also ordered to tear up railroads and destroy locks on the James River canal, which carried Confederate supplies. They must move quickly because Lee, holding off Grant with his Petersburg fortifications, could still strike out in his rear.

Custer raided to within eleven miles of Richmond. Marching back, he was surprised by Early and Rosser, who had mustered some men since the Waynesboro retreat. In the skirmish Custer's Jack Rucker fell, pinning him down. Fortunately the horse was stunned and lay still. Chaplain Holmes thanked a merciful God while aides pulled Armstrong out from under. Custer replied with "Amen," leaped on a fresh mount, continued to direct the fight, and ended it with a prayer of thanks and a resolution to "glorify Him and keep His commandments."[14]

On March 19, 1865, Sheridan reached White House Landing and rested five days. Custer quartered himself in a comfortable house, placed his flag over the gate and arranged the captured ones — seventeen in all — along the fence. Correspondent Paul showed Armstrong the report he was sending the *New York Times*. It said, "General Custer deserves the credit for planning and executing one of the most brilliant and successful fights in this or any other war." Chaplain Holmes came to headquarters and bade Armstrong good-by with the assurance that God had created him, Custer, as the special military genius of the war. Armstrong liked the Reverend Mr. Holmes and didn't think he would deceive a fellow. Reveling in the flattery, he wrote Libbie: "Your Bo has won new laurels. . . . Oh, my angel, I have the most glorious Division. They behaved splendidly." He told her, too, that he had not sworn a single oath since he left her, not "even in thought." *

The march from White House Landing across the Peninsula was tedious. Half of Sheridan's cavalrymen walked, their horses unfit for service. At the James River they tramped over a pontoon bridge spanning the broad waters, and on March 26 joined Grant's army near Petersburg. The Union line extended west of them for fifteen miles behind elaborate fortifications of logs, sandbags, and wickerwork, with side trenches, bombproofs, bristling abatis, and chevaux-de-frise. In this muddy maze of defenses the Union Army had stagnated since Sheridan's cavalry rode away last summer. But as soon as the roads dried this spring a decisive offensive was sure to start.

Sheridan, as well as Custer, wanted to join the final chase, but Armstrong's immediate concern was mail from Libbie. A bundle of letters and a package containing socks and underwear awaited him. Here was a letter from Judge Bacon, who had been slow to approve of his son-in-law but who now joined in the general adulation, writing that even a horse which had been owned by the Boy General was worth more than other animals.

A letter from Libbie said that the Waynesboro flags had arrived in Washington and she had gone to the War Department to see their

* The *Times* article was published March 20, 1865. Armstrong made a similar boast about not swearing in mid-August, 1864. M. Merington, *Custer Story*, pp. 114, 141–142. During the buffalo hunt in 1872 with the Grand Duke Alexis, Custer is reported as being fluently profane. Others say not. Like accounts of Lincoln's smutty stories, the fact is controversial.

formal presentation. The Secretary of War had been most kind to her, and at the end of the ceremony she told Stanton that she had been waiting a long time for a letter but felt recompensed after witnessing this presentation. She said Secretary Stanton replied: "General Custer is writing lasting letters on the pages of his country's history." *

Yes, indeed, and Secretary Stanton must know what he was talking about. The same thing was being said by Sheridan, by Chaplain Holmes, by Judge Bacon, by the national press, and by many others. Unquestionably they were right. No doubt about it!

18 Appomattox

CUSTER READ THE ORDER AND SHOOK BACK HIS CURLS WITH A QUICK jerk: the cavalry was to move to the extreme left of Grant's line — a day's march along the confusion of redoubts, trenches, bristling abatis, squalid supply depots, parks of muddy wagons. The country beyond the last fortification reminded Custer of the Wilderness — dreary, flat, scrub pines, dirt roads, worn-out land, ragged tobacco patches. Officers gossiped, as soldiers always do, about their destination. Was Sheridan being sent by a southern route to join Sherman? Some said, "No. We'll only circle south and west of Richmond, cut the last two railroads supplying Lee's army — the Southside to Lynchburg and the Richmond & Danville." These railroads crossed at Burkeville, sixty miles west of Richmond and Petersburg. If Union troops took that junction Lee would have to come out and fight, or be starved into surrender.

On March 29, 1865, the head of the cavalry reached Dinwiddie Court House. Custer, however, rode far in the rear, accompanying the wagon train. Cold rains drenched the countryside. The scrubby pine

* The *New York Times,* March 22, 1865, reports 17 enemy flags coming with Custer to Washington. Libbie told the incident about Stanton in a letter to Armstrong, March 26, 1865. In her "Beau Sabreur," p. 301, she seems to have confused it with the reception of Custer's flags after Saylor's Creek.

forests were soggy, the roads soft as mush. Armstrong detested his routine job but performed it philosophically. War hero that he was, he still accepted drudgery without complaint — especially when assigned the task by his adored Sheridan.

With three brigades, Custer corduroyed the roads, helped mules which sank belly-deep in the mud, joked with the men as he helped toss sacks and boxes out of mired wagons. Night overtook the train. The animals were unharnessed and fed. Armstrong lay down to rest and immediately fell asleep, as he always did. He awoke to find himself in two inches of water, got up and made a new bed of fence rails — hard, but dry.

In the morning as the wagons floundered by, Eliza looked at Custer's pallet and laughed, "Oh, I 'spect you wanted Miss Libbie with you . . . and she just as willing, and she'd have said, 'Oh, isn't this nice!' " [1]

All day long, and the day after, March 31, rain poured on the lumbering wagons, but an order from Sheridan brought Custer relief, and the prospect of exciting service. The general told him to leave one brigade with the train and come with two to Dinwiddie Court House — and fast.

Armstrong found the settlement of Dinwiddie Court House to be less than a dozen shabby buildings clustered around a dilapidated courthouse with timbers propping up one side of the roof.[2] He noticed a small church, and a tavern with gallery beside the muddy road — apparently the only dry place in town. Some "soiled doves" were making merry with officers there. But out of sight, on the drenched fields north of the squalid settlement, Sheridan's dismounted troopers were bombarding an almost invisible enemy. How many, no one knew! Evidently Lee had discovered the Union advance and had sent enough men to nip it at birth. He might succeed, too, unless Grant's infantry arrived quickly.

To encourage the embattled soldiers Sheridan, Merritt, and Custer rode out into the shrouded fields and along the barricades, each under his battle flag, with staff around him. Custer's standard was a new one which Libbie had made for him — red and blue silk with crossed sabers embroidered on both sides. In the tip of one of the points she had stitched her name. The gleaming silk seemed incongruous above the mud-caked riders.

At dark a heavy fog blanked out the fields and stopped the firing. Sheridan reported good news. He had received a telegram from Grant saying that General Warren, "Warren of the Topogs," should arrive with the V Corps by midnight — impossible, according to a court of inquiry later, but Custer did not know that when Sheridan ordered him to picket the line until morning.

Another wet night of long, dreary hours without sleep! Finally dawn paled the milk-white atmosphere, but no Warren had appeared. Instead, Sheridan rode out of the mists, his swarthy face wet under his pork-pie hat. Yes, by God, Warren was late, but he was coming in on side roads to get behind the enemy. The cavalry must advance, push whoever it was out there back onto Warren's approaching columns.

Custer started his line forward. Firing began almost at once. The Confederates retreated slowly, fighting as they went. Custer listened in vain for the volleys behind them which would tell him that Warren had come. After sunup the fog dissolved. Custer saw the enemy now — Confederate infantry, he believed, with temporary fortifications here and there. Some held their ground. Others were withdrawing along paths in the shiny-wet pine woods. Men who surrendered belonged to Pickett's corps. So Lee had sent out a wing powerful enough to annihilate Sheridan's cavalry! *Where was Warren?*

Custer advanced another two miles. Then the van of Warren's V Corps appeared — not behind the enemy, as expected, but on the Union cavalry's flank. At least that saved Sheridan's thin line of horse. Custer increased the fury of his charges and pushed the enemy back six more miles. A reporter for the *New York World,* George Alfred Townsend, watched Armstrong at this time and noted that the glamorous young man looked tired and haggard. Four days with little sleep and food had taken its toll, but the Boy General still waved his long straight sword over every unit which advanced.[3]

At noon Custer saw ahead of him a road junction known as Five Forks. In the gloomy pines stood the unmistakable line of breast-works — logs, rails, embankments. The fortifications stretched along the road for two miles, and somewhere behind them must be Hatcher's Run and the Southside Railroad with trains running to Lee's main force at Petersburg.

An aide from Sheridan rode up. He said Warren's infantry was to storm those works this afternoon, if enough of the V Corps came in. Custer should remain on the extreme left, bluster, make a noise, hold the enemy's attention, and be ready to cut around his flank while the infantry struck at the other end of the line.

Custer dismounted part of his division. Next to it Devin deployed his, on foot. Beyond him stood the first masses of Warren's infantry. More were arriving continually.[4]

Hour after hour Custer's men waited — the usual lull before battle. Custer set his bands to playing lively airs — "Nellie Bly," "Yankee Doodle," "Hail Columbia." Grant's aide, Horace Porter, rode up. The commanding general had sent him to observe the battle. Today's fight would be as important as any in the war. The two schoolmates talked a few minutes. If the North won this field, Lee would have only one supply line left — the Richmond & Danville Railroad. He could not depend on that alone, would have to evacuate Richmond and come out from behind the Petersburg fortifications which had protected him since last summer. Armstrong also learned that all of Warren's men had arrived at last, although they seemed slow getting in position. In this emergency every hour counted, because Lee might send rein-forcements on the Southside Railroad. Grant didn't trust Warren, didn't like him, and had indicated to Sheridan that Warren's removal from command would be acceptable.

At four o'clock distant bugles sounded the Union advance. Drum-beats throbbed along the line. Flags began to move as blocks of infantry went forward. The footmen bore the shock of this battle, far from Custer's position. Over there, whenever the lines faltered, Sheridan spurred in on black Rienzi, shaking his fist, encouraging, threatening, cursing, praying, insane with battle fury. Once he snatched his own standard from the color bearer, and jumped Rienzi over the earthworks into the midst of frightened Confederate gunners, who threw down their arms. By dark the whole enemy line was cut to pieces, and Custer clattered off beyond Hatcher's Run, rounding up prisoners and herding them back down the road like sheep. Lee had lost a whole wing of his army, and its commander, Major General George Pickett, barely escaped capture.

However, the victory failed to bring rejoicing to all the Northern soldiers. At the height of the battle, Sheridan had removed Warren from command — ostensibly for tardiness. No worse fate could befall a professional soldier. Warren, who had shown outstanding ability at Gettysburg, perhaps saving the day there, protested the removal and asked Sheridan to reconsider.

"Reconsider? Hell!" Little Phil snapped. "I don't reconsider my decisions. Obey the order!"

Sheridan had no good reason for dismissing a general at the moment of victory, thus ruining his military career when the war was practically ended. However, Grant wished it, and future favors might come from kowtowing to the great man's whim. Custer could have profited by noticing this weak streak in tough Phil Sheridan, but few men see the flaws in those who appreciate their own best qualities. Certainly Armstrong had seen nothing but good in McClellan and Pleasonton.

Sheridan gave Warren's V Corps to Griffin, Custer's teacher of tactics at West Point. That cadaverous, bean-pole lieutenant was a corps commander now! News correspondent Townsend visited Sheridan's bivouac in the pines that night. He found Little Phil sitting by a fire, examining a map. Gay as a chipmunk, the bulletheaded general wanted to talk, explain the battle. Close by lay Custer, trying to sleep — long hair over his face. The gaunt figure of General Griffin moved back and forth in the firelight. His new command presented many problems, many things to learn, and he constantly consulted aides and orderlies.[5]

At Five Forks Lee suffered his worst defeat thus far in the war and Sheridan, hero of the Shenandoah Valley, won new fame. With Pickett's five to seven thousand Confederates captured, the Army of Northern Virginia now had only two corps — Ewell's and Longstreet's — plus Fitzhugh Lee's cavalry with Rosser and Munford. This remnant could not hope to survive long. Horace Porter left the battlefield and galloped back to Grant's headquarters shouting the good news to roadside soldiers. One man raised his open hand to his face, thumb to nose, and replied, "No, you don't — April fool." [6]

That night of April 1 the sky above Petersburg trembled with red flashes. Grant had learned about the victory, and was beginning to bombard the enemy works preparatory to an assault. Custer was too sleepy to watch, but at dawn he was in the saddle, ready to go once more. His division, on the extreme left at Five Forks, had the van this morning and rode north across the Southside Railroad tracks. The day was fine after the rain, with blue sky, white cumulus clouds; creeks babbled bank-full, submerging beds of mint and watercress. Before noon Armstrong learned that Grant had won the Petersburg works and found them sparsely manned. Lee had gone. He must be racing for some western station on the Richmond & Danville Railroad — his last supply line. Custer hoped that his division would earn everlasting glory by being the first to catch him — a grand fox hunt. Surrounded by his red-necktied staff, Armstrong trotted along the road, restless as a game animal, popping his whip on his boot, whistling a tune to the accompanying band, his sharp nose turning watchfully from side to side with quick jerks that flipped his long hair.

Lee's army moved west on many roads, leaving a trail of broken-down horses, abandoned guns, and stragglers hiding in the woods. On April 3 Custer skirmished with gray-clad soldiers at Namozine Church. In the charge Tom Custer captured a battle flag and fourteen prisoners, three of them officers, thus earning a brevet captaincy and the admiration of his elder brother.

Next day, April 4, Armstrong scoured the country roads north and west, hunting Lee. At 7 A.M. on the fifth he rode into Jetersville, a station on the Richmond & Danville Railroad. The town consisted of a blacksmith shop, a store or two, a post office, and a few residences. Sheridan was here already; he reported that Lee's army was five or six miles up the track, at Amelia Court House. The Confederates lacked rations and could get no more unless they came down the railroad and routed the Union cavalry.[7]

Sheridan put his riders to work building fortifications across the tracks to hold back Lee. He also called in his other divisions on the double-quick, and sent word for the infantry to hurry. If the VI Corps would join him the war might end here!

But Lee did not come as expected. So General Crook led his division north, hunting him. Early on April 6, he reported that Lee had crossed the tracks at Amelia Court House and was marching west, evidently planning to bypass the Federal cavalry and return to the railroad beyond them at High Bridge, Farmville, or Appomattox Station, if he could march that far without supplies.

Sheridan sent his cavalry after him. They were to snap at the Confederates' heels, harry their trains, look for a weak spot in Lee's flank where part of the army could be cut off and held until the infantry arrived.

In midmorning Custer stopped to water horses. An aide galloped up saying that he had discovered what appeared to be a gap in Lee's line. Armstrong did not wait for the horses to finish drinking. His division dashed away. He found a large wagon train, with Ewell's corps behind it as rear guard. The exhausted teamsters dozed in their seats, too tired to do any driving — and none was needed. The mules followed the wagons in front of them, stopped and started with them. Custer's division charged, overturned the whole cavalcade, setting fire to wagon boxes and supplies. Thus Ewell's corps was cut off from Lee's army.

Old Baldy heard the commotion and sent Generals Custis Lee and Joseph B. Kershaw with their men to save the train, while he formed for a defensive action behind Saylor's Creek. Crook and Devin overtook him there and attacked, as the VI Corps streamed in for a knock-out blow. Custer, busy with the wagons, came late to the firing line and looked across the fields toward the enemy. Windrows of white smoke showed Ewell's position but the Union cavalry had been unable to break it. Custer ordered his bands to play and led a charge. Perhaps it was Custer luck, perhaps, as jealous enemies would say, he waited until other divisions had weakened the enemy. In any event, his musical whirlwind broke the line. Tom Custer leaped his horse over the enemy breastworks and reached for a battle flag. The color bearer shot him in the head. Tom fired his pistol at the man and handed the cap-tured flag to a follower. "Armstrong," he shouted, "the d——d rebels have shot me, but I've got my flag."

Tom turned his horse to charge again, but Armstrong stopped him. The bullet had entered Tom's cheek and come out his neck. Burnt powder pitted his face. After the first shock, blood began to flow. No matter! Tom wanted to go on. Armstrong put him under arrest and sent him to the surgeon, but he was very proud of Tom. That boy had taken two battle flags in three days. For his gallantry he received a brevet colonelcy and the Congressional Medal of Honor — a citation more distinguished than Armstrong ever received, but Autie showed no hint of jealousy. To a Custer it was always one for all and all for one. Armstrong would say that Tom, not he himself, should be the general.[8]

By dark the entire enemy defenses broke in confusion. Custer rode among the smoking ruins, dead horses and mutilated men. Disorgan-ized Union pillagers had been ahead of him. Frightened Confederate prisoners stood among the debris. Armstrong saw a little group of horsemen turn uncertainly this way and that, obviously at their wits' end. All were poorly mounted; some horses were straddled by two men. Their gray uniforms looked mussed and ragged.

Custer rode up to them. The party asked sullenly to be taken pris-oner, said they had been robbed by riotous Yankees who had taken their watches and gone on. The leader of this motley band was elderly, pop-eyed, one-legged Baldy Ewell, strapped on his flea-bitten charger, with a crutch under his arm. This legendary warrior, whose cannon had thundered in Custer's ears for two days at Gettysburg, looked pale and whipped today. The war had ended for him and he said it was ended for Lee, too.

With Ewell the once-invincible Army of Northern Virginia lost another seven or eight thousand men — the largest aggregate captured without negotiation during the war. Lee now had only Longstreet's corps, some odds and ends in a second corps under John B. Gordon, and Fitzhugh Lee's and Tom Rosser's bobtailed cavalry. Why fight longer? [9]

Among the prisoners were three notable generals — Robert E. Lee's son Custis; Paul Semmes, brother of the commander of the *Alabama;* and Joseph B. Kershaw, a South Carolinian who had served in the secession convention and in many battles of the war. He had watched Custer's charge at Cedar Creek last fall and said, now, that when Custer's flag appeared in the afternoon he had told his gunners to shoot it down, for he considered it the most dangerous on the field.

Custer's aide, who heard the story, laughed and replied that Kershaw's gunners had succeeded only in killing one of Custer's best horses.

Among other prisoners, Custer recognized a familiar face. Lieutenant Colonel Frank Huger had been an upperclassman at West Point who hazed "Fanny." Like his fellows, Huger looked tired and half-starved. Custer invited him and Kershaw to dinner. Eliza would prepare some delicious Southern dishes for them all.

The reaction of these two South Carolinians — Kershaw and Huger — to Custer's hospitality reveals their characters. Kershaw, for the rest of his life, would be a Custer admirer, proud to say that he had surrendered his sword personally to such a gallant soldier. Frank Huger, on the other hand, whined forever after, claiming that Custer took his spurs, and entertained him only to display his own superiority. Such diverse judgments of Custer's every act were polarizing now, and prejudices for and against him would crystallize in the years ahead. No one seemed able to interpret him as a human being with both good and bad characteristics. He was either an "egotistical show-off" or a spotless Sir Galahad.*

Next morning, April 7, Custer selected, for his bodyguard, troopers who had distinguished themselves in the last battle — his usual custom. As he marched off, passing acres of prisoners, he ordered his bands to play "Dixie," and he waved his hat to the forlorn men. They responded with cheers. His troopers tossed hardtack to them as they rode by — a gesture of friendship which depleted their own rations.[10]

As yet nobody knew how best to get ahead of the remainder of Lee's army. The Burkeville junction was behind them now, but Lee might be headed for one of the railroads beyond, and thus escape to either Danville or Lynchburg. Sheridan again sent Crook on Lee's trail. Merritt was ordered to take Custer and Devin southwest, get ahead of Lee in case he crossed the Southside Railroad. Custer's division led the way. At Prince Edward Court House, a messenger came from Merritt telling Custer to halt, rest his men, and await further orders. Crook had struck the enemy's rear but could not stop him. The final battle might be fought somewhere close.

Custer, always averse to inactivity, was pondering this order when his guard brought in a Confederate straggler. The fellow said that supplies for Lee were being unloaded at Appomattox Station, twenty miles ahead. Lee's army must be headed that way.

Custer decided to evade Merritt's order to halt. He sent a courier to him, telling about the trains at Appomattox Station, and saying that he would go after those supplies unless he received contrary orders. Then he swung his division into the road and set off at a fast trot — much too fast for "contrary orders" to overtake him.

* F. Whittaker, *Complete Life of . . . Custer . . .* , p. 303. Kershaw's account is printed in M. Merington, *Custer Story,* p. 153. See also E. Eliot, *West Point in the Confederacy,* p. 358, E. P. Alexander, "Lee at Appomattox," p. 929, and J. C. Haskell's "Reminiscences," p. 124. In fairness to Huger it should be noted that his disparaging remarks are what Alexander says he said.

Darkness had almost fallen when Custer heard, through the pines on the hills ahead, a train's whistle. Appomattox Station at last! He ordered a charge and with the first two regiments dashed forward.

Four trains stood on the track, with wagons beside them being loaded with rations by lantern light. A Confederate advance guard fled up the dark road into the pines. Custer manned the locomotives with troopers who understood wood-burning engines and enjoyed hearing the trains bump up and down the track, whistles blowing. A sudden explosion — a sheet of flame and breath-taking concussion — staggered the dismounted Union soldiers deployed at the station. Enemy artillery in the woods across the tracks were so close that they had overshot their mark. In the darkness Custer ordered an immediate attack. Perhaps he was charging into Lee's main army? No matter! His confident voice rang out. Troopers hearing it groped forward with blind courage, bugles in every troop blowing a charge.

Custer audacity won the field. He captured a park of artillery — twenty-five guns — and followed the retreating Confederates along the dark road through the pines. He came to meadows, fought his way across them to a brook. Beyond it — two miles now from Appomattox Station — his men reached the stage road running west from Appomattox Court House to Lynchburg. He found gray-clad soldiers here, but they retreated both up and down the pike. A cannon opened fire from the direction of Lynchburg. Which way was Lee's army?

It was recklessly dangerous for Custer to go on, but he knew Devin would be coming close behind him on the road. So he divided his division, adding to his peril. He ordered one unit to charge west toward the cannon flashes. The rest of his men skirmished east along both sides of the highway toward Appomattox Court House, still two miles away. At 8 p.m. Custer saw, above the red flashes of his own skirmish line, the yellow lights of the village — five houses, the courthouse and jail. On the dark hills beyond glowed myriad watchfires. Lee's entire army! The Confederates' only possible avenue of escape was along the Lynchburg highroad, which Custer held. His line was very thin, his men and horses very tired. Yet he faced greater odds than at Gettysburg.

Now if ever he needed the music of his band playing "The Battle Hymn of the Republic":

> *He has sounded forth the trumpet that shall never call retreat;*
> *He is sifting out the hearts of men before His judgment-seat;*
> *Oh, be swift, my soul, to answer Him! be jubilant, my feet!*
> *Our God is marching on.*

Armstrong warned his men what lay ahead and placed them across the road as carefully as he could; then he spurred off to find Sheridan, who must be with the oncoming columns. He found him in a little frame house near Appomattox Station, and explained his men's position.[11] They had headed off Lee's army but could not hope to hold it.

Sheridan understood at once, ordered all his cavalry forward on the road to Appomattox Court House, and sent word for the nearest infantry to hurry. A special courier carried a message to Grant, describing Custer's success. It concluded: "If General Gibbon and the Fifth Corps can get up to-night *we will perhaps finish the job in the morning.*"[12]

Custer galloped back to his line. Lee had not moved during his absence, and at midnight Devin's relief column arrived. Armstrong withdrew his men, then rode to the field hospital to console the wounded. The surgeon reported that he had never before received so many severe cases in so short a time.* The night fight had been costly, but if Custer had not dared it Lee would have got his supplies from the trains and been well on his way to Lynchburg by this time. As things stood now, Lee might still force his way through the thin cavalry line across the stage road unless the infantry arrived.

Custer, nervously impatient, rode back to Sheridan's headquarters. Little Phil was still awake. Like Custer, he could not sleep. Horsemen were still coming in and the infantry's van was reported close behind. Marching feet thumped continually past headquarters. Custer stayed only a few minutes, then galloped back along the column. He wanted

---

* The heavy casualties are reported by H. E. Tremain, *Last Hours of Sheridan's Cavalry,* p. 231. Custer, in his report, *O. R.,* I, XLVI, pt. 1, p. 1132, says his loss was slight.

to be sure that the thin line across the road was holding and that his own men would be rested and ready to reinforce it when necessary.

A misty dawn found Custer trying to inspect the enemy's position — almost impossible in the fog. Bugles in both armies began blowing reveille. Soon Confederate cannon set the mists whirling. Confederate cavalry appeared on the Union left. Dismounted Union horsemen stopped them, but drew back, too weak to countercharge. The fog was lifting now, and Custer saw Lee's Army of Northern Virginia advancing in battle formation on the road from Appomattox Court House, Gordon's corps leading the way, determined to open the road. Those veterans knew that cavalry could not withstand a massive infantry thrust.

Custer watched the dismounted bluecoats give way, after stubbornly resisting the host. He formed his division in columns of squadrons to charge the enemy flank as its line advanced. Then he beheld a welcome spectacle. At his left, behind the withdrawing horse, blue-clad infantry streamed out of the pines on the road from Appomattox Station. The van of Edward O. C. Ord's Army of the James had outmarched Gibbon to the scene. Ord's aide-de-camp was Peter Michie, the laughing Buckeye whom Custer had liked at West Point. Sheridan, too, had come with this army, and now aligned it impressively across the road, then drew off the last of the retreating cavalry. Custer remained in position to charge the rebel flank as they met the infantry. He ordered sabers drawn — a glittering sight on that fine April morning. Then across the field an unusual movement attracted his nervous eyes. A horseman bearing a white flag galloped toward him. The Confederates, seeing the solid wall of blue infantry before them, knew that their last chance was gone.[13]

The flag-bearer introduced himself to Custer as Captain Simms of Longstreet's staff, and said he had come from Lee to request a suspension of hostilities. Custer sent the word immediately to Sheridan. What happened next is controversial. Longstreet, in a book published in 1896, said that Custer rode into his lines with the flag of truce, claiming that he and Sheridan were independent of Grant and that they wanted immediate and unconditional surrender. According to an article written by E. P. Alexander, who was not present, Longstreet decided to bluff Custer by threatening to have Pickett deploy his corps and wipe out Custer's division. Longstreet said, further, that this threat of a force which no longer existed made Custer back down meekly.

The weak point in this story is that Armstrong knew as well as any man in the Union Army what had happened to Pickett's corps at Five Forks, and neither Longstreet nor anyone else ever scared Custer with a dead horse. Longstreet's story became still less credible in 1903, when General Gordon claimed that the peculiar request for surrender came to him, not Longstreet. The story was further discredited by Custer's chief of staff, Edward Whitaker, who recalled that he was present when the flag of truce arrived. He stated that Custer sent him back with the flag of truce — certainly a natural thing for a major general to do. If Pete Longstreet bluffed anybody, it must have been Chief of Staff Whitaker, whom he mistook for Custer.*

Another sidelight on Custer at the surrender appears in a story told by his friend, Alexander Pennington. He remembered how the two armies waited for Lee to meet Grant after the flag of truce had been

* This is another of the many controversial incidents in Custer's life. Douglas Southall Freeman, *Lee's Lieutenants*, III, p. 737, gives four sources for it, W. M. Owen, J. C. Haskell, E. P. Alexander, and J. Longstreet. Freeman notes that none qualify as contemporary eye-witnesses. Longstreet told the story in *From Manassas to Appomattox*, p. 627, thirty-one years after it was supposed to have happened to him. The first published account appeared in Owen, *In Camp & Battle with the Washington Artillery*, twenty-five years after it could have happened. Haskell's account in the Virginia Historical Society Library was typed in 1903. Certainly the best evidence does not indicate that Custer went back with the surrender flag as Longstreet says. Sheridan's official report at the time, *O. R.*, I, XLVI, pt. 1, p. 1110, says Custer, on receipt of truce flag, "sent the information to me at once" and he, General Sheridan, rode over with an escort to consult with the enemy. Sheridan's aide, Michael Sheridan, also scouts the Custer surrender story. Custer's chief of staff, Edward W. Whitaker, tells his story in a letter to Mrs. Custer, dated February 6, 1899, and in articles in the *Washington Post*, January 29, and February 12, 1899. See also P. V. D. Stern, *End to Valor*, pp. 250–251 and 393–394.

delivered. A ditch, he said, separated the blue and gray soldiers where Custer sat his horse. Armstrong turned to him, saying, "Let's go see if we can find Cowan."

The two officers rode to the edge of the stream and called to an officer in gray. The man knew Cowan and said he would send for him.

Soon Cowan came on horseback and jumped the ditch.

"Hello, you damned redheaded rebel," Custer laughed, and they all shook hands affectionately. While chatting, Pennington said, there was a stir in the Confederate camp. Lee, in his resplendent uniform, came down a nearby road and crossed a bridge over the ditch. He saw the Blue and Gray conference and ordered it broken up. There must be no communication between soldiers before he met Grant. As soon as Lee had gone, the officers came together again, and were still chatting when Lee returned.[14]

Custer might have behaved in this manner, but Pennington's story, like the others, cannot be accepted wholly. True, there was considerable fraternizing between enemy officers on that fine Sabbath morning of April 9, 1865, but when Grant met Lee at the McLean residence in Appomattox Court House, Custer was there, along with Sheridan, Ord, and Merritt.

These second-rank generals waited below the board steps to the porch of the two-story brick house. The front yard was twenty feet across and Lee's orderly held his gray horse, Traveller, there. The man had taken the bit from the horse's mouth so he could nibble the fresh grass.

When the conference in the house ended, Lee appeared on the porch — a statuesque figure, handsomely dressed in full uniform, embroidered belt, dress sword. Apparently not noticing the officers below him, he paused a moment, smote his gauntleted hands together in an absent-minded way, came down the steps, mounted his horse and gathered the reins. Shabby little Grant followed him and passed in front of the big gray horse. The little conqueror looked up at the resplendent man he had vanquished and touched his hat. The gray man on the gray horse answered the salute, then reined away.

As soon as both commanders' backs were turned, the waiting officers crowded up the steps and into the house, scuffling for relics. The house owner, Wilmer McLean, offered to sell the furniture. Sheridan paid twenty dollars for the little oval-topped table on which the surrender terms were written, then presented it to Custer. General Gibbon rode up in time to see Armstrong skipping down the steps with it on his shoulder. Sheridan smiled as he watched his favorite swing up into the saddle and ride away balancing the furniture on his head. With the gift, Sheridan sent a note to Libbie saying: "My dear Madam — I respectfully present to you the small writing-table on which the conditions of the surrender of the Confederate Army of Northern Virginia were written by Lt. General Grant — and permit me to say, Madam, that there is scarcely an individual in our service who has contributed more to bring this about than your very gallant husband." [15]

The afternoon was pleasantly busy for Custer. Generals Griffin and Merritt were assigned the task of paroling the Confederate Army. Armstrong hunted eagerly for old friends. He found Gimlet Lea and invited him to dinner. Gimlet had been exchanged since Armstrong stood up at his wedding but was now a prisoner of war again. Custer also found Fitzhugh Lee. A fellow officer reported seeing the two cavalrymen roll on the ground together, laughing like schoolboys. He supposed they had been classmates at West Point instead of pupil and teacher.[16]

Where was Tom Rosser? Custer asked, but he failed to find him. Rosser had escaped before the surrender, cutting across fields north of the Union Army with two brigades. Munford was with him.

That night Custer wrote a congratulatory address to his men which must have kept him busy into the late hours.

It began formally:

> With profound gratitude toward the God of battles, by whose blessings our enemies have been humbled and our arms rendered triumphant, your commanding general avails himself of this his first opportunity to express to you his admiration of the heroic manner . . . which to-day resulted in the surrender of the enemy's entire army.

Then he itemized the division's victories, saying "the record established by your indomitable courage is unparalleled in the annals of war." He closed with:

And now, speaking for myself alone, when the war is ended and the task of the historian begins; when those deeds of daring which have rendered the name and fame of the Third Cavalry Division imperishable, are inscribed upon the bright pages of our country's history, I only ask that my name be written as that of the commander of the Third Cavalry Division.[17]

In the morning, rain deluged the scattered encampments. Custer was ordered up the tracks to Prospect Station, where the 3d Division made camp in dreary wet pines. As soon as Armstrong got under shelter with dry paper he wrote his first letter to Libbie since the surrender: "My Darling — Only time to write a word. Heart too full for utterance." He had to be careful not to blot the ink with wet hands, but continued: "Thank God *Peace* is at hand. And thank God the 3d Division has performed the most important duty of this campaign. . . . Oh I have so much to tell you, and no time. . . . Hurrah for Peace and my little Durl."

Armstrong folded the letter and handed it to the orderly who was carrying the mail. As soon as it was gone he received a telegram. Libbie was in Richmond, less than a hundred miles up the railroad track. Senator Chandler had arranged an excursion to the fallen capital for members of the Joint Committee on the Conduct of the War and their wives. Libbie had come with them and was staying in the Executive Mansion. She had slept in Jeff Davis's bed.

Next morning, before Libbie was awake, Autie strode into her room. He had not stopped to get permission for a furlough. "So, after all these years of fighting," he quipped, "you beat me into Richmond."

Libbie thought he looked very thin and tired. She got up and they examined the flag of truce which Autie had received — the fringed linen towel that had brought the Civil War to an end. After she dressed they prowled through Jeff Davis's mansion and pronounced it handsome but overfurnished with mirrors and draperies. Mrs. Davis had taken the silver and linen but left her china, which Libbie believed to be Sèvres.[18]

Armstrong and Libbie went back to the army camp. She liked to remember that she was the first woman to ride the Southside Railroad after the evacuation of Richmond. He also arranged for her to accompany the column on its march across Virginia to Washington. Mrs. Pennington also had joined her husband, so the trip promised to be festive. Armstrong rode a new horse, a fiery four-mile racing stallion named Don Juan, picked up on the march to Appomattox and bought from the government, he was careful to add. For Libbie he had a smooth-gaited pacer he called Custis Lee. The animal, captured at Five Forks, had belonged to one of Lee's staff members. A carriage was provided for Libbie when she tired of the saddle. Eliza, with her jolly stories and sheet-iron stove, accompanied them in her own antiquated vehicle.

The column rode north leisurely. Maytime in Virginia: lilacs, azaleas, dogwood glowing in every wood lot, every hill and meadow recalling some experience to Armstrong. Together they rode through Trevilian Station (still in ruins), crossed the Rapidan, passed Brandy Station where he had captured the battery and got that wound which earned him the furlough that led to their marriage. At Bull Run, Autie probably pointed out where he, as a boy lieutenant, had tried to deliver a message to McDowell. And Libbie, unlike so many wives, was not bored with his tales. No need for him to want grandchildren who would listen, saucer-eyed. But Libbie still hoped for them.

On May 23 a grand review of all combat forces was scheduled in Washington. Only about half of the army could be spared, but that was enough for a spectacular parade. Custer's men were to lead the column. The day before the ceremony his division camped at Bladensburg. Rain pattered on the tents all night as troopers polished brass buttons and blacked boots. Some of them were looking forward to civilian life, some were not. For many, the army had become a profession. Their young legs were bowed to the saddle. Their hearts beat time to drums. They liked the soldiers' trade. Moreover, every private knew now that with peace he would never be a corporal. Sergeants would go home to face the girls without a commission.

The rain stopped at dawn and the sun rose on a city of clean-washed brick buildings, the sweet smell of fresh earth and green lawns. At nine o'clock a cannon blast started the parade. General Meade led the way down the hill past the Capitol. The dome was finished now — white as alabaster against a clear blue sky. The Union it stood for had been saved. School children packed the grassy slope, their shrill voices piping above the ripple of passing hoofs.

Sheridan was absent — on special duty in New Orleans — so Wesley Merritt rode in his place. Young, handsome, straight in the saddle, he was as fine a cavalryman as Custer, perhaps, but he lacked color. Journalists had not found him a good subject for news, although he sometimes wrote reports as flamboyant as Custer's — but all to no purpose, it seems. The crowd scarcely knew him.

At the foot of Capitol Hill, the horsemen wheeled onto Pennsylvania Avenue in a column of platoons, sixteen horses wide, sabers drawn — the formation in which they had charged on many a field. Tattered banners bore the names of Antietam, Gettysburg, Winchester. Custer rode at the head of the 3d Division in somber major general's skirted coat. The boots on his bowlegs had square toes and heels run over on the outside, but they were polished until the leather shone like obsidian. Beneath his saddle pranced the mottled bay, Don Juan, gleaming like mahogany, with prominent veins etching his impatient legs. White foam tossed from his champing bit. Over his flowing mane and pointed ears Custer looked up Pennsylvania Avenue. Housetops were black with people, all windows bulging with heads thick as grape clusters. The packed sidewalks, dotted with little parasols and waving handkerchiefs, were as gay as petunia beds. Small boys in the trees along the avenue screeched for attention. Behind him Custer heard the bands — his skirmish-line bands. Today, the sun shone on polished brass trombones and trumpets. The big bass drums bobbed along on sedate horses. The 3d Division's lifeblood pulsed with those bands.

The crowd began to cheer. People had recognized his broad hat, the red tie tossed debonairly over one shoulder and the mist of red ties on the men behind him — proudest badge in the Army of the Potomac. The roar of recognition frenzied Don Juan. Custer could feel between his knees the animal's heart pound with terror, but the Boy General was used to fractious mounts. He sat easily in the saddle, his lithe body a part of the curvetting horse, his blue eyes dancing as he smiled at the crowds. Women waved. Fathers held up little boys to see him: *There he is. Look! That's Custer! Old Curly, greatest cavalryman who ever lived. Twelve horses shot under him. See his broad hat? A bullet creased it. He had a lock of that hair clipped off by flying lead. Got wounded in a charge at Brandy Station. Clap for him! Yell!*

Cynics in the crowd who knew Custer's big eccentricities and little conceits admitted that, with all his faults, the people loved him. It was true, too, that when dangerous work must be done and others quailed, Custer did the job, and did it merrily.

At 15th Street the van of the 3d Division turned around the Treasury Building. Pennsylvania Avenue, all the way back to the Capitol, was filled now with advancing horsemen, a stream of blue centaurs flowing lavalike between human banks. Ahead, Custer saw the White House. The President's reviewing stand stood at the top of the hill. As the column wheeled, three hundred girls in white rose to their feet, showered Custer with flowers and began to sing. He leaned over to catch a bouquet. For a moment his reins slacked, and in that split second Don Juan bolted.

Racing ahead, horse and rider passed the marshals and the van. At the President's reviewing stand Custer tried to give a saber salute, but instead he hit his hat, lost it and his saber, too. Then, with both hands free, he brought the frantic beast under control.

Scoffers would accuse him of inciting the animal to make a grand display — the old Custer show-off trick. Who can say? His admirers called attention to the mastery with which he conquered the fiery steed.[19] A *World* reporter, with no prejudice for or against Custer, wrote his paper: "In the sunshine his [Custer's] locks unskeined, stream a foot behind him. . . . It is like the charge of a Sioux chieftain" — ominous simile. Since boyhood, Custer had been likened to an Indian warrior.

All day long and all next day the Army marched along Pennsylvania Avenue. Then the show was over. A few workmen cleaned the deserted street, swept away scraps of dirty paper, withered flowers, and horse manure. The war had ended, and when Custer rode out to bid good-by to the 3d Division at its encampment he faced the most difficult ordeal of his life. Never did he try harder to be brave.

Somebody in the serried blue ranks before him shouted: "A tiger for Old Curly!"

Deep-throated cheers rocked the air. The solid formation boiled with képis, tossed up from ranks. The Boy General froze to attention, lips quivering. He dared not look at Libbie when he rode back to the place where she awaited him.

"We shall soon be enjoying the rich blessings of peace,"[20] he wrote his sister. Of course he meant every word of it. . . . Or did he?

19 Texas

DURING THE WEEKS FOLLOWING WAR'S END, LIBBIE WORRIED ABOUT ARM-strong's haggard looks, his exhausted condition, the lassitude so different from his characteristic enthusiasm. He had nothing to look forward to, no plans to interest him. The boy who had become a brigadier at twenty-three and a major general at twenty-four, who had received the Confederate surrender flag, and was accustomed to seeing his name continually in the newspapers, had become a forgotten man. Then one day he received a letter from New Orleans marked CONFIDENTIAL. As he read it, Armstrong's spirits revived. Phil Sheridan, commander of the area west of the Mississippi and south of Arkansas, wrote to inquire if Custer would accompany him on an expedition into Texas against Kirby Smith. The last rebel general still defied the United States Government. Libbie did not know that Sheridan might be sent to invade Mexico also, to drive out the French — who had disregarded the Monroe Doctrine in setting up an empire there under Maximilian while the North was engrossed in civil war.

Custer accepted Sheridan's proposal at once, and soon received the official order. Tired as he was, he would recuperate more rapidly if not fretting about his future. With Libbie and staff — including Eliza, of course — he boarded a westbound train, planning to embark on an Ohio River steamboat.* The trip was a holiday for these irrepressible young men. They began it by playing a practical joke on the train men. According to railroad rules, special coaches were reserved for ladies. No man unaccompanied by a woman was allowed in them. This separated Armstrong and Libbie from their official "family." Passengers had to change cars often and the young officers determined to thwart regulations. Libbie joined the fun. At the next change she distributed among the aides her hand baggage — cloak, umbrella, gloves, shawl, and lunch-basket — before she and Autie boarded the waiting ladies' car. Then, as the train whistled for departure, the aides came running. At the car steps they waved the feminine baggage in the brakeman's face, said the ladies had gone ahead, mounted the steps, and entered the sanctuary.

The passengers were all in holiday mood. The war was ended and the train was packed with soldiers. At every stop, bands and parades welcomed home-coming heroes. Custer's aides kept the coach in a hubbub. They sang war songs and wandered endlessly up and down the aisle. Like country boys on a vacation, they shouted jokes from end to end of the car, hoping everybody would hear and join the hilarity. Beneath

---

* Custer presumably received this order May 22, 1865, the day before the review (O. R., I, XLVI, pt. 3, p. 1195). In 1887, Libbie Custer (Tenting on the Plains, p. 50) says they embarked on the steamboat at Louisville. In 1876, co-operating with F. Whittaker in Complete Life of . . . Custer . . . , she let him say (p. 320) that they embarked at Parkersburg, West Virginia.

her gaiety Libbie felt homesick, but she did her best to hide it. She sincerely wanted to go back to Monroe for a few days of glory; but she had made her choice of a husband, and his interests came first.

As night settled over the rocking train it entered the mountains. The aides turned up their collars to sleep, as they had done on many a battlefield. Two of them, wanting to lie across the entire seat, evicted their civilian seatmates by an old trick. They said that their overcoats had been taken from smallpox victims [1] — the rural hoax used later, with variations, in stories by Mark Twain and Owen Wister.

At an "eating stop" in Ohio the restaurant keeper refused to serve Eliza on account of her color. Custer had a Southerner's prejudice against the colored race, but he also had a Southerner's affection for Negro individuals he knew. He insisted on having Eliza served and dared the proprietor to throw him and his staff out of the dining room.

The first real relaxation for Armstrong began on the Ohio River after he climbed up the gangplank to the lofty decks of a steamboat. Here was a new world of luxury for him and Libbie. She beamed at the long avenues of comfortable deck chairs, the spacious ladies' parlors, the paintings of doves, wisteria, and fair maidens on all stateroom doors, the glittering chandeliers in the dining saloon, the Negro waiters in their white coats. Hour after hour, she and Autie watched the wooded shores of the Ohio River slip past them as the great ship glided down the stealthy current into the Mississippi.

Out on the broad expanse of the Father of Waters the steamboat wheeled south. Armstrong and Libbie, in their deck chairs, watched the black smoke from the steamboat's twin stacks trailing over the water behind them as the North they knew receded below the sky line. Ahead, over the southern horizon, they watched northbound vessels loom up, grow in size as they approached, whistle recognition and pass — some side-wheelers, some with stern wheels throwing white showers of spray.

After the first day or two, Armstrong became his old restless self again, striding along the decks, up and down companionways, two steps at a time. He prowled around the dark boiler room below water level, inspected the horses: Jack Rucker and Libbie's Custis Lee. Never able to stay long in one place, he climbed to the airy pilothouse on the texas. Military sites that he had read about in the newspapers interested him — Island No. 10, Fort Pillow, Vicksburg. At one landing he saw a man swing up the gangplank on crutches.

"That's General John B. Hood," somebody said.

Custer galloped down the steps to see him. The two veterans sat together and talked cordially about their battles — no bitterness, no regrets. Armstrong sent for Libbie. Hood had trouble rising on his crutches and wooden leg to meet "the little lady," but she immediately put him at ease and took care not to interrupt the conversation.

As the steamboat glided into the deep South — Louisiana and Mississippi — Libbie and Armstrong noticed how the fields disappeared behind levees. Only occasionally could they see the tops of trees. In the evenings, as darkness settled over the river, they smelled fragrant orange blossoms and watched the reflections of stars on the creeping waters. Now and again a ship, spangled with lights, went by, headed back to the distant world they were leaving.

New Orleans appeared to them as curious as a foreign city. They marveled at quaint gables surmounted by chimney pots, and the lacy ironwork on lofty galleries. Mysterious entryways revealed vistas of tropical plants in brick courtyards. Together they visited the *Vieux Carré,* listened to the French patois, watched sailors, Negroes, priests, and strutting pigeons. They laughed like children when Autie nodded toward a fat Cajun woman, hinting that Libbie — always embarrassed about the slimness of her figure — might want to look like that. The sight of a bright turban on a colored mammy prompted Armstrong to tell Libbie to buy one like it for Eliza. They dined in all the famous restaurants. Armstrong had tasted oysters first in the Peninsular Campaign. Here he ate them again, fresh from Pass Christian. He introduced Libbie to bouillabaisse, crab gumbo, crawfish bisque, and shrimps *à la Créole.*

On shopping sprees they breezed through fashionable stores. Armstrong watched Libbie try on hats in the most exclusive shops. She, never Armstrong, objected to the prices. He always showed the same enthusiasm for her clothes that Libbie, in turn, showed for his horses and guns.

They learned that General Winfield Scott was staying at their hotel. Custer presented his compliments. Gallant "Old Fuss and Feathers" asked to meet Mrs. Custer, explaining that age would prevent him from raising his great weight to an erect position for the introduction. With this understood, Libbie went in, but the aged general's gallant training would not let him remain seated. He struggled to rise, even got halfway to his feet with an awkward bow which discomforted Libbie. She felt compassion for the gigantic, decrepit figure, so unlike the heroic picture of him which had always hung in her father's Monroe home.

The Custers dined with Sheridan in his mansion. The grim little man with the cannon-ball head lived lavishly. Surrounded by a legion of servants, he still retained the colored cook who had served him during the war. After dinner Armstrong and the short-legged general sat on the gallery, without Libbie, and talked of the future. Sheridan had something to say which might distress her. Kirby Smith had surrendered, but the United States Army was to be prepared now to invade Mexico and drive out the French. Pontoons for crossing the Rio Grande had been sent to Alexandria, up the Red River in Louisiana. Forty-five hundred troops were disembarking there, too, and Custer must organize them for a march to Texas. Wesley Merritt was leading another column to San Antonio. In case the invasion failed to materialize, the troops were to stay and maintain order in the recently rebellious South.[2]

Before Custer and his staff left New Orleans they spent all their money, and had to purchase on credit their passage up the Red River. Such predicaments never worried these boy officers. Libbie remembered how one of the aides swaggered around the transport's deck jingling his last twenty-six cents against his penknife to prove he was solvent.

The boat trip up the Red River lacked the luxury of the Mississippi River passage. The scenery was monotonous, also. Spring floods had inundated both banks and the tree trunks now wore stockings of gray mud. Above the old waterline dreary, gray moss hung in mournful streamers from the concave branches of half-dead cypress trees.

Days passed with no variation from the stinking waters except an occasional squalid camp where the steamboat docked for wood. But Custer and his youthful staff always seemed happy. They congregated under the deck awning, played their guitars, and sang war songs. Armstrong practiced shooting his favorite rifle at alligators which basked along the steamy shore. Aides added to the fun by teasing Eliza, telling her that 'gaters hid in the ship's hold and came up at night hunting colored folks.

Late in June the steamer arrived at Alexandria. As the vessel tied up at the levee Armstrong and Libbie joined the crowd near the purser's office, waiting their turn to land. Both wrote letters home during the delay, Libbie to her father, Armstrong to his brother and sister. These letters were to be left on board for mailing down-river on the boat's return trip. Libbie had learned from Autie this habit of writing home whenever there was a moment to spare.

The Boy General and his wife stepped down the gangplank. On the levee a tall, thin man raised his broad-brimmed planter's hat. Libbie, pleased always at being noticed, saw something familiar about him. He introduced himself and she recognized the Southern beau of her Monroe school days. The slender boy had aged greatly in five years, but after Libbie recovered from the shock he appeared to be unchanged.

The Custers moved into a vacant house which had been General Banks's headquarters during the war. In the days that followed they rode out to see the plantation owned by Libbie's romantic Southern friend and received another shock. That fabled mansion with its magnolias and mocking birds was shabby, like most things in the South. Indeed, Libbie was much impressed by Southern shabbiness everywhere. The houses all lacked the little comforts she expected — simple things like running water. She blamed this on slavery. These people, accustomed to being waited on constantly, had eschewed laborsaving conveniences. She found the Negroes here in the deep South much more backward, more bestial, than the Virginia darkies.

Libbie sensed that the many diplomatic problems confronting her husband might be too much for his impetuous nature. She complained, years later, that a boy of twenty-five was expected to act the subtle part of a statesman, to conciliate Southern citizens and at the same time punish unremittingly all evidences of rebellion.[3]

Strange as it seems, Custer had more trouble with his own men than with the conquered foe. The war had ended and the volunteers assigned him wanted to go home. None of them had ever been subjected to rigid discipline. They considered officers their equals, pillaged the farms of citizens whom Custer hoped to conciliate, were constantly absent without leave, and deserted at every opportunity. One colonel told Custer that his men wanted the general to explain the reason for his last order. Another regiment sent Custer a petition for the dismissal of their colonel. Armstrong had stepped from the Academy into high command and only knew how to inspire disciplined soldiers. These rough Westerners considered him a marionette. At one inspection a regiment turned out in grotesque costumes. Some had on caps, some hats with brims turned up or down. Some wore boots, others shoes covered with ashes. Some wore jackets, some stood in their shirt sleeves. Some had their breeches stuck into their boots. Some carried their cartridge boxes upside down — all very funny to a Western volunteer, but Custer, the practical joker, was not amused.

He escaped from this constant insubordination by riding away every evening with Libbie — she in her stylish lead-weighted riding habit on Custis Lee, Armstrong beside her on Jack Rucker. Together they cantered out of the dusty encampment and its frustrating problems. For an hour or more they forgot shabby Alexandria, its sultry streets flecked with cotton scraps, the levee piled high with dirty bales awaiting steamboats. After the hottest day the countryside seemed cool and fragrant. Roses and Osage oranges hedged the fields for miles. Custer reveled in the picturesque scenery, the gorgeous sunsets, and he never forgot to include little Libbie in the magnificence of the sky. As an eminent fighting man he dared admit appreciation of aesthetic things without fear of being called effeminate. Libbie responded, glowing with pleasure when she saw him happy.

On one ride they went to the old, ornate schoolhouse with turreted corners called Sherman Institute in honor of its antebellum principal, William Tecumseh Sherman. Reconstruction politicians had not yet inflamed the people against him, and Sherman's name was still respected in the South. Libbie thought that the desolate stone building seemed out of place in the dreary pine forest where it stood.

The Custers' carefree rides were always shadowed by threats of mutiny in camp. Two soldiers were court-martialed, one for desertion, the other for refusing to obey a superior officer, and both were sentenced to be shot. The troops protested, threatened to shoot the general instead of the prisoners. Custer ignored the threats and prepared to carry out the sentences. The more menacing the soldiers became the more he determined to be obeyed. No questions! No back talk! One man against a regiment were the odds he liked.

The day of execution came. It was whispered that Custer would be shot before his order was carried out but he rode off fearlessly to the place of execution. Libbie, in quarters, buried her head in a pillow so as not to hear the shots which might mean the death of Armstrong or of the culprits. Out on the parade ground both prisoners were blindfolded before a firing squad. Armstrong stood at one side, daring any mutineer to do his worst. Then, at the last moment, he led aside the least guilty of the two and let the deserter — a bad man, disliked by the troops — be shot down. Thus the Boy General demonstrated that his word was law and no man could intimidate him. The incident might be dismissed as necessary military discipline, but Custer would get in trouble during the years ahead for executing deserters. This early experience may have influenced his later actions.*

After six weeks in Alexandria, the time came to start a 150-mile march west to Hempstead, Texas. (Custer, in a letter home, said the

---

* Libbie Custer's memory can never be depended on. She was not a trained observer. An effort to check the true details of this incident has failed.

distance was 250 miles.) Libbie induced him to cut off his long hair, so he would be more comfortable in the hot weather. But she did not try to break him of the small-boy manner of wearing his clothes with reckless abandon, his hat balanced perilously on his head. Instead, Libbie laughed indulgently, just as his mother had at the first child to survive from her marriage to Emanuel.

Dozens of Negroes asked to follow the column west. Custer told them they could not come along. He also refused the proposals of cotton brokers who wished to use the army to protect their speculations. Libbie remembered later that one man offered her husband twenty-five thousand dollars for the privilege of accompanying him,[4] but Custer, guilty of nepotism, of seeking political favors, of enhancing his own exploits, had never yet been accused of graft. Whether he would continue to withstand this temptation, in the era of corruption in Grant's administration ahead, remained to be seen.

On the march Libbie and Armstrong slept in an ambulance converted into a bedroom. Special receptacles had been built in the curtains for her toilet articles, shoes, and shawl. The regimental saddler had stitched LADY CUSTER in cavalry yellow on the canvas cover of a regulation canteen. In camp the ambulance was parked in front of Custer's tent. Every night and morning the general lifted his wife in and out of her "room." A lady could not modestly get up or down any other way. Libbie also had to be lifted on and off Custis Lee's saddle.

Soon after leaving the Red River's flower-scented valley the army, in column of twos, traversed flat and monotonous pine barrens. The few log houses along the road interested Libbie. She noticed that they were all double cabins joined end to end with a roofed "trot-way." This was a style of architecture new to the Michigan-reared girl, and she amused her companions by prophesying that the next residence would be exactly like the last.

Midsummer in western Louisiana was piping hot with air smelling of dust, stagnant water, horse sweat, and turpentine — unpleasant odors which Libbie learned to like because she was always happy with Autie.

Fortunately, his troublesome army quit complaining on the march and everyone seemed content. Armstrong rode at the head of the column with his old swagger. The longest, hottest day never seemed to tire him. Libbie marveled, night after night, when he called for a fresh horse after the evening meal and trotted off with the dogs for a hunt. But always, before he left, he arranged a smudge in one end of the ambulance to keep mosquitoes away from Libbie. She thought that the smoke was sometimes worse than the insects, but laughed about it. She was smart enough to know that her husband's life was horses, hunting, and fishing. Her job was to adjust and help him enjoy them.

At reveille every morning Libbie always feared that she might not be ready to march on time. The horror of keeping thousands of men waiting while she fumbled in the predawn for hairpins made her shudder. Always she brushed her hair straight back, wasting no time to part it. She said later that she learned to bathe and dress in seven minutes. Armstrong fretted once, "It is easier to command a whole division of cavalry than one woman," but she consoled herself with the knowledge that the injuries which make a man really suffer are the ones he keeps to himself, not those he jokes about.

Sleeping in the ambulance made it impossible for Libbie to kneel beside her bed for prayers. She had to wait until she crawled under the covers. The prayers were brief, "since I had nothing to ask for, as I believed the best of everything on earth had already been given to me."

At Hempstead, Texas, they established permanent camp. This was on the Brenham-Galveston railroad. There they learned that France had withdrawn from Mexico. Good! That expedition was canceled. Custer's brother, Tom, and his father, Emanuel, came by boat from Galveston, the former to serve as the General's aide, the latter to be his forage agent — good pay and not much work. Armstrong looked out for his own. To headquarters also came big, jolly Nettie Humphrey, now Mrs. Jacob Greene. Her husband had tried selling insurance at the end of the war but was glad to get back under the army umbrella and serve as assistant adjutant general for Custer. The Greenes' tent was pitched near the Custers', and soldiers constructed a "bowery" connecting them. Both families were together much of the time. Armstrong scratched away on his letters and reports while the women chatted over their sewing and Emanuel read aloud to himself. When Jacob Greene's flute began to squeal and the brass band added to the din, fidgety Custer seemed best able to concentrate!

Trouble broke out among the troops again as soon as they stopped marching. Once more Libbie looked forward each day to the relaxation of an evening ride. The Greenes, Emanuel Custer, and the staff usually went along, adding to the fun. Armstrong and Tom were forever playing rough practical jokes on their father. The old man learned to be on guard whenever they rode on opposite sides of his horse and leaned over endearingly. Such professed affection usually screened a sly kick in his horse's flank to make him buck. At other times, when loose stones lay scattered along the road the sons might dash away. Their horses' flying hoofs would shower the old man with rocks — unless he could outrun them and let his horse's hoofs pelt them.[5]

Once when Emanuel wanted to see an alligator which was reported dead in the neighborhood, the boys sent him on a long detour to see the body of a very putrid mule. At another time Armstrong came from the office with an official-looking paper which he said was an order transferring his father to a Negro regiment as chaplain. The old man's one aversion was the colored race.

Emanuel scored his best return-joke on the boys by getting them to bet with Libbie in a horse-judging contest. He whispered the answers to his daughter-in-law. With the winnings, she bought a silk dress and swished proudly around, delighting them all, for the boys were as game sportsmen when outwitted as was their father.

Emanuel Custer enjoyed the hunting in Texas as much as his sons did. Libbie went with them occasionally, but she knew that a woman is usually more appreciated when she welcomes the returned hunters with hot coffee than when she goes along and gets in the way. Armstrong soon accumulated a pack of dogs — both coursers and trailhounds which followed him as faithfully as Ned Hazard's dogs did in the book he had read at West Point. Sport-loving Texans added hounds to his pack constantly. He made friends with the planters — was their kind of man — but his troubles with the volunteer soldiers continued. Finally he wrote a "private letter" to Sheridan asking if his disciplinary methods — lashing and head-shaving — were too severe. Both these, and branding, too, had been punishments during the war.

Sheridan came out by boat from New Orleans, inspected the situation, and evidently approved Custer's methods, for he recommended his promotion to major general in the regular army, thus supporting Congressman Bingham's request.[6] He also ordered the column to march to Austin, one hundred and twenty-five miles farther west.

Libbie welcomed the change because tents were chilly homes in November. Besides, moving always made men in the ranks forget their troubles. Officers, too, liked to march. At night she sat with Armstrong and his staff around a big open fire. Smoke made her eyes smart, but the laughing young men assured Libbie that smoke sought beauty.

In daytime the marching column serpentined across dreary wastes of mesquite thickets, bare now and looking for all the world like a vast neglected peach orchard. Here and there clumps of prickly pears, tall as a man on horseback, glistened like tin plates in the wintry sun. Now and again the road crossed open prairies of russet grass. Sometimes a jack rabbit would bound off with his peculiar lopsided lope. If Custer's greyhound, Byron, spied the hare he shot away like an arrow. Armstrong would push his cap back from its precarious perch over his left eye, tighten it down on his head, and follow. Father Custer and the rest joined the race. Libbie gloried in the sight and wrote later, describing the flowing music of Byron's actions: "Each bound sent him flying through the air. He hardly touched the elastic cushions of his feet to earth, before he again was spread out like a dark, straight thread. This gathering and leaping must be seen, to realize how marvelous is the rapidity and how the motion seems flying."

As the army neared Austin, Libbie noticed that the country was more thickly settled, with more land in cultivation. Negro workers sat along the fences, like blackbirds, watching the dusty column, eyes rolling, big mouths laughing at the soldiers' sallies. The city ahead looked attractive under its evergreen live oaks.

Custer established headquarters in the deserted Blind Asylum, a large two-story stone house with rooms for the staff, a suite for himself, a special sewing room for Libbie, and a piano where restless Tom could lay his half-burned cigarettes.

Law-abiding citizens welcomed the soldiers, as they had at Hempstead. Austin was the capital of Texas. It had no railroad, but the Custers felt that they were back in civilization — a great mistake, Libbie learned later. The weather was comfortable on sunny December days and the staff sometimes rode to Mount Bonnell. They had to dismount and scramble up the last few feet, but the view from the top was magnificent. Below them lay the city, its surrounding cotton fields, and the broad silvery band of the Colorado, meandering through riverbottom sand bars. Armstrong liked to bring out the band to play the "Anvil Chorus" while he and his friends picnicked on the height.

The Austin people bred fast horses and Armstrong won their friendship racing with them. In a grandiloquent letter home, he said that he now owned fourteen horses. Libbie, in a letter she wrote, said that they had three horses and a fast pony. If people in Monroe compared notes they probably understood. And it is likely that Libbie may have shrunk the number as much as Custer inflated it: he was writing to a humble family that would enjoy his opulence; Libbie was writing to an opulent father who disapproved of extravagance — especially in race horses.[7]

Libbie enthusiastically supported Armstrong's interest in the track. For their mulatto jockey she stitched red, white, and blue silks. As she sewed, Armstrong interrupted her constantly. She would hear him storm into the big old building, bumping the edges of furniture, catching his spurs on chair-rounds until he strode into the sewing room. Here he snatched his little wife from her seat, sent the lapboard flying, spools of thread rolling, while he carried her away to the corrals to see a new horse. And Libbie enjoyed every minute.

On Christmas she trimmed the big stone house with boughs. A tree was decorated and mistletoe hung over all the doors. Armstrong dressed as Santa Claus and distributed presents — some genuine, some "dry sells" or teases. Thus Tom got a jew's-harp with a note: "Give the piano a rest." Emanuel got a Negro baby doll, and a pack of cards to shock his Methodist principles. When the laughter stopped he unwrapped the conventional man's presents — handkerchiefs, neckties, and tobacco.

After Christmas, Armstrong and Libbie visited San Antonio, 85 miles south on the broad, sandy Alamo Creek. In this old Spanish town they bought presents, Autie for his sister Lydia, Libbie for her stepmother. On January 31, 1866, Custer received the bad news he had dreaded: His volunteer commission had expired. Sheridan's recommendation had been futile, and Custer was reduced to his rank in the regular army — a captain in the 5th Cavalry, back East.[8] He showed the order to his staff. This automatically returned them all to their various units. They began packing at once. Custer sold all his horses except Custis Lee, Jack Rucker, his beautiful Black Phil Sheridan, and the race mare. He gave away most of his hounds.

With Libbie, Eliza, and the jockey, who like most waifs wanted to stay with him,[9] and with his staff and baggage, he set off for the railhead at Brenham. There the little party boarded a rickety old train which Libbie was sure had not been repaired since before the war. At Galveston they waited for a boat to take them to New Orleans. The sojourn proved a pleasant one. They enjoyed the smell of salt water, exercised the horses on a long white crescent beach and refused to worry about the future.

The boat, when it came, was as dilapidated as the train, and their passage on her proved rough. Armstrong became deathly seasick. Libbie and others feared shipwreck, but at New Orleans * they quickly forgot their discomfort and planned a new fling in expensive shops.

For the festive life Libbie donned her best dress, the one with the broad belt above the hoops. She added a big Mexican buckle which

* Records in the National Archives indicate that the party was in Galveston February 13, and in New Orleans February 20, 1866.

made her slim waist look even slimmer, like the stem of a wineglass. Stepping proudly out on the street, she was unprepared for that first horrible day.

Libbie forgot that she had been away from civilization for almost a year. Styles had changed and her magnificent wardrobe was hopelessly dated. Modish ladies had even discarded hoop skirts. The bonnet Libbie wore on the back of her head to frame her parted hair was completely passé. Libbie did not want to be seen in her "rags" even when purchasing proper clothes. What would the sales people think? Moreover, she shouldn't buy anything now because Armstrong's salary had been cut from eight to two thousand dollars a year. But he never worried about money, said they had saved a thousand dollars in Texas, and urged her to purchase what she pleased. They dined, as they had before, in gorgeous restaurants. Father Custer puzzled over the French menus, tried to pronounce the names, and kept them all laughing.

Libbie, the economical member of the family, was glad when they were all on the Mississippi steamboat splashing upriver toward home. The boys seemed as gay as ever, unperturbed by the sudden change in Armstrong's fortunes. With no apparent cares on earth, they teased Emanuel as usual, bantering with him constantly. At table they got the old man started on politics. As he lost himself in argument, they exchanged one of their empty plates for his untouched dinner — and the waiter carried it out. Another time they stole his ticket and then induced the purser to ask for it and threaten to put the old man off as a stowaway at the next wood-yard. Once Armstrong picked his father's pocket and fled to his own stateroom. Father Custer pounded on the door, demanding admittance, until his son poured a pitcher of water on him from the transom. Next morning the boys assured the old gentleman that he had pounded on the door of a lady passenger, who had done her best to protect herself. They pointed out his victim and urged him to apologize lest the scandal reach the Methodist congregation in Monroe.

The old man paid them back at the next landing. When rural Southerners trouped up the gangplank he scuffled with his sons, shouting for help, complaining that these ruffian boys were robbing him. Bad characters were common in the river towns and Emanuel Custer's "playacting" deceived the new passengers. To save his own boys from possible lynching he had to confess it was all a joke. Yes, Father Custer could be counted on to give as good as he took.

Some of Custer's official family left him at Cairo, Illinois. Others parted from him at Detroit. At Monroe, he and Libbie moved into the Bacon mansion and wondered what to do next. Custer had applied for a thirty-day leave of absence to seek something better than a captain's pay. The leave was granted on April 28, 1866.[10] He did not know where to go or what kind of work to attempt. His fellow veterans who craved continued glory were going into politics. Kilpatrick had mounted the hustings and Custer's name surely equaled his in popular appeal. Other veterans, who preferred affluence to glory, were entering business. Custer was offered vice-presidencies in several firms which considered his name an asset, but he could not picture himself in a commercial career. He never had known the value of a dollar and he did not care to learn. He wanted to be with Tom, and he realized that their pranks would never fit in a conservative business establishment.

The perplexed youth decided to go to Washington and talk with Secretary of War Stanton — the old, though not intimate, friend of the family. He would also call on Grant. These great men might have something suitable for his talents. To save money, Libbie remained in Monroe. Always ambitious for her husband, she lamented the injustice of seeing her Autie go away as poor as when he left Monroe with the rank of captain in 1862.

20 Swing Around the Circle

THE WASHINGTON TO WHICH CUSTER RETURNED IN THE SPRING OF 1866 was a stinkpot bubbling with corruption. Peace seemed to have rotted everybody's morals. Many army officers had tried a year of civil life and now clamored desperately to get back in service. Custer was disgusted with the slick-tongued claim-agents who lurked around hopeful applicants, offering, for a price, to get them commissions. Five hundred dollars was not considered exorbitant to obtain the favor of a senator.

Armstrong called on Secretary of State Seward. The wizened little man's face and neck still showed the knife scars received on the night Lincoln was assassinated. Custer went next to see Secretary of War Stanton. Armstrong had won a major generalcy by brevet for his service at Appomattox, and he knew that both Congressman Bingham and General Sheridan had written Stanton urging the commission without the brevet.[1] The Secretary welcomed the boy from his home town, asked him to stand at attention while he walked around the room, head bowed, eyes looking over the tops of his little glasses at the young man's military carriage. Custer asked for, and got, commissions in the regular army for Tom and George W. Yates. Both boys had failed to find congenial work in civil life. The record does not disclose what, if anything, he requested for himself.

Chief Justice Chase invited Custer to a dinner party and he was photographed there. Senator Chandler took the Boy General home for a visit with his family, then asked him to testify before a Reconstruction Committee about conditions in Texas — a great bore, lasting day after day and consuming time which Custer wanted to spend looking for a job. Only late at night could he find leisure to write Libbie. This was like life in the army, but his midnight hours here were not punctuated by distant cannonading. Instead, he heard only the rhythmic clump of a passing cab horse or the sudden burst of drunken conversation from homebound revelers. His long letters contained the usual meticulous details. He described his room, told what he said to old friends and what they said to him, passed along compliments to Libbie — and to himself. He said he was fortunate to have obtained that commission for Tom. The boy must not let them down. "Urge Tom to study Tactics," he wrote. Armstrong also told Libbie about the latest styles — a new kind of hair net, birds on ladies' fans — and said that he had not indulged in his favorite pastime, the theater, except when taken by friends. He missed her very much, he said, and reminded her again to have Tom study "Tactics." [2]

Custer toyed with the idea of seeking a diplomatic appointment — a usual political reward. Then he heard that the Mexican republicans wanted to employ a top-ranking cavalry officer to help expel Maximilian — much better than having the United States Army do it. The pay was twice that received by a major general. In Texas Custer had sympathized with the republicans. Sheridan, although officially neutral, had done many things to help them. Here was a chance for service which Armstrong understood. He asked Grant to give him a letter of recommendation to the Mexican minister, Señor Don Matias Romero, and Grant wrote most flatteringly, saying: "There was no officer in that [the cavalry] branch of the service who had the confidence of Gen. Sheridan to a greater degree than Gen. C., and there is no officer in whose judgment I have greater faith than in Sheridan's." [3]

With this appointment practically assured — in his mind — Custer applied for a leave of absence from the army, but it was denied. He hesitated to resign. The Mexican job might last only a year or two, and commissions in the United States Army were valuable. Armstrong went to New York hoping for some more permanent and equally remunerative employment there.

Life in Manhattan proved much gayer than in Washington and also more expensive. Friends took him driving behind the finest horses he had ever seen. When he visited Wall Street the Brokers' Board adjourned to give him three cheers. At his hotel he found a special table reserved for the military, and one of the waiters was a man who had served in his brigade. Custer met Pleasonton and went with him to dine at the Manhattan Club. He saw several West Point schoolmates, all eager to renew old frolics and see the latest shows. As in Washington, it was usually late at night when Armstrong wrote Libbie. He told her the names of all the plays he had seen, and described his visits with the actresses, experiences with the boys in shooting galleries and "pretty-girl-waitress-saloons." Artless and outspoken always, he wrote his wife: "We also had considerable sport with females we met on the street —'Nymphes du Pavé' they are called. Sport alone was our object. At no time did I forget you." He attended a masquerade ball at the Academy of Music and told Libbie that he dressed in a devil suit with a black mask, red silk tights, and black velvet cloak. Two upright feathers on his cap represented horns. "Our fancy-dress party at the Humphrey House," he concluded, "was more choice." However, he enjoyed seeing a picture of himself at the "Bal Masqué" in *Harper's Weekly*.[4]

On May 18, 1866, Judge Bacon died.* Armstrong hurried home. Libbie was the sole heir to his estate, but the will provided that sufficient property be sold to raise five thousand dollars. This sum was to be loaned at interest, which would be paid to her stepmother for life. Thus Libbie realized little immediate cash, but her father's real property promised good future returns. She felt very much alone now and joined Armstrong when he returned to Washington, seeking employment. Armstrong learned that the mounted service was to be expanded, thus creating a new position of Inspector General of United States Cavalry. He applied for the job but, instead, was offered a commission as lieutenant colonel in the 7th Cavalry † — quite a comedown for a major general who had been feted everywhere by great men, though better than the captaincy he now held. He and Libbie decided to accept it, but to continue hoping for something better.

They found the capital agog with a bitter political fight concerning reconstruction of the Southern states. President Andrew Johnson and the National Union Party, on whose platform he and Lincoln had been elected, favored restoring self-government to all the states which had seceded, providing only that they abolish slavery and submit to a few minor requirements. Radical Republicans bitterly opposed this plan, and Custer's best friends were Radicals. Men like Zach Chandler

---

* Date from gravestone in Woodlawn Cemetery, Monroe, Michigan, furnished me by Dr. Lawrence Frost.

† Custer wrote this letter July 6, 1866. His commission as Lieutenant Colonel is dated July 28, 1866.

and John A. Bingham, Custer's most ardent supporters, insisted on treating the South like a conquered province, disenfranchising the most prominent whites and giving the vote to Negroes. As practical politicians they knew that the President's plan of reconstruction would destroy the Republican Party as well as their own political careers. A majority of the American people had been Democrats before the war and still were. The only possible way for the Republicans to stay in power was to insist that the Southern states enfranchise the freed slaves. Without their votes the Democratic Party, North and South, would take over the nation.

Armstrong Custer had seen the masses of liberated field hands in Texas and Louisiana, and to give them the vote seemed to him ridiculous — a travesty on democracy. If the Republican Party could be saved only by the "slave vote," he believed that it deserved to perish. Other prejudices, no doubt, helped influence his decision. Many conflicting emotions usually combine to make what men call their "objective conclusions." But one thing is certain: Armstrong decided against his personal interests and dared defy his friends, the Radicals, in order to do the right thing as he saw it. Already he had differed with his father's reactionary Democratic views but he also differed with the Radicals' vindictive plan. Summing up his political views on reconstruction he said:

"I believe that every man who voluntarily engaged in the Rebellion forfeited every right held under our government — to live, hold property. But . . . for the Government to exact full penalties, simply because it is constitutionally authorized to do so, would, in my opinion, be unnecessary, impolitic, inhuman, and wholly at variance with the principles of a free, civilized and Christian nation, such as we profess to be." [5]

Having thus expressed himself publicly Armstrong attended a mass meeting in Detroit on August 9, 1866, to endorse the National Union platform, and was appointed one of four delegates to the national convention scheduled to meet in Philadelphia on August 14.

At this meeting in the City of Brotherly Love, he mingled with many

of the nation's foremost generals, as well as politicians and humanitarians, all intent on healing the wounds of war. Some eccentrics were
also present. The notorious George Francis Train occupied a suite at
the Continental Hotel. During the war he had harangued British audi-
ences, urging them to favor the North. Now, in Philadelphia hotel
corridors, he addressed all who would listen. At the convention's opening session delegates from South Carolina walked into the hall arm
in arm with delegates from Massachusetts. Armstrong heartily approved. He always liked Southerners.

The Radical press deplored this mingling with defeated traitors and
even said, incorrectly, that the guerrilla, Mosby, was among the delegates. Evidently falsehood, and perhaps violence, would be used by the
Radicals to discredit the National Union Party and Johnson's reconstruction plan. But Custer was not intimidated. Quite the reverse. He
had made his choice and the reckless cavalryman determined now to
grasp time by the fetlock and hold on to the end. With five others, he
proudly signed his name to a call for all ex-soldiers and sailors to attend
a grand rally in Cleveland on September 17, the anniversary of Mc-
Clellan's victory at Antietam.[6]

Having parted with his Radical friends to join the National Union-
ists, Armstrong had to look now to this party for advancement in his
career. He wrote directly to President Johnson, his "Commander in
Chief," applying for a colonelcy — even a colonelcy of infantry, he said,
but he wanted only white troops.[7] The President replied by inviting
him and Mrs. Custer to join the presidential party on "a swing around
the circle." Ostensibly the trip would be made for the purpose of
placing the cornerstone on a monument being erected to Stephen A.
Douglas in Chicago, and of visiting Lincoln's tomb in Springfield,
Illinois, thus paying homage to both Democrats and Republicans. But
President Johnson had an ulterior motive. He wanted to explain his
reconstruction policy directly to the people, and thus to influence them
to vote for lenient treatment of Southerners and against the Radicals in
the fall elections. He would be accompanied by members of his cabinet,
by high-ranking generals including U. S. Grant, and by foreign min-

isters including Señor Romero. Certainly any man looking for advancement could ask for no better opportunity to make important acquaintances. Custer accepted at once.[8]

Armstrong and Libbie were in the West when the party left Washington on August 28. It traveled first to Philadelphia, then to New York. On the march up Broadway an ex-officer, wounded at Antietam and imprisoned at Andersonville, presented the President with a white silk flag inscribed: WE WHO FOUGHT AND GAVE OUR BLOOD TO PERPETUATE THIS UNION, WILL NOT PERMIT IT TO BE SEVERED BY SUMNER, THAD STEVENS, AND OTHER CO-CONSPIRATORS.

In the evening the presidential party dined at Delmonico's. Generals Wesley Merritt and Alfred Pleasonton were present. Libbie and Armstrong, with Byron, the greyhound, joined the group at Manhattanville where a steamboat waited to take them to West Point. The guests were still laughing over a race through Central Park between the six horses drawing the President's carriage, and the six driven by Grant. The General's hitch won.

The trip up the Hudson was delightful, the weather magnificent without a cloud in the sky. A river breeze fanned the excursionists' faces. Boats whistled and dipped colors as they passed. Libbie met the notables — Secretary of State Seward, with his sharp nose and sharper tongue; bewhiskered Gideon Welles, Secretary of the Navy; Admiral Farragut, and all the rest. She noted, with her usual gentle sarcasm, that Farragut's spouse could never take her motherly eyes off the eminent seaman. While sewing, or conversing with other ladies, Mrs. Farragut always watched to see where he was or where he went.

At West Point, carriages conveyed the distinguished guests up to the Plain. Cadets, wearing their white pantaloons, marched in review past the President, platoon after platoon, every chin, every elbow, every bayonet-point aligned as perfectly as in a paper of pins.

Traveling westward from the Point, the party stopped frequently to greet assembled crowds. Grant and Custer always received more applause than the President. At Niagara Falls, Major General Thomas — the "Rock of Chickamauga" — joined the party. President Johnson held a public reception, followed by a grand ball. General Grant, according to the *New York Times*,[9] sat outside sampling whisky. Generals Custer and Lovell H. Rousseau stood for two hours surrounded by what a reporter called "the beauty and intelligence of the city." Scheming politicians who watched them decided to run Custer for office — for governor of Michigan, or congressman at least.

When the special train reached Buffalo the crowd called for Grant. Secretary Seward stepped out of the car and announced that Grant was ill. They called next for Custer. Amid waving hats and cries of "Speech" Armstrong told the throng that he was no speechmaker, but he had fought four years to uphold the Constitution and save the Union. Now, he hoped the people, come election, would vote for the Constitution "as it is" and the Union "as it was." The crowd seemed to like his soldier bluntness.

On the train again, politicians asked Custer about running for office. Last year, when the war ended, he had declined political opportunities, but he was a major general then, not a lieutenant colonel with nothing ahead of him except a possible assignment somewhere on the dreary plains.

In every city more people got on the train. Committeemen, correspondents, office seekers, and politicians stood in the aisles or sat on baggage. General Grant lay stretched out on a trunk in the baggage car, his head on a carpetbag. At Erie and other stops, he did not appear when called for by cheering crowds. Perhaps he really was ill. Perhaps he had drunk some whisky to cure his illness. In any event the situation gave Libbie a good opportunity for one of her amusingly sarcastic observations. But ever since her marriage, Armstrong had warned her against maligning his fellow officers. That was an exclusive privilege of his own. Certainly in this instance she held her witty tongue. Grant, after all, had written a fine letter to Señor Romero.

Trundling across Ohio toward Cleveland the passengers purchased newspapers. This was Custer's native state and it was also the domain of Senator Ben Wade, the Radical whom Custer had defended at West

Point five years ago, even though he represented Father Custer's political opponents. "Let there be a fair fight," had been Armstrong's code always — so he thought. Now Ben Wade controlled the politics of Ohio along with many newspapers in it. He opposed the President's reconstruction policy, and denied him a fair fighting chance to present it. Stooping to all the undemocratic practices too common in democracies, he did everything in his power to discredit the "swing around the circle." He printed falsehoods in the press. His henchmen were instructed to create disturbances and heckle the speakers. Libbie read with shocked surprise that "General Custer and his associates" were consorting with "subjugated traitors." Readers were reminded that Armstrong had ordered lashes meted out to his officers without trial [10] — a sample of the lies which would get into print about Custer. Libbie also learned that three of Chicago's biggest newspapers, the *Tribune,* the *Republican,* and the *Post,* planned a hostile demonstration when the presidential party reached Lake Michigan. Perhaps trouble might even start sooner.

At Cleveland the station crowd cheered cordially. Rain threatened but the gloomy streets to the hotel were lined with waving hats and handkerchiefs. No apparent trouble here! The hotel management greeted the distinguished guests with festive Chinese lanterns. A crowd gathered outside, calling for the army officers to appear at the windows. Each was cheered in turn — all except Grant. He could not be found. Someone explained that he had boarded the boat for Detroit, where he would rejoin the party. Secretary of the Navy Welles told his diary that the general had expected trouble in Cleveland and left to escape it.[11]

President Johnson stepped out on a balcony to address the crowd. Ben Wade's plug-uglies started shouting, making hideous noises to overpower anything he might say.[12] This disturbance set the pattern for the rest of the trip across Ohio. The party was annoyed and menaced on the street going back to the station, and at all stops along the line. If Armstrong was planning a political career, he saw now what to expect.

At Detroit, in Zach Chandler's Michigan, the party got some relief. From here the special train backed up the track to Monroe. Custer was to be given a triumphal entry into his home town. At the familiar station a crowd awaited the train. Secretary Seward stepped out on the rear platform and, with his best stump oratory, shouted to the upturned faces, "I find that General Custer has a difference in the way he enters towns. When he enters an enemy town he goes in straight forward and the enemy backs out. When he brings us into his own town he backs us in."

The crowd laughed politely, as political crowds usually do at the wit of their own partisans. Seward finished his short introductory speech with: "I give you the two great cities of ancient and modern times — Nineveh and Monroe — both distinguished for light horsemen before the Lord — Nimrod and Custer." [13]

Libbie, in the sanctuary of the ladies' car, must have peeked through the curtain as her husband stepped out the car door to be greeted with "three cheers and a tiger."

The rest of the trip across Michigan and Indiana was unpleasant. Libbie read in a newspaper: "We advise loyal citizens to avoid him [the President] as they would any other convicted criminal." Arriving in Chicago she rode beside her husband in one of the carriages which took the party down to the Douglas Monument on a bluff overlooking Lake Michigan. Grandstands had been erected for the cornerstone-laying ceremony. The day was brilliant, with no waves on the sky-blue lake which stretched to the eastern horizon. Armstrong and Libbie were always sensitive to nature's splendor. Perhaps it was only coincidence that, on this beautiful day in the open, they decided definitely against going into politics. Back in their hotel Armstrong wrote a card to the Detroit *Free Press* stating that he would not accept the nomination as congressman from Michigan, although he personally endorsed the National Union platform. [14]

Next day the party boarded a special train on the Alton Railroad for Springfield to visit Lincoln's tomb. General John A. McClernand, now back in politics, outfitted a flatcar with a cannon and planned attaching it to the presidential special in the town of Lincoln, thirty miles north of Springfield. He was a supporter of Johnson's platform and wanted to announce the President's arrival in the Illinois capital with resounding salvos — and reminders to vote for his, McClernand's, candidates, of course. However, the train crew either failed to see the signal, or being Republicans feigned blindness, so the presidential special of four cars rolled into Springfield unaccompanied by artillery. Lincoln's home town did not approve the Lincoln-Johnson National Union Party platform. The city fathers were Radicals and refused to vote any money for the President's reception, but some three thousand people assembled at the station to see him — just curiosity, perhaps. When Johnson stepped out on the car platform and came down the steps the applause was meager, but it roared enthusiastically as Grant, Farragut, Steedman, and Custer appeared.

Libbie and the other ladies accompanied their husbands in carriages to Oak Ridge Cemetery. They drove down in the hollow under great trees and stopped before a brick retaining vault — a dugout on the hillside. Overhead the foliage was beginning to turn red, yellow, and brown. The President and his companions alighted from the carriages to walk solemnly around the sepulcher, their feet shuffling in the damp leaves underfoot. Then they signed their names in a visitors' book and drove back to town. Black clouds were blowing in from the east. That evening, on a St. Nicholas Hotel balcony, local politicians delivered addresses in the rain. Custer and other military heroes were introduced, but when Johnson tried to speak, hecklers interrupted him. To quiet the disturbance someone called for music.

"Play the Rogue's March," a voice in the crowd answered.[15]

In the morning the presidential party walked to the station and boarded their train for Alton. From there a flotilla of gaily decorated steamboats carried them down the Mississippi twenty-five miles to St. Louis, where General Hancock's staff waited on the levee. Up in the city, Johnson spoke again but the audience was unsympathetic. He lost his temper, heckled the hecklers, complained that Thad Stevens,

Charles Sumner, and Wendell Phillips likened themselves to the Christ and called everybody else Judas.[16] The crowd replied with boos. An ingrained coarseness in Johnson, product of his illiterate background perhaps, repelled a discriminating audience.

From St. Louis the party started back to Washington. At Terre Haute, Indiana, a mob attempted to derail the train. A torchlight procession in Indianapolis ended in a riot. The crowd tore down illuminated transparencies. Pistol shots cracked in the streets. One man was killed. When Johnson tried to speak voices shouted, "Shoot the damned traitor."

Custer, standing with Farragut and Grant, noticed that the police refused to interfere. Grant strode forward and shouted, "For the credit of your city, hear us all speak."

It did no good, and Grant made no more appearances on the trip. He left the party shortly thereafter.

At Louisville, a Revolutionary soldier met the train to greet the President. The mob hooted. Custer had held his temper for days, but this was too much. He brushed past his wife and shouted from the platform, "Wait until next October and more groans than these will be heard."

That night, at eight o'clock, the party boarded a steamboat for Cincinnati, arriving next morning. This was back in Ben Wade's Ohio again and soldiers lined the street along which the President must drive to the Spencer House. Grant's father, and Sherman's father-in-law, Thomas Ewing, both stood with the reception committee,[17] but Wade's henchmen kept the mob in a turmoil.

The next planned stop was at Scio, Ohio — nearest railroad point to Custer's birthplace. Armstrong wired his uncle that they were coming. As the train pulled into the hill town Custer looked out at the familiar landscape, the rough pastures dotted with sheep. This was Congressman Bingham's bailiwick and Autie saw, at the station, glaring anti-Johnson placards held by a waiting crowd. The engine panted to a stop. Cheers were given for Grant and for Custer, but none for Johnson. Custer stepped out on the platform and swung to the ground. He shook hands with people who introduced themselves as friends of the family. He heard ugly remarks made about the President, some so loud that Johnson could hear them in his car. Custer straightened up and faced the mob. "I was born two miles from here, and I am ashamed of you," * he shouted. Then he climbed back on his car and signaled for the conductor to start the train. As they pulled out he told Libbie he would never visit Scio again — a resolution he kept. Sitting down beside her he reached for pen and paper — his antidote for nervousness — and wrote the Scio citizens a furious letter, saying that he considered the reception a personal insult. Still angry when the train steamed into Steubenville, he hurled furious defiance at the mobsters who hooted Johnson.

The Custers left the presidential party at Steubenville and returned to Monroe. Armstrong then hurried back to Cleveland to prepare for the Soldiers and Sailors Convention he had helped call. On the opening day, September 17, 1866, many delegates failed to appear. This was discouraging, but Armstrong felt sure that they were delayed by the heavy rains. He moved that the meeting be postponed. A discussion followed and Custer withdrew his motion. General Gordon Granger was elected chairman. Generals Custer, James B. Steedman, and Colonel L. D. Campbell escorted him to the chair. A dispatch was read to the meeting from ex-Confederate soldiers in Memphis who wished the convention success and agreed to abide by any rules of reconstruction laid down for them by "the soldiers of the Union." Among the signers was Nathan Bedford Forrest, ringleader of the Ku Klux Klan which had been organized to defy the Federal government. The letter was misleading, for it indicated that the Klan might be in league with the National Union Party. At least that was the interpretation given it by the Radical press. Chairman Granger, Custer, Steedman, and others signed a congratulatory but noncommital reply. Propagandists, enlarging on the meeting's apparent sympathy for the South, reported

---

* C. G. Bowers (*Tragic Era*, p. 137) quotes Custer as saying "two miles from here." Three miles is more nearly correct. Custer's experience at Scio on this trip is also recounted in M. Ronsheim, *Life of Custer*, p. [63].

that Custer introduced Forrest in person to the convention [18] — another of the palpable lies which people were beginning to tell about Armstrong. He gained more warranted criticism when he ended the session by calling for three cheers for the Fenian Movement — an organized effort to gain independence for Ireland favored by many Irish-Americans who had fought in the Civil War. A circular, presumably issued by the Radicals to counteract this appeal, blamed Johnson for interfering with the Movement.

The Cleveland convention led to the famous "round robin" letter, signed by many officers, denouncing Secretary Stanton, but Custer's name was not among them. He and Libbie had had enough of politics. Already Armstrong was much too prominent for his own good in the bitter postwar struggle for power which would lead to the impeachment of the President. Life in the army — even on a lieutenant colonel's pay in the dreary West — offered more satisfaction although the Great Plains in 1866 were considered the Siberia of America. Writers like Owen Wister, painters like Frederic Remington, soldiers such as Custer, had not yet made the West romantic. If there were any glory to be found out on those dreary wastes, Armstrong and Libbie did not know about it.

21 "Not the Death of a Soldier"

In THE FALL OF 1866 ARMSTRONG CUSTER BOARDED THE TRAIN FOR FORT Riley, Kansas, where the 7th Cavalry was being organized. Libbie accompanied him with a curly-headed Monroe schoolmate, Diana, who looked forward to meeting officers. The Custers also took their cook, Eliza, and the colored jockey they had brought from Texas. In a stock car Armstrong shipped four horses — Jack Rucker, the Virginia colt Phil Sheridan, the pacer Custis Lee, and his Texas race mare. He also transported Byron, the greyhound; Turk, a hideous white bulldog; and several trail hounds. Tom Custer was left behind, and Libbie worried because a woman, much older and wiser than that boy, seemed to have set her cap for him. Armstrong promised to have Tom transferred to his regiment as soon as possible.[1]

At St. Louis they stopped for a last fling before burying themselves on the Plains. An exposition was in full swing. Custer enjoyed the prize animals, the exhibitions of horsemanship. He and Libbie attended a play, *Rosedale,* in which Lawrence Barrett took the part of "Elliot Grey." Armstrong liked the scene where the hero pretends that his wound is worse than it is, so the heroine will continue dressing it. The music particularly appealed to him. After the performance Autie walked backstage to the actor's dressing room. Barrett invited him in. The star noticed that the general seemed bashful, reticent, yet his sharp blue eyes were peculiarly direct and penetrating. Custer's voice, according to Barrett, was soft and earnest. His words tumbled out with nervous quickness, almost a stutter. He asked Barrett to come to the hotel and meet Libbie. The actor accepted. Thus began a long friendship, and Armstrong, who had longed for years to be an author, henceforth hoped to be an actor, too.*

Custer's holiday soon came to an end and the entire retinue traveled westward. The Union Pacific Railroad, Eastern Division, was still ten miles short of Fort Riley, so they finished their journey in wagons. When the little cavalcade drove up out of the deep valley of the Kaw onto the Plains, the first sight of the fort dismayed Libbie and Diana. Before them stood a quadrangle of cream-colored stone buildings, a story and a half high.[2] On all sides the tawny grasslands stretched away flat and endless as the ocean — a red-yellow ocean now, in November. None of them had seen anything like it before, and this was to be the Custer home for as long, perhaps, as five years. Armstrong, the perpetual optimist, marveled audibly at the panorama. So did

---

* There are two different accounts of this meeting, one by Libbie Custer in *Tenting on the Plains,* pp. 344–347, the other by Lawrence Barrett in F. Whittaker, *Complete Life of . . . Custer . . . ,* pp. 631–633. I have used the Barrett account.

Libbie, although less enthusiastically after she saw the bare, barnlike rooms in the officers' quarters. She especially disliked the wind, which blew all day long, sifting sand into the houses, even into food and bedding.

Fort Riley was in the Department of the Missouri — one of four departments composing the Division of Missouri, which included the Great Plains from Canada to the Gulf, all under the command of William Tecumseh Sherman. The department to which Custer was assigned was commanded by General Hancock, of Gettysburg fame. He had established headquarters in Fort Leavenworth and assigned the 7th Cavalry to Fort Riley where it could protect construction crews as they laid the rails westward. The 7th Cavalry was a new regiment still being organized. Its colonel, Andrew Jackson Smith, was a tough old regular with a long military record in Mexico, on the Plains, and in the Civil War. Over fifty now, he refused to admit his age and gloried in hardships which made younger men flinch. Like a veteran "top kick," he left routine management of regimental affairs to Lieutenant Colonel Custer.

Armstrong had seldom trained green men, and he disliked the job. He had failed with citizen-soldiers in Texas, and the enlisted regulars in 1866 were of a much lower order, many of them ignorant immigrants. The native-born Northerners in the ranks had been selected for physical stamina with little regard for moral or mental attributes. They were men willing to soldier for fifty cents a day at a time when the country was entering a period of tremendous expansion and opportunity. However, Armstrong seems to have succeeded with them at first, for Colonel Smith, watching his progress all winter, recommended that Custer's appointment be approved, saying, "I can't well do without him." [3]

Armstrong's troubles in the 7th Cavalry began with his fellow officers. Many of them suffered, as he did, from a feeling of unmerited inferiority, a realization that life in the army was looked down on, and that war had unsuited them for any other career. [4] The ranking major was Wyckliffe Cooper, a Kentuckian with a meritorious war record but bad drinking habits. Another of these regulars was Robert M. West, a brigadier general during the war, cited for bravery at Five Forks, and now reduced to a captain. Then there was Captain Frederick Benteen, a taciturn, sardonic fellow who had won his first commission at Wilson's Creek in 1861, and had stayed in the army because that was the easiest way to make a living. He was six years older than Armstrong, had no ambition for military glory and no intention of doing anything more than was required by military regulations, but he knew them thoroughly, and was careful never to transgress. He and Armstrong probably disliked one another at first sight.

Among Armstrong's favorite officers was his Monroe friend, Captain George Yates, whose troop was known as the "band box company." Another was Captain Louis McLane Hamilton, grandson of the great Alexander, a jaunty chap with hedgehog mustache, who wore his képi recklessly over one eye. Other loyal supporters were Captain Myles Keogh, an Irishman with smiling eyes, impressive imperial, and unquenchable thirst. A professional soldier, he had served in the Papal Guards, distinguished himself at Gettysburg, and always squandered every paycheck as wantonly as the lowest private. Myles Moylan was another Custer man. He had a questionable record, including a dismissal from the army in 1863, but there was no doubt about his fighting qualities. He had enlisted three times as a private, once under an assumed name, and always rose quickly to officer status. Now only a sergeant major, he was evidently planning his next step toward a commission. Canadian-born Lieutenant William W. Cooke was another Custer adherent. He had enlisted at the age of sixteen in a regiment of New York cavalry, and participated in the Shenandoah campaign. In the closing battles around Richmond he attained a lieutenancy. Custer knew the young man well and made him adjutant of the 7th Cavalry. Cooke added distinction to the assignment by cultivating side whiskers like General Torbert's.[5]

Thus the regiment, like so many isolated organizations, split into two factions, one for and one against Custer. Yates, Hamilton, Keogh, Moylan, and Cooke were prominent in one clique; Wyckliffe Cooper,

Robert West, and Frederick Benteen in the other. Libbie watched with apprehension as her husband worked with these officers, forming the recruits into a regiment. She feared more than anything else that Armstrong would fail to adjust himself to the monotonous routine. But here, as in Texas, she relaxed with him on horseback rambles across the Plains. She had been out of the saddle almost a year, and riding gave her a "pain in the side" at first; but she smiled and gritted her teeth until the pain left her.

Armstrong never outgrew the adolescent boy's delight in making girls scream. Of all his horses Libbie liked Custis Lee best. His smooth racing pace gave her the feeling of floating on air. Once when she and Autie sped across the Plains together, he reached out his strong arm and lifted her from the horse's back, then put her down again on the thumping saddle. A man as strong as Custer could hold petite Libbie out at arm's length, but the experience was breathtaking for her. To enjoy it, she must relax and have perfect confidence in her husband. Perhaps Libbie's ability to do this was the secret of her love.

Diana thoroughly enjoyed life at Fort Riley, with so many beaux. Autie gave her one of the cavalry mounts as her very own. Then one day he and Libbie made a discovery and had great fun with the young lady. Custis Lee was having his corns treated, so Libbie rode Diana's mount. The animal persisted in snuggling up against the horse beside him. No cavalry horse should act that way. Where did this one learn such a trick? Custer remembered how the fellows back in Monroe had been embarrassed when they took a girl buggy-riding and the animal insisted on stopping at another girl's gate. Horses could not keep secrets, and Diana blushed prettily when they teased her about it.

The winter was enlivened to some extent by a visit of prominent journalists from the East, among them Charles Godfrey Leland, who wrote in his memoirs: "There was a bright and joyous chivalry in that man [Custer], and a noble refinement mingled with constant gaiety in the wife, such as I fear is passing from the earth." [6] Eastern sophisticates, young men much traveled in Europe, always described Custer in the most glowing terms.

Everyone at Fort Riley knew that an expedition would be sent against the Indians come spring. Railroad construction across the Plains was due to start in earnest then and the red men were sure to fight. Sherman ordered his Department commanders to make the Indians submit to white man's rule. If they failed to abide by their peace treaties, show them no mercy. If they wanted war give it to them.

General Hancock determined to establish authority and settle the Indian problem in his department with a grand expedition—foot, horse, and artillery. On March 1, 1867, it started from Fort Leavenworth before new grass had come. Passing Fort Riley, the column picked up the 7th Cavalry, Colonel Smith and Lieutenant Colonel Custer commanding. A new major had just joined the regiment, a man who would have tremendous influence on the rest of Custer's life. Joel H. Elliott had enlisted as a private and worked up to a captain in the Civil War. He had recently taken examinations for commissioned officers and passed with an outstanding record that earned him a majority, thus putting him above many older officers.

Unusual publicity would be given Hancock's Indian campaign because it was accompanied by accredited journalists. Henry Morton Stanley represented the *New York Herald* and *Missouri Democrat*. Theodore R. Davis reported for *Harper's*. During the war he had worked with Al Waud, and called him Pop. Armstrong invited Davis to join his mess. The two young men had first met at West Point when the journalist visited there. Now Davis bunked in an A-tent with Lieutenant Charles Brewster, who had been captured by Mosby's men and drawn lots which saved him from being hanged.[7]

Always sociable, Custer rode along the marching column, hunting army friends. Among the guides and scouts he noticed Wild Bill Hickok, dressed fantastically in Zouave jacket and buckskin leggings. Wild Bill perfumed his long hair, and could, it was said, tie the ends of his sweeping mustache behind his neck. He was a handsome man withal, stood straight as an arrow and carried two ivory-handled revolvers which assured him due respect.

Riding farther along the column, Custer recognized an old friend with the 4th Artillery. Charles C. Parsons had been in his class at West Point and was now a captain. A quiet, thoughtful man, he was unhappy in the army, like so many others. When a student he had been quite religious and might well have been called "Parson" Parsons.

The column marched west along the Smoky Hill stage road toward Denver until the riders saw, across the dead-level of the Plains, a stockade of one-story, mud-plastered huts known as Fort Harker (four miles from present-day Ellsworth, Kansas). One observer said that dried weeds, standing on the flat roofs, looked like a scared man's hair.[8] Here the column turned south until it came to the Santa Fe Trail along the Arkansas River. General Hancock established headquarters at Fort Larned, one hundred and sixty miles from Fort Riley — much farther from Libbie than Autie liked to be.

The Indians had been notified to assemble here on the Arkansas for a council, but they did not appear. A large village of Dog Soldiers — a warrior society composed of Sioux and Cheyenne — was known to be on Pawnee Fork, some thirty miles away. Hancock sent word for the head men to come, saying, tartly, that if they did not do so he would go out and council at the village site — a threat no Indian would like. That night two chiefs, Tall Bull and White Horse, rode into camp with a dozen warriors. Hancock assigned them a tent and ordered a great fire kindled for a council.

These red men were the first wild Indians Armstrong had ever seen. How much did they differ from the "redskins" he had written about in that essay at West Point? Certainly they bore only slight resemblance to James Fenimore Cooper's Leatherstocking Indians, but they were men of dignity — grim, pagan-eyed, spear-throwing lords of war and the chase. Their faces were painted with finely etched designs in brilliant colors. Beads and trinkets jingled from their slit ears and from necklaces. They walked with slow delibertaion, placing their feet carefully. Haste might tear the beads from leggings and moccasins. All wore army overcoats, issued by Indian agents, and in addition these chieftains wrapped woolen blankets around their bodies in a peculiar manner which left the right arm free. Each had his scalp lock bound and decorated with silver ornaments — a challenge to get it if you could.

For the council, officers donned their dress-uniforms with gold epaulets. Hancock, tall, gray, firm-faced yet genial, made a magnificent appearance. Artillery officers wore their new helmets with the red horse-tail plumes — a trifle incongruous, perhaps, with Parsons's religious countenance. The warriors, both red and white, sat down facing one another across the fire. An Indian produced a calumet and filled the bowl from a fringed and beaded tobacco pouch.

Armstrong noticed the peculiar way the Indians inhaled and exhaled the smoke through nose and mouth with short rhythmic puffs. When his turn came he put the moist stem in his mouth and tried it. The other officers did likewise.

General Hancock opened the parley by saying that he had come to maintain order. If the Indians wanted war, he would give it to them. If they wanted peace, he would maintain it. Good Indians who wanted to live in peace would be protected. Bad Indians who persisted in killing and robbing must be surrendered by their people for the white man's punishment. The interpreter translated this. Then Hancock complained because so few Indians had come to the council. He said he had sent word that he wanted to talk to the whole village. As the village had not come in, he would march out in the morning, go to it and talk to all.

Tall Bull replied. Armstrong noticed his fine warlike countenance and his evasive speech. He alluded to the scarcity of buffalo, his love for white men, hinted that presents would be acceptable, and said he did not know why the village had failed to come.

Next morning, Hancock, true to his word, started the column on the thirty-mile march to the village — a two-day trip. On the way, they encountered an Indian battle line stretched across their road. Three hundred warriors had ridden out to meet them on prancing ponies. Armstrong delighted in the savage brilliance, the waving blankets, ornamental shields, spinning feathers, rifles gleaming in the sun. Hancock deployed to meet them. The cavalry drew sabers. The artillery unlimbered, Parsons commanding with the precision he and Armstrong had learned at the Point.

An Indian rode forward with a white flag. Armstrong learned later that this was Roman Nose. Behind him on painted war ponies came Sioux and Cheyenne chieftains, among them Pawnee Killer. Hancock told the red leaders that he was ready to fight if they wished it. If not, he would go on to the village and meet the people in council there. To this the chiefs agreed, so the army moved up the creek close to the village. But at the time appointed for the council no Indians appeared. Hancock waited all day. From his encampment he could see the tips of Indian tepees under the misty green of budding cottonwoods. That night Armstrong went to bed wondering what Hancock planned to do next. He had watched the General in a worse predicament before the Battle of Williamsburg; Hancock had acted wisely then. During the night Armstrong was awakened by an aide, who told him to report at headquarters immediately.[9]

General Hancock had learned through his scouts that the Indians had deserted their village and fled. He could hardly believe it, for at dusk last night smoke was still fanning from the peaks of the tepees. However, he wanted Custer to take the 7th Cavalry, surround the village and find out. This must be done stealthily, lest the Indians be stampeded if they were still there.

Armstrong assembled his men in the dark and rode away. When the village was surrounded he dismounted and beckoned to three men — an interpreter; the regimental doctor; and Sergeant Major Moylan, the soldier who could always earn a commission but had never been able to hold one. (On this expedition he would earn a lieutenancy.) With these men Custer walked toward the nearest tepee. The interpreter warned him to be careful. His wife lived in the village and he suspected an ambush. Armstrong ordered the man to call out in the Indian tongue, say they were coming as friends, not enemies. The interpreter shouted this message but the only reply they heard from the darkened village came from barking dogs. That was alarming, for if the dogs were there the Indians must be also.

Custer drew his revolver and with his little party slipped forward. He admitted later that he was very nervous but too proud to turn back. Lest they be seen against the stars, the men dropped on all fours and crawled up to the first tent, watching, listening for any sound. Armstrong put his ear against the elkhide tepee wall but could hear nothing. He opened the door flap and crawled in. Fire embers glowed in the center of the lodge and he smelled wood smoke and stewing meat.

Buffalo robes lay on the floor. Back rests (Indian chairs) of willow wands looped from the upright tepee poles. Rawhide containers, geometrically designed, stood in their accustomed places. But the inhabitants were gone. Other tepees were empty, too. In all the village, there remained only an old man, too feeble to travel, his squaw, and a demented white girl of eight or ten who had been brutally raped by some of the younger bucks before they left. Correspondent Stanley, who knew the slums of London, inspected the village next day and noted the filth of this, his first Indian encampment — "so foul, indeed, as to defy description." The robes on the floors, he said, were a mass of filth and vermin. Custer, in his description, made no comment on the lack of cleanliness. He noted only the picturesque equipment — typical, certainly, of Custer's romantic views of the Civil War and of life, itself.[10]

When General Hancock learned that the Indians had fled, he ordered Custer to take the 7th Cavalry and pursue them. Colonel Smith was retained for detached service. Correspondent Davis went with the pursuit column. If there was any action he knew Custer would be in it, but Davis had no confidence in the troops under him — so different from the soldiers he had known in the war. The men in this army he found to be mostly bums or broken-down adventurers, some of them ex-Confederate soldiers seeking free transportation to the Colorado mines. They showed no interest in the service or in Indian fighting, and would certainly desert at the earliest opportunity.[11]

The Indians' trail led north. Custer tried to follow it, but the pony tracks soon fanned out and there was no single trail to guide him.

Davis noted that Armstrong seemed much depressed. This was his first independent command since coming to the West, and it promised to be a failure. But Old Curly would not give up. He knew that somewhere north of them across the horizon, seventy or eighty miles away, the Smoky Hill stage road ran east and west from Fort Riley to Denver. The fugitives would have to cross that road if they went north. Drivers and stationkeepers would be sure to see their tracks. Custer determined to ride north and find out.

The little column wormed its way over the ocean of grass. One day Armstrong saw a distant black speck — his first buffalo. He rode Custis Lee toward it, a lone horseman on the Great Plains, but he felt confident that he could outrun any hostile Indians, and he did want to bag that bison. The chase took longer than he expected but the final run was exciting. At the moment he pulled the trigger to kill the lumbering beast, Custis Lee tossed up his head and the ball hit him between the ears. Armstrong picked himself up out of the dirt, shaken by his fall, bewildered and mortified. On all sides the horizon lay flat and treeless without landmarks, and he had no idea which way to walk, seeking the army. He dared not light a signal fire, lest it attract Indians. Fortunately the army found him, but in his next letter to Libbie, tenderfoot Custer could not bring himself to say that he had killed her favorite mount.

The column reached the stage road at last and learned that Indians had crossed it, sacking stations on the line as they passed. Evidently the redskins who had fled from their village were now on the warpath. Custer ordered his column to march east along the road. He found deserted stage stations every ten or fifteen miles. At intervals groups of stationkeepers had gathered for defense. These men told horrendous tales of Indian atrocities and they pointed to a pillar of smoke where the road crossed the eastern horizon. Custer pushed toward it.

At Lookout Station, fifteen miles from Fort Hays, he found the buildings in ashes, but still smoldering. No Indians could be seen on the vast surrounding plains. Near the burned debris lay three charred bodies. Custer dismounted to look at them. The victims had been scalped and mutilated, probably tortured before death.*

Armstrong hurried on to Fort Hays, arriving on May 3 with his horses exhausted. To his great disappointment he learned that the post lacked adequate horse feed. Custer could do nothing except report to Hancock and await supplies. Of course he wrote Libbie, too. She replied from Fort Riley that she and Diana wanted to join him. The railroad had been pushed sixty miles west of Riley since last winter, and she was sure they could ride from the railhead in a supply wagon to Fort Hays.

Armstrong agreed, so the two girls and Eliza made the trip. Libbie found Fort Hays much more primitive than she expected. Miserable log shanties with stone chimneys stood in a square around what passed for a parade ground. A little stream at the bottom of a wash almost encircled the post. In the best cabins canvas had been tacked under the pole-ceiling to catch sand sifting down from the dirt roofs. Occasionally a rattlesnake dropped into this billowing ceiling and remained trapped for weeks, startling the people below with its threatening whir.

Libbie found other things equally unpleasant. Four or five horses died daily from starvation. The men complained about their rations, too, and deserted whenever they saw a chance. General Hancock came to inspect the fort, saw the revolting conditions, agreed to send hay, oats, and suitable food for the men. Then he returned to Leavenworth, acknowledging his Indian campaign a failure.[12]

---

* Custer, in *My Life on the Plains,* p. 94, says he found three bodies. H. M. Stanley (*My Early Travels and Adventures,* p. 241) says only two. The Indians' defenders have claimed that these massacres were retaliation for Hancock's burning their village. The weight of the evidence (H. M. Stanley, *My Early Travels and Adventures,* p. 241; Custer, *My Life on the Plains,* p. 95; G. B. Grinnell, *Fighting Cheyennes,* p. 244) indicates that Hancock burned the village *after* he heard about the massacres. Of course the Indians who plundered the stage route may not have been Dog Soldiers from the village. Stanley's description of the village is found in his *Early Travels and Adventures,* pp. 39, 41, 43.

After resting almost a month Armstrong decided that some of his men and horses had recovered sufficiently to march. He still hoped to retrieve something from the campaign's failure. The renegades must be somewhere on the plains north of him, between the Smoky Hill road and the Platte River, along which the Union Pacific Railroad was being built. Armstrong ordered three hundred and fifty of his best troopers to ride north on June 1, with twenty wagons, and hunt the Indians. Correspondent Davis looked forward to a "scoop," but, having watched the unhappy enlisted men, he wondered if the whole regiment might mutiny and desert when they reached the railroad.

The column marched away from the post under the ranking officer, Major Wyckliffe Cooper, a member of the regimental clique which opposed Custer. Cooper was leaving a wife back in civilization who expected their baby to be born in his absence. He seemed much depressed and was drinking heavily.

Armstrong watched the column go, then dallied one more day with Libbie. At midnight, accompanied by a little escort of only seven scouts and soldiers, he galloped after it — a glorious moonlight ride he remembered later. They reached the encampment at reveille, in time to join the next day's march. Thirty-six hours without sleep seldom bothered Custer.

After Armstrong assumed command he amused himself by hunting, scouting across the Plains, studying the habits of wild animals — coyotes, prairie dogs, burrowing owls, rattlesnakes. The peculiar Indian burials on scaffolds, with the deceased warrior's favorite horse lying dead underneath, interested him. His men could not desert out here, but he worried about Cooper. The man's drinking increased with the distance he rode from the post.

Then an unfortunate thing happened. Correspondent Davis told later about that night of June 8, 1867. He was sitting at Custer's mess, he said, as the sun dipped below the rim of the Plains. Armstrong noticed the vacancy at Cooper's place and said someone should be with the Major. Custer knew that Cooper disliked him personally, so he turned to Davis. "Possibly you should be the person," he said.

Davis rose to go, but before he left the table they all heard a pistol shot. Armstrong put a restraining hand on Davis's arm. He sent Tom, who came back reporting a suicide. Custer assembled all his officers. At his tent door, he told them what had happened, concluding, "Gentlemen, this is not the death of a soldier — it is unnecessary, standing as we do in the presence of such an example, that I should say more."

Custer turned and strode away. Correspondent Davis said, later, that the only time he ever saw the general hesitate and knit his brow was when fellow officers consulted him about Cooper's funeral. Evidently the decision was a hard one. For a man to die in action, face to the foe, and be buried with inspiring military ceremony, seemed a proper and satisfying end of life for Armstrong Custer, but suicide . . .*

When the column reached the Platte River near Fort McPherson, Custer rode out on the bluff and looked over the broad, timbered valley, flat as the Plains and a level lower. He could see the Union Pacific tracks reaching westward, and the telegraph line which already carried messages to California. The overland wagon road passed here, too, and, seventy miles to the west, it branched, one prong leading to Denver, the other to Oregon. Forts, stage stations, and ranches stood along this highway. Custer telegraphed Sherman, Commander of the Division of the Missouri, for further orders and began loading supplies. Sherman replied that he would come to see Custer.

Armstrong established camp twelve miles from Fort McPherson and waited. Shortly thereafter, Indians appeared on the southern Plains and signaled for a parley. Pawnee Killer, from the Dog Soldier village, wanted to talk. With him and his chief warriors, Armstrong held his first council, smoking the pipe of peace as he had seen Hancock do. Pawnee Killer expressed great friendship for the whites. Custer shook his hand and urged him to bring his people to the fort and live in peace. The chieftain grunted assent, accepted presents of coffee

---

* This account of Cooper's death is from T. R. Davis, "With Generals in Their Camp Homes," p. 130. The record in the National Archives gives his death date as June 8, 1867, "from excessive drinking."

and sugar which Armstrong gave him, and jogged back over the horizon.

Armstrong felt pride in his diplomatic victory, and when Sherman arrived told him about it, but that nervous, excitable, wrinkled redhead was unimpressed. He did not trust Indians, or Custer either, for he wrote a friend that Armstrong was "young, very brave even to rashness, a good trait for a Cavalry officer," but he added that he considered him lacking in "much sense"; he thought it inexcusable for him to be mixing in politics. Sherman told Custer that Indian promises were worthless, and the red men must be taught a lesson. All who refused to obey the white man's law must be killed. He ordered Armstrong to begin by cleaning out the renegades in the Republican River watershed — a favorite hunting ground south of the Platte. In case they attempted to escape by moving north of the railroad they would be taken care of by "General" John Gibbon — now reduced to colonel — who had two thousand men in the Department of the Platte.*

Custer set off with orders to report for his next instructions at Fort Sedgwick, one hundred miles farther up the road (near where Julesburg, Colorado, would stand). Riding southwest with the regiment was like shoving off from the shores of civilization. The little column soon passed out of sight of "land" on that ocean of grass — green now, in late June, and springy under the horses' hoofs. Scouts rode over the horizon constantly, but reported no Indians. Armstrong finally camped, as ordered, on the Republican. He was very anxious to find the hostiles, and almost desperate now to see Libbie. He estimated that he had ridden about seventy-five miles southwest from Fort McPherson, that it was another seventy-five miles northwest to Fort Sedgwick, where he was to report for orders, and only seventy-five miles south to Fort Wallace on the Smoky Hill road from Fort Hays to Denver. Why not send the wagons south to Wallace, instead of northwest to Sedgwick for sup-

---

* R. G. Athearn, in *William Tecumseh Sherman and the Settlement of the West*, p. 105. General C. C. Augur commanded the Department where Gibbon was campaigning.

plies? With them he could send word to Libbie at Fort Hays to come west to Wallace and then ride the wagons north to camp. Armstrong even convinced himself that the southern route was smoother and more suitable for vehicles. Having reached this conclusion, he ordered the wagon train to march in charge of his adjutant, the dignified side-whiskered Lieutenant Cooke. A guard, under Captain Robert M. West, would accompany it. The lieutenant, as Custer's personal aide, thus temporarily ranked the captain — a humiliation which must have rankled in Captain West's heart and no doubt contributed to his determination to humiliate Custer as soon as the campaign terminated.

When the wagons had trundled across the southern horizon, Custer sent Major Elliott with a detail of eleven men to Fort Sedgwick to pick up any orders Sherman might have sent to him there. On the night after both detachments had gone, Indians attacked the main camp but Armstrong fought them off. He wondered if they had waylaid his two little parties. Next day the red men appeared again and signaled for a parley. Armstrong met them and learned that last night's enemy was his erstwhile friend, Pawnee Killer, smiling today in the most ingratiating manner. Furthermore, the chief, during the parley, tried to trap Custer away from his men. Failing in this, a little band of warriors appeared near the camp, daring the soldiers to follow them. Custer let Hamilton give chase with his troop, and they were promptly led into an ambush — but luckily escaped.[13] Armstrong was learning his first lessons about Indians. He was also wondering what might happen to Libbie if she came with the wagons.

Fortunately Elliott and his detail returned from Fort Sedgwick without trouble. However, the train had to fight its way north from Fort Wallace, the wagons in double column, saddle horses inside, the dismounted troopers in a circle around the slowly moving vehicles, shooting at the feathered warriors who swept daringly past them. Libbie was not with the train. Autie's letter had failed to reach her. She had been forced to go back to Fort Riley when a flood inundated Fort Hays.[14]

The experience was unpleasant, but it may have saved her life, for officers were under orders to kill women rather than risk the possibility of their capture by savages.

Elliott brought orders from Sherman for the regiment to march on, up the Republican, hunting Indians. The soldiers could get supplies anywhere along the Denver road west of Fort Sedgwick.

Custer set off at once, and immediately displayed the willfulness and lack of judgment which seemed to increase with his advancing age. Perhaps his boyish traits were only becoming more noticeable as he reached man's estate. However this may be, he certainly knew that his men differed from Civil War soldiers, but instead of tempering the rigors of army life Custer ordered a series of forced marches — morale-building exercises, he believed. A commander must at times force his men to the limit, yes; but Custer's weakness was not knowing the limit of these men, not realizing that they lacked military ambition, and that a day's ride on one of his thoroughbreds was not comparable to the same experience on an "issue" horse. Then, as though this were not error enough, he unwisely selected the main-traveled road to the Colorado mines for his camping place after a sixty-five-mile waterless march.

The men began deserting at once, slipping away two or three at a time. Disregarding this, Custer visited a nearby army post and learned that he had missed some orders from Sherman which Lieutenant Lyman S. Kidder had tried to deliver to him on the Plains. In fact, Kidder was still out there seeking him now, and as he was accompanied by only a guide and ten soldiers he might be "rubbed out" by the first party of Pawnee Killer's warriors who spied him. Armstrong telegraphed for a duplicate set of orders — which told him to proceed to Fort Wallace — and on receiving them, ordered the command to prepare to march at dawn. Lieutenant Kidder and his party must be saved, but it would take more forced marches to do it.

When Custer's order to prepare for a renewed march at dawn was received, thirty or forty more men deserted before reveille. Armstrong learned about this latest defection when handed his morning report on July 7, while the regiment prepared to march. The penalty for desertion in time of war was death. He could probably overtake the fugitives, but that would have meant abandoning Kidder. Armstrong ordered the column to proceed.

At noon, after a fifteen-mile march, the regiment halted to unsaddle, rest horses, and boil coffee. Custer had been told, as he rode at the head of his regiment, that many more, perhaps a third of his men, planned deserting after dark. Wholesale desertions had become common in many other regiments, especially those close to the mines, but he was determined that no such defection would happen in his outfit. He was not prepared for what he saw at the noontime halt.

Out across the Plains, in sight of the whole regiment, fifteen men, seven of them on government horses, were riding back to the stage road. Something must be done at once! Armstrong shouted to Officer of the Day Henry Jackson in a shrill, excited voice which the whole regiment could hear: "Stop those men. Shoot them where you find them. Don't bring in any alive."

The horses belonging to Tom Custer, Major Elliott, and Adjutant Cooke were still saddled. These men started in a race to see who could be first to overtake the deserters. A bugler galloped after them. Twenty-five minutes later distant shots were heard and bugle notes called for a wagon. Five prisoners were brought in, three of them wounded — none dead. Ten had escaped. Soldiers gathered around the wagon to see the victims.

"Don't go near that wagon, Doctor," Custer shouted. "I have no sympathy with those men. Adjutant, have all troop commanders continue the march."

Surely such a lesson would stop future plans for desertion, but Custer was taking no chances. That night he ordered officers, not enlisted men, to walk post, and to shoot to kill anybody who dared come out of his tent. The precaution was needless. The regiment was now thirty miles from the tempting highway, and the spirit of mutiny had been crushed — except in the hearts of some officers who lost a night's sleep walking post, and now began to plot revenge. Chief among them was Captain Robert M. West, who had been humiliated by serving under a lieutenant.

On the next day's march Custer forced the pace, getting every mile he could from men and horses. He knew that Lieutenant Kidder was somewhere along the trail across the grasslands and that if not rescued soon he would be exterminated. On the fourth day after leaving the Platte, scouts found the couriers' trail, headed for Fort Wallace, still eighty miles south. The chance of their reaching it alive seemed slim. Not a minute must be lost. The column pushed ahead. Within a few miles Custer spied something on the plain. It was a dead horse, stripped of all accouterments. Custer was not sure that it belonged to the couriers until he saw the "US" brand. Two miles beyond lay a second horse, and the guide found unshod pony tracks. Indians! From here on the tracks of the couriers' horses showed them to be galloping. This was bad. The couriers had evidently been running like buffalo from the Indians.

Custer quickened his pace. Ahead, he saw vultures circling and in the tall grass along a draw he found the men's bodies — stripped of their clothes, horribly mutilated, and scalped. Arrows stuck from the corpses like quills on a porcupine. The remnants of the collar of a black-and-white shirt around the neck of one victim was the only clue to the men's identity.[15] Custer ordered them buried with proper military ceremony — the pomp dear to his heart. Then the column marched on southward across the plain until it arrived at Fort Wallace, a cluster of log cabins and dugouts on the stage road from Fort Riley to Denver.

Here Armstrong learned that cholera had broken out at Fort Riley. Libbie wrote that she was frightened and very anxious to see him. Riley was only a little over three hundred miles east along the stage road and Armstrong decided to go at once. Of course it was contrary to orders and through dangerous Indian country, but Libbie needed him. Besides, he had a plan for getting there which he was confident would work.

22 Court-martial

CUSTER'S EXCUSES FOR LEAVING FORT WALLACE WITHOUT PERMISSION IN July, 1867, will always be controversial. His horses were undoubtedly worn out by the long march north to the Platte and back again. To Armstrong that alone seemed reason enough to prevent him from following orders to continue harassing the Indians, using Fort Wallace as his base. Just how the pick of such tired horses were in condition to make one of his greatest forced marches — toward Libbie — he did not say. Another, and perhaps better excuse, was the lack of adequate supplies at the fort at a time when hostile red men prevented wagon trains from coming through. In addition the garrison was threatened with cholera, the dread disease which was reported also in Fort Riley, where Libbie had gone shortly after Custer left Fort Hays. These things justified Armstrong, in his own mind, in rushing back to learn how his wife was faring. His enemies would maintain later that he made these excuses as a pretext for visiting Libbie.

When Custer made a decision he acted instantly, whether in a charge or in a personal problem. To get supplies and thus save the post he selected a hundred of his best mounted men. He would lead them as an escort for the empty wagons on the march east along the stage road for 150 miles to Fort Hays. In case provisions were unavailable there, he would go an additional 70 miles to Fort Harker, the temporary railhead. If, on arriving at Harker, Armstrong boarded a train to Fort Riley he could see Libbie and get back by the time the wagons were loaded. Up on the Republican last month he had altered the campaign in an effort to see Libbie. Why not try it again?

At sunset on July 15, 1867, the wagon train and escort started across the Indian-haunted Plains. They marched all night, all next day, and the following night, passing several wrecked stage stations. They stopped only long enough to feed horses and boil coffee — never more than an hour each time. At Downer's Station, an "eating stop" on the stage route when it was running, they found an infantry patrol. Custer called a halt. He was only thirty-five miles now from Fort Hays. His men were nodding, blurry-eyed, and their horses' heads drooped, hocks knocking together. Armstrong slid off his mount, curled up in a doorway and fell asleep. Within half an hour he was aroused from his stupor by a report that Indians at the rear of the column had cut off some of his men who had failed to come into the station. Two cavalrymen had been killed.

Custer ordered his bugler to sound Boots and Saddles. Then he notified the infantry commander about the casualties, and instead of going back to investigate, he plodded ahead. Nine or ten hours later, at 3 A.M., the column staggered into Fort Hays. Armstrong was proud of his record. It was better than his sixty-five-mile waterless march to the South Platte. This time he had covered 150 miles in 60 hours with only six hours' rest.* Feats of endurance like this had made him famous in the Civil War. They tested the stamina of his men. However, Armstrong was not yet ready to quit. Supplies were inadequate at Fort Hays and the knowledge that Fort Harker, on the railroad leading to Libbie, was only another sixty or seventy miles down the road prevented him from resting. The dangerous Indian country had been left behind. Armstrong told Captain Hamilton to follow at a slower pace with the train and guard. Custer would go ahead and have supplies ready to load at Fort Harker when they arrived. With this arranged, Armstrong, brother Tom, Adjutant Cooke, and two privates swung up on their horses and rode off. Next morning at 2 A.M. they shuffled into Fort Harker. The train for Riley — and Libbie — left at three. Custer went at once to Colonel Smith's headquarters and knocked at his bedroom door. The sleepy old soldier let him in. Armstrong, in his excited way, said the wagons were coming, would arrive in a day or two, must have supplies. In the meantime he wanted to catch the morning train

* In *My Life on the Plains*, p. 211, Custer said he marched 150 miles in 55 hours. According to the court-martial records in the National Archives he seems to have consumed five more hours.

for Fort Riley, would be back when the wagons came in, hadn't seen his wife for six weeks.

Colonel Smith liked Custer, had said he could not "well do without him." Sleepily he acquiesced in the exuberant officer's natural desire, told him to take his own best regards to the ladies and went back to bed. Before noon that day Libbie heard on her gallery a quick, nervous step and the clank of a saber. The door burst open and in came Autie bubbling with life, talking excitedly, words tumbling from his mouth. The lovers were so glad to be together — but they soon learned that the tryst was expensive both in money and in military prestige. Old Colonel Smith thought things over after he awoke that morning. What authority did he have to grant Lieutenant Colonel Custer a leave of absence outside his jurisdiction? Why was the young man not with the 7th Cavalry fighting Indians? Smith wired for Custer to return at once. Armstrong took the next train back to Fort Harker, knowing that he was headed for trouble, but Libbie could say twenty years later that the short time they spent together after a summer of anxiety and worry over cholera, floods, and hostile Indians was for her "one long, perfect day." [1]

On July 28 Custer was placed under arrest. His immediate superior, Colonel Smith, and the disgruntled Captain Robert M. West preferred charges against him. They accused him of leaving Fort Wallace without permission, of excessive cruelty and illegal conduct when he ordered his officers to shoot deserters; of abandoning the two soldiers who were killed by Indians near Downer's Station; and of marching men excessively. Captain Robert Chandler, of Hancock's staff, was appointed judge advocate for the trial.

To all outward appearances the threat of court-martial did not worry the Custers. Surely a hero with Armstrong's Civil War renown could do nothing wrong! Libbie wrote home that such unpleasantnesses were a routine part of army life. But both of them were whistling in the dark, for Armstrong usually became religious when facing danger, often communing with his chaplain. To defend him in the court-martial, he selected the religious Captain Parsons, of the 4th Artillery. The two officers held long conferences. Libbie became acquainted with her husband's counsel, liked him very much and derived comfort from the fact that he was a church man. She took special interest in his reminiscences of West Point days with Armstrong. He said that he first noticed Custer in chapel that time when Armstrong put his fingers in the red hair of the boy ahead of him and pretended to burn them.

Parsons and Custer discussed the charges and decided to select as witnesses Armstrong's best friends, Adjutant Cooke, Major Elliott, Captains Hamilton and Thomas B. Weir — the latter a war veteran who had risen from lieutenant to captain since Custer commanded the 7th. Of course Tom Custer was also to testify for his brother. Armstrong, always happier when he could write, jotted down notes for consideration by Parsons, describing what his witnesses would say — notes which Libbie kept for the rest of her life, as she did everything else her husband touched.*

Of all the charges, Armstrong feared most the one which accused him of shooting those deserters. Of the three wounded, one had died. Ever since the end of the war, discipline had been Custer's greatest problem. But shooting a deserter before a firing squad in Louisiana had brought him no trouble; and in Texas Sheridan had backed him when Armstrong resorted to whippings for other offenses. Desertions were more numerous now than they had been then, and the quality of the enlisted men was inferior. Flogging had been revived as a regular punishment. It was not unusual to end the chastisement by "spread-eagling" the culprit in the sun for additional torment by buffalo gnats.[2] Such brutal punishments were condoned, but when a man died under them the officer in charge might be held accountable. Armstrong wrote Sheridan, asking him to testify in his behalf,[3] but Little Phil had reasons of his own for not appearing.

Custer's defense on all counts was weak. He did not deny facts. Instead, he tried to justify his acts. Excessive marches, he said, must be covered by cavalry. He cited forced marches during the war. When Jeb Stuart made his spectacular circle around McClellan's army, Union

* These notes are now at the Custer Battlefield National Monument.

pursuers rode 90 miles in 24 hours, almost 4 miles per hour, while he, Custer, coming from Wallace to Hays, rode less than 3 1/2 per hour. He did not say, however, that he had maintained this pace almost twice as long.

• Armstrong had no trouble proving that Colonel Smith wished him *bon voyage* before he boarded the train for Fort Riley. The old fellow admitted as much, but why had Custer left Fort Wallace without permission? Armstrong explained this by citing the lack of supplies and stating that Sherman, up on the Platte, had given him carte blanche to go where he deemed best, "to Denver City or to hell if he wanted to." [4] That sounded like Sherman and Armstrong could repeat it with a chuckle, although it sounded flippant for a court-martial record, perhaps too flippant for Armstrong's own good. Curly's sunny disposition had a way of breaking out in the darkest situations.

Custer explained leaving the two men who were killed by Indians at Downer's Station by saying that they had disobeyed orders by dropping behind the column and after they were dead he could do no more for them. The Indians had vanished. His own horses were too tired for action. To stop and stumble around through the hills instead of getting supplies back to Fort Wallace might jeopardize the whole command.

This seemed a poor excuse, for the dead men may well have dropped from the column through sheer exhaustion. The case against Custer for shooting the deserters seemed even worse. His enemies testified that when Armstrong saw, out across the plain, the fifteen deserters, he shouted to Officer of the Day Jackson, "Bring back none of those men alive." It was also alleged that when the wounded deserters were hauled into camp, Custer said, within hearing of the whole regiment, "Doctor, don't go near those men. I have no sympathy for them." Then he loaded his greyhounds into a wagon to protect their feet from prickly pears and started the column, thus showing more concern for the comfort of his dogs than his men. His enemies said, further, that two days elapsed before the doctor dressed the men's wounds, a delay which may have caused the death of one of them.

The regimental surgeon was called upon to testify. He corroborated the statement about Custer's shouting to him not to treat the wounded men, but the doctor added that Custer told him, when the crowd could not hear, "You may attend them after a while." As soon as the column started, the doctor said, he examined their wounds. He did not dress them for two days because he lacked clean water, not because Custer ordered a delay.

When Armstrong was called on to defend himself against this charge, he admitted the allegations, saying that it was necessary to threaten brutality in order to prevent half or more of the regiment from deserting. He did not intend to carry out these threats, he said, and his officers understood this, otherwise they would have brought in the fugitives dead. Moreover, the only person he ordered to shoot the deserters was Officer of the Day Jackson, who never fired a shot. The culprits were wounded by Elliott and Cooke who went voluntarily and shot, no doubt, in self-defense, when attempting to make the arrests.

None of Custer's defenses impressed the court. He was convicted on all counts and sentenced to a year's suspension from the army with forfeiture of all "proper pay." Armstrong, debonair always, consoled himself with the cheering knowledge that he would have time at last to write — especially his memoirs of West Point and the war. Libbie heard the verdict with equal external composure, saying later, "When he [Autie] ran the risk of a court-martial in leaving Wallace he did it expecting the consequences . . . and we are determined not to live apart again, even if he leaves the army otherwise so delightful to us." [5]

General Grant approved the sentence, with the notation: "The reviewing officer, in examining the testimony in the case, is convinced that the Court, in awarding so lenient a sentence for the offenses of which the accused is found guilty, must have taken into consideration his previous services." [6] To make matters even worse, the friends and relatives of Major Cooper now blamed his death on Custer, seeking redress in the War Department. It was even intimated that Armstrong might have employed someone to shoot the major.

23 Battle of the Washita

CUSTER MIGHT HAVE LEARNED A LESSON FROM HIS CONVICTION IF SHERI-
dan had let him alone. What that general did next to the headstrong
boy was enough to spoil anyone. After the eulogies lavished on Armstrong in the Shenandoah Valley and at Appomattox, it was becoming
constantly harder for him to conceive of himself as doing anything
wrong. The court-martial publicity had not been so humiliating as
Libbie feared. His disgrace was not even mentioned in the illustrated
article about his part of the Hancock campaign which T. R. Davis
wrote for the February, 1868, issue of *Harper's Monthly Magazine.*

Suspension from duty gave Custer ample time to keep posted on national affairs, and the situation in Washington was not to his liking.
The radicals who advocated a vindictive reconstruction of the defeated
South had got control, and in March they impeached President Johnson. Old Zach Chandler had been prominent in forcing the trial and
Congressman Bingham delivered the closing address for the prosecution. Armstrong was luckily free from that imbroglio.

Also in March, Sheridan assumed command of the Department of
the Missouri, and he was determined to succeed where Hancock had
failed. Little Phil had achieved a victory in the Shenandoah Valley
after several generals had lost their reputations there. Surely he could
do as much against Indians out West. But to Sheridan's dismay, his
heavily loaded cavalrymen always failed to overtake raiding war parties. In a period of only sixty days, Indians had killed one hundred
and twenty-four settlers in Kansas, Colorado, and Texas. General Sherman, commander of the division, raged at the army's incompetence:
"The more we can kill this year," he said pointedly, "the less will have
to be killed the next year for the more I see of these Indians the more
I am convinced that they will all have to be killed or be maintained as
a species of paupers." [1]

Sheridan decided to try a new plan. He would beat the Indians at their own game, fight fire with fire. He moved his headquarters from Fort Leavenworth to Fort Hays, close to the renegade Indian country, now reached by the railroad. Here he authorized George A. ("Tony" or "Sandy") Forsyth, his trusted aide in the Shenandoah campaign, to organize a troop of frontiersmen — scouts inured to the Plains, men who could meet the Indians on their own terms.

On August 29, Forsyth marched out of Fort Hays with fifty-one men — more fighters than he might expect to meet in any war party. Three weeks later two frightened and bedraggled couriers from this troop straggled into Fort Wallace. They reported that Forsyth and his entire detail were surrounded on a branch of the Republican, and were fighting for their lives. Unless help reached them immediately all would be massacred.

Sheridan dispatched a relief expedition and before waiting to hear from it, he wired Washington to remit Custer's sentence. He needed the Boy Wonder. Sheridan also sent another wire to Monroe. Armstrong and Libbie were dining at a friend's house when the telegram arrived. Custer opened it and read:

> HEADQUARTERS DEPARTMENT OF THE MISSOURI,
> IN THE FIELD, FORT HAYS, KANSAS
> *September 24, 1868*
>
> GENERAL G. A. CUSTER, MONROE, MICHIGAN:
> Generals Sherman, Sully, and myself, and nearly all the officers of your regiment have asked for you, and I hope the application will be successful. Can you come at once? . . .
>
> > P. H. SHERIDAN
> > *Major General Commanding*

Armstrong did not wait for orders from Washington. Instead, he wired Sheridan that he would board the next train. Evidently the United States Army could not conquer the Indians without him! As he stuffed a change of clothes into a bag he resolved to send a copy of Sheridan's telegram to all the court-martial officers who had condemned him. But he never did. After a ten-months' forced vacation he was too eager to get back in service and chase Indians. Action was always more fun than revenge.

Armstrong left Monroe on the first train with two Scotch staghounds, Blücher and Maida, and a new pointer. At the Fort Leavenworth ferry he found General Sheridan's carriage and baggage wagon at his service. Custer got his own horses out of pasture, loaded them on a stock car, and dropped a note to Libbie telling about all the special courtesies Little Phil had arranged for him. Then he boarded the westbound train, passing Fort Riley, and Harker — where he had made his fatal mistake — then on to Fort Hays where Sheridan awaited him.

Winter had already come to the Great Plains. A cold wind blew from the snowfields, out of sight across the western horizon, freezing picket ropes stiff as wire, numbing human flesh to the bone. Sheridan told Custer that he planned a winter campaign. He believed the only way to subdue the Indians was to attack their villages after snow came and their ponies were too weak to travel. If the Indians' supplies were all destroyed they would have to come into the reservations or starve. Sheridan said he had proposed such a winter campaign to his scouts and guides. They were against it; said white men would perish in the blizzards.[2] What did Custer think?

Custer was not a man to make excuses or say, "It can't be done." He liked Sheridan's plan. "How soon do I start?" No wonder Ol' Curly was Sheridan's pet!

Little Phil explained that the 7th Cavalry was at Fort Dodge, across the Plains ninety miles southwest of them. He planned to establish another fort in the heart of the Indian winter range, one hundred miles farther south — some two hundred miles from their present location. At this proposed Camp Supply, Custer must wait until cold weather weakened the enemy's ponies. Then he could strike.

Armstrong wrote Libbie to move to Fort Leavenworth, bring a companion who would enjoy meeting officers. He would run in to see them at every opportunity. Posting this letter, Armstrong, with a small escort and his big dogs at heel, rode to Fort Dodge in two days, "rather good for someone out of practice," he told Libbie in his next letter. Stamina, endurance, energy had cost Custer a court-martial, but they were the things he admired, demanded of himself, of his horses, dogs, and men. In this same letter he said Indians attacked the garrison while he was eating dinner on the day he arrived. He leaped on a fresh horse, called out the regiment and chased the savages until long after dark.

No doubt Armstrong liked to think of himself as a cyclone — and compared to other commanders he may have been — but the records indicate that he did not act so fast as his letter implied. Instead of opening his campaign on the day of his arrival he seems to have waited four days before taking command. Perhaps "careless reporting" is a characteristic of reckless men. Certainly Armstrong did not exaggerate more than the fabulous Will Cushing, who acted so heroically in the Civil War. Imagination, or lack of it, may be a necessary part of gallantry. Custer's peculiarity was that he always claimed to be energetic but cautious, said that he took only calculated risks — another exaggeration!

Most of the officers in the 7th Cavalry seemed glad to see their old commander. Major Elliott, Captains Yates, Keogh, and Weir, Lieutenants Moylan, Cooke, and Tom Custer welcomed a renewal of the old hilarious days of horseplay and practical jokes. Tom could hardly wait to tell his brother about a skunk which had tangled with his dog "Brandy." To be comforted, the unfortunate canine had jumped on him and Captain Hamilton. After that they both amused themselves the rest of the night by visiting other officers' tents, stinking them out of their cots. Armstrong wrote Libbie all about it. He also described the good hunting. Blücher killed a wolf. Maida caught a jack rabbit alone. Together they took hold of a buffalo.

Custer found it difficult to be cordial with the clique which had opposed him, especially Captain West, but he determined to do his best and wrote Libbie, "My official actions shall not be tarnished by a single unjust or partial act."

To train the regiment for the winter campaign Custer ordered a shakedown march, with target practice twice a day. He organized his best marksmen into a corps of forty sharpshooters under Lieutenant Cooke — favoritism again, grumblers like Captain Fred Benteen were sure to say. He also enlisted a party of Osage to serve as guides, and some white and mixed-blood frontiersmen to act as interpreters, scouts, and couriers. Among these was a flat-nosed, squat-bodied Mexican with thick Negroid lips who spoke Cheyenne, having married into the tribe. Romero was his name, and his unromantic features prompted fun-loving Armstrong to call him Romeo.

The scouts were paid seventy-five dollars per month and Custer promised an extra one hundred to the first man who led the regiment to an Indian village. As Chief of Scouts he employed "California Joe," a giant mountain man whose real name was Joe E. Milner. Joe's head was covered with curly hair which coiled on his shoulders. A dingy briar pipe gurgled in his tangled red whiskers. Soldiers said he was "brass-mounted." Armstrong relished his picturesque clothes and quaint lingo. He wanted that kind of man in his outfit. The 7th Cavalry must have character and individuality.

Custer equipped himself for the expedition with special overshoes of buffalo hide with the hair inside. He experimented with heavy woolens under buckskin shirt and breeches — a warm combination for freezing weather, but in rain the shirt would stretch to his knees. Daily, Armstrong hardened himself by hunting on the plain, shooting wild fowl on the Arkansas sloughs. Bagging a pelican, he sent it to the Audubon Society of Detroit. One day he was hurt. A rearing horse struck him over the eye, opening his flesh to the bone. The surgeon bandaged his head leaving only one eye open but not quenching his eagerness to be off.

In November Grant was elected President of the United States. Custer showed no enthusiasm. Libbie liked Grant when they met in Virginia, and he had written that good letter to the Mexican minister, Señor Romero, but Armstrong detested Grant's tricky tactics during the impeachment of his friend, President Johnson, and Custer was always stubbornly loyal to a friend or an idea. Sheridan, on the other hand, took inordinate interest in the election. Perhaps he foresaw promotion for himself in case Grant won. In any event, he neglected plans for the winter expedition while the electioneering progressed. Some officers in the West said that he had lost his nerve concerning the winter campaign, would give it up. Armstrong defended him stoutly, would never admit publicly any weakness in his idol, but when he wrote Libbie he admitted his doubts and consoled himself with the prospect of seeing her soon. "I do not long for glory or fame," he wrote with his usual exaggeration, and added, "My reward is centered on ending this trying separation" — a more exact statement, no doubt.

Finally, however, Sheridan ordered the expedition to set off and establish Camp Supply. On November 12, 1868, four hundred wagons crossed the Arkansas, consolidated into a column four abreast with an infantry guard and plodded southward across the undulating plains. Custer's cavalry scouted the country ahead. General Alfred Sully commanded the column. On the sixth day's march he ordered a halt. Around the covered wagons spread an expanse of undisturbed grass, cured on the stem — ideal winter pasture. A mile above the place where Wolf and Beaver Creeks join to form the North Canadian, a fort was staked out, with bastions at alternate corners. Two or three days later Sheridan arrived with more troops. He ordered Custer to leave on November 23, find Indians and destroy them if he could. He was to take eleven companies — about eight hundred men — and the Osage scouts. A minimum number of wagons would transport tents and supplies.[3]

The night before departure was warm, threateningly warm. Plainsmen knew this foretold a storm. After dark all lights were out except in a few tents where officers wrote last letters home. At four in the morning reveille sounded. Custer noticed an unfamiliar hush in the camp. The roof of his tent sagged suspiciously. He parted the tent flap and looked out. A foot of snow covered everything. Soon Adjutant Cooke stamped in out of the darkness with the morning report in his hand and snow in his black side whiskers. "How's this for a winter campaign?" he asked sarcastically.

"Just what we want," Custer told him.

Horse grooming was hurried and perfunctory in the feathery atmosphere. Men ate breakfast around campfires. The order to take down tents and store the clammy canvas in wagons added to their misery. The sky was still black above trembling flakes when company officers reported their troops ready to march. Bugles sounded Boots and Saddles. The men shuffled through snow to the picket lines, and Custer galloped, with an orderly, across the plain to Sheridan's tent. Big snow crystals pelted his face. Little Phil heard the sentry challenge him and called from the warm yellow interior of his tent, asking about the storm.

"Just what we want," Armstrong called back. "If this stays on the ground a week, I promise to return with the report of a battle with the Indians."

"Keep me informed, and good luck," the general replied with his usual accompaniment of cordial oaths.

At the flap of another tent Armstrong saw a staff officer wrapped in a buffalo robe. "Good-by," the man called. "Take care of yourself."

Custer rejoined his regiment. Snow lay on the men's hats, on their shoulders, in the wrinkles of their blue uniforms, and it covered their saddles faster than the men could brush it off. Armstrong told the bugler to blow Prepare to Mount, then Mount. The men swung up. Custer paused a moment. Everyone in the general's tents must be listening. Armstrong turned to the band. It sat in position on the gray horses. He gave the final order, Advance, and the column marched into the wavering curtain of falling flakes, the band playing "The Girl I Left Behind Me."

All men were cautioned to remain within sight of the column, for if anyone strayed a few hundred feet in this storm he might be lost forever. The guides reported that they would not be able to find the proposed camp site on Wolf Creek, but Custer carried a compass and the creek ran east-and-west. Thus it was impossible to be lost so long as they stayed north of the stream.

Shortly after noon, having marched twelve or fifteen miles, Custer wheeled the column south into the creek-bottom timber. Horses were picketed and fed. Soldiers swept away snow-covered leaves to clear spaces for the tents. Dinner was cooked. After eating, Custer lay back on his buffalo robe bunk with his staghounds, warm and affectionate bedfellows. His officers reported the men in good spirits, proud of their hardiness in the storm.

At four next morning the camp was astir. Stars twinkled brilliantly and eighteen inches of snow blanketed the ground. California Joe said, "The travelin' is good overhead."

Custer led the column up Wolf Creek, often riding far in advance. The storm had driven buffalo into the shelter of the trees, and the men lived well. Once the staghounds, Blücher and Maida, bayed an old bull in the deep snow. Armstrong dismounted and, with a drawn knife, ran in on foot and hamstrung the animal, then killed it with his pistol.

The weather moderated and at the end of the second day Armstrong saw, across the southern rim of the Plains, a group of five peaks — the Antelope Hills — on the South Canadian (near what would one day be west central Oklahoma, close to the Texas border). These peaks, ranging from one hundred and fifty to three hundred feet in height, were the Indian guideposts of this vast vacancy. Custer ordered the column to leave Wolf Creek and ride straight for the peaks. He knew that any war party returning from the Kansas settlements would travel in sight of the Antelope Hills. The column reached them at dark and camped on the north bank of the Canadian. Armstrong called Major Elliott to his tent and explained his next plan: The major must take three troops with guides and Indian scouts, provide them with three days' rations and one hundred rounds of ammunition, and march in the morning along the north bank of the Canadian for fifteen miles. The mud and melting snow would make trailing easy and, if he found that Indians had crossed going south, he was to follow the tracks but send a courier back with the news. In the meantime the main column would cross the river and travel south slowly. Their trail would be plainly seen by the messenger.

At dawn Elliott rode away with his squadron. Custer spent several hours locating a suitable wagon ford — no easy task in the freshet of melted snow. The Canadian's banks were steep and the quicksands treacherous. He finally found a place where the lead wagons crossed without mishap. He ordered them to park and wait on the south bank until all joined them. The regiment, as it came over, must dismount and rest horses. Then Armstrong rode to the top of a nearby peak. The panorama was magnificent. A flat world stretched, saucerlike, around him, with no landmark except the bed of the Canadian, a red scar through the grasslands, from horizon to horizon.

By midmorning Armstrong saw, below him, that the last wagon had crossed the river. He started to ride down to his men when he noticed a distant speck. The tiny black figure rocked as it progressed across the white plain — evidently a rider was coming at a gallop. Could Elliott be sending a man already?

Custer raised his glasses to see better. As the figure grew in size he recognized Scout Corbin's horse. Surely an Indian trail had not been found so soon! What had happened? Armstrong rode to the foot of the hill and waited nervously. The man seemed a long time coming, but at last he pounded in and swung to the ground. The horse stood trembling, nostrils distended and red as blood. Yes, a hot trail had been found, Corbin said. A hundred and fifty warriors had gone south not more than twenty-four hours ago! They were probably headed for a village on the Washita, the next stream south.[4]

Custer ordered the scout to get a fresh horse, return to Elliott and tell him to follow the Indians until 8 P.M., then wait for the column. When it arrived they would all go on together in the dark.

The courier trotted off. Custer assembled his officers, "front and center," to explain his plans. Speaking in his quick, almost stammering manner, he said eighty men would be left with the wagon train, all others must prepare to march at once. Each must take one hundred rounds of ammunition, a little coffee and hard bread, but no extra blankets. Wear overcoats and expect to bivouac in the snow. Custer took out his watch and held it in his thick hand.

"In twenty minutes, gentlemen," he said, "the Advance will be sounded. You are excused."

The officers galloped to their commands, scattering soft mud and snow. Ammunition was distributed, mess chests opened for hard bread. Here and there a flash of red flannel showed where a trooper was putting on an extra undershirt for the ordeal. Weak horses in each troop were relegated to the wagon guard.

The Officer of the Day happened to be cocky Captain Hamilton. His duty was to guard the wagon train while his company marched into action under a lieutenant. He appealed to Custer but Armstrong would make no exception to the rule unless some officer was willing to exchange places with him.

Hamilton rode away. He found a man who had been incapacitated by snow-blindness and they traded assignments. Thus Captain Hamilton rode with his troop when the regiment started. No time had been allowed for dinner. The weather turned hot and the men, in addition to being hungry, perspired inside their bunglesome clothes. Under the melting snow, water seeped through the dead grass. Horses slipped in the mud. Bare patches of sod appeared on the south slopes. The wagon train followed but was soon left far behind on the horizon. Scouts galloped off hunting Elliott's trail. The sun sank to within a hand's breadth of the sky line, and still no trail had been found. The mud was beginning to freeze now and would soon be hard as rock. Then horses would no longer make tracks that could be followed.

As the sun set, Custer saw one of his scouts, far out in front, signal that he had found the trail. But when Armstrong reached it, he could see no sign of Elliott's men on the horizon beyond. Custer ordered one of his best troops to go ahead — slow gallop — while it was light enough to see, overtake Elliott, and wait until the regiment caught up.

At nine o'clock all the troops had joined Elliott in a small timbered draw, out of sight from the plain. It seemed to be the Washita River bottom or a tributary. Both men and horses showed fatigue, but Custer never tarried long. He ordered the horses unsaddled, watered and fed. The men might boil coffee but all fires must be in the bottom of the gulch, invisible to spying Indians on the flats.

The Osage scouts wanted to wait until morning. Custer asked them why. Getting no satisfactory reply, he decided that they were reluctant to attack before they knew the number of their enemy.

Custer's rule, all through the Civil War, had always been to attack first and, if outnumbered, cut his way back afterward. He had done this repeatedly: at Beverly Ford, at Gettysburg, and at Trevilian Station. No superstitious Indians could bluff him! At 10 P.M. the column left the line of trees and rode downstream on the flats. Moonlight helped them see the way. Two Osage walked ahead. Behind them, three or four hundred yards, their fellow scouts followed in single file, leading their mounts. California Joe rode his mule at the rear. The snow had crusted since dark, and the horses made so much noise that it was necessary to keep the cavalry a quarter- to a half-mile behind the scouts. All riders were ordered to strike no matches, speak only in whispers, and keep the tin cups which dangled under the saddlebags from rattling.

An hour or two had passed when Custer saw, against the midnight sky, the two lead scouts stop. He rode forward.

"What is it?" Armstrong asked.

The Osage spoke little English. "Me smell fire," he replied.[5]

Custer sniffed with his long nose but was uncertain. He told the red men to advance — but cautiously.

A half-mile farther, red coals were spied under a clump of trees at the left. Were Indians sleeping there or had the column frightened them away? Armstrong sent a man back to halt the regiment while the scouts, with guns ready, stalked off to investigate. They came back out of the darkness and reported no Indians there. The fire must have been left by boys tending the pony herd during the day. This, of course, meant that the village was close.

The two lead scouts advanced stealthily again, one ahead of the other. Armstrong rode behind the second one. At the crest of a ridge he saw the front man crouch suddenly, then creep back. Custer dismounted, handed the reins to the second scout and went forward. At the crest he peered into the dark line of trees ahead. He saw a herd of something. Were they horses or buffalo? He watched and listened. A dog barked in the distant trees and Armstrong heard the tinkle of a bell. That convinced him. War parties are unaccompanied by dogs. . . . This must be the village. As Armstrong turned he heard a baby cry.

The hour was now past midnight. Custer sent a scout back to bring all officers forward. The commanders trotted in, dismounted, and huddled around him, like players listening for the signals. Armstrong explained that the regiment was to be divided into four units. Each must advance from a different direction and strike the village, which apparently was in the trees near the horse herd. Major Elliott was to take three troops and circle behind the village. Two other columns of two troops each were to come in from the sides. Custer would keep four companies, as well as the sharpshooters under Cooke, the Osage scouts, and the band. The encircling detachments had ample time to get in place. The attack from all sides would begin at dawn.

As usual, Custer found waiting harder than marching or fighting. He divided his four troops into two squadrons, one under Hamilton and the other under West — captains of the pro- and anti-Custer factions. Excitement united them all. Even the usually lethargic Captain Benteen stopped his sardonic grumbling. The night was bitter cold, especially for those men who had drenched their clothes with sweat during the heat of the day. Custer wrapped the cape of his greatcoat around his head and lay down by the warm bodies of his staghounds. He awoke in an hour and looked at his watch. Still two hours before dawn! He strode off through the crusted snow to inspect his men. Soldiers huddled in groups at their horses' heads, some nodding, some mumbling to one another. He found the Osages squatting under the low branches of a tree, muffled in their blankets. They knew that in open country, any windbreak, no matter how small, made the warmest place to camp. The red men complained. They did not like this white man's way of charging into an unknown number of enemies.

Next, Custer walked to the white scouts' bivouac. These men were in better spirits. California Joe wanted to talk. Romero, the Mexican-Negro mixed-blood, grinned cheerfully. They looked forward to a big haul of Indian ponies, come morning.

As dawn approached, the moon disappeared and the stars burned brighter. The cold hours dragged. A peculiar red light over the village made Custer fear that the Indians had discovered him and sent up a rocket for help. Watching it apprehensively, he soon realized that this unusual light was only the morning star shining through frosty mist from the Washita. Finally the sky began to pale. The day was breaking!

Custer ordered his men to mount and form line, the band and Cooke's sharpshooters in center. A sharp breeze cut like a knife but Armstrong ordered coats off, and haversacks dropped from saddles. A guard was left with this duffel. The shivering line rode over the divide at a walk and started down toward the pony herd. Custer led the way, followed by Captain Hamilton, the lucky fellow who had traded guard duty for action. In the uncertain light the distance seemed longer than Armstrong had estimated. The Indians were sure to hear the horses' hoofs break the snow crust. Soon Custer spied the peaked tops of tepees among the bare trees, but he saw no sign of life. Had the red men evaded him as they had a year ago on Hancock's futile campaign?

A rifle shot rang out somewhere in the village. The alarm? Custer turned to the band leader and ordered him to play "Garry Owen."

The rowdy air blared across the snow:

> *We'll break windows, we'll break doors,*
> *The watch knock down by threes and fours;*
> *Then let the doctors work their cures,*
> *And tinker up our bruises.*

The music stopped. Saliva had frozen in the instruments,[6] but the defiant melody opened the battle. Custer heard answering cheers from three sides of the village. Bugles beyond the frosty trees sounded the Charge. Horsemen pounded in from all sides, guns booming. On the hurricane deck of a galloping horse the cold air made a man's eyes water. Captain Hamilton disappeared. Armstrong saw, through streaming eyes, the terrified pony herd thunder among the tepees, racing past blue-coated troopers. Snowballs from flying hoofs pounded the leather tent walls. Red men bounded among the stampeding animals, or fell sprawled in the trampled snow. Some escaped to the creek bank, jumping half-naked into the icy water. Others hid in sinkholes and soon opened fire. Custer directed Cooke and his sharpshooters to clean them out. He detailed a guard to round up the pony herd, and he established a field hospital among the tepees.

Before ten o'clock quiet had been restored except for a few pockets of embattled warriors being attacked by Cooke's men. Armstrong rode in to see the wounded and dead in the hospital. Captain Hamilton's body lay there, shot in the back. Was he killed by accident or by a disgruntled trooper? This was a chance every officer must take. Albert Barnitz, a troop commander, lay seriously wounded. The surgeon said he would surely die. Tom Custer and another lieutenant had received minor wounds. Eleven enlisted men had also been hit, none hurt seriously.

Custer saw a boy bugler sitting on a stack of robes. He noticed two holes in the boy's head — one over the eye, the other over the ear. Surely a bullet could not have gone through without killing him! Custer asked about this peculiar wound. The lad said he had been struck by an arrow which glanced around his skull, the point coming out over his ear. He explained how the surgeon had drawn out the shaft, letting the skin stretch back into place, thus leaving two holes. Custer asked if the boy saw his assailant.

"If anybody thinks I didn't see him," the lad replied, "I want them to take a look at that." He held up a fresh scalp.

Captain Benteen rode in waving a beautiful pair of boy's moccasins.

He said he had met their owner coming down the creek, tried to take him prisoner, but the red youth would not give up. Instead, he shot several times at Benteen, and that officer had to kill him to save his own life. Plucky little cuss!

Armstrong, in his memoirs, commended Benteen for displaying such patience and gallantry — a compliment that illy matched the way Benteen was soon to treat Custer.

Other soldiers came in with a grimmer story. They had met a squaw trying to escape with a small white boy — a captured prisoner worth several hundred dollars in ransom money. When prevented from getting away with the lad, she drew a butcher knife from the folds of her blanket and disemboweled him before the horrified soldiers.

Other troopers looting the tepees found pictures, daguerreotypes, fragments of letters, bits of bedding from Kansas homesteads brought in by the war party, and the dispatches carried by one of Sheridan's couriers who had been killed. Custer kept these relics to show Little Phil.

Before noon Armstrong rode through the wrecked tepees and inspected his lines. On the bare hills beyond the village he saw something which must have chilled the blood in his veins. All around his regiment a multitude of warriors were assembling — evidently from other villages, unknown to him. His own men were now low in ammunition. If cut off from their wagon train they might be wiped out here among the lodges which they had captured. Certainly no time must be lost in deciding what to do next.

Custer rode back to the center of the village, told his interpreter, Romero, to assemble all the captured women and children — some fifty of them. An important-looking squaw came to him with a friendly smile. She said that this village had belonged to Black Kettle, who now lay dead with other warriors. More villages, she said, stood along the Washita — villages of the Kiowa, Arapaho, Comanche, and Plains Apache, in fact all the hostile Indians. Some were only two miles away, the farthest about ten. The woman enjoyed talking, said she was Black Kettle's sister and that she had repeatedly warned him to stop his young men from raiding white settlements. As she talked on and on, Custer realized that the warriors might be gathering in dangerous numbers. Indeed, she might be purposely holding his attention to gain time. At the end of a melodramatic speech she stepped up to him, leading a pretty Indian girl whose hand she placed in his. Armstrong turned to the interpreter and asked, "What is this woman doing, Romeo?"

No matter how tense a situation Armstrong must have his little joke.

"Why, she is marrying you to that young squaw," "Romeo" grinned.

Custer dropped the girl's hand. In this emergency, with Indians gathering to attack, there was no time for dalliance. Later he would say that he approved the "peace policy," but not to that extent. Besides he already had a wife more to his liking at Fort Leavenworth.

Custer realized that it would take some hours for warriors to come from the farthest village. To defend his position he extended his line around the village. As the men marched out to their stations, an ammunition wagon rattled in behind six heaving mules. The quartermaster back at the wagon train had sent it. Now Custer had sufficient ammunition. The teamster and escort said they barely evaded the encircling warriors. Guards who had been left with the soldiers' overcoats and rations at dawn that morning also came in, leaving the clothes and food to the savages. In the excitement Custer's dog, Blücher, raced away after the red horsemen and did not come back.

Custer feared that the wagon train might be ambushed, thus leaving the regiment without support in the wilderness. He abandoned the idea of saving the horses he had captured and hoped only to get the regiment out alive. He ordered the women prisoners to select mounts to ride in the retreat. The rest of the animals, eight hundred and seventy-five all told, must be killed — an unpleasant task for a cavalryman — but Sheridan had ordered a scorched-earth program. The Indians must be impoverished.

Soldiers began to tear down and burn the tepees. Over one thousand buffalo robes were destroyed, together with seven hundred pounds of tobacco, great quantities of dried meat, guns, pistols, bows and arrows. Lieutenant E. S. Godfrey later recalled tossing into the flames a beautiful beaded buckskin gown decorated with elks' teeth. No souvenirs could be kept.[7]

As the sun sank in the cold western sky Custer drew his command into formation under the bare trees. Major Elliott and fifteen men were missing.* A thorough search of the village and the ground outside the lines failed to show any trace of them. Several people remembered seeing the major lead a squadron in pursuit of a little party of Indians, but no one knew what had happened to him. Custer, in a hurry to get away, ordered the regiment to horse. With the band playing, he started along the creek toward the next village — a pretense of assurance to conceal his fears. He was pleased to see the Indians on the hills melt away, evidently scampering off to defend their villages. His bluff was working.

After dark Custer ordered the column to countermarch. Silently it returned through the burned village; then on to the divide where the Indians had captured the soldiers' overcoats and rations; and still on across the dark plain. At 2 A.M., far from the battlefield, the column halted, built big fires and rested. The men were hungry, having eaten nothing for over twenty-four hours, but all they could do now was tighten their belts and like it.

By daylight the men were again in the saddle. At ten o'clock that morning they met the wagon train with food for all. Now the expedition was a success! Tents were pitched and Custer wrote his report to Sheridan. He planned to send it ahead of the column by California Joe. The scout prepared to leave as soon as darkness hid him from view. Custer wrote Sheridan that the fight was "a regular Indian Sailors Creek." The 7th Cavalry had defeated the celebrated chief,

---

* Authorities do not agree on the exact number left with Elliott. G. A. Custer (*My Life on the Plains,* p. 389) gives nineteen enlisted men killed. Randolph Keim, who was with Custer on the expedition, reported in *Sheridan's Troopers on the Border,* pp. 144–145, that Elliott and sixteen men were found. C. C. Rister, *Border Command,* p. 109, says Elliot and eighteen men.

Black Kettle, reinforced by the Arapaho under Little Raven and the Kiowa under Satanta — slight exaggeration! Armstrong concluded by asking the general to communicate with Mrs. Custer. He said approaching darkness prevented him from writing her before the courier must start.

Four days later, the 7th Cavalry marched triumphantly into Camp Supply. Sheridan rode out to review them. The Indian guides led, savage faces painted for war, chanting a victory song. Next came the white scouts in their fringed buckskins, then the mounted prisoners in their brilliant blankets. The regiment followed in column of platoons, the band playing "Garry Owen," which from now on would be the 7th Cavalry's own:

> *We'll beat the bailiffs out of fun,*
> *We'll make the mayor and sheriffs run;*
> *We are the boys no man dares dun,*
> *If he regards his whole skin.*

As Custer and his officers passed Sheridan, they saluted with their sabers. Little Phil lifted his cap. He liked that man Custer — always did. The army had been frustrated on the Plains for three years. Now Custer led it to victory — the Shenandoah Valley over again.

Sherman telegraphed congratulations.[8] So did Secretary of War John M. Schofield, the one-time West Point teacher who was dismissed.

24 Wild Indians, New York Society, and a Grand Duke

BACK EAST, HUMANITARIANS DECRIED CUSTER'S WASHITA BATTLE OF NO-vember 27, 1868. They said that Black Kettle had always been a friend of the whites, that he influenced many warlike chieftains to sign peace treaties, and repeatedly brought in white captives held for ransom by savage villages. The Indian Bureau confirmed the humanitarians' statements, even augmented them. The rivalry between the Indian Bureau and the War Department was bitter. Propaganda to discredit every army act must be expected.

Sheridan gritted his teeth when frustrated. He disliked civilian complaints, but he knew Black Kettle's Indians to be bad. He had seen the gruesome relics, bits of bedding and daguerreotypes from sacked Kansas homesteads found in their camp, and was sure that Custer had given the Indians the medicine they needed — the same dose which cured Confederates in the Shenandoah Valley.

Armstrong had certainly enhanced his reputation for getting things done, but an ugly bit of gossip started a few months after the fight. Captain Benteen, Custer's enemy and a chronic whiner, knew that Armstrong had been court-martialed after riding away from his dead troopers at Downer's Station. Now Benteen wrote a letter which was published, unsigned, in the *St. Louis Democrat*,[1] criticizing Custer for making no effort to save Elliott and his men. In due time a copy of the newspaper came to camp. Custer read it, called his officers to his tent, and slapping his whip on his boot top said he intended to horsewhip the author. Lieutenant John F. Weston, who was present, remembered later that Captain Benteen shifted his revolver to a handy position in his belt and said, "All right, General, start your horsewhipping now. I wrote it."

Custer seemed dumfounded, hesitated a moment, then hurried from the tent.*

In his memoirs Custer excused himself for abandoning Elliott by saying that the major had ridden off without authority and that a scouting party failed to find him. Moreover, the total lack of shots indicated that all his party must be dead. In addition, haste in getting

---

* See C. C. Rister, *Border Command*, p. 114; C. F. Bates, *Custer's Indian Battles*, p. 16. Note that Libbie Custer (*Tenting on the Plains*, p. 113) tells a similar story as happening in Texas when a newspaper article maligned Armstrong's father. It is probable that Libbie gave such fanciful interpretations to several of her husband's acts.

away was imperative lest the Indians capture Custer's wagon train and thus leave the whole regiment helpless in the wilderness. These excuses are notably similar to those Custer gave to the court-martial when he abandoned the two dead troopers at Downer's Station.

Armstrong's anxiety about the wagon train is also open to criticism. In the first place, he should have realized that the Indians did not know a train was coming. In the second place, it had an adequate guard. Certainly, in 1867, his wagon train, guarded by an equal number of soldiers, had kept moving on the trip north from Fort Wallace in spite of attacking Indians.

Custer has also been censured for overestimating the number and hostility of the Indians on the Washita. Although many warriors assembled around him they invariably retreated before his every advance. This, critics say, should have shown him that they were observers only, not dangerous antagonists. Moreover, the warriors available in all the hostile villages numbered only one thousand to fifteen hundred — surely no match for 700 disciplined cavalrymen. Custer, of course, did not know this. All he knew was that his regiment was very far out in a very desolate desert in midwinter, surrounded by many savages. His enemies would say that he either became frightened or so elated over victory that he wanted to get back regardless of Elliott's fate. Who can analyze motives?

When Custer returned to Camp Supply with his victorious cavalry he wrote Libbie at once referring to the complimentary citation he received from Sheridan. "Oh, is it not gratifying to be so thought of by one whose opinion is above all price?" He also assured Libbie that he had obeyed her throughout the battle, never needlessly exposing himself. He closed by saying that he hoped to see her before long. Sheridan had promised to send him to Fort Leavenworth as soon as he completed one more march down the Washita, gathering recalcitrant Indians and taking them to their reservation at Fort Cobb.[2]

To help in this last undertaking the 19th Kansas Cavalry had come. This regiment of volunteers was commanded by Ex-Governor Samuel

Crawford. The Kansans had lost their way on the Plains in the recent storm. They had also lost their horses — but not the spirit of revenge which they hoped to wreak on the savages who had raided their frontier settlements. The 19th Kansas, together with Custer's 7th Cavalry, should be able to corral and whip all the renegade Indians in the Southwest. Sheridan proposed to go with them on the expedition. He had brought staghounds to the Plains, so he could match their fleetness against the speed of Custer's Maida.

Armstrong suggested taking along three of the captured squaws. They knew the country and could help mightily in dealing with their own people. For this job he selected Black Kettle's talkative sister, another woman about her age, and a young girl named Mo-nah-se-tah.* She was the daughter of Little Rock, a chief who had been killed in the Washita fight. Custer described her as "an exceedingly comely squaw, possessing a bright, cheery face, a countenance beaming with intelligence, and a disposition more inclined to be merry than one usually finds among the Indians. She was probably rather under than over twenty years of age. Added to bright, laughing eyes, a set of pearly teeth, and a rich complexion, her well-shaped head was crowned with a luxuriant growth of the most beautiful silken tresses, rivalling in color the blackness of the raven and extending, when allowed to fall loosely over her shoulders, to below her waist." [3]

This description is noteworthy because gossips would have much to say about Custer's relations with Mo-nah-se-tah.

The three Indian women followed the column in an ambulance. Scouts led the way, and California Joe kept Armstrong laughing at his humorous remarks. As the army approached the Washita battleground, Sheridan and Custer rode ahead with a squadron to examine the field. Topping the ridge where the soldiers had left their overcoats before

---

* Libbie states that this Indian girl was the same as the one to whom he was almost married during the Washita battle (E. B. Custer, *Following the Guidon,* pp. 49, 90, 94, 97). Armstrong, in his *Life on the Plains,* does not say she was the same person, but he does not deny it.

the charge, they found the body of Custer's dog, Blücher, bristling with arrows. Below them stood the bare trees white with frost. The men rode closer. Crows flew up but a few half-wild Indian dogs still skulked around, sniffing at grisly remains. To search every foot of the ground for miles around Sheridan deployed the squadron. Two miles from the charred wreckage they found the bodies of Elliott and his men, all badly mutilated. Certainly it would have been difficult to have found them at the close of the fight while an unknown number of hostile Indians were congregating.*

Next day the brigade marched down the Washita, passing the sites of the villages whose warriors had threatened Custer. All were deserted. Only round circles of dry earth in the mud showed where tepees had stood. Charred fagots, scraps of buckskin, battered kettles, worn moccasins, broken shields, and torn parfleche indicated that the Indians had moved in haste. In one deserted camp lay the battered bodies of a white woman and her baby. The Kansas volunteers recognized her as a captive who had written pathetic letters urging that she be ransomed. Mo-nah-se-tah came from the ambulance, prowled about the deserted encampment examining broken implements and the design on discarded clothing. She said the village belonged to Satanta, the Kiowa.[4]

Grimly the column resumed its march down the Washita, day after day, meeting no opposition except from icy winds which whistled across the plain stinging the men's faces, numbing their hands, penetrating woolen clothes, but not buckskins like those worn by Custer and the scouts. Seventy-five monotonous miles below the battlefield, Indians swarmed over the river bluffs to meet them — red men armed for war! Custer deployed the brigade. He had twice as many men now as he had for the Black Kettle fight. What a chance to teach these renegades another lesson! Then the survivors would learn to stay on their Fort Cobb reservation, as Sherman had ordered.

* Letter, Armstrong to Libbie, December 19, 1868; C. C. Rister, *Border Command*, p. 115. To find a few bodies on the winter plains two miles away is a more difficult problem than Custer's maligners want to admit.

The soldiers moved forward slowly, the Kansans caressing their rifles, the regulars in a disciplined line, imperturbable, inflexible as a great machine. A chief rode out from the Indians. He smiled cordially, extended his brown hand to Sheridan, said he loved white men, loved peace. His name was Satanta. Custer warned Sheridan to be on guard. Satanta was as jolly a rogue as ever scalped a white man.

A messenger from Fort Cobb rode into the soldiers' lines and handed Sheridan an official letter. Little Phil, on his big horse, read the missive. It said that these, and all other Indians from here to Fort Cobb, were peaceable. "That settles it," Sheridan must have concluded as he handed the paper to Custer.

Armstrong took the letter in his square hand. The signature at the bottom was W. B. Hazen. Custer remembered the name. Lieutenant Hazen had placed him under arrest for not stopping a fight at West Point in 1861. Hazen was a major general now, on special duty with the Indian Bureau — stopping another fight.

"Tell them, Romero," Sheridan said to the interpreter, "if they are our friends, to come with us to Fort Cobb and settle down."

Satanta's face brightened. "Yes. We come. Call in *soldado*."

Sheridan remembered Custer's warning. "Tell Satanta the chiefs must ride with us," he said. "Let the village follow. Then we will believe, and call in the soldiers." [5]

The Indians agreed to this. The head men came in and rode along with the soldiers, but every day one or two chieftains disappeared. At last only Satanta and Lone Wolf remained. It was plain now that they, too, planned escaping. The village had not followed, and the whole performance had been a ruse to help the Indians get away. Sheridan lost his temper. He saw an Indian waving a signal from a hill.

"Tell that man to go to his village, explain to the people that we will hang the two chiefs in our hands unless they are all at the fort tomorrow night," Sheridan said.

Satanta, thoroughly frightened now, called in the red courier, talked

Only known picture of Custer before he went to West Point. The lovelorn lad holds a picture of the girl he never married. *Published here by courtesy of Milton Ronsheim, Cadiz, Ohio.*

Cadet George A. Custer, photographed for 1861 classbook.

Cadet Custer, probably taken immediately after graduation. The weapon in his left hand is a Colt "sidehammer" model 1855, never used at West Point. This may have been the pistol he bought in New York. If so, the hot weather down there in July explains the wilted collar, which would not have been allowed at the Academy.

B-6074

Courtesy Custer Battlefield National Monument,
Dept. of Interior

Brigadier General Custer, the bridegroom brushed and
garnished.

General Custer, his wife, and faithful servant Eliza. The General's haggard cheeks indicate that this picture was taken on the march north from Appomattox.

Courtesy Custer Battlefield National Monument, Dept. of Interior

Major General Custer, his wife, and younger brother, Tom.

Courtesy National Archives

The Blue and the Gray: McClellan's Aide-de-Camp Custer, right, and James Washington, prisoner of war, left. They were together at West Point.

Generals George A. Custer and Alfred Pleasonton

Custer and the Grand Duke Alexis in 1873. The Czar's son enjoyed hunting buffalo and singing about love.

Grizzly bear bagged at edge of Black Hills, 1874. *Left to right:* Bloody Knife, Custer's favorite Arickaree scout, killed two years later on the Little Big Horn; Custer; an orderly; Chief of Engineers William Ludlow. All three of those named claimed to have killed the bear. George Bird Grinnell and Luther North were eating berries on a nearby hillside. They hear the bombardment but arrived too late to claim that their shots dispatched the monster.

Black Hills Expedition, 1874: Six mules haul each covered wagon. Note beef herd at upper left.

Black Hills Expedition: Custer's wagon train passing through Castle Creek Valley on or about July 28.

Original Anheuser-Busch picture of "Custer's Last Fight," painted by
Cassilly Adams, now a collectors' item. In the real fight, Custer carried
no sword and his hair was cut short.

Indian painting of "Custer's Last Stand." On the left are Custer's embattled soldiers, on the right Reno's. Custer's horses were stampeded, as
the picture shows.

earnestly with him, then watched him gallop off. The village was already fifty miles away and its people could not possibly return before the deadline, but enough of them did stream in to convince Sheridan that all were coming. He was also more convinced than ever that Custer understood Indians. As for Hazen, that man had acted the way the Indian Bureau always did. This war would have been settled long ago if renegades failed to get protection from the Indian Bureau every time the War Department caught them.

At Fort Cobb the wintry weather moderated. Mail from Camp Supply brought Armstrong a dozen letters from Libbie. He replied that he longed to see her. Sheridan had promised him "for the fiftieth time" that he could go East at the first opportunity, but the job here must be finished. The mail also brought Sheridan reports of more white women held for ransom by Indians. A letter from Sherman said: "I am well satisfied with Custer's attack. . . . I want you to go ahead; kill and punish the hostiles, rescue the captive white women and children, capture and destroy the ponies." [6]

Custer and Sheridan lay on the grass in the December sunshine discussing how best to carry out these orders. On Christmas, 1868, they dined together, laughing and joking. Little Phil saw now that he had been tricked, and he regretted not punishing Satanta when he had the chance. [7] He knew that other wild bands were wintering in western Indian Territory near the Panhandle of Texas. He decided to establish another post — Fort Sill — over there by the Wichita Mountains, a group of isolated peaks thrust through the Plains.

That winter, while Sheridan was establishing Fort Sill, Custer led two expeditions after renegade Indians. On the first, in January, 1869, he was gone for sixteen days, with only a small party of picked men. Before leaving he wrote Libbie a long letter, not mentioning the proposed campaign lest she worry, but he did tell her to prepare Eliza for another pet in the Custer menagerie. Mo-nah-se-tah had a baby!

The date of this letter, January 14,[8] is important, because Armstrong's maligners would call him father of this child, although he had known Mo-nah-se-tah less than two months.*

Custer's first expedition failed. True, Armstrong sent in Little Raven's village of Arapaho in the custody of Captain Weir, a man Custer was finding dependable since his promotion. However, villages of Cheyenne and Kiowa, known to have white prisoners, evaded him. Armstrong's little party almost starved — ate their horses — before they reached Fort Sill.

At the post they slept, rested, filled their stomachs. A tintype photographer offered to snap their pictures. Custer posed for one, wearing beard and buckskins. He sent it to Libbie. On their anniversary he wrote, "I am sorry we cannot spend it together, but I shall celebrate it in my heart." †

Custer rested a few days, then set off again, taking both regiments and Mo-nah-se-tah with her baby. This expedition, like the previous one, entailed great hardships. The column ran out of rations, lived on mule meat, had to abandon and burn some wagons. Armstrong demonstrated outstanding plainsmanship, knowledge of Indian psychology,

---

* Mari Sandoz, in her magnificently written Western books, assumes that Custer fathered a baby by Mo-nah-se-tah. She has generously given me her citations for this assumption, based on records she saw in the National Archives. These records have been moved since she saw them in 1937–1938 and a repeated search has failed to reveal them, so it is necessary to rely only on the Sandoz notes concerning their contents. She also states that the Fort Sill Medical Records showed Custer and other officers to have been treated for syphilis, 1868–1869 — a commendable caution rather than an indictment. In the Fort Hays records, also now missing, she reported a reference to a son born in the stockade to Mo-nah-se-tah, no date. If the child referred to by Custer was born in January, this second baby becomes extraordinary. There can be little question about the January child, for he is also referred to by Benteen as an example of how the despised Custer was cuckolded. Until the various documents are found, then, and show more than has been reported from the Sandoz notes, the Custer-baby stories must be considered Indian gossip. It should be remembered, too, that the Indian Bureau would not have been averse to circulating tales against the army.

† Letter, Armstrong to Libbie, February 9, 1869. A copy of the tintype is reproduced in C. F. Bates, *Custer's Indian Battles,* p. 15. Miss Agnes Bates spent the winter of 1875 at Fort Abraham Lincoln with Mrs. Custer.

and remarkable ability to control the Kansans who had enlisted to get back their kidnaped women and wreak revenge on the Cheyenne. He had learned Indian ways rapidly and never acted with more courage and sagacity than he did this winter.

Scouts finally located the Cheyenne village, and Custer surrounded it; but instead of attacking, as he had on the Washita, he held back his vengeful volunteers, because he knew that the first shot fired would be the signal for massacring the white prisoners.

When the Indians saw that they were surrounded, they invited Custer to visit their chiefs. Armstrong went boldly to the meeting — a very dangerous thing to do — thus putting himself in their power, but he had a sly plan of his own. The Indians tried first to kill him by witchcraft but the medicine man's charms failed. Next the chiefs came to Custer's camp with entertainers, hoping to divert attention while the village slipped away with its white prisoners. This gave Armstrong his opportunity. He seized the chiefs and offered to trade them for the kidnap victims.

The villagers sulked — "no trade" — until Custer started to hang the red men. This brought results. The white women were released from the tepees where they had been hidden, and the whole village agreed to pack up and come to Fort Sill as soon as the ponies were strong enough.[9]

On these trips Custer broke the monotony of daily life with rude jokes, laughing as coarsely as any cowboy when a man was bucked off his horse. To test a scout's appetite he once fed him meat from a starved horse, claiming it was buffalo. Occasionally he realized that such practical jokes were beneath the dignity of his rank, but the boy in Armstrong was slow to die. Yet, always, in the midst of privations or of horseplay, he could compare the wild scenery, the sunsets, the purple shadows of horses in white sand, with paintings by artists he had known. As he rode along he hummed:

> *The bold dragoon he has no care*
> *As he rides along with his uncombed hair.*

The band played triumphantly as the regiment marched back to Fort Sill again. "Custer fed us on one hardtack a day and 'The Arkansas Traveler,'" a Kansas volunteer said ruefully. Perhaps so, but "Garry Owen," not "The Arkansas Traveler," had become Armstrong's favorite tune.[10]

Sheridan had gone to Washington, so he was unable to review the troops as he had done at Camp Supply after the Washita fight. Since Grant became President, Sherman had been elevated to general, and Little Phil to lieutenant general. If Custer hoped to go up a step, too, he was disappointed, but he may have derived some satisfaction from learning that Captain West, who had preferred those court-martial charges against him last year, resigned on March 1, 1869. He was in very bad health and died in September — from excessive drinking, it was said. Colonel Smith, who had joined West in bringing the charges, and General William Hoffman, president of the Court, both retired in May. Thus the worst of Custer's enemies seemed to be out of his way. However, he read that Marcus Reno had been assigned to him as a major.* Reno and Benteen could make trouble, and Hazen, of course, with his Indian Bureau backing, was always a threat, especially now since Sheridan had gone.

All renegade Indians on the Southern Plains were believed to be under control by the spring of 1869, except one band led by Tall Bull which had ridden north when the grass greened. Custer was ordered to disband the Kansas volunteers and march the 7th Cavalry to the railhead at Fort Hays. The regiment would stay there all summer. Armstrong went to Fort Leavenworth to help Libbie move to her "summer home." Before returning, the Custers attended a military hop. Custer had become a famous Indian fighter now and people watched him curiously. Dr. Robert H. McKay, a newcomer to the army, was disappointed in his looks, thought him undersized, too slender. Long hair

---

* M. Ronsheim, *Life of Custer*, p. 27; F. B. Heitman, *Historical Register of the United States Army*, p. 35; Godfrey Papers. Reno was assigned as of December 26, 1868, but he had not joined in June. Letter, Custer to Sherman, June 29, 1869.

gave him an effeminate appearance. But the doctor admitted that Armstrong was a graceful dancer and that there was something arresting about his face, something of boldness, dash, a quick eye. His every movement showed energy. No doubt he was a whirlwind in action.[11]

The Fort Hays to which the Custers returned was completely new and strange to Libbie. Since the flood which drove her out two years ago, the post had been rebuilt. Officers were now quartered in a fine row of two-story frame houses, each with a porch and a little fenced yard in front. Here and there a few spindly trees had been planted. To Libbie the everlasting Plains were the only familiar thing left and there was one spot on them which she always remembered with a mixture of fright and laughter. Once after Autie had ridden north with his men in '67 she and Diana had gone for a walk out of bounds. A nervous sentry mistook them for Indians and opened fire. To protect themselves the two girls lay flat on the ground. Libbie, for the first time in her life, rejoiced in her slenderness, and now that the ordeal was over could say of Diana: "The pretty, rounded contour of the girl, which she had naturally taken such delight in, was now a source of agony to her, and she moaned out, 'Oh! how high I seem to be above you!' "[12]

Those days were gone forever, and the new post held only memories of them. The 7th Cavalry was assigned a camp site two miles away and the Custers lived there, too. The post commander, General Nelson A. Miles, became much attached to both Armstrong and Libbie — a friendship which would last as long as they all lived. To make them as comfortable as possible, he provided an assortment of tents, one for a bedroom, another for a kitchen, and a large hospital tent for a parlor. An Indian tepee was erected for Eliza. Libbie added domestic touches to stiff army chairs by draping them with gay Indian blankets and skins. Armstrong stretched a canvas fly over their outdoor dining table. A "striker" stood guard before meals to prevent the staghounds from stealing food. Armstrong adopted some unconventional manners when dining outdoors. To cause laughter, he poured the last of the water in his glass on the ground or flipped a prune seed over his shoulder —

habits which embarrassed him at least once later when dining in a house.

The inactivity soon bored Custer. He wanted to go East for a change and applied for the position of commandant at West Point.[13] Failing to get this, he enjoyed himself shooting wild turkey, antelope, and elk. He pronounced buffalo chasing almost as exciting as leading a charge. Many distinguished men came to hunt with him, among them Lords Waterpark and Paget. The latter sent Armstrong a handsome pistol "in remembrance of the very happy time spent at Fort Hays while buffalo hunting in Sept. 1869."

At night, even after the hardest hunt, Armstrong continued his writing, finally having articles published in *Turf*, in *Field and Farm*, and in *Forest and Stream*, signing them NOMAD. Later in the fall, as winds from snowfields below the horizon curled around Fort Hays, the regiment moved to Fort Leavenworth. In December Armstrong went to Monroe on business. He stopped in Chicago to see Sheridan, who was convalescing from an illness. Tony Forsyth and other aides were there. The old comrades went to the theater together. Custer laughed at Joe Jefferson "until his sides ached." He watched Lydia Thompson play in *Blondes* at the Opera House, and the *Times* reported him to be chasing blondes instead of Indian maidens. Armstrong wrote Libbie that the "boys" were tormenting him and he enclosed the clipping. The "boys" also seem to have outplayed him at euchre, for he resolved to forgo cards as long as he remained married.[14]

Next summer, Armstrong and Libbie went back to Fort Hays with the regiment for another tour of drilling, hunting with Easterners, and writing. The following winter, 1870–1871, they returned to Leavenworth. They had lived for five years on the Plains now, and both wanted a change. Armstrong considered resigning from the army, but decided to ask only for a leave while he sought other employment. He was granted one hundred and twenty days — four whole months![15] With Libbie he went to Monroe. They had been married seven years now and once again Libbie watched him go East alone seeking a livelihood. This time he headed for New York with a bear cub for the Zoological Society, a pearl-gray stovepipe hat of the latest fashion on his head, and a packet of mining stock which he hoped to sell. Like his old commander, U. S. Grant, Custer thought he might succeed in the financial world.

As usual, Armstrong was feted by old friends and when he wrote Libbie he complimented her on what a popular husband she had married. He dined at Delmonico's, attended the theater with General O. O. Howard and his family. General Torbert invited him to visit his Delaware home. On Fifth Avenue, Armstrong saw General Merritt alight from an omnibus and help down a stylish young lady. He introduced her as his wife, and invited Armstrong to call. All jealousy over those guns at Cedar Creek seemed forgotten — if that were possible while both remained in the army!

At a banquet Armstrong sat between Horace Greeley and Bayard Taylor, who was recently back from central Africa. Whitelaw Reid, Charles A. Dana of the *Sun,* and the Wall Street banker-poet, E. C. Stedman, were at the table. Armstrong wrote Libbie later that Stedman had said her husband was the Chevalier Bayard of the Civil War, "Knight *sans peur et sans reproche.*" Having bragged in this manner Armstrong ended by saying: "I repeat this *to you alone.*" [16]

Custer received an invitation from Vinnie Ream, a child wonder, to attend the unveiling of her statue of Abraham Lincoln in Washington. Custer declined, writing, "You are young and have obtained a foothold upon the ladder of fame far in advance of your years and to attain which others in your profession of acknowledged genius have been compelled to devote a lifetime. Go on dear friend conquering, and to conquer, your victories are lasting and unlike mine are not purchased at the expense of the lifeblood of fellow creatures leaving sorrow, suffering and desolation on their track." [17]

Armstrong sold his mining stock, sent Nevin Custer a down payment for a farm where he could be near his parents in Monroe, and found he had money left. Armstrong asked for additional leave — and got it. During the summer of 1871 he traveled between Monroe and New

York several times. The luxury of post-Civil War Manhattan fascinated him. He did not gamble, but he visited and described to Libbie the lavish gambling parlors, the faro banks, tables for playing baccarat and rouge-et-noir, all so different from the squalid gamerooms in Hays City. He shopped for army friends, bought gold sleeve-buttons for one officer — the result of a bet — and sent flowers to profligate Keogh's ladylove, at that officer's request. For himself and Libbie he bought musical scores which they could play and sing together.

In July, Custer learned that Captain Robert Chandler, who had served as Judge Advocate in his court-martial, was in an insane asylum. That whole gang — Smith, West, Hoffman and all — seemed to be getting their deserts. Armstrong expressed no regrets and no sympathy, but he did ask for another thirty days' extension of his vacation. Again he got it. He saw much of actor Lawrence Barrett and still toyed with the idea of going on the stage himself. He was a guest several times in the box of the singer, Clara Louise Kellogg, and wrote Libbie about her, saying, "Miss Kellogg is very dainty in regard to gentlemen." [18] Another theater patron, Larry Jerome, entertained him. Larry laughed about keeping a box at the opera instead of a pew in church — said it was cheaper entertainment. With the Jeromes — Larry and Leonard — Armstrong went to Saratoga for a few days at the races. He wrote Libbie that he enjoyed everything except being away from her. "How I wish you were here," he said, "to 'double my joys and quadruple my expenses' in this enchanting place." Then he added, "pardon the quotation — it seemed the place to bring it in. But you never seem any expense to me." [19]

Custer knew that Sheridan had gone to Europe to observe the Franco-Prussian War. He was expected back early in September. Armstrong happened to be sitting in a box with Miss Kellogg when notified that the general's ship had docked — a day late. He excused himself and went that night to Sheridan's hotel. The two sat talking until 1 A.M. The little general said, "Custer, I wish you had been with me. . . . You and that 3d Division could have captured King William six times over." [20]

Such sweet tunes always thrilled Armstrong and he repeated them to Libbie. When next he wrote, he said that Sheridan wanted him to accompany him to Boston. The general would telegraph the War Department for permission.

Even Sheridan, it seems, could not prolong Armstrong's leave. After many extensions, during eight months, his holidays came to an end. He was ordered to report on September 3, 1871, at Elizabethtown, Kentucky. The 7th Cavalry had been brought in from the Plains and distributed by company and squadron in seven Southern states. Custer dreaded duty which he knew would be partly political — suppressing Ku Klux Klanners, enforcing federal taxes on distilleries — but when there was no way of evading a direct order he always obeyed cheerfully.

Only two companies of the 7th Cavalry were stationed at Elizabethtown. Libbie joined her husband there. They lived in one of the small brick cottages connected with the Hill House. Libbie made it homelike, and Armstrong hung his favorite pictures — Libbie in her wedding dress, McClellan, Phil Sheridan, and himself as a major general. The Custers ate their meals with "Aunt Beck" Hill. Her guests all sat at one big table, while a little colored boy pulled the rope on a punkah. Its red streamers waved flies off the apple sauce and hot bread served at every meal. Kentucky seemed as foreign to Libbie as New Orleans, and very different from other places where she had lived. She was reared in a country village but Monroe people did not come to town riding two and three on one horse, bare feet kicking.[21]

In October, 1871, after the great Chicago fire, Sheridan and his aide, Tony Forsyth, were called on to police the stricken city. Tradition says that Custer helped them, but the records indicate that Armstrong was on detached service at this time, inspecting horse purchases in the South. Indeed, he seems to have spent little time in Elizabethtown until after May 22, 1872.[22] While traveling between horse markets, he wrote diligently — no longer stories about hunting, but a long account of Hancock's campaign against the Indians, which he hoped *Galaxy* magazine would publish serially. On a train at night, or in the bare room of a dingy Southern hotel, he plied his pen as industriously as he had by candlelight on the eve of battle. Only when he got a chance to speed north and see Libbie did he break this routine.

In Elizabethtown he would pop into Captain Yates's home to play with the baby, say the little fellow was "barefooted on top," like his dad. He bantered Lieutenants Varnum and Moylan about attending a Methodist revival, accusing them of going for the same reason others went to the circus. Always he schemed to get friends into the 7th Cavalry. He wanted to make it "a big family." To be happy, Armstrong must be surrounded by intimates, joking, teasing one another as he and his brothers had done in his father's household. He requested that Lieutenant James Calhoun be assigned to the 7th. Calhoun was a handsome, blond six-foot Ohioan who had worked his way up through the ranks to a commission. Besides, he was engaged to marry Armstrong's sister, Maggie.

In January, 1872, Sheridan ordered Custer to quit inspecting horse purchases and accompany the Grand Duke Alexis on a buffalo hunt. The son of the Czar wanted to try the sport, and every courtesy was being shown him as a gesture of international good will following the purchase of Alaska. Sheridan planned going along. Tony Forsyth was in charge of all mess arrangements, with orders to supply the best.[23] Sheridan had employed picturesque Will Cody as guide. The dime novelist, Ned Buntline, had recently made him famous as "Buffalo Bill." The Grand Duke's party was to detrain at North Platte, Nebraska.

Libbie shook the mothballs out of Armstrong's woolen clothes, packed his fringed buckskins, and kissed him good-by. The expedition promised to be spectacular. In addition to providing covered wagons and a stagecoach, Sheridan arranged to have Spotted Tail bring along his village to add local color.

The nineteen-year-old Russian was a skilled horseman and good shot. He bagged his buffalo and relished the company of older experts. One stock hand, who had never seen Custer before, noted that he rode with a stiffer seat than the cowboys, and that the fluency of his profanity was the envy of all.*

After the hunt, Custer remained with the ducal party. At Louisville, Alexis was entertained with a grand ball. Libbie came up from Elizabethtown, danced with His Highness and won all hearts with her beauty and soft musical voice. A reporter described the little lady — she was thirty now — as "a dark loveliness." [24]

Alexis invited the Custers to accompany him on the steamboat trip down the Mississippi to New Orleans. The *Galaxy* magazine had accepted Armstrong's account of the Hancock campaign, and the first installment was in the copies now on the stands. Thus "G. A. Custer" had become something of a literary personage as well as a cavalier among the foreign dignitaries and American attachés.

The entourage was gay, with midnight revelry and late rising. Libbie delighted in coffee and rolls in bed, a substantial breakfast at noon, and the evening dinner with three kinds of wine — all so different from the American way. She enjoyed chatting with the Europeans and listening to their amusing accents. She noticed that the Grand Duke's tutor coached him constantly on American history, geography, and economics. The young prince listened politely but seemed more interested in humming music-hall ballads. "If efer I cease to luf" [25] was his favorite verse. Autie could join him in the refrain with appropriate theatrical grimaces. The two had a hilarious time.

At a ball given the party in Memphis, the Custers met their old army friends, the Parsonses. "Colonel" Parsons had served Armstrong sympathetically as defense counsel in the court-martial. Libbie noticed that his wife's clothes looked woefully shabby and out-of date. Parsons explained that he had resigned from the army to become minister of a little mission church. They were very poor but both of them were finding satisfaction they had never known in military life, by serving God through their fellow men.

The Custers barely had time to get back to Monroe on March 7, 1872,

* Had Armstrong forsaken his resolution to quit swearing, or were these recollections the imaginings of envious minds?

for Maggie's marriage to Lieutenant Calhoun, now assigned, at Custer's request, to the 7th Cavalry. At the conclusion of the ceremony Armstrong and Libbie returned to Elizabethtown. An accumulation of mail awaited them. Some came from readers of the *Galaxy* article. One letter from General Mitchell, of Hancock's staff, commended Custer's interpretation of the unfortunate Indian campaign.[26] Another bore the imperial crest of Russia. Alexis sent friendly greetings — the last echo of a glamorous experience. Libbie cherished memories of it but the hour for Cinderella's awakening had struck. Looking out the window, she could see the dusty road between shabby brick houses, a farmer in tattered straw hat, and a few ragged Negroes. Armstrong seemed bouyant as ever. He had purchased two race horses, Bluegrass and Frogtown, which engrossed his attention although he complained, with a chuckle, that he lost ten thousand dollars on them which he needed for payments on Nevin's farm.

Elizabethtown marveled at Custer's many changes of costume. Sometimes he would be seen in military uniform, then in fringed buckskins, occasionally in civilian clothes.[27] Having purchased that dove-gray topper in New York, he liked to wear it.

The town was mildly pleased when another dramatic figure, Lawrence Barrett, came for a visit. As a "bread-and-butter" gift he presented Armstrong with a handsome cameo ring. Libbie hoped it would fit her finger best.[28]

The brick house seemed empty after Barrett had gone. Armstrong tried to concentrate on articles for *Galaxy*. He fidgeted, played an old organ in the parlor — no good for "Garry Owen." Constantly his thoughts dwelt on the subject of his stories — the Great Plains. He realized now, as never before, that he belonged out where the wind swept free — wind pure as spring water, bracing as old wine. A man was the center of his own universe, out there.

In February, 1873,[29] after almost two years in Elizabethtown, Armstrong strode into Libbie's sewing room, snatched her from her chair, waltzed her around the room, singing, laughing, knocking over furniture. One chair crashed into the kitchen to notify Eliza. He had received orders to reunite the 7th Cavalry and take it to Dakota Territory. The Northern Pacific Railroad was being built across Sioux country, and a guard would be needed to restrain belligerent warriors. Service again in the great silent places . . . *Whoopee!*

25 Yellowstone

THE 7TH CAVALRY ASSEMBLED AT MEMPHIS THE LAST WEEK IN MARCH, 1873. From here three steamboats were to take them on the first part of their journey to the Indian country. It was a time of great hilarity for all. Armstrong and Tom Custer, Yates, Cooke, Moylan, Keogh, and Calhoun would be together again. Armstrong's sister, Mrs. Calhoun, was traveling with them. Black Eliza had got married and left, but the Custers had a new colored couple, Mary and Ham. At Cairo, Illinois, the regiment changed to railroad cars and chuffed northwest into late winter weather. The railroad ended at Yankton, just inside Dakota Territory. Libbie was glad to get off the train and stretch her legs — "limbs," they were called by proper ladies. A cool breeze cut through her muslin clothes. Armstrong rode off to superintend placing the encampment. She waited by the tracks arranging their personal baggage — boxes, barrels, Armstrong's leather trunk with COL. G. A. CUSTER stenciled on the end,* his four favorite pictures — as a windbreak for the cages of mockingbirds and canaries, along with the baskets of puppies which always accompanied Custer's headquarters.

That evening a storm struck with blizzard fury. Even in mid-April the snow can pile high in Dakota. Custer rode in, white with wet flakes, slid from his horse, and collapsed with one of the short illnesses to

* This has been preserved with other personal relics at the Monroe County Historical Society Museum.

which he was subject. He was helped into an empty house and here Libbie nursed him during the night, as snow sifted through cracks in the walls.

Next day the sun shone on a dazzling white world. The snow soon melted and water gurgled down all the gullies. Armstrong recovered quickly. The regiment pulled itself together in the mud and started on a three-hundred-and-fifty-mile march up the Missouri to Fort Rice, twenty-five miles below the Northern Pacific railhead at Bismarck (now North Dakota). At the head of the column with Armstrong and his adjutant rode Libbie and her sister-in-law, Maggie Calhoun, in their tailored riding habits. Before noon every day Custer usually galloped ahead with the guidon carrier from each troop. He placed these men where he wanted the company tents pitched as the regiment marched in. When the girls arrived Autie lifted them down from their horses, unsaddled their mounts, and as the encampment rose around him, he usually lay down, often in the broiling sun, for a nap. The staghounds lay beside him; sometimes a gigantic head would rest affectionately on his chest.[1] The girls washed in a tin basin and combed their hair before a wobbly mirror on a tent pole.

On June 10, 1873, the column arrived at Fort Rice. Custer reported the 7th Cavalry for duty to General David S. Stanley. The Yellowstone expedition to guard the Northern Pacific surveyors was to start from here.

Libbie and Maggie, with an escort, rode on to Bismarck, where they boarded the train to St. Paul; then they returned to Monroe.

For ten days the 7th Cavalry practiced brigade drill with the eleven companies of infantry and two batteries of artillery stationed at Fort Rice. The column would contain fourteen hundred and fifty-one men and seventy-nine officers, with two hundred and seventy-five wagons. Tony Forsyth and Sheridan's new aide-de-camp, Frederick Dent Grant — the President's son — were assigned to the expedition. Since the election, a coolness had arisen between Sherman and Grant, and the former refused to take Fred Dent on his staff; but Sheridan, a much rougher man, though parodoxically obsequious, agreed to do so, and sent young Grant as one of his two representatives on the expedition.

The usual motley crew of red and white scouts and guides had been hired. Among them was "Lonesome Charlie" Reynolds, a taciturn mountain man with the high forehead of an intellectual, and a reputation for being "big friend of redskin." A man of mystery, gossips whispered that he had an aristocratic past. Among the red scouts was Bloody Knife, a savage-looking man with high cheekbones, long hair matted on his shoulders, and a reputation for being "big friend of paleface." [2] Seven hundred beef cattle were to be driven along for the commissary. A steamboat, the *Far West,* would take supplies up the Missouri and Yellowstone rivers to a point where the expedition, following a more direct route across the Plains, would meet it. Armstrong planned to take Mary, his cook, and the sheet-iron stove necessary for her Southern dishes. He also arranged for a sutler named Balarian to accompany his regiment with two wagonloads of trade goods and liquor. General Stanley had ordered Balarian out of Fort Rice for selling whisky to soldiers. But Custer, who did not drink, felt sure he could manage him, and thought liquor in moderation might be good for his regiment's morale.

The expedition started on June 20, 1873. Armstrong donned a bright red shirt made for him by Libbie, thus becoming the most conspicuous mark in the brigade. But he could say, sardonically, that he had taken out two life insurance policies, one payable to his parents, the other to his wife.[3] The surveyors who were to be protected from the Indians had already pushed out over the western horizon, but they would be overtaken long before they drove their survey stakes on the banks of the Yellowstone. As soon as Fort Rice was left behind, General Stanley learned that Balarian was with Custer's regiment. At the first encampment he sent Aide-de-Camp Grant back to search the sutler's wagons and confiscate any liquor he might find. Young Grant stopped at Custer's tent and explained his errand. In fact, he stayed there long enough for Custer to send word to the sutler — who promptly distributed his load, a case here, a keg there, to all the more temperate officers. When

Grant finally reached Balarian's wagons there was nothing incriminating left. The sutler, the officers, and Lieutenant Grant all seemed to admire Custer's adroitness.

As the column crawled westward Armstrong began writing to Libbie. Every night he added to the letter until it contained forty-four closely-written pages. General Stanley, in his tent, also began writing his wife. A comparison of the two men's letters makes a study in contrasts. Custer described the good times his officers were having, told how they gathered in his tent every evening for jokes and songs: "I am prouder and prouder of the 7th, Libbie; not an officer or man of my command has been seen intoxicated since the expedition left Fort Rice. H—— [veterinarian John Holzinger] and I have our periodical official tussles, as usual, but I see a great deal of him and like him better than ever."

Compare this with Stanley's letters: he wrote that the weather for the first seventeen days was terrible, simply terrible — a downpour during fourteen of them. Custer, writing Libbie about the same days, said: "Our march has been delightful. Such hunting I never have seen." Then he told about the good shots he had made at running antelope, said he liked his new hexagonal-barreled 50-caliber Remington better than his Winchester.

Both officers discussed each other in their letters home. Stanley said Custer was exasperating — had a reputation throughout the army for insubordination, for usurping authority, but on this trip he was under the wrong man for such tricks. "I have seen enough of him to convince me that he is a cold-blooded, untruthful and unprincipled man," Stanley wrote. "He is universally despised by all the officers of his regiment excepting his relatives and one or two sycophants. He brought a trader in the field without permission, carries an old Negro woman, and cast-iron cooking stove, and delays the march often by his extensive packing up in the morning. As I said, I will try, but am not sure I can avoid trouble with him. . . ."

As Stanley wrote the above, Armstrong was writing Libbie: "General Stanley is acting very badly, drinking, and I anticipate official trouble with him. I greatly regret this, but fear it cannot be avoided." The trouble came almost at once. Stanley wrote his wife:

> I had a little flurry with Custer as I told you I probably would. We were separated 4 miles, and I intended him to assist in getting the train, his own train, over the Muddy River. Without consulting me he marched off 15 miles, coolly sending me a note to send him forage and rations. I sent for him, ordered him to halt where he was, to unload his wagons, and send for his own rations and forage, and never to presume to make another movement without orders.
>
> I knew from the start it had to be done, and I am glad to have so good a chance, when there could be no doubt who was right. He was just gradually assuming command, and now he knows he has a commanding officer who will not tolerate his arrogance.

Custer came back when he received this order and set to work building a bridge over the Muddy. In his letter home he made no mention of the reprimand and wrote only about the amusing way the regiment utilized empty kegs for pontoons to float upturned wagon boxes.[4]

The bridge was finished on July 1 and the infantry began to cross. Stanley notified Armstrong that his cavalry must henceforth ride at the infantry's rear and as additional punishment Custer must consider himself under arrest. Confinement was the one thing Armstrong could not tolerate, but as usual he accepted the order as an opportunity to catch up on his sleep. He lay dozing in camp when he heard a strangely familiar voice outside say, "Orderly, which is General Custer's tent?"

Custer would have known that voice in Babel. He sprang up on his long spindly legs and strode out to shake hands with Tom Rosser — his best friend at West Point and worst enemy in the Shenandoah Valley. Rosser was chief engineer on the Northern Pacific survey now. His wife, back at St. Paul, had tried but failed to intercept Libbie and Maggie as they went home.

All that day and late into the night, the two friends lay on a buffalo robe recounting war experiences. Rosser smiled admiringly as he remembered that the worst defeat he ever suffered was from Custer on October 9, 1864. That morning he had watched through his field glasses as the Union forces deployed. He recognized Armstrong's long hair and told his generals to beware. They did their best and thought they had Ol' Curly licked, Rosser said, until the bluecoats came whooping in from the side, the one place where they were not expected, and the Confederates panicked.

As the two old friends talked, Rosser warned Armstrong to watch General Stanley, said that he had found him undependable, a heavy drinker — once so drunk that his fellow officers carried him to his tent. When Rosser learned that Custer was under arrest and his regiment condemned to tail the column, he resolved to see Stanley in person. His surveyors wanted cavalrymen hunting for Indians out front, not plodding behind the infantry.

Custer was soon released and, in his brilliant red shirt, he led the way across the horizon toward the Yellowstone. Rosser came to ride with him often. Sometimes Myles Moylan joined them. True to form, Myles had worked up quickly to a captaincy, which he might yet lose on some wild prank. He had once been captured by Rosser's Laurel Brigade and he wanted to talk and joke with the "general." [5]

In the evenings, after tents were pitched, officers of the 7th Cavalry often played cards — all but Armstrong. He kept the resolution made after that euchre game in Chicago. His brother-in-law, James Calhoun, had continual bad luck. Skilled players always beat him, but he never seemed to learn. Tom and Armstrong both tried to dissuade him. They refused to loan him any more money for play, and told him he would need his summer salary to live properly at the post next winter. They even teased him in public, suggesting that he resign from the army and join a Wild West show. Buffalo Bill and Texas Jack had given their first theatrical performance last winter. Calhoun was as fine a physical specimen as either of them; perhaps he should go on the stage, too, billed as "Antelope Jim." [6]

When the column reached the Yellowstone near the mouth of Glendive Creek in Montana Territory, the steamboat *Far West* had already arrived. Officers and men eagerly sought the mail and latest newspapers. Young Grant learned that his grandfather had died, and he decided to take passage back to civilization. Supplies were unloaded and a stockade was constructed on the riverbank. Custer detailed Captain Benteen to stay here as a guard with two companies — a good routine job for the soldier who cared nothing for military adventure. The remainder of the 7th Cavalry and all the infantry were ferried to the north shore of the Yellowstone. Then the *Far West* dropped downstream.

The column started westward with the cavalry ahead. Next came surveyors with maps, tapes, and transits, then the infantry. Sometimes they followed the river bed, riding across grassy meadows between groves of cottonwoods. Deer bounded up from clumps of wild roses and disappeared behind the frosted silver walls of bullberry thickets, tall as a man on horseback. Now and again the column serpentined up onto the great flats which rolled away endlessly to the north. Progress was tedious, requiring much manual work to cut a roadway for wagons. On July 31, 1873, they encamped north of the mouth of the Powder River. Custer always scouted ahead, picking the column's route. On August 4 he nooned with a squadron of eighty-five men and five officers opposite the mouth of the Tongue (where Miles City would be built). The day was hot and the men pulled off their saddles under giant cottonwoods. Custer, with his saddle for a pillow, napped in the shade of rustling leaves. He had taken off his buckskin shirt to cushion the hard leather. It was soft as velvet and smelled of fragrant willowsmoke. To cool his feet he pulled off his boots. A shot aroused him.

"Indians! Indians!" sentries shouted.

Men ran for their horses. Custer snatched his Remington and strode off in socks and underwear. Looking across the plain, he saw six warriors. The little brown figures rode about nervously, wild as antelope, but they showed no disposition to run away. Evidently they were looking for a fight. Armstrong told Calhoun, now his adjutant, to form the brigade. Then he pulled on shirt and boots. He called for a detail of twenty men, gave them to brother Tom, and assigned the main command to Captain Moylan with instructions to stay where he was. Next Custer beckoned to Bloody Knife, and with him joined Tom at the head of his detail. They rode toward the gamboling warriors.

The little figures darted away, then back again, always beyond rifle-range, but temptingly close. Armstrong suspected them of being decoys to lead the soldiers into a trap and decided to investigate personally. He halted Tom's detail, called for two volunteers on fast horses, and rode toward the Indians with them — Custer and two men under the vast dome of sky. Hiding Indians were sure to pounce on such a tempting prize.

The six warriors continued their frolics, but Custer noticed that they were edging toward cottonwoods along the river. He knew better than to follow them there, and stopped. For a few moments everything was quiet. Then the Indians sprang their trap. Three hundred warriors dashed from the trees — a long line of racing horses, painted bodies, fluttering feathers, shrill war cries. The cavalry stood divided in three groups, and the Indians evidently hoped to surround each group and kill them all. Custer and his two men sped back toward the regiment, the ground streaming beneath their horses' racing hoofs. Long-legged cavalry mounts could usually outrun Indian ponies in a fair match. The three units combined without mishap, and dismounted in tall grass for defense. They were outnumbered three to one, but felt confident so long as ammunition lasted. Soldiers lying flat on the ground made uncertain targets, while a mounted warrior was conspicuous as he dashed by.

Armstrong signaled Bloody Knife to follow him. Together they crawled off to a point where they hoped to get a shot. Lying in the grass they heard the throb of pony hoofs galloping toward the soldiers' line. The Indian rider fired his rifle, then swept away, quick as the flight of a swallow.

"If he does that again, let's see who's the best shot!"

Waiting, their faces in the sweet, warm earth, they heard again the throb of hoofs. Louder, louder. He's coming again! Both men saw above them a flash-view of a brown body, a painted shield, a horse. Both fired. The savage hit the ground with a thud.[7] Each man claimed the lucky shot, said the other could not hit a tent when inside it. Bloody Knife had a sharp tongue, wasn't afraid to use it, and always gave as good as he received. Armstrong liked the boasting, teasing red man. He was as jolly company as Tom! Or his father!

The only thing which seemed to worry the embattled cavalrymen was their dwindling supply of ammunition. That could become serious. Armstrong's lifelong remedy was to charge. He ordered his men to mount, formed them in line, and raced toward the biggest concentration of Indians. The red men scattered, just as they always did in Kansas. Custer was convinced more than ever that when disciplined cavalry hit and hit hard, disorganized Indians fled.

After the fight Custer's officers assembled to review their action and the infantry marched into the bivouac and pitched camp. One cavalryman had been killed and one was missing. A search was made of the terrain — no Elliott would be deserted here — but instead of finding the troopers, scouts found the bodies of Dr. John Holzinger, Armstrong's amiable veterinarian, and sutler Balarian.[8] They had evidently wandered unarmed from the column before the fighting began. To them the great sweep of grasslands must have looked peaceful and empty. These tenderfeet had not learned the mountain man's maxim: "Where there ain't no Injuns is where you'll find 'em thickest." Both men made poor trophies for an aspiring warrior — no scalps. One was bald-headed and the other wore his hair cropped short.

For the next five days Custer trailed the retreating Indians up the Yellowstone. Stanley followed with the infantry at a slower pace. Often Armstrong marched at night, hoping to surprise the hostile encampment. He picked up ragged coffee sacks and other articles which indicated that the savages who had attacked him were reservation Indians — probably followers of Sitting Bull, a medicine man who was inciting many peaceful red men to revolt. Following the Indians' trail along the north side of the river, Custer looked across at the great greasewood flat — greener than grass this time of year — which marked the mouth of the Rosebud. The walls of the butter-colored bluffs stood close together here. The Yellowstone swirled between them, churning through countless cottonwood-capped islands.

On October 9 Bloody Knife showed Armstrong where the Indians' trail had crossed the river, going south. This was only three miles east of the Big Horn. Custer worked all next day trying to force his horses to cross at the same place, but when pushed into deep water they repeatedly swam back to the north side.

On the following day, October 11, Armstrong tried again until he saw, to his surprise, that he was being watched. The carved bluffs on the south side were dotted with Indians! As Custer scrutinized them, he also noticed lines of red men coming down the slopes. Soon little white clouds of smoke appeared in the willows across the river. Bullets smacked against the dirt bank near him. Armstrong ordered the horses driven back from the riverbank into the cottonwoods, where they would be out of sight. This did not help much, for shots from the bluffs north of the river announced that other Indians had crossed, and the soldiers were now surrounded.

Custer had whipped these same red men last week when they outnumbered him three to one. He would do so again! He placed his men in an arc with their backs to the river, faces to the bluffs where puffs of smoke disclosed Indian marksmen's hiding places. The shooting had become continuous — bullets humming, cutting twigs overhead, snipping off round cottonwood leaves which spun to earth. Armstrong's orderly, a sharpshooter he prized highly, crumpled to the ground with a bullet through his head. Lieutenant Charles Braden fell. A ball had broken his thigh.

In this ugly military situation Custer was unable to resort to his usual charge. The ground was too rough for horse. South of him, across the Yellowstone, he saw that the bare hills were black with Indian women, children, and old men, come to see him destroyed.

Armstrong ordered Lieutenant Varnum to slip toward the hidden

Indians with his sharpshooters, watch for enemy gun smoke, and place a bullet where it came from. Then Custer turned to Tom, telling him to prepare his troop for an advance. Two companies under Yates and Moylan would support him. The rest of the regiment must be scattered out as flankers, to prevent the Indians from isolating Tom's unit. With all arrangements made, and flankers slipping off into the rough country, Armstrong rode among the waiting troops. Bullets still pinged around them. Adjutant Calhoun's horse was shot down. A moment later Armstrong's own horse stumbled. By habit, Custer jerked the bridle reins; but the animal collapsed. This was a real battle, a desperate fight! Custer waved to Tom and pointed forward. He shouted to the band, "Play 'Garry Owen.'"

All that was left of the regiment started forward against what Armstrong believed to be at least twice their number. The shooting swelled into a roar. Custer, watching from a fresh horse, looked behind him down the Yellowstone. He saw a towering column of golden dust against the turquoise sky. The infantry was coming. No need for flankers now! Armstrong called them in and, with the whole regiment — 450 men — he advanced.[9]

The Indians melted away, as they had done before. Little parties splashed back across the Yellowstone to safety. Others skimmed across the plain. Blue-clad troopers followed, some of them for eight miles — far below the mouth of the Big Horn. All day long these victorious soldiers came trotting back with captured ponies, painted shields, bits of savage finery thrown away in the retreat, and — more important — they brought in many discarded rifles of the latest model issued to the red men by the Indian Bureau.

Custer spent all next day doctoring the wounded, inspecting horses. Then he marched on up the Yellowstone, to Pompey's Pillar — a rock-capped pinnacle beside the river, so named by William Clark when he explored this country with Meriwether Lewis in 1806. Here the column turned north, leaving the river for the great grasslands drained by the Musselshell River. In this rolling country they found their first buffalo.

Custer killed four and carefully preserved their heads. He had learned taxidermy from scientists with the expedition, and on some nights omitted his writing to sit, with sleeves rolled up, preparing his skins. Some hunters brought in grizzly bears, but Custer failed to shoot one. In a notebook he kept records of his shots, jotting down distances. Later, in a letter he wrote the Remington Arms Company endorsing their sporting rifle, he said that the forty-one antelope he had killed were hit at a distance averaging over two hundred and fifty yards — perhaps another Custer exaggeration.[10]

Armstrong suffered his usual troubles when working under strict orders. He knew this weakness of his, and asked permission to strike across the Plains in a straight line toward the stockade on the Yellowstone — a daring trip, for the temperature registered one hundred and ten degrees in the shade at noon and none of the Indian guides knew whether water could be found in that vast country.

Perhaps Stanley was glad to be rid of Custer. Perhaps he saw the importance of adding a bit of geographical discovery to his expedition. In any event, he retained two troops of the 7th Cavalry and gave Custer permission to take the surveyors and strike off with the rest of the regiment — six companies in all. Armstrong left the middle branch of the Great Porcupine and in five days traveled one hundred and fifty miles — another of those forced marches which had once cost him a court-martial. Forage ran out and the horses subsisted on less than quarter-rations, but Custer reached the Yellowstone without abandoning a single wagon. He found that Benteen had guarded the stockade satisfactorily, and in due time the infantry arrived by the longer route. A new steamboat, the *Josephine,* ferried the brigade south of the river. She had come up the Yellowstone with mail, including four letters from Libbie, who had heard some gossip about Autie's arrest and wanted the details.

Custer replied that he was sorry she had heard about it — "Suffice it to say that I was placed in arrest for acting in strict conscientious discharge of what I knew to be my duty — a duty laid down expressly in Army regulations. . . . Within forty-eight hours Genl. Stanley came to me, and apologized in the most ample manner, acknowledging that he had been in the wrong, hoping I would forget it, and promising to turn over a new leaf. . . . With his subsequent faithful observance of his promise to begin anew in his intercourse with me, I banished the affair from my mind. Nor do I cherish any but the kindliest sentiments toward him, for Genl. Stanley, when not possessed by the fiend of intemperance, is one of the kindest, most agreeable and considerate officers I ever served under." [11] Whatever the facts, this is undoubtedly what Libbie believed, and any reader must admit that Custer, with all his impulsiveness, displayed more charity toward his enemies than did such superiors as Stanley, Sheridan, or even Grant. Armstrong also wrote Libbie that he had been assigned exclusive command of a post for the winter. He, with six companies, was to occupy Fort Abraham Lincoln — now under construction. She must join him as soon as the work was finished.

After posting this letter in the steamboat mailbags, Custer set off overland with his regiment for Bismarck, one hundred and ninety miles away as a crow flies. He covered that distance in eight days. Bismarck was a wretched railhead hamlet of wooden buildings and broken-board sidewalks, with the dissolute women and drunken men who congregate at such places. Fort Abraham Lincoln was being built on the other side of the river, four miles below. Here the Custers were to have their first house all to themselves, a two-story building standing above the long log barracks around a parade ground — the conventional plan for western forts. Stretching out from the fort in every direction lay the wide Missouri River bottoms and the Great Plains, "flat as God's pancake." But it would be "home," and Armstrong wrote extravagant letters describing its magnificence. Libbie knew enough about the army and about her lord and master to question its grandeur, and she must have smiled when she read that Autie had induced the quartermaster to put two large wardrobes "in our room. Otherwise I knew I should find the hooks at my disposal dwindle until I found my garments hanging over the back of a broken chair." [12]

26 Black Hills and Threatening Clouds

IF I WERE AN INDIAN," CUSTER WROTE, "I WOULD GREATLY PREFER TO CAST my lot among those of my people who adhered to the free open plains rather than submit to the confined limits of a reservation, there to be the recipient of the blessed benefits of civilization with its vices thrown in without stint or measure."

This opinion, much more tolerant than that voiced by his superiors, Sherman and Sheridan, was to be broadcast in Custer's serialized account of the Indian war published in *Galaxy* magazine. These articles gave him a crescendo of publicity, and also began his controversial downfall.

Immediately after returning from the Yellowstone expedition in the fall of 1873, and while still working on his *Galaxy* articles, Armstrong went back to Monroe and brought Libbie out to Fort Abraham Lincoln, along with another of those unmarried friends who might enjoy meeting officers.[1]

The Custers' new home was a spacious three-story residence. Every room had a fireplace. Heavy draperies hung at the windows. Overstuffed sofas, chairs, and many footstools adorned the parlor. Fancy kerosene lamps were suspended from a high ceiling. Libbie arranged bird cages and flowerpots in the sunny windows.* In this house Custer concluded his *Galaxy* series, stating that, as he wrote, an expedition was being outfitted for the Black Hills, "a region of country as yet unseen by human eyes, except those of the Indian." [2]

Custer exaggerated, of course. The Black Hills had been seen by white adventurers, but the country was relatively unexplored and the Sioux considered it sacred territory. In their treaties with the government they insisted always that these mountains remain inviolate. To

* The Custers' first house at Fort Abraham Lincoln burned, and the one described was the second. (E. B. Custer, *Boots and Saddles,* p. 115.)

explore them was contrary to the government's pledge, but the Indians had broken their promise to stop killing overland travelers, so Sheridan felt justified in ordering Custer into the forbidden area. He was particularly anxious to find a suitable location for a fort where he might station soldiers who would teach recalcitrant Indians to respect white men's lives.

As Custer prepared his expedition, he got into an argument with General Hazen through the columns of the *New York Herald* and the *Army and Navy Journal*. Hazen had become a petulant fellow who liked to voice his opinions, especially when they were polemic. Moreover, his statements were usually scrupulously correct. He had already caused trouble for Sheridan and Custer in the pursuit of Satanta. Now he objected to Custer's report which stated that the Yellowstone country was suitable for cultivation.

An argument ensued, but it was terminated temporarily by Armstrong's engrossment in preparations for his Black Hills expedition. He was to be sole commander. Success would give him due recognition, perhaps an advancement in rank. He checked every detail, including a recheck of his life insurance policies.[3] He also invited actor Lawrence Barrett to accompany him — to enjoy magnificent scenery and plentiful game. The cost for two months, he wrote, would not be so much as a week in a hotel. Besides, think of the opportunity to wear out old clothes! Barrett declined the invitation, writing that he envied the free life of a cavalryman far from "the starched horror of a hotel-table," but he could not get away.

Fred Grant had returned from the East and was going with Custer again. So was Tony Forsyth, the great Indian fighter.[4] In addition there would be Bloody Knife, the Ree scout; taciturn Charlie Reynolds, the mystery man; and Luther North, famous commander of the Pawnee battalion. Yale University was sending ethnologist George Bird Grinnell with a corps of scientists. Altogether the journey promised to be most interesting.

The expedition left on July 2, 1874 — ten troops of the 7th Cavalry, the band, two companies of infantry, and a photographer equipped to take stereopticon views. Over a hundred wagons and ambulances, a herd of beef cattle, three Gatling guns, and a three-inch cannon brought up the rear.

The Badlands east of the Black Hills were reported too rough for wagons. Armstrong hoped to find a road around them, but in case he failed, an adequate supply of packsaddles was included in his equipment. On the first day he marched only thirteen miles, the wagons trundling four abreast. From this camp he sent back a letter to Libbie. With it the courier carried a young curlew which Autie had caught. He wanted her to take care of it for him. All she need do was to catch sufficient grasshoppers every day to keep it alive!

Armstrong steered a course westward midway between the Badlands and the route to the Yellowstone which he had followed last year. After the second day, antelope became plentiful. An hour seldom passed without sighting the pale amber creatures along the sky line. Out on the Plains the heat became intense. A wind burned the men's faces, chapped their lips until they bled. Swirling hot sand plagued the horses. Distant columns of smoke told the soldiers that Indians were watching. Armstrong and Tom amused themselves by teasing "Bos." Their younger brother, Boston, had joined the expedition for his first Western experiences. They tried to deceive him with mirages, sent him on impossible errands, hoped to scare him by tossing clods on his bed at night, did their best to lose him on the Plains and then, from ambush, shot over the bewildered boy's head — all true Western pranks.

At last Armstrong beheld his goal — sixty miles away. With luck, the column should reach it in three days. The Black Hills did not look black at all, nor were they hills. Instead, Custer saw a long ridge, bumpy on top. Its color, as the sun set, was dark blue, almost purple, somewhat like the Blue Ridge in Virginia.

As the column approached the highlands the way led through shallow valleys edged with a thin growth of pine — just the thing for camp-fires. Grass underfoot became better. The cattle herd put on flesh, bucking and kicking when started in the morning. Each day the mountains loomed higher in the sky. Dark clouds brooded over the gloomy crests.

On July 20, 1874, the column entered the Black Hills through a curtain of drizzly rain. Flowers stood knee-high in the meadows, and the air was sweet with their fragrance. Soldiers plucked them as they rode along, decorating their hats and their horses' bridles. On both sides of the advancing horsemen, ridges of red rock glistened with silver sheets of falling water. Ragged clouds drifted across mountainsides ahead, disclosing green parks, trembling aspens, and gloomy pines. Armstrong wanted, above all else, to kill a grizzly bear. Surely yonder bare slopes formed an appropriate range for those monsters.

For nineteen days Custer explored the mountain wilderness. With friends he rode ahead of the column, and climbed the highest peaks, firing salutes with his Remington from the summits. Almost daily he saw gray wolves — distinguishable from coyotes by the way they carried their tails, proudly aloft, not sneakingly horizontal. Several times Armstrong found carcasses of deer killed by mountain lion. The big cats invariably covered their kills with trash. Bloody Knife explained that the lion would rest nearby and return after dark every night until the carcass was consumed. Other scouts reported grizzly-bear tracks, but no one got a shot. In the afternoons camp was pitched in some green valley where beaver dams, like stairsteps with mirror surfaces, reflected the towering crests beyond. In this idyllic wilderness Armstrong sat before his tent in the evenings surrounded by his military family. As the sun disappeared, the band played and shadows crept out from beneath mountain walls.

On August 3 Custer decided to send out dispatches. Lonesome Charlie Reynolds volunteered to take them seventy-five miles south across the Indian-infested Plains to Fort Laramie on the Platte in Wyoming. He would ride at night on a horse with shoes nailed on backward. In daytime he planned to hide, hoping that any inquisitive red warriors would follow his trail the wrong way. Custer sent with him an official report, a popular article for the *New York World,* and a letter to Libbie.

In the first two, he described the beauty of the country, its suitability for settlement, and the abundance of the game. He also said that the geologists had brought in samples of gold. In Libbie's letter, he bragged about the morale of the 7th Cavalry, praised Bloody Knife, and added that he found himself as strong and tireless as any Indian, said he had never been in better physical condition, weighed one hundred and sixty-four pounds, all muscle and sinew.

As soon as the messenger started, Custer headed his column for home by the northern route, close to the one by which he had come. His exploration of the Black Hills had been completed and only one thing marred his happiness: he had failed to kill a grizzly.

Then a new obstruction threatened the expedition's success. As the party approached the edge of the mountains, four Cheyenne met it. These proud, naked savages brought grim news. They were traveling, they said, from Sitting Bull's camp to the reservation. Before leaving the hostiles they had learned that renegades planned intercepting Custer on his way out. Better be careful!

Armstrong smiled under his sweeping mustache and six-weeks-old beard. He had become used to threats of Indian massacres. For seven years he had proved repeatedly that well-trained cavalry could defeat many times its number of Indians. The important thing was for soldiers to take the initiative. Let Sitting Bull attack if he felt lucky!

Next morning the long line of white-topped wagons continued northward. Custer rode ahead with a small detail. They would soon be out of the mountains. Already he smelled the hot breath of the surrounding Plains. In the sagebrush-covered foothills on August 7, Armstrong beheld what he had been looking for — a grizzly sidling up a bare hillside. Custer, William Ludlow, the chief engineer, and Bloody Knife swung off their horses and opened fire. The monster was hard to knock down. Luther North and George Bird Grinnell were eating berries on a nearby hillside. They heard the bombardment, and came running. When they arrived the enormous animal lay dead. His pelt was glossy black except for brownish-yellow hair on his head and the lower parts of his shoulders. He must have been very old, for his canine teeth were worn to stubs, his molars to the gums. All three hunters, like sportsmen generally, claimed to have fired the fatal shot.

In the days that followed, the column pushed out on the Plains, skirting east through the edge of the Badlands — a fantastically eroded country of low peaks and concave slopes, striped black and red, white and gray, like gigantic Bedouin tents. Custer scanned these buttes and mesas constantly for enemies. When the column finally emerged on the open Plains they found great areas burned by the Indians — evidently to stop the soldiers. Charred grass stood thick and glossy like the grizzly's hide. The marching column stirred up great clouds of soot which blackened the men's faces and filled their noses with the smell of charcoal. To reach fresh grass for the horses Custer forced the column to march thirty miles a day for five days. Such hardships always caused complaints. Men said that Custer made them get out of ambulances and walk so his sore-footed staghounds could ride. Armstrong paid no attention. He knew that an officer must expect resentment and ignore it just as he must disregard the hazard of being shot in the back by his own men in every charge.

On August 30, at 4:30 P.M., the column marched into Fort Abraham Lincoln with the band playing "Garry Owen." It had been gone just sixty days.[5] Custer dismounted at his quarters to greet Libbie and to find himself more famous than ever. Not only was he recognized as a great Indian fighter and a popular writer, but his discovery of gold in the Black Hills had caused great excitement. A rush was sure to follow. But there was an unpleasant aspect to this renown. Humanitarians had censured him for attacking Black Kettle. Now he was also blamed for discovering gold on Indian land and thus precipitating a new war. Another group, headed by Hazen, questioned whether he had actually found the precious metal, warned the public that Custer was untrustworthy, that he habitually enlarged the truth.

Custer responded, and the old controversy began again in the stilted language of two gentlemen who secretly regretted it. The feud was reaching a nasty-nice climax as Armstrong and Libbie traveled East to attend the wedding of Frederick Dent Grant in Chicago on October 20, 1874.

Armstrong also enjoyed the experience of seeing his magazine articles published in book form with the title *My Life on the Plains*. He decided to write his memoirs, beginning with West Point experiences. In stores he purchased little gifts for friends back at Fort Abraham Lincoln, including a present for Bloody Knife. On their return to the fort, they brought along Maria Reed — Armstrong's favorite niece, "Riley" — to meet army officers.

The winter was gay at Fort Abraham Lincoln, with a continual round of entertaining in a limited circle. Armstrong rented a grand piano from St. Paul, and a harp added elegance to his parlor. Tom spent too much time drumming on both; but Libbie, having no son, had become much attached to him, even persuading herself to enjoy his annoyances. Charades were popular at the Custer home. Libbie liked to overdress in furbelows and feathers to take the part of "Flora McFlimsey with Nothing to Wear." She rigged Tom in a gigantic stovepipe hat or with frayed-rope curls to represent a judge's wig. On one occasion Armstrong played the principal male part in "Buffalo Bill and His Bride." The real Buffalo Bill and Wild Bill, both of whom Custer knew, were becoming more famous as actors on the stage every year.

Armstrong spent much time alone in his library. He began now to make up for his academic indifference at West Point. Besides working on his memoirs, he studied Napoleon's campaigns — especially Napier's six-volume *War in the Peninsula*.[6] Spain resembled the West so familiar to Custer. He was a slow reader, often rereading a single paragraph several times. Thus Custer, at the age of thirty-five, was trying to master the principles of military science in spite of having already won distinction without this knowledge. And Libbie learned not to interrupt; for when she did, he had to begin again at the top of the page, an embarrassing retreat for a captain of horse.

Custer decorated his library, as most boys do their rooms, with all his trophies. First and foremost were the pictures of McClellan and

Sheridan, Libbie in her wedding dress, and himself in major general's uniform. Among these portraits hung heads of antelope, bison, and grizzly — the latter from the Black Hills. Hunting caps and field glasses dangled from antlers. A snowy owl which he had mounted himself watched a rampant snowshoe rabbit. A sand-hill crane stood above the gunrack. These specimens collected dust and revealed juvenile taste.

Custer had no desk. He wrote on a table with a few reference books open on chairs around him. His leather-bound dictionary showed signs of hard usage. William Tecumseh Sherman, now the highest-ranking officer in the army, encouraged Custer to continue writing his war memoirs. He and all his family, he said, had read Custer's *Life on the Plains,* and thought it the best account yet written about the Indian fighting. Sherman may have been particularly pleased with the author's criticism of Grant's Indian policy, for he differed radically with the President on this subject. Sherman's own works had just been published and he admonished Custer to prepare for an author's fate: "I have received such hard knocks about my *Memoirs,*" he wrote, "that I should suppose you had been warned." [7]

Surely no aspiring writer was ever deterred by such forebodings, much less a Custer. Hour after hour he scratched away with the pen between the first and second fingers of his square hand. Always loyal to friends, he praised McClellan, his generalship and wisdom, recklessly ignoring that general's unpopularity.

Libbie, busy with management of the house, stayed out of his room. The dear man must be undisturbed. Besides, he had a pet field mouse which crawled over his papers, his arms and shoulders, as he wrote.

In January, 1875, Lonesome Charlie Reynolds reported that he had heard, at the Standing Rock Agency, an Indian named Rain-in-the-Face boast about killing the veterinarian and the sutler on the Yellow-stone expedition — chubby Dr. Holzinger, and the popular liquor seller, Mr. Balarian. Armstrong ordered Captains George Yates and Tom Custer to take one hundred men and catch the murderer.

This was a tough assignment in the dead of winter, but the two officers came back with their man. They had ridden fifty freezing miles down to the windswept agency where, in the trader's store, Tom mingled with the red men, all blanketed to their eyes. Finally he recognized Rain-in-the-Face and, slipping behind him, pinioned the Indian's arms. Soldiers hustled the prisoner back to the fort before his red brothers had time to recapture him. With the culprit in the guardhouse, the 7th Cavalry chalked another heroic achievement on its proud standard. People would later pronounce Rain-in-the-Face innocent, stating that he was captured to enhance the regiment's glory and was later allowed to escape.[8] Who knows? Jealousy between the regiments as well as between the Indian Bureau and the War Department had reached a state where anything might be said.

In February people in Dakota liked to say, "As the days grow longer the cold grows stronger," but they also watched for signs of spring. Roads to the post melted into mudholes in the afternoon and froze as hard as iron before morning. Out on the Plains, the south slopes became bare. Then one night the post was aroused by a dull whistle, like a swish of silk. Libbie and Armstrong knew what this meant and after breakfast they hustled into warm clothes to drive down to the river: the familiar white expanse, half a mile wide here, had become a churning chocolate mass, sweeping southward. The sight was fascinating, but a person became dizzy from watching it too long.

The summer of 1875 seemed unusually tedious for the Custers — no campaigns for the 7th Cavalry, just routine drill. Gold seekers swarmed into the Black Hills. This violated Indian treaties, but the 7th was not ordered to stop them. Custer told Indians, and also white reporters who visited Fort Abraham Lincoln, that the red men's rights should be respected.

Libbie and her friends, sewing and chatting together, planned new wardrobes. Most of the officers' wives were still young enough to sit on the floor or on stools when they worked. It was fashionable to wear "over-dresses" — sometimes three skirts, one draped over the other.

Bustles were truly magnificent. Riding habits must be shaped like hourglasses, and were usually worn under stovepipe hats adorned with gay veils which blew, bannerlike, when the horses galloped. Libbie preferred a little Robin Hood cap with feather, which sat forward on her head, her knot high behind it. Little bangs covered her forehead.

The inactive summer gave Armstrong time to read the newspapers — too much time for his own good, perhaps. Democratic victories pleased him. The sordid ethics of Grant's administration contrasted shockingly with Johnson's courageous honesty, and Custer, like many other supporters of the National Union Party, became a Democrat again. He was delighted to read that Ex-President Johnson had been elected to the United States Senate, and wrote him a letter of congratulation.[9] The Democrats, now in power, promised to make a thorough investigation of Grant's corrupt administration and elect their own President in the fall. Good! Custer had seen plenty of graft right here at Fort Abraham Lincoln. His own men complained about the high prices charged by the sutler while the same goods could be bought cheaper in Bismarck, four miles away. Yet army regulations forbade service men from making purchases there. Custer had investigated and was told that the sutler kept only three thousand dollars of his fifteen thousand dollars' annual profit. The balance was sent to grafters in the War Department. Maybe the Secretary himself took a cut. Congressmen who were hunting for corruption could start profitably at Fort Abraham Lincoln.

Secretary Belknap visited the Fort during the late summer of 1875. On the day of his arrival the sutler sent Custer a basket of wine for the distinguished visitors. Armstrong returned it. He did not drink wine and he did not intend to be cordial with an official whom he believed corrupt. He ordered the salute required by regulations, but instead of meeting Belknap at the reservation boundary he waited in his office for the Secretary to call.

Armstrong made himself equally unpopular with corrupt officials in the Indian Bureau. He had seen both military and Indian reservations enlarged apparently for the sole purpose of dispossessing private merchants and giving their trade to the government monopoly. He had heard repeatedly that many Indian agents were selling, for their personal profit, the goods sent them for issue to the Indians. He was told that some agents even made a practice of falsifying their rolls in order to get more goods to sell.[10] No wonder reservation Indians constantly joined the renegades on the Plains under Sitting Bull. Things were getting so bad that malcontents were now joining another band of hostiles under a Cheyenne warrior named Crazy Horse. Custer did not blame them.

Perhaps the corruption provoked Armstrong excessively because he was getting bored with idleness. Both he and Libbie longed for a change. He applied for two months' leave, and got it. Shortly after Belknap's visit, Armstrong took the "Old Lady" to New York for a fling. He always looked forward to wearing civilian clothes, but a tight collar annoyed him, so he wore a loose-necked shirt with a narrow bow tie. Middle age was sharpening his features. His eyebrows were beginning to jut out like shelves above his pointed nose, and his mustache completely covered his mouth. His red-gold hair was thinning. He parted it far to one side, brushing long locks over the top of his head. Golden curls still clustered behind his ears but no longer fell over his coat collar. Ginger-colored sideburns adorned his cheeks. Such hirsute adornment was not unusual for civilian males, but there was something about Custer's appearance which made those who looked at him always see the dashing figure in buckskins, even when he wore his pearl-gray topper, cutaway coat, and striped trousers.

The theater season was in full swing. Operatic music entranced Armstrong. Listening, he became unconscious of his surroundings, lost in ecstasy. Libbie, beside him, realized that she was sitting alone until the music stopped. On evenings when she felt tired and wanted to rest, he would go to Booth's Theater, where Lawrence Barrett was playing the lean and hungry Cassius in *Julius Caesar*. The two friends joked together in Barrett's dressing room. Armstrong struck Barrett's armor, making the tinware ring. That night back at the hotel Autie awakened his "Old Lady" to laugh with her about what he had done.[11]

Reveling in city entertainment, the Custers forgot the jealousies and worries about promotion which were a part of army life. But other troubles followed Armstrong into Gotham. Hazen printed his denunciation of Custer's report on the Yellowstone in a pamphlet entitled *The Barren Lands.* He said that it was unthinkable to expect more new and populous states to be carved from the Western Plains and that encouragement of emigration was "wicked beyond expression." This came very close to calling Custer names but Hazen did not stop here. He published another pamphlet entitled *Some Corrections of "My Life on the Plains,"* which excoriated Custer's account of the Washita fight, showing by agency records that the warriors present were not so numerous as Armstrong said.[12]

Fortunately for Custer, the turbulent Hazen now turned his attention to bigger game. His latest victim was the Secretary of War. Hazen had accused Belknap, three years ago, of taking bribes from the Fort Sill sutler. For this Hazen had been punished by assignment to the worst posts in the Northwest, places unlikely to cure his wounds. Now, however, while victorious Democrats were investigating the War Department, he would be heard.[13] Armstrong forgot his quarrel with Hazen in the prospect of seeing justice done Secretary Belknap. He even joined the clamor, telling people in the East things he knew, or thought he knew.

In November, 1875, Custer applied for an extension of his leave. He and Libbie had sentimental reasons for wanting to celebrate Thanksgiving in the city. They had first met on that day and might never spend another together, because the corruption in high places was goading the Indians to desperation. Sitting Bull's hostiles were sure to start an Indian war come spring. The newspapers and everybody in the streets admitted it. Moreover, Alfred Terry, commander of Custer's department, had promised Armstrong the honor of rounding up the renegades. Redpath's Lecture Bureau offered Custer an engagement after the summer's campaign — if he survived. The pay would be two hundred dollars per evening, five nights a week.*

Custer's request for leave extension was granted. He was running low on money now, so he and Libbie moved into a room across the street from the Hotel Brunswick where they ate their meals and got their mail. They went to parties by horse car instead of hansom cab, but still enjoyed it all. In January, 1876, Armstrong requested still another extension, stating, truthfully, that snow made it all but impossible to reach his post. Custer was always reluctant to return to duty. In February, he asked for a third extension but the adjutant denied it.[14] The couple bade friends good-by at a last circle of parties, and boarded the train for Bismarck. On the Plains west of St. Paul the locomotive stuck in snowdrifts. Food and fuel ran low and snow continued to pile up around the cars. The passengers worried. Men could take it — but for a woman! Then one day Libbie heard a shrill cry out in the flying flakes — the Custer shout she knew so well! Tom had come, with a bobsled. Libbie was carried through the drifts and laid in the straw beside the staghounds. The sled lurched off into the storm. She was reasonably warm between those animals, but feared that the driver might lose his way in the blizzard.

Arriving safely at the fort, the Custers had barely warmed their fingers and toes, hung their clothes up in cold closets, and greeted friends, when a telegram summoned Armstrong back to Washington. Evidently he had talked too much about what he knew concerning War Department corruption. Congressman Hiester Clymer wanted him to testify in an investigation. Armstrong did not wish to go. He wanted to begin preparations for the spring campaign and feared he might be supplanted if not present. He offered to give his testimony under oath at Fort Abraham Lincoln, but this was not acceptable.

Libbie dreaded the sled journey back to the train but she began to

---

* F. Whittaker, *Complete Life of . . . Custer . . .* , p. 638. In January Custer attended a reception at the New York Historical Society and enjoyed meeting "a group of young men over eighty." (*New York Times,* July 12, 1876; and letter, Armstrong to Tom, in M. Merington, *Custer Story,* p. 277.)

repack her dresses. Armstrong stopped her. She must take no such chance. He would go alone. Friends called, asking him to take messages or make purchases for them back East. Mrs. Yates gave him a list of baby clothes she wanted. That family was still increasing. Libbie warned Armstrong, when she kissed him good-by, to guard his tongue. Remember that Old Zach Chandler was still a power in the Senate and he had been good to them in the old days.[15]

On the way to Washington, Custer stopped in New York to see his publisher. *My Life on the Plains* was selling well and he wanted to discuss publication of his *Memoirs*. The impending investigation had stirred up much bitterness. Republicans tried to embarrass Custer at every turn. Relatives of the deserters whom he had ordered shot over eight years ago attempted to discredit him.[16] But prominent Democrats lauded him as a hero and invited him to soirees. William C. Endicott, who later would be Secretary of War under Grover Cleveland, described Armstrong in a letter to a friend as "that nice young General Custer who dined with us." [17]

In Washington, General Rufus Ingalls offered to share lodgings with Custer. Ingalls was a short, stocky man with a wisp of hair plastered over a balding pate. He had been Grant's chief quartermaster during the war, and was now on the presidential staff. Custer knew him as the best poker player in the army, and also here in Washington, where Congress boasted some card experts. Ingalls confided to Armstrong that he was afraid of the Clymer investigation. Nobody knew what cards that committee held in the hole.

Custer might have learned from Ingalls when to "stand" and when to "pass," but he was not a card player. He met and enjoyed the company of many people, mostly Democrats — Grant's enemies — in and out of politics. He breakfasted with Sherman. At dinner with Senator Thomas F. Bayard of Delaware, he met former Confederates now holding office or lobbying for friends. Among them was the "Duke of Sonora," as the ex-senator from California, William Gwin, was called. A startling article in the *New York Herald* was being discussed. Entitled "Belknap's Anaconda," it accused the Secretary of War of selling army post traderships in Dakota. Custer, having just come from the Territory by way of New York, was accused of being the author. He denied it.[18]

Escaping the political hurly-burly one evening, he attended a reception at Vinnie Ream's studio and was charmed by the little artist, who could say "A new dress helps get commissions — even from the clergy." With characteristic absent-mindedness he lost his purse — that old habit of his. Early next morning he wrote Miss Ream:

> My dear Vinnie:
> Pardon me for disturbing you at this early hour. Please have your servant examine the floor of your studio to see if my wallet (not my pistol) was not dropped there last night. If so return it by bearer and, in any event, do not chide me, even mentally, for interfering with your much needed morning nap.
>
> Faithfully yours,
> G. A. CUSTER [19]

Custer testified before several congressional committees — but never to his credit. Talkative always, and not a lawyer, he seemed unable to differentiate between personal knowledge and hearsay evidence. He dared link the President's brother, Orvil Grant, to Belknap's crooked deals. Enemies confronted him with the *Herald* article denouncing Belknap, accused him of writing it and, to prove their point, produced a draft for one hundred dollars in his favor which presumably paid for it. Armstrong had an explanation for this and the authorship was not proved. He was happy when excused from further testimony.[20]

During all these frustrating proceedings Armstrong fretted. He knew that he should be outfitting his expedition for the summer campaign. He requested officially that the four troops of the 7th Cavalry which were still stationed in the South be sent to join the expedition. He also applied for the transfer of Calhoun's brother, Fred, from the infantry to his regiment. Fred had married Armstrong's niece, Emma Reed. Let all the Custer clan be together if possible! There were already four Custers in the 7th — Armstrong, Tom, Boston, and Autie, the last two employed as civilian helpers. Libbie made five. James Calhoun had a Custer wife, also a sister and a brother at the post, making nine altogether. The adjutant refused to add more.[21]

Custer's impatience grew with the spring flowers. The Capitol lawn showed fresh greenness, and trees along Pennsylvania Avenue burgeoned with delicate leaves. Cottonwoods on the Missouri must be doing the same. The Belknap impeachment began on April 17. Custer's evidence had already been ruled out as hearsay. Why hold him longer? He appealed to Alfred Terry in the West. That general wanted Custer as much as Sheridan had in 1868. The nation's senior Indian fighter, General Crook, had been trounced by the Indians in March. Terry hoped to outdo him, just as Sheridan had outdone Hancock in '68, but to do so he needed Custer. The managers of the Belknap impeachment agreed to Custer's release, but President Grant now held up his clearance. Grant had, no doubt, read the criticism of his Indian policy in Custer's popular *My Life on the Plains*. Certainly he had read Custer's testimony before the congressional committees, knew about the *Herald* article, and resented the accusations against his brother, as well as those against his Secretary of War. Repeated charges of corruption were exploding in Grant's bearded face, exasperating his usual equanimity. He determined to punish Custer. Let the Sioux expedition go forward under Terry without Custer's aid.

When news of this decision reached Fort Abraham Lincoln, Major Reno immediately applied for command of the 7th Cavalry, but soldiers in the regiment hoped that Custer would be restored. They had confidence in him as an Indian fighter. Reno was untried. The Democratic press across the country howled about "Grant's revenge," cited it as another example of his corrupt administration. Thus Custer became a political issue in this election year.

Armstrong decided to see Grant personally and try to explain his case. In the White House anteroom he waited several hours. Finally General Ingalls came out and explained that the President did not want to see him. Armstrong penciled a note, saying that unjust inferences had been drawn from his testimony. He asked Ingalls to give this to the President. Then Custer strode from the White House. He would go by the first train to Fort Abraham Lincoln and join his regiment. On the way to Chicago he stopped in New York for a last call on friends at the *Herald*.* The editor wrote later:

> General Custer blew into the *Herald* office like a fresh breeze. Dressed in mufti, citizenized as far as just clothes could do it, there was something so fine and broad and free in his carriage, in the laughing blue of his eyes, in the curl of his yellow hair that one's heart went out to him. It was privately arranged that he was in certain events to write of the expedition for the *Herald*. In this I was to have a part.[22]

Getting off the train at Chicago, the resilient Custer received another blow. One of Sheridan's aides handed him a telegram — arrested again! This time for leaving Washington without proper permission. The expedition was to go forward under Terry and without Custer. Once more the Democratic newspaper fulminated about Grant's pettiness. In the midst of this new tumult Armstrong wrote the President: "I appeal to you as a soldier to spare me the humiliation of seeing my regiment march to meet the enemy & I to not share its dangers." Once more Terry interceded. Always, in a crisis, generals wanted the indispensable Custer. Sheridan endorsed the request grudgingly, an obsequious deference to Grant. Sherman, who kowtowed to no man, asked Grant to reconsider.[23] The President and his political advisers may have read the following, or some of the other articles appearing in the press:

* O. L. Hein, *Memories*, p. 108. This call in New York may have been before the return trip. See F. Whittaker, *General George A. Custer*, p. 362. The exchange of correspondence concerning this trip is printed in F. Whittaker, *Complete Life of . . . Custer . . .*, pp. 553–560. An excellent summary appears in E. I. Stewart, *Custer's Luck*, pp. 130–132. See also National Archives, Doc. 2568–1876; *Index to Reports of Committees . . . First Session of the Forty-Fourth Congress*, p. 155; C. F. Bates, *Custer's Indian Battles*, p. 26. J. M. De Wolf in letters to his wife (April 25, May 8, 1876) shows his preference for Custer over other commanders (J. M. De Wolf, *Diary*, p. 33).

There is a degree of gallantry and manly pride in General Custar [*sic*] that we can but admire. He was a gallant soldier when in the field; honest in all his acts, and his opponents can but give him credit for military honor; and yet when he tells the truth, (because he is a Democrat) the Chief Executive of our Government attempts to disgrace him.²⁴

Few executives — and fewer military men — like to reverse their orders. Grant now showed greatness by surrendering.

Custer would lead the 7th Cavalry to meet the enemy and Terry would command the entire expedition. Democratic politicians would watch every step for opportunities to ridicule the administration, point out Custer's superiority, and oust Grant and his party in the fall elections.

The good news came to Custer along with newspaper editorials calling the President "imbecile Grant," and deploring the fact that the gallant Custer must be compelled "as it were, upon bended knees, to beg of his inferior." He returned to Fort Abraham Lincoln on the train with Terry, who had also been East. They were greeted with a thunderous salute which must have gratified Custer. No doubt he felt additional pleasure if he read in a Western newspaper: "The honest man [Custer] will live in history, the brute [Grant] will be consigned to historic oblivion and disgrace." ²⁵ Such praise had not been heaped on Custer since the Shenandoah and Appomattox days. To understand Custer it must be remembered that he was surrounded often by admirers singing such exaggerated acclaim.

27 Custer's Last Stand

ON MAY 17, 1876, THE EXPEDITION AGAINST THE RECALCITRANT SIOUX and Cheyenne left Fort Abraham Lincoln with the band playing "The Girl I Left Behind Me." Officers' wives on their verandas tried bravely to hide all emotion. Enlisted men's wives in Laundress Row mopped

their eyes with apron corners unashamedly. Their urchins beat on tin
pans and pretended to be going along. As the column swung by the
Indian scout village, the marching red men chanted war songs. Libbie
and Margaret Calhoun went with the column the first day. Armstrong
had his hair cut short, wore a red tie, broad-brimmed white hat, and
fringed buckskin shirt. He rode beside Brigadier General Alfred
Terry, commander of the expedition. Terry was a tall, cadaverously
thin man. His black beard and hat contrasted strikingly with Armstrong's white sombrero, ruddy complexion, and golden-red hair, so
lustrous with health.* Beside these leaders rode bearded Adjutant
Cooke on a white horse. His black beard had grown into two long
streamers like the points of the letter "W," prompting Armstrong to
call him the "Queen's Own." Bloody Knife and Lonesome Charlie
Reynolds accompanied some forty scouts; Rees dressed in unkempt is-
sue-uniforms, Crows — ancient enemies of the Sioux — in native dress.[1]

At the first stopping place out on the Plains the soldiers were paid.
They were now so far from Bismarck's fleshpots that they could not
squander their money and become too drunk to march next day. That
night Armstrong and Libbie camped together for the last time. Before
dawn he left their tent to supervise the packing. After breakfast his
"striker," John Burkman, lifted Libbie up on her horse. "Good-by,
John," she said to him. "You'll look after the general, won't you?"

Then she and Margaret turned to follow the paymaster's "Doughtery
wagon" and escort back to Fort Abraham Lincoln. They rode along
the advancing column, past faces headed westward — among them
some, like Benteen's and Reno's, dark with hatred of the commander;
other faces glancing at the young women with admiring eyes. There
was Captain Yates from Monroe, whom Armstrong had got Pleasonton to appoint on his staff, and roguish Tom Custer with the scarlet
spot on his cheek from that bullet at Saylor's Creek. And there was
handsome Captain Calhoun, Margaret's husband, and the smiling
ne'er-do-well Keogh, always popular with the fair sex, riding his fa-

---

* A brilliant lock of hair, said to be Custer's, is in the Myrick Collection.

vorite horse Comanche. Armstrong had bought flowers once for Keogh's ladylove. Next came Captain Weir, the lieutenant who had testified for Armstrong in the court-martial and shown bravery and dependability in the Washita battle and campaign which followed.

Behind the twelve troops of the 7th Cavalry marched three companies of infantry, a platoon of Gatling guns on pack horses, and the wagon train — twenty-seven hundred men, including one hundred and seventy-six civilians. Among the latter rode forage master Boston Custer. Autie Reed, now in his upper teens, helped drive the beef herd.

The column was two miles long and, when the last face passed, Libbie, not daring to look back, repeated a line of poetry she once learned:

> *But this I've seen, and many a pang*
> *Has pressed it on my mind —*
> *The one who goes is happier*
> *Than he who stays behind.*

It was fortunate that Libbie did not turn, for Custer's orderly remembered later that when his commander rode out from the column and watched his wife and the paymaster's detail recede across the prairie, Custer's face was very white and solemn under his freckles. "A good soldier has two mistresses," he said in a low voice as he rejoined the column. "Whilst he's loyal to one, the other must suffer." *

Custer had crossed these Plains four times, and he plotted his course just as a sea captain does. The renegade Indians were believed to be somewhere south of the Yellowstone and two other columns were converging on them. General Crook, after his setback in March, was coming again from the south with thirteen hundred men. The other column — under John Gibbon, Armstrong's West Point artillery teacher — was marching down the Yellowstone from Forts Ellis and

* This incident is from C. F. Bates, *Custer's Indian Battles*, pp. 28–29. It appears also in J. E. Remsburg, *Charley Reynolds*, p. 48. E. B. Custer, *Boots and Saddle*, p. 265, says she and Maggie rode out one day. Mark Kellogg, in his *Diary* (p. 86), notes Custer's driving energy.

Shaw in Montana, with four companies of cavalry and two of infantry — four hundred in all. Terry and Custer expected to march two
hundred and fifty to three hundred miles before they met these
columns.

On June 3 a party of scouts appeared on the western horizon, bringing news from Gibbon's column, which they had left near the mouth
of the Rosebud eleven days ago. No word had been received from
Crook, but the renegade Indians must be somewhere on the head-
waters of the Powder, Tongue, Rosebud or Big Horn rivers — probably
on all of them.

The scouts returned to Gibbon with the information that Terry and
Custer were coming by the most direct route. The scouts carried with
them an installment of Custer's memoirs for *Galaxy* to be sent to the
publisher by the first supply steamboat. Armstrong carried a file of
notes in his equipment and he had written almost nightly, no matter
how long or hard the march. He had now completed his life story up
to the time he had been assigned to Lieutenant Bowen of the "Topogs"
and had watched Hancock disobey an order, thus winning the Battle
of Williamsburg.

More than two weeks passed before Terry's column met Gibbon's.
On the westward march Custer had ridden off one day without permission, taking four companies on a forty-five-mile scout up the Little
Missouri. Terry told his diary he disapproved, but he did not place the
irrepressible lieutenant colonel under arrest as Stanley had done. Later,
on the Powder River, Terry sent Major Reno with his right wing on a
scout up that stream and down the Tongue where he was to rejoin
the regiment. This time Reno disobeyed orders and instead of coming
down the Tongue, crossed it and came down the Rosebud, sending
word that he was camped at its mouth on the Yellowstone. Again
Terry wrote that he was displeased. But in both cases he seems to have
said nothing to the disobedient subordinates. He was a genial man,
well liked by both officers and men. A lawyer by training, he had risen

to his generalship during the Civil War, and success was more important to him than the discipline incident to it.

Reno had good reason for his disobedience. He had discovered an Indian trail — over three hundred lodges — and, hoping to overtake and destroy the village, had followed it farther than specified by his orders. Reno reported that it was headed for the Greasy Grass, the Indian name for the eastern tributary of the Big Horn, known as the Little Big Horn. This may have excused Reno in Terry's mind. After all, a worthy commander could disobey an order to gain a victory. Custer, when he heard the report, thought that Reno's men should have kept on going. He wrote Libbie: "I fear their failure to follow up the trails has imperilled our plans by giving the village an intimation of our presence. Think of the valuable time lost." [2]

Terry moved the regiment up the Yellowstone and joined Reno on the Rosebud. Gibbon's column camped across the river. Headquarters was established on the steamboat, *Far West,* in the stream. On June 21 a signal from the ship summoned Custer to come aboard. A boatman rowed him out. Armstrong climbed over the rail, saluted Terry, and shook hands with Gibbon. The three commanders walked to the cabin and sat down around a map. Scouts had examined much of the surrounding country now, and all agreed that the hostiles must be up the Rosebud, or on the Little Big Horn, or the Big Horn proper. According to reports, there might be 1000 to 1200 warriors. Custer estimated 1500 — more than either of his colleagues.* In any event, they should be no match for a regiment of cavalry. None of the officers considered the possibility of defeat. Their problem was to prevent the Indians from slipping away. To them the red men were like game — fine game, elusive and dangerous. The Indian trail had already been discovered on the Rosebud by Reno's wing of Custer's regiment. Let Custer follow it with all his men. The steamboat would ferry Gibbon's

---

* The above estimate is from J. McLaughlin, *My Friend the Indian,* p. 127. All trustworthy accounts agree that the soldiers had little idea about the number of hostile Indians. Certainly many more than suspected had left their reservations.

column to the south side of the Yellowstone and go with them up the Big Horn as far as navigable. Thus the Indians would be caught between pincers. Terry said that he would give Custer written orders tomorrow. The tall, thin man was almost exhausted after his march with Custer's column[3] and would direct the campaign from the steamboat.

Custer warned his officers to be ready — light marching order, no tents. Box all sabers for shipment on the steamboat.[4] From here on, men would sleep in overcoats and saddle blankets. Inspection would be held in the morning.

Armstrong, always restless, told everybody to hurry. He arranged to have his staghounds left with the wagons. He transferred Boston Custer and Autie Reed from the quartermaster department so they could accompany him. All Custers must share the fun! On the steamboat, the sutler did a big business selling tobacco, snuff, shirts more comfortable than army flannel, and straw hats for hot summer days. Terry gave him permission to tap the whisky kegs, with the usual result among the enlisted men. Some officers filled their canteens for that "extra tired time." During the evening many of them played cards on the steamboat — last chance for some time to take money from Gibbon's men. Major James S. Brisbin, second to Gibbon in command, found Armstrong on the forward deck under the stars, and talked with him for a long time. Custer said that he had decided to leave the Gatling guns behind. He was confident the 7th Cavalry could handle anything it met.[5]

On the morning of June 22 Custer received his orders from Terry. He read:

> COLONEL: — The Brigadier-General Commanding directs that as soon as your regiment can be made ready for the march you proceed up the Rosebud in pursuit of the Indians whose trail was discovered by Major Reno a few days since. It is, of course, impossible to give any definite instructions in regard to this movement, and, were it not impossible to do so, the Department Commander places too much confi-

dence in your zeal, energy and ability to wish to impose upon you precise orders which might hamper your action when nearly in contact with the enemy. He will, however, indicate to you his own views of what your action should be, and he desires that you should conform to them unless you shall see sufficient reason for departing from them.

After this preface, Terry explained his "views": If the Indian trail led toward the Little Big Horn, Custer should swing to the south, thus keeping the Indians between his column and Gibbon's. Terry also wanted Custer to scout the upper branches of Tullock's Creek as he rode south and "endeavor" to send a scout to Gibbon telling what he found. He also asked Custer to plan to meet Gibbon's column in fifteen days.[6]

This order is important because Custer would be accused of disobeying it, of failing to meet Gibbon for a joint attack on June 26, as planned — an agreement of which there is no contemporary record. Gibbon's chief of scouts, Lieutenant James H. Bradley, wrote in his diary that Terry expected the two columns to reach the Indians at about the same time, but it was understood that if Custer arrived first he was at liberty to attack if prudent. Terry, in his report to Sheridan written on the steamboat, was also specific. He described how Custer was to go up the Rosebud, and Gibbon up the Big Horn. He concluded: "I only hope that one of the two columns will find the Indians. I go personally with Gibbon." Newspaperman Mark Kellogg, who accompanied the column, also wrote that Custer was to follow the recently discovered trail and "overhaul the Indians." Kellogg picked Custer's column as the likely winner, and went with it. All agreed that the most important thing was to prevent the Indians from escaping.[7] But each commander, like a true professional soldier, hoped that his outfit would bag the game.

When Custer received Terry's written order to march "as soon as your regiment can be made ready," he sent his compliments to Terry and said the regiment would start at noon. Did the commanding general care to review them before they left? Custer hoped so. He loved reviews and he had won the admiration of every commander he ever served, by always being ready.

After sending his reply Armstrong worked furiously. Rations and ammunition must be drawn, faulty saddle-gear repaired, worn clothing replaced. Pack animals would carry salt, forage, extra horseshoes. Every man must take both bridle and halter, picket rope and pin. He must also take a nose bag, twelve pounds of oats in the grain bag on his cantle, and his haversack filled with rations. In this last minute of worry and fluster both Armstrong and Boston wrote letters home. Armstrong's to Libbie said:

> MY DARLING — I have but a few moments to write as we start at twelve, and I have my hands full of preparations for the scout. Do not be anxious about me. . . . I hope to have a good report to send you by the next mail. A success will start us all toward Lincoln.
>
> I send you an extract from Genl. Terry's official order, knowing how keenly you appreciate words of commendation and confidence in your dear Bo. . . . [Then Armstrong copied the opening lines of Terry's order.] Your devoted boy AUTIE.

To the west, black thunderheads glowered above the Yellowstone. Storms could be bad on the high Plains — but never too bad for Custer. By noon the column was ready to be reviewed, every man in his saddle, the pack train loaded. Promptness, action, no excuses. Let's go! This was Custer at his best.

Generals Terry and Gibbon came over from the steamboat and sat their horses beside Armstrong while the column filed past. The 7th Cavalry boasted fewer foreigners than many regiments. Most of the officers were seasoned Civil War soldiers, though the rank and file had had little battle experience. Their first fight would be the last for many of them. But three hundred and fifty miles of marching from Fort Abraham Lincoln had already given them the appearance of veterans. Summer sunshine had tanned their faces the color of mahogany. Their uniforms had been slept in for a month. Rain had stained their blue blouses green or purple. Some men appeared in checked shirts bought from the sutler. Coarse issue-boots showed in open oxbow stirrups of the McClellan saddles. Adjutant Cooke, Captains Tom Custer, Calhoun, and Keogh were dressed in buckskin. So was Boston. Major Reno had on an old army blouse and a straw hat. Only the horses showed uniformity. Armstrong was always careful to put all of a color together — bays, sorrels, blacks, and grays. Each animal wore a blue saddle blanket with orange border. The men were all armed with 1873 model Springfield .45–70's. The officers carried .45 Colt Peacemakers. Less than half of this regiment would be alive three days later.[8]

On the first afternoon the regiment marched twelve miles. At 4 P.M. it bivouacked in the deep narrow valley of the Rosebud. Custer's trumpeter, John Martini, an Italian lad who had been drummer boy for Garibaldi and who spoke only broken English, came to all officers telling them to report to the commander. They would find his headquarters flag in a bullberry bush upstream.

Answering this summons, the officers trudged past the dismounted troops, clustered now in the bushes. Some were doubled up in sleep. Others stared stupidly at the stratified bluffs. Unshaved cheeks bulged with tobacco quids. At Custer's headquarters, Adjutant Cooke, the side-whiskered Canadian, checked to see that all officers were present. Then Custer said: "We are now starting on a scout which we all hope will be successful." He spoke in his quick, nervous manner. "I intend to do everything I can to make it both successful and pleasant for everybody. I am certain that if any regiment in the Service can do what is required of us, we can."

Now, for the first time, Custer outlined his plans to the officers and he warned them that the Indians would escape unless surprised. Great caution must be used. No men must stray from the column. There must be no shooting, no unnecessary noise. Commands would be given vocally, never by trumpet. "I will be glad to listen to suggestions from any officer of the command," he said, "if made in the proper manner.

But I want it strictly understood that I shall allow no grumbling, and shall exact the strictest compliance with orders from everybody — not only mine, but with any order given by any officer to his subordinate."

Having given these instructions, Custer blurted out what seemed to be troubling him. He said that it had come to his attention down on the Yellowstone that some officers whined to each other about his official actions instead of filing regular complaints. He held up a copy of *Army Regulations* in his stubby hand, opened and read the paragraph concerning this offense. "In case of its repetition," he said, "I shall take the necessary steps for punishment."

"It seems to me you are lashing the shoulders of *all*, to get some," Captain Benteen said. "Now, as we are all present, would it not do to specify the officers whom you accuse?" Benteen could show sarcasm and hatred in the tone of his voice, and he knew that *Army Regulations* prescribed no punishment for vocal inflections. The chronic joking grumbler had bluffed Custer when the general threatened to horsewhip the writer of the disparaging letter after the Washita battle. He'd go as far as he dared again.

"I want the saddle to go just where it fits," Custer told the circle.

Benteen fidgeted. He asked if Custer ever knew of any criticism or grumbling from him.

"No," Custer told him. "I never have, or on any other [campaign] on which I have been with you."

Custer dismissed the group. They trudged back to their troops in the bullberry brush along the Rosebud. A few gathered at Lieutenant Edgerly's flag to sing. The melody of "Annie Laurie" was heard by a troop or two lying along the creek. The officers closed with the Doxology, and separated A few irrepressible ones went to their bivouac singing, "For he's a jolly good fellow, which nobody can deny."

Benteen, fighting mosquitoes in his shelter tent, with the cape of his army overcoat over his head, heard the music and lamented with a grim smile, "Why make the night hideous with song? Let a fella rest! What the hell is this man's army coming to?"

Next day, June 23, the regiment marched thirty-three miles — a stiff

hike but not excessive.* The column had done as much on another day
coming out from Fort Abraham Lincoln. But Major Benteen growled
to himself. A man in this army was entitled to all the comforts possible.
Why suffer unnecessary hardships? Maybe Custer got fun and excitement out of a victory over the Indians. He, Benteen, wasn't out for
"glory-going purposes." [9]

Custer's other battalion commander, Marcus Reno, had no diary, so
he kept his opinions inside his square, stolid head, but he certainly disliked Custer as much as Benteen did. Of the two, Reno's steady eyes and
determined jaw made him appear to be more dependable if danger
threatened.

Before midday Armstrong came to Indian "sign." News of the discovery passed along the files of men. Ranks closed, intervals shortened,
the pace quickened. The regiment became a unit — a living thing, like
a ship in a fresh breeze. Libbie had described this electric tremor in a
marching column by quoting Longfellow:

> She starts, — she moves, she seems to feel
> The thrill of life along her keel. . . .

Armstrong exulted in the prospect of piloting such a craft into the
hurricane of battle. During the afternoon his regiment passed the sites
of three deserted villages. These must have belonged to the Indians
Reno had trailed. The savages had not been gone long, for the leaves on
the branches covering their wickiups were wilted but not yet crispy-
dry.

* The reports of the three days' marching by different individuals, as outlined in F. Whittaker, *Complete Life of . . . Custer . . .* , p. 579, are enlightening. Reno, the ranking survivor, reported marching 12–33–28 miles on the first
three days, then added the forced night and day march of 27 miles, making a total
of 100 miles. Benteen, the grumbler, reported the marches as 12–25–45, plus 33 on
the last night and day, making a total of 115. Nelson A. Miles, who knew the
country and studied the battle, said in his *Personal Recollections,* p. 205, that
Custer marched 12–33–28 and on the last night and day marched 35 miles, making a total of 108. Grant would condemn Custer later by saying that he marched
83 miles during the last twenty-four hours. Custer was evidently not the only
man who saw things to his own advantage.

That night some of the officers and men bathed in the Rosebud.[10] Benteen grumbled about their scaring away the fish. He had set a seine and hoped to supplement army rations.

Next day, June 24, the column marched twenty-eight miles while watching constantly for Indians. They came to the site of a village larger than any yet passed. Armstrong halted, sent out scouts to investigate in all directions, and called his officers. They assembled in twos and threes around the headquarters flag. Scouts straggled in to report, with sign-language and broken English, that although they had seen no enemies the grass for acres around had been close-cropped by a big pony herd. Moreover, the frame of a deserted sun-dance lodge stood over yonder. A white man's scalp hung on one of the poles.

Custer ordered the officers to have men cook rations at once on small fires, make no smoke, and be sure that all flames were extinguished before dark. As the sun sank behind the cañon walls the men ate, then smoked. Some dipped their bedtime quid in snuff and curled up in overcoats for sleep. Captain Myles Keogh, beaming Irishman from the Papal Guards, invited Captain Benteen to his tent — a little canvas-fly over a bush — where some of the officers planned sitting together in the dark to tell stories, perhaps empty a canteen.

Benteen groped his way to the rendezvous. He found the officers huddled behind glowing cigarettes. Lieutenant Charles Camilus DeRudio, an Italian patriot, was describing a hairbreadth escape with Mazzini. DeRudio and Keogh had fought on opposite sides in Italy but were good friends now. Benteen listened awhile, then told the shadowy figures that they had better get some rest; be prepared for a fight tomorrow, maybe next day. He stumbled back to his bivouac and sat down to pull off his boots.

Out of the night stepped Custer's trumpeter. That "damned little Eye-talian Martini" brought an order from the commanding general to form the regiment immediately — prepare for a night march. . . . More lost sleep!

The night was as black as the inside of a cave. For over an hour the regiment stood in ranks, each man waiting to join the single file ordered to march up a side-gulch. At last Benteen's turn came to start his squadron. He complained, with his usual chuckle, that he could not see the way and kept his place only by listening to the rattle of tin cups dangling from the saddle-pockets of troopers ahead. At 2 A.M. the column halted in a deep defile close to the divide between the Rosebud and Little Big Horn — an excellent place to hide. The men built small fires to boil coffee, but the water stunk of alkali. Horses curled their upper lips in disgust when they drank it.

At daylight on June 25 the soldiers looked up to the edge of the deep basin in which they hid. Pine trees rimmed it and patches of them also grew down the steep slopes toward the bottom. Finally the sun peeped over the east rim. Custer, a beaded knife in the belt of his buckskin shirt, rode his horse, Vic, bareback among the resting men. The fringe on his breeches swung with his dangling legs. The sorrel's blazed face turned alertly from side to side, ears up, watching for something to shy at. Custer stopped before each company, Vic arching his thoroughbred neck, pawing the ground. Custer told the officers that scouts had spent the night on the ridge. They claimed to have discovered the village, maybe twelve or fifteen miles away. He had ridden up there, himself, this morning, but could see nothing even with field glasses. Indian scouts were as fallible as other humans, so it seemed best to move closer, but remain hidden.

Lieutenant Godfrey was not with his troop when the commander passed. He learned later that Custer had made the rounds, so he rode over to headquarters. He found Armstrong, Bloody Knife, and several Rees squatted in a circle, talking. Godfrey noticed that Custer seemed unusually grave and preoccupied. Bloody Knife cut in with a guttural remark. Custer turned, with his characteristic quick jerk, to the interpreter. "What's that he says?"

"He says we'll find enough Sioux to keep up fighting for two–three days."

Custer smiled, his old beaming self again. He knew Indian scouts to be cautious. The Osage had acted like this before Washita. "I guess we'll get through with them in one day," he said.[11]

Shortly before noon the column wormed out of the cañon and crossed the divide. For a moment each rider glimpsed a grand panorama — limitless plains carpeted with soft green, and in the distance, fifty miles away, pale snow-capped mountains. The Little Big Horn River was invisible, but a wide draw ahead of them, known later as Reno Creek, sloped gently toward a depression in the flats where the river must be.

The column halted in a pocket west of the divide, hiding again in pine clumps. The feed was good, with green grass under the waving buff of last year's growth. Here and there sego lilies twinkled like garden flowers back East. Officers tightened saddle girths, idly pulled their mounts' foretops over bridle brow-bands, wondered what Custer planned to do next. His usual method of attack was to surprise a village at dawn. Perhaps he planned doing so tomorrow. By that time Gibbon's column coming up the Big Horn would be close.

As the regiment waited, Captain Yates discovered that a pack mule had lost a box of hardtack. He sent Sergeant Curtis with a squad back to hunt for it. They found the box along the trail. Three Indians were chopping it open. The troopers drove them off and Yates reported the incident to Custer. Certainly the hostile village would know any minute now that soldiers were in the country. Custer ordered Martini to sound Officers' Call — the first time a bugle had been blown for two days.

Officers trotted to the headquarters flag. They knew without being told that immediate action would be ordered. The time for secrecy had passed. The sky was slightly overcast and a light breeze kept the weather cool enough for hard riding.* Custer cautioned his officers to

---

* Lieutenant Godfrey reported this weather condition (Godfrey Papers, June 25). Note that Bailey, in letter to his wife (July 22, 1876, in Godfrey Papers) thought that the column was to hide west of the divide and strike on the morning of the twenty-sixth, and that the Indians' discovery of the soldiers made immediate action imperative. Lieutenant Edgerly (W. A. Graham, *Custer Myth*, p. 219) evidently believed the same. Like others, he seems to have known nothing about a meeting date on June 26.

be sure that every man carried a hundred rounds, then form column. He called for six men and a noncom from each troop. These, with Troop B, under Captain Thomas McDougall were to guard the ammunition mules at the rear. Benteen was to take three troops — about one hundred and twenty-five men — and Reno three more. For his own personal command Armstrong kept five companies: F, I, and L made up of bay horses, C of light sorrels, and E, the white-horse troop. Autie Reed would ride with his uncle.

"I give the honor of the advance position to that troop which has best obeyed my order against grumbling," Custer piped in his high, penetrating voice.

"I take it then," Benteen blurted out. Looking continually for an affront, he thought Custer seemed surprised.

"Well, Colonel Benteen," Custer stammered, "your troop has the advance." *

The column started down the draw. It had gone only a short way when Custer galloped to the van with Adjutant Cooke beside him on his leggy gray. Armstrong said that Benteen was setting too fast a pace, and took the lead himself, stocking-legged Vic prancing under the curb bit. After a few miles the draw opened into wide rolling plains and Custer called a halt. As the troops closed intervals Custer and Cooke, on their sorrel and gray horses, consulted some papers. Benteen, always critical, wondered what they were studying. Finally they nodded for him to join them. Custer waved a fringed arm toward the southwest and told Benteen to lead his battalion in that direction, watch for the Indian village, and if he found it, "pitch in."

Benteen trotted off with his squadron. A few miles ahead of him stood some steep, grassy knolls. Perhaps the Little Big Horn and the Indian village were beyond them. As soon as Benteen had gone Custer ordered Reno to lead his battalion down the south side of the draw,

* T. M. Coughlan, "The Battle of the Little Big Horn," p. 15; E. S. Godfrey, *After the Custer Battle*, p. 4. Benteen told a somewhat different story at the Court of Inquiry (W. A. Graham, *Abstract of the Official Record*, p. 135). The Indians' discovery of the soldiers and the division into battalions may have occurred east of the divide. Accounts disagree.

through which the regiment had come. Custer followed with his five troops on the north side. Between them a thread of trees indicated the bed of the stream. Thus the 7th Cavalry's twelve troops advanced toward the Little Big Horn in three roughly parallel columns, with the ammunition mules well in the rear. No one knew which of the three would be first to spy the Indians.

Custer's column came to a lone tepee. Armstrong halted, swung to the ground and opened the door-flap. A dead warrior lay on a scaffold inside — not an unusual burial for an Indian. On a knoll, near the tepee, scout Fred Girard signaled. He had ridden up there ahead of the troops and shouted that he saw Indians, forty of them, racing away on ponies. The village must be on the Little Big Horn bottom which cut the plain ahead.

Armstrong turned to Adjutant Cooke and snapped a few commands. Cooke and Captain Keogh galloped across the draw to Reno's column. The two officers rode with Reno at a spanking trot. Fred Girard joined them with his scouts. After swinging along for three miles, the column came to the Little Big Horn. No village in sight! The river bottom stretched out a mile wide, and the stream meandered through trees at the foot of the bluffs on the east side. A cloud of dust a mile downstream indicated that the Indians might be there.

Adjutant Cooke told Reno: "General Custer directs that you take as fast a gait as you deem prudent and charge afterward, and you will be supported by the entire outfit." *

Reno's battalion broke ranks to ford the stream. Cooke and Keogh waited on the east bank as the three troops waded out on the west side, deployed and started down the river-bottom meadows. Bloody Knife, Charlie Reynolds, and other scouts rode on the extreme left. Cooke and Keogh watched them start, then turned their horses back, toward Custer, whose five troops waited about three quarters of a mile up the draw. Riding slowly to meet the general, they heard a horse's hoofs

---

* Just when and where this order was given is controversial. Note W. A. Graham, *Custer Myth*, p. 263.

pounding behind them. Fred Girard brought word from Reno that he had already met the Indians — lots of them. He could see their naked bodies as they rode to and fro in the river-bottom brush. He also saw the tips of tepees in the trees beyond them.

Cooke told Girard that he would report this to Custer. And here the first mystery of the Little Big Horn battle begins, for no one knows whether he did so. Only one of the men who might have heard survived and he understood little English. However, it seems probable that Custer received the message, for he turned his troops abruptly from the draw and rode north. Without doubt, he planned whooping in on the Indians' flank or rear as they attacked Reno. This was his usual offensive in the Shenandoah — one that had always worked.

On the tableland behind the river bluffs east of the stream, Custer halted his command and rode over to the rim. Bugler Martini, Adjutant Cooke, and Autie Reed followed him. Together they looked down on the mile-wide river bottom. Far to the left, Reno's line was almost undistinguishable in the brushy meadows, but below them and to the right stood circle after circle of tepees — lodges of the Northern Cheyenne, and of Oglala, Miniconjou, and Hunkpapa Sioux. Here was the largest assemblage of hostile Indians ever to congregate on the Plains. Instead of containing possibly twice the fighting strength of the 7th Cavalry, this village exceeded it four or five times. However, Custer knew from nine years' experience that Indians did not stand to fight. They were brave enough individually, but unorganized. Each man was his own general and masses of them were subject to panic. What he did not know was that this vast encampment had just been augmented by the same Northern Cheyenne who had recently whipped Crook a second time, over at the head of the Rosebud, and now believed themselves invincible.[12] In addition, reservation Indians, with rifles given them by the Indian Bureau, had been streaming into the hostile camp all summer.

From the blufftop the village circles looked peaceful enough. A few ponies stood with drooping heads. Here and there a squaw in voluminous buckskins trudged among the conical tents. All the little figures were women — no men! Bugler Martini, who watched his master with the worshipful eyes of a boy looking at his first sweetheart, stated later that Custer said: "We've caught them all asleep."

Martini knew little English at the time of the fight. What Custer probably said was "We've caught them napping." He turned abruptly in his saddle and waved his broad-brimmed hat for his five waiting troops to see. "We've got them," he shouted. Custer set his hat over one eye and pressed it down in his peculiar manner, then spurred down the slope to his men. The column started forward at a fast trot, breaking into a gallop across depressions, to close intervals. Custer turned in his rocking saddle and said to Martini, "I want you to take a message to Captain Benteen. Ride fast as you can, and tell him to hurry. Tell him it's a big village, and I want him to be quick, and to bring the ammunition packs." Custer turned to the column. His shrill commanding voice called: "As soon as we get through, we will go back to our station." Thus his last recorded words may have concerned a reunion with Libbie.

Martini reined his horse away. Adjutant Cooke stopped him. "Wait, orderly," he said. "I'll give you a message." He knew that the bugler was still learning English, might deliver a confused order. Cooke opened his notebook and wrote:

> BENTEEN: Come on. Big village. Be quick. Bring packs. W. W. COOKE. P. S. Bring packs.*

Cooke tore the page from his book and handed it to Martini. The boy reined his horse back up the trail. Regaining the high ground where he had sat with Custer, he looked at the departing column. The van had already disappeared down a draw which must lead to a crossing

* The story of this document, before it came to rest in the U.S. Military Academy Museum, is told by M. F. Perry in "Come on! Be Quick!", pp. 14–15. See also W. A. Graham, *Custer Myth*, pp. 287–300. Accounts of other men, who claimed to be survivors, notably Scout Curly and Sergeant Knipe, have been discredited. Custer's last spoken words are taken from Martini's testimony at Court of Inquiry (W. A. Graham, ed., *Abstract of the Official Record*, p. 130).

of the Little Big Horn. As he watched, the white-horse troop followed. This was the last sight any white man had of Custer's men.

Martini rode south along the edge of the bluff. Looking down on the river bottom where Reno was advancing, he heard rapid firing and saw many little brown figures dashing along on ponies. Reno had them on the run, he thought. Then, from behind him in the grasslands where Custer had gone, he heard a tremendous bombardment. He must hurry, so Benteen could bring that ammunition to Custer. As he rode he saw a distant horseman galloping toward him from the south. The rider wore buckskins, but was white. He disappeared in a swale; then came in sight, closer and larger. Martini recognized Boston Custer. The forage master had been left behind, probably with the pack train.

"Where is the general?" Boston shouted, his sapphire Custer-eyes dancing excitedly.

Martini pointed back toward the bombardment. Boston lunged away —the last man to join Armstrong's doomed column.

Martini's horse was tired — ears hanging sideways, hocks bumping —but the trumpeter forced him onward. The sound of distant shooting came to him from two directions — Reno's and Custer's. This would be a great victory surely! Would his horse carry him and his message through? The boy on the faltering horse seemed but a speck in the grass under the bowl of sky. Prairie flowers — purple, yellow, and white — nodded about him in the June breeze.

Emerging at last, on the edge of the draw down which the regiment had come earlier that afternoon, Martini saw many little horsemen across the green basin. They rode in formation, must be soldiers. Benteen, of course! Martini turned his horse down the slope toward him.

At about 4 P.M. the Italian trumpeter handed the message to Benteen, who, having found no Indians, had already turned to rejoin the column. On the way he picked up the ammunition train and came on, slowly, with it. When he read Martini's note he hurried to the bluffs ahead, to observe the battlefields. Here he met Reno's men, disorganized, breathless, bleeding. Reno was hatless, a handkerchief tied around his square head, his face speckled like a guinea egg with dried blood. He said that he had advanced in open order down the river bottom. The enemy had flanked him. To save the command, Reno stopped, consolidated his three companies in a patch of timber, but the Indians slipped through his lines, shot Bloody Knife so close to him that hot blood sprayed his face. In desperation Reno ordered a retreat at full run — as inviting to Plains Indians as a buffalo hunt. In the race for these bluffs a third of his men, among them Charlie Reynolds, had been killed.

Where was Custer? Nobody knew. As Benteen and Reno talked, Captain Weir, of Benteen's command, marched his troop south to find out. Weir had admired Custer since fighting with him at the Washita.[18] Armstrong had always relied on Weir, trusted him, promoted him, and Weir was not one to wait and wonder. He led his men forward cautiously, heard a thunderous bombardment about four miles away, in the direction Custer had gone. He deployed his men as skirmishers and kept going. Within a mile, bullets began to hum around his thin line, whistling overhead. He halted and consolidated for defense. Benteen overtook him here. The two officers discussed the situation. They did not know how many enemies lay hidden ahead, but Reno's mauled battalion behind them certainly needed support. Benteen ordered Weir's troop to return. It was now 7 P.M. They found Reno fortifying himself as best he could while bullets buzzed like yellow jackets around his men and horses. Soldiers crouched behind piles of equipment, boxes of hardtack, dead mules. Red marksmen, invisible behind the gently sloping ridges, fired at any white man's head which dared appear.

The deadly fusillade lasted until dark. Then silence.

Reno now displayed a distressing weakness of character. The man with the firm jaw who had been cited for gallantry at Cedar Creek proved deplorably wanting in resolution. Benteen, on the other hand, took over heroically. Although second in rank, this gossipy and garrulous fellow, like the Duke of Austria in Shakespeare's "King John," found that "courage mounteth with occasion." He ordered foxholes dug, rearranged duffel for defense in case the Indians renewed the attack tomorrow. The soldiers, having marched most of last night and the day before, dropped asleep even as they toiled. Benteen worried about keeping sentries awake and had to prop open his own eyes. Many men nodded sleepily even as they watched, with horror, the big fires down in the Indian village where warriors celebrated their victory, dancing and singing over scalps already taken and others anticipated in the morning.

The embattled troopers criticized and cursed Custer. Had he abandoned his men as he did Elliott on the Washita? Lieutenant Godfrey, walking his rounds, heard men say, "What in hell does Custer care for us! You bet he's all right, somewhere with water and grass." [14] The stories Benteen had been sowing for eight years bore fruit at last. True or not, they heaped appalling retribution on a dead commander.

Before that night of threatening horrors passed, Lieutenant Godfrey heard an unbelievable proposal. Reno called his officers together and said that the only hope of saving the entire command from massacre, next day, was for them all to slip away in the dark — save themselves. Benteen was too good a soldier to consider such a procedure. The United States Army might have left its wounded to the enemy in the Civil War, but it would not leave them to be tortured by savages.* The desperate officers continued to walk their rounds.

During the night thirteen men straggled into camp. They had been left behind by Reno in the river underbrush, having failed to hear his order to retreat.

At dawn the Indians attacked as expected. The cavalry horses could not be protected behind makeshift barricades, and many were killed. Occasionally Indians crawled close enough to pick off soldiers. Once more Benteen displayed his courage. He cleaned out these nests of red

---

* This aspersion on Reno's character must be accepted with reservations. There is only one witness to the incident (W. A. Graham, *Custer Myth,* p. 333 ff.). Fred Dustin, who did much research on Custer, but never without subjectivity, discredited it.

sharpshooters by leading charges against them on foot. There was no doubt about the old curmudgeon's ability when necessity demanded action.

At noon all shooting stopped. Soldiers peered over the barricades. Down in the river bottom where the village had stood, they saw a vast horde of horses, pack animals, and shouting red men. A multitude of ponies estimated at fifteen to twenty-five thousand, and God only knew how many Indians, flowed westward across the Plains toward the pale mountains. The village was escaping! Where was Custer?

That night the ragged, starving, besieged soldiers heard a distant bugle call. Could that be Gibbon's column? Before morning four more refugees who had hidden in the brush when Reno made his retreat straggled in. Among them were Fred Girard and Lieutenant DeRudio, the latter with a more exciting story of escape than any he experienced under Mazzini.[15]

Next morning, June 27, the soldiers saw a column of dust on the rolling Plains to the north. As they watched, it grew higher and wider. A scout from Gibbon's column rode up to the barricade. He told the soldiers that Custer had been massacred. The 7th Cavalry troopers did not believe it. Other mortals died, but surely not Custer.

Only an hour or two earlier, Lieutenant James H. Bradley, commander of Gibbon's scouts, had found all that was left of Custer's five troops. As he rode up the east bank of the Little Big Horn, he had seen a dead horse and turned toward it. White objects dotting the hillside ahead had attracted his attention. What were they? Riding closer he saw, scattered across the reddish-brown grass, the naked bodies of more than two hundred and fifty men — white as marble except for mahogany-colored faces and hands. A few wore bloody undershirts. Some had on trousers, and many wore white socks. Squaws had taken practically everything else from the corpses. The women particularly coveted bootlegs for moccasin soles, and had thrown aside the lower parts. Children, looting with their mothers, had found rolls of green-and-white paper in dead soldiers' pockets. They saved some of these greenbacks to decorate their toys.[16] Only a few bodies had been mutilated. Mark Kellogg lay dead in his civilian clothes but any recent dispatch to his newspaper, if he wrote one, was gone.

Lieutenant Bradley could not identify the bodies, so he called for the officers from Reno's command to come and help him. Calhoun's body was found behind those of his men. They had died in skirmish formation. Tom Custer, terribly mutilated, lay on his face. Scalped several times, he had been left with hair only on the nape of his neck. His skull was crushed and his body bristled with arrows. His heart had been cut out. Keogh was identified by the crucifix he wore around his neck. His thick black hair, still parted in the middle, had not been "lifted" by the redskins. His wounded horse, Comanche, was the only living thing left on the battlefield.

Armstrong's naked body was found on the highest point of the field — sitting in the angle between two dead soldiers, one lying across the other. His arm rested on the topmost corpse. His face lay in the palm of his hand. When the body was rolled over and laid out, Lieutenant Godfrey remarked that the colonel looked exactly as he did when taking one of his frequent cat naps.[17]

Two small wounds were found on Custer's body — a bullethole through his left breast and another in his left temple. There were no powder marks, no signs of a hand-to-hand struggle, no indication that he had even seen his assailants. The whole battalion may well have been shot down by Indians concealed in the deep gulches traversing the field. The last thing Custer must have beheld before he died was the spectacular panorama of sweeping plain with pale, shining snowfields in the distance — breathtaking, magnificent, yet strangely reminiscent of the view from the back stoop of the farmhouse in New Rumley, Ohio, where the little boy, Armstrong, had placed a tin washbasin on his yellow curls to amuse the family.

28 A Wounded Thing Must Hide

ON THE NIGHT OF JULY 5, 1876, THE "FAR WEST" DOCKED AT BISMARCK to telegraph the tragic news East. Then it floated down to the fort to notify the next of kin, and unload wounded survivors of Reno's column. Libbie was aroused next morning by a knock at the back door. She heard a deep voice tell the cook to summon Mrs. Custer.

Libbie slipped on a dressing gown, called Margaret Calhoun and Maria Reed. In the parlor they met Captain William S. McCaskey, Lieutenant C. L. Gurley, and J. V. D. Middleton, post surgeon. The Captain read a formal announcement of the tragedy. All three women stood dazed. The July sun was sultry hot but Libbie chilled to the bone and asked weakly for a shawl. Margaret's senses revived with equal slowness. She had lost a husband, three brothers, and a nephew. Of the close-knit Custer family only she, the old folks, and Nevin remained. She ran after the departing captain, calling, "Is there no message for me?"

Twenty-six women * in the fort had been struck by the disaster. Libbie must stand by as the grim announcement was read to them all, first in Officers Quarters, then down on Laundress Row. She must be a model of bravery, as Autie would wish. She shuddered.

Autie did not wish anything now!

Libbie had not recovered from the shock when she realized that she was no longer in the army. She must give up her home. After twelve years as an officer's wife her pension would be thirty dollars per month.

Another shock came to Libbie when she read the newspapers. General Terry had sent in two reports of the Little Big Horn fight. The

---

* This number is from E. B. Custer, *Boots and Saddles*, p. 268. W. A. Graham, *Custer Myth*, p. 148, quotes Godfrey as saying that thirty-nine women were bereaved. The scene described above is from Graham's book, p. 282, and M. Merington, *Custer Story*, p. 323.

first, dated June 27, told the simple facts. The second, dated July 2, blamed Custer's death on his own disobedience of orders, on the fact that he had tried to show off by racing away to beat Gibbon's column to the Indians.

Only the first had been intended for publication. The second sounded very much like Terry's excuse to his superior for dividing his command and suffering a defeat. But the fact that the second report was published by mistake did not help Libbie. She knew her Autie to be impetuous. In his *Galaxy* article he had told how General Hancock disobeyed an order and won the Battle of Williamsburg. Perhaps Armstrong disobeyed orders when he thought it advisable. Had not Clausewitz said, "Pity the warrior who is content to crawl about in the beggardom of rules! . . . What genius does must be the best of rules." Surely there was no higher authority than Clausewitz. However, in this instance Armstrong had broken no rules; she had read Terry's order and she knew.

Libbie left Fort Abraham Lincoln and returned to Monroe. She was thirty-four years old now, still slim and beautiful. With her on the train from Bismarck came the other Monroe girls, Margaret Calhoun, Maria Reed, and Annie Yates with her children dressed in the clothes which Armstrong had purchased for them on his last trip to Washington.

Many women had been widowed by Indian fights before Custer's time, and it was not unprecedented for red men to wipe out entire units. Major William Fetterman's command had been exterminated in 1866, and J. L. Grattan's in 1854. Libbie had seen at West Point the monument to Major Francis Dade and his men — one hundred and ten killed by Seminole, with only four escaping. But Custer's case was different. He had ridden to defeat amid political controversy. Enemies of the administration already pointed accusing fingers at Grant, blaming him for Custer's death, urging voters to settle with Grant and his party in the fall elections. To save themselves the Radicals were bound to strike back and the blows from both sides would hit Libbie. The most malicious of them all came from President Grant. He, like other politicians, had to defend himself and his party. Without reading Terry's order carefully he accused Custer of disobeying it. Grant also claimed that Custer marched farther than he really did, thus over-exerting himself and his men to deprive fellow officers of their share of victory.

Libbie had been in the army long enough to know that professional jealousy would set military tongues wagging. Interested bystanders would soon join in the controversy. She was not surprised when Custer's enemies began telling how he had boasted that he would ride away from Terry as he had from Stanley. General Gibbon even re-membered that he warned Custer to wait for him and not be greedy. Such remarks wounded Libbie deeply, but she found some comfort in a friend's announcement that he remembered Terry's last words to Custer as being, "Do what you think best if you strike the trail." *

Libbie should have known that none of these statements, either pro or con, were credible except as examples of the frailty of human memory. Perhaps her greatest solace came in letters from McClellan and Rosser, Democrats both, but men well qualified to judge Custer. The former pointed out that the critics who now accused Custer of rashness would have blamed him for timidity had the Indians escaped. Rosser wrote that any cavalryman worth his oats must take the chances that Armstrong did. Tony Forsyth, a more experienced Indian fighter than either of them, said Custer acted well within his orders.[1] In the South, which Custer admired so much, the Richmond *Whig* praised his bravery and fighting ability. William Rowan, who had fought

* A letter dated July 16, 1878, in the Illinois State Historical Library, from Ben Grierson, famous for his Civil War raid, blamed Custer's death on his own recklessness. Grierson, as a commander of Negro troops, met Custer at Fort Sill in 1869. Gibbon, a good soldier, was not a disciplined observer. Note that he gets the sequence of events mixed in his *Personal Recollections*, p. 939. Other pronouncements for and against Custer may be found in C. T. Brady, *Indian Fights and Fighters*, p. 223; T. M. Coughlan, *The Battle of the Little Big Horn*, p. 14; W. A. Graham, *Story of the Little Big Horn*, Appendix, pp. 15, 32; C. E. De Land, *Sioux Wars*, pp. 372, 430; G. B. McClellan's *Own Story*, p. 365; N. A. Miles, *Personal Recollections*, p. 205.

against Custer in the war, offered the services of a regiment of former Confederates to avenge his memory. A Confederate who had captured Custer's cap and sash at Trevilian Station in 1864 sent them to his widow. In the North, Buffalo Bill closed his theatrical performance to go West and take the "first scalp for Custer" — grand publicity for his fall opening. The Metropolitan Life Insurance Company added to the widespread interest in Custer by publicizing his farsightedness in taking out an adequate policy. Calhoun and Keogh had also insured their lives.[2]

During this period of alternate accusation and praise a strange man called at Libbie's house. Speaking with a slight English accent, he said that he had served in the Army of the Potomac until wounded in the Wilderness. He had met General Custer when working on the editorial staff of *Galaxy*. Now Sheldon & Company, who published Custer's *Life on the Plains,* wanted him to write a biography of the General to be delivered in the early fall. Would Mrs. Custer help him?

The name Frederick Whittaker was familiar to Libbie. She had seen it signed to an article in *Galaxy* which praised her husband for gallantry and blamed his defeat on an overwhelming number of Indian opponents.[3] Oh, what a chance to end the terrible "disobedience" charge and put the blame where she believed it belonged — squarely on the heads of Grant, Reno, and Benteen! This time her dear husband could not stop her, caution her to be tolerant and kind. Yes, indeed yes, she would help Mr. Whittaker as much as she could. Thus Libbie got deeper and deeper into trouble in an effort to exculpate her Autie.

Whittaker's book was a fully illustrated biography of 648 pages hastily prepared to take advantage of the popular interest in Custer. Some of the narrative's personal touches, added by Libbie and glamorized by Whittaker, would be accepted uncritically by many historians. The most flagrant error concerned Custer's military heritage. Libbie believed Custer to be of German descent, probably Pennsylvania-Dutch. Armstrong knew little about his ancestors and cared less, but on his last trip to Washington he had received a letter from a Custer in the Orkney Islands who claimed relationship, even listed many odd spellings of the name as far back as 1647. Custer had joked about this with Libbie.[4] Now she told it all to Whittaker and that imaginative writer described the General as the great-great-grandson of one Küster, a Hessian officer in the Revolution who remained in Pennsylvania.

Libbie pronounced the book, with all its Custer-praise, a poorly written one. But she may have been responsible for convincing Whittaker that Reno spoiled Custer's battle plan by failing to charge the Indian village. Had Reno continued his pursuit, the great body of Indians opposing him would not have dared to ride off and attack Custer. Whittaker also asked, in his book, why Benteen, when ordered to "Come quick. Bring packs," stopped as soon as he reached Reno, thus preventing more than seven companies from rescuing Custer and his five isolated ones.

This devastating query may also have originated in Whittaker's conferences with Libbie. Armstrong was never averse to taking all the credit available, but it is doubtful that he would have approved — publicly at least — of Whittaker's forthright statement: "Had not President Grant, moved by private revenge, displaced Custer from command of the Fort Abraham Lincoln column, Custer would be alive today and the Indian war settled. . . . Reno and Benteen would never have dreamed of disobeying their chief, had they not known he was out of favor at court."[5]

The book's disparaging chapter on Grant probably had little effect on the election of 1876, although Libbie may have derived some satisfaction from the party's near-defeat that fall. Certainly the book contained many statements which were bound to start controversy — to Whittaker's delight, perhaps. Some military experts maintained that Reno's entire battalion would have been exterminated had he charged the village instead of dismounting to fight on foot. Others dissented. Who can say? Such Indian authorities as George Bird Grinnell and James McLaughlin, who knew Custer and the wild Indians as well, agreed with Libbie and Whittaker. Unorganized Indians, they said, would have scattered in panic had Reno continued his charge.

With the coming of cold weather Libbie moved to New York, to lose herself in the great crowds, she said. An overpowering emotion consumed her every thought: she must vindicate her husband's memory, discredit his enemies. Autie had always curbed her natural impulse to gossip and accuse. Now she was unrestrained, could let herself go. Moreover, Mr. Whittaker seemed eager to continue working with her to force a military investigation, and thus give Custer his true deserts.

Libbie's first problem after arriving in the city was to make a living. Her insurance money would not last forever, and "ladies" did not work in 1876. However, she read in the newspapers a notice which gave her an idea. Some well-to-do, civic-minded New Yorkers were organizing what they called "The Society of Decorative Arts," to display and sell artistic handiwork of talented but "decayed gentlewomen" — and some not so talented although certainly decayed — who needed extra money but could not leave the sanctity of their homes.

Libbie, a little slip of a woman in widow's weeds, called on the president of the organization and applied for the position of secretary. Mrs. David Lane looked down at her wistful, smiling face framed by the ruching under her black crepe bonnet and around her neck. She was favorably impressed and reported her interview to members of the board. They disapproved of employing the widow of such a widely publicized individual as George Armstrong Custer, but Mrs. Lane, being a strong-minded woman, employed her anyway. Though the salary was meager Libbie accepted it, and within a short time won the hearts of board members who had disapproved her appointment. In Virginia during the war she had shown tact and sensitivity in letters to bereaved parents, telling herself, always, that the message she sent was Autie's "in all but the manipulation of the pen." Now, her letters to forlorn women who hoped to sell their handiwork showed equal compassion.

Moreover, she seemed never dismayed by the accumulation of correspondence which piled up daily on her desk.[6]

Interest in the Little Big Horn Battle was revived during the following summer by Custer's disinterment in Montana for reburial with military honors at West Point. At this time, General Nelson A. Miles, the Custers' lifelong friend, visited the battlefield with twenty-five Sioux and Cheyenne warriors and investigated it thoroughly. He became convinced that Reno and Benteen had betrayed Custer, just as Whittaker claimed in his book.

Spurred by these constant reminders, Libbie sorted the accumulation of clippings and letters she had saved concerning her husband. She remembered that Armstrong, on his last trip to Washington, had sat for a bust by Vinnie Ream. The little sculptress had been a favorite of his. Libbie wrote her a long, chatty letter asking about the bust and disclosing her own disappointments, frustrations, and determination to clear her husband's name. "There is still before me an awful day of dread," she wrote, "and until that is ended it seems impossible for me to leave the seclusion in which I have hidden myself in this great city." [7]

The "day of dread" was the reburial of General Custer at West Point on October 10, 1877. Father Custer and his daughter Nettie (now Mrs. Smith) traveled East for the services. Libbie came up from New York with Mrs. Lawrence Barrett.

The smell of autumn tinged the air. Forest trees on the ridge behind the officers' residences blazed with color. Gloomy cedars etched zebra stripes across the brilliant slope. Libbie entered the little Ionic chapel on the arm of General Schofield, commandant of the post, and sat facing the mural of Mars above the altar. This was where the Reverend Mr. Parsons had first noticed the boy Fanny playing pranks.

Custer's coffin was covered with the Stars and Stripes. On top lay his sword and plumed dress-helmet, which he seldom, if ever, wore. At the conclusion of the services, pallbearers carried his body to a caisson and he was trundled away, under the elms, along the road over which Cadet Custer had watched Lieutenant Griffin lead the artillery that frosty morning in 1861. A horse, blanketed to the ears, followed the funeral procession. From the animal's withers hung spurred boots pointing to the rear. At the cemetery, soldiers lowered the coffin into an open grave. Libbie heard the hollow thud of a few clods dropped ceremoniously on the metal box, the chaplain's solemn words, a sharp command, and the roar of a volley fired above the tomb. Minutes later, it seemed, the echo answered from Storm King Mountain and the Crow Nest. Then the young widow was led away with her cherished memories, feeling somber consolation in the knowledge that Armstrong slept "where his comrades had laid him." [8]

During the winter of 1877–1878 in New York, Libbie and her old friend, Frederick Whittaker, persisted in their efforts to secure an official inquiry into the circumstances surrounding Custer's death. Perhaps Whittaker hoped to stimulate sales of his book. Perhaps he felt genuine resentment against Custer's critics, for Whittaker was a soldier and Armstrong had a gift for engendering tremendous loyalty in his supporters. Perhaps Libbie's own relentless enthusiasm was behind it all. In any event, on May 18, 1878, Whittaker wrote Wyoming's delegate to Congress, W. W. Corlett, urging a congressional investigation, then gave a copy of his letter to the press for publication.

Confronted with this disparaging publicity, Major Reno asked for a military Court of Inquiry to pass on his actions during the battle — certainly a more authoritative body than a congressional committee. The hearing was set for January 13, 1879, in Chicago. When the Court convened, Libbie's aunt, cousins, and Margaret Calhoun came from upper New York and from Michigan to be with her during the ordeal. Together they would watch every day's report. Libbie read that Wesley Merritt was to be one of the three officers composing the Court. Good! She remembered that he and Armstrong had served together in the Army of the Potomac. Later she had entertained him at their quarters on the Plains. With naïve, feminine trust, she was confident that such a gracious gentleman would uphold Armstrong's good name.

Many officers, enlisted men, and two civilian packers — twenty-three men in all — were summoned as witnesses for the Inquiry. Reno, on the stand under oath, defended his actions by blaming Custer for not telling him the battle plans. His only orders, he said, were to charge the village and "You will be supported by the whole outfit." Reno said he thought that this meant Custer would follow him. Instead, Custer circled to strike the Indians' flank.

This seemed like a poor defense. Since Shenandoah Valley days, Custer invariably opened an attack on one front and, when well engaged, charged in on the flank. If Reno did not know this he was an ill-informed officer. If he failed to see Custer wave his hat from the bluff on his right, he was an unobserving one. If he could not fathom what Custer planned, he was stupid. Perhaps the most damaging thing about Reno's defense was his contradiction of his own story. In his official report immediately after the battle he had said that he expected Custer to support him on the flank. Now, two and a half years later, he said he expected support from the rear.

Reno maintained that his flight, in which a third of his men were killed, was a charge. Such military semantics could not disguise a rout, especially since Reno had left in such a hurry that part of his men never heard the command and stayed behind. As these men were unharmed and joined the battalion after dark, the prosecution asked Reno if the entire unit might have dug in and stood its ground. Reno thought not.

All officers, when cross-examined at the Inquiry, refrained from calling Reno a coward. Good men occasionally lose their heads and Reno was a fellow soldier. Lieutenant Godfrey asserted that he showed "indecision" and "nervous timidity" — probably the worst accusation at the hearing. One of the civilian packers, who was struck by Reno, testified that he was drunk.

The verdict displeased the prosecution as well as the defense. With carefully chosen words the Court decided: "The conduct of the officers throughout was excellent, and while subordinates, in some instances, did more for the safety of the command by brilliant displays of courage than did Major Reno, there was nothing in his conduct which requires animadversion from this Court." [9]

To a sensitive officer this was the blackest kind of whitewash. To Libbie it was a defeat. Now, more than ever, she missed Armstrong, wanted him to be with her. She must buy that Vinnie Ream bust if she could scrape together enough money. She wrote again to the sculptress, and Vinnie replied, asking her to come to her Washington studio and supervise the finishing touches. Libbie, still hurt by the trial, lacked courage to show her face in public. "A wounded thing must hide," she wrote Vinnie, "and I cannot go to Washington and stay among the General's friends." Final decisions on the bust must be made by mail.

Vinnie inquired if Mrs. Custer wanted her husband dressed in buckskins. Libbie decided not. "I feel attached to his real western suit," she wrote, "but since frontiersmen have become showmen and the sensational papers have spread broadcast the buckskin clothes I do not like to think of Autie, as represented for all time in them. I have a sentimental & tender love for the styles of dress that he adored. . . . Others could not [enter] into that sentiment."

Libbie was very tired. Every accusation against her husband increased her fatigue. Margaret Calhoun's bright curly hair and sunny disposition reminded her of Autie and cheered her days, but Maggie had her own life to live and could not stay forever. Libbie rented "a little dot of a flat with a widowed friend" and continued to augment her modest funds with the Society of Decorative Arts' pittance. Her one purpose in life now centered on purchasing the Custer bust and she confessed that every letter from Vinnie Ream set her "heart beating like a drum." Yet she worried lest she could not afford to purchase it when completed. Perhaps she could get a plaster cast?

In this highly emotional state she received what was to her "a crushing blow." An equestrian statue of Custer had been erected at West Point without her knowledge. According to the accounts she heard, her Boy General looked sixty years old. Moreover, she was told that he held a pistol in one hand and a sword in the other — an untrue picture of her Armstrong. "His most brilliant charges," she explained to a friend, "had been made without firearms."

During the summer of 1879, Libbie mustered sufficient money and courage to go to Washington. She was delighted with Vinnie's progress and with Vinnie, too. The bright-eyed little artist had married, and Libbie enjoyed calling her "Mrs. Hoxie" and telling her how good it was to "know that you have entered the paradise that a man's loving heart opens to his wife." Gazing at the bust, Libbie wondered if a bronze copy might be put on a pedestal beside Armstrong's grave. Then people could walk past that equestrian horror and see Armstrong's "strong, fine face" as it really was.

Back once more in New York, she wrote an appreciative letter to Vinnie. "When will I forget the day I spent those hours with you!" she said. "I could not speak fast enough. I had so much to say to you — and you a stranger." [10] She enclosed one hundred dollars she had earned herself and promised to send fifty dollars later.

In the spring of 1880 she learned that Major Reno had been dismissed from the army for drunkenness and conduct unbecoming an officer and gentleman. Gossips said that he had ordered a subordinate away on special duty and in his absence made improper advances to his wife. [11] Maybe so, maybe not. Libbie did not like him anyway. Less sordid and more heartening news came to her from West Point. Lieutenant Godfrey had delivered a lecture there commending Custer's part in the engagement. Hurrah! Armstrong always said that everything would come out all right in the end.

Next year, 1881, Libbie purchased a little home for herself and that marble bust — as soon as it was finished and paid for. On Memorial Day she steeled herself for another visit to West Point, though she trembled a little lest she break down. Everything looked so familiar. Leaves on the elms around the Plain were burgeoning. White flower-clusters glowed on the honey-locust trees with all the spring freshness and delicacy which Armstrong loved. The grass stood velvet green, like river-bottom meadows out west. Time to prepare for a summer campaign! Libbie, in a new hat and full skirted dress with balloon sleeves, walked from the library out to the cemetery. As she passed the equestrian statue of her husband she turned her head proudly aside. Armstrong's grave, among his fellow soldiers, seemed dignified and comforting. If only she could get rid of that bronze monstrosity!

Returning to New York, Libbie appealed to Actor Barrett. Could he induce influential friends to remove that statue? She wrote to Secretary of War Robert Todd Lincoln, and to General Sherman. The fury of her enthusiasm knew no bounds. In a letter to Sherman she blamed General Merritt for blocking her appeals. He had been jealous of Armstrong in the war, she said, and had shown it in his conduct at the Court of Inquiry. "Armstrong would not approve of my saying this or anything against him," she concluded, "but I saw it." [12]

Libbie made her final trip to Washington in the fall of 1881 to get that marble bust. In the capital she called at General Sherman's office to ask him to exert his authority toward having her pension increased from thirty dollars to fifty dollars a month. The government must realize that the cost of living was going up!

Sherman met her graciously, asked her to take a chair. Libbie, sitting before the grizzled, straight-backed redhead, lost her nerve. Money was such an unladylike topic and the General's conversation did not lead into it. Later, at Vinnie's, she felt more at ease. The bust was finished now, so she paid her precious money and started back to New York with it. The marble was heavier than Libbie anticipated. At Jersey City she had to employ a porter to carry it on and off the ferry across the Hudson and then to her little home. Having a big man to serve her again seemed like old times. Libbie gushed appreciation — the enthusiasm which had stimulated enlisted men who used to work in her garden.

Home again, all by herself, ecstatic Libbie unpacked the bust. Then she took out her mourning-bordered notepaper and wrote appreciative letters to friends down in Washington. She thanked Sherman for his interview and dared ask him now — as she had not when sitting before him — to do what he could about raising her pension. She was in serious need of the money. With due humility she signed the letter, "Desolate me."

Then Libbie started another letter, a much easier one to write. It was to Vinnie, saying that she was delighted with the bust. "Just above my desk," she wrote, "that grand face looks up as if ready to face any future!" [13]

Libbie, too, began to feel like facing any future. The old sorrow was no longer acute and she received two financial landfalls. First, her pension was increased to fifty dollars. Then her stepmother died and the income the judge had left his wife reverted to Libbie. How wise Armstrong was when he said things turned out all right in the end! Libbie had reached her fortieth year now. She was not rich but free at last from financial worries. She decided to take a trip to Europe.

When this vacation ended, Libbie returned to New York and set to work on a new project. She would write a book about her Dakota days, army life at Fort Abraham Lincoln, and that last tragic summer. *Boots and Saddles* was published in 1885 and soon sold well over twenty-two thousand copies — more, Libbie said, "than my wildest midnight dreams." Three hundred letters came to her from appreciative admirers. In one delivery Libbie recognized Vinnie Ream Hoxie's handwriting and tore open the envelope. It was so good to be remembered by the little sculptress.

Libbie answered Vinnie's letter at once. "I suffered so in writing *Boots and Saddles,*" she said, "that every kind word written or spoken to me, is treasured as my best wealth."

Indeed the greatest recompense she received from the book was the realization that it kept alive the public's interest in her husband, an interest which would surely lead to his complete vindication. For a short rest she went to Mexico. A new dictator, Porfirio Díaz, welcomed Americans, both tourists and capitalists, to bolster his economy. After this vacation she started on her second book, with Armstrong's bust always before her. *Tenting on the Plains* described her life in Texas and in Kansas, ending with her husband's surprise visit to Fort Riley which had caused his court-martial. She did not mention his conviction and year's suspension from the army, but she did describe those fatal twenty-four hours by saying: "There was that summer of 1867 one long, perfect day. It was mine, and blessed be our memory, which preserves to us the joys as well as the sadness of life! — it is still mine, for time and for eternity."

Libbie worked diligently for eighteen months on this volume, taxing her strength and her memory to the utmost. Nineteen years had passed since they left Kansas. Many things had become dim, she said, "except the partings and anxiety and suspense." Libbie found it hard to keep the story "rushing," but always buoyed herself with the joy of serving Autie. When the book was safely in press she went to Europe again for four months.[14]

During the next three years she worked on her third book, *Following the Guidon,* and ironically enough, now that she no longer needed extra money, her pension was increased to one hundred dollars. Her last book, like its two predecessors, was dedicated to Armstrong. This time she worded the message: "To one who has followed the guidon into that realm where 'the war-drum throbs no longer and the battle-flags are furled.' "

The volume began with the Battle of the Washita and ended with the summer in Kansas before Armstrong was ordered to Kentucky. Libbie described the details of a woman's life in camp: how to live without running water, without a door to lock, without a mirror — except a tiny one on a tent pole. She described all the improvisations necessary to make a tent a home. This volume was published in 1890 when homesteading was popular in the West. Every year hundreds of women were experiencing the hardships she described with such comforting gusto. Moreover, Sitting Bull was killed in December of that year, and Terry died next day — events which would, no doubt, stimulate sales of a Custer book. Sitting Bull, when he traveled with Buffalo Bill's show, had been advertised as the man who killed Custer. People conversant with the facts knew better. A great many other

Indians claimed the same honor, but, of course, nobody knew whose bullet killed the general, especially since the Indians did not know they were fighting Custer until told later by white men.

Fourteen years had now elapsed since the fight. Crazy Horse, Chief Gall, and many other participants had been interviewed and reinterviewed. Sitting Bull and Reno had discussed the fight at length. There was no longer anything of historical value to be learned from the Indians — albeit ambitious writers would "discover" for easily-duped readers the "true story" of the massacre for over three-quarters of a century. More remarkable still, as memories became dimmer, preposterous tales were accepted, the most extraordinary being that Custer's body was not mutilated because the Cheyenne hid it from the vengeance of Rain-in-the-Face, then put it out again for the soldiers to find.[15]

In the 1890's Elizabeth Custer's books began to appear in new editions, and she was called on for "readings" of her works. She met writers, painters, patrons of the arts. When an artists' colony called Onteora was started in the Catskills, she built a rustic cottage there. The owners called their summer homes picturesque names like "Wake-Robin," "Pennyroyal," and "Larkspur." Libbie named hers "The Flags." The literary people at Onteora included playwright Brander Matthews, Mark Twain, John Burroughs, and the small, melancholy-eyed Frank Stockton, then famous as the author of *Rudder Grange* and *The Lady or the Tiger*. Richard Watson Gilder, editor of *Century Magazine,* owned a cottage there; so did Mary Mapes Dodge, editor of *St. Nicholas*. Libbie's face, set in a becoming sunbonnet, was painted among the artistic "pioneers" on the plaster wall inside one of the first houses. In this congenial settlement she worked, played, picnicked, and watched the sun set behind the mountains.[16]

Libbie spent many a summer at Onteora. In the wintertime she experimented with several residences. She and Autie had planned the home to which they would retire and often discussed its details. Now Libbie, alone in her fifties, sought endlessly for the home of her dreams. She purchased one on Seventy-eighth Street, and as soon as she got her curtains hung, began looking for another. Never could she realize that life differs from the things dreams are made of.

Then occurred one of those amazing mishaps which did much to immortalize George Armstrong Custer. In St. Louis the brewing firm of Anheuser-Busch foreclosed a mortgage it held on a saloon. Among the furnishings their agent took a gigantic painting entitled "Custer's Last Stand," evidently painted, with due elaboration, from an illustration in Whittaker's book. It pictured Custer with long hair and a cavalry saber — both errors. The life-sized composition had been painted in the 1880's as a cyclorama for a traveling show, but had failed to attract customers. Anheuser-Busch decided to reproduce copies of it for display in their customers' barrooms. This got them into immediate trouble. The artist, Cassilly Adams, saw the reproduction and objected. He had never sold the picture, he said — merely stored it in the saloon. Anheuser-Busch settled the case by paying him a handsome sum, probably thirty thousand dollars, for the original picture. The painting was then presented to the 7th Cavalry, and eventually was burned in the fire which destroyed the Officers Club in El Paso in 1946. Shortly after the purchase from Adams, another artist, F. Otto Becker, copied Adams's composition, adding variations. In this second painting Custer holds his sword above his head instead of thrusting it forward into an Indian. Anheuser-Busch reproduced some one hundred and fifty thousand copies of these two paintings for distribution to their customers. Copies of the Cassilly Adams picture have become collectors' items.*

The "Last Stand" picture undoubtedly did much to perpetuate the Custer story, which received another fillip in January, 1892, when Libbie's friend, Richard Watson Gilder, published in *Century Magazine* the lecture which Captain E. S. Godfrey had given at West Point. The article exalted Custer at the expense of other officers in the en-

---

* The history of these pictures has been worked out with care by Don Russell in *Sixty Years in Bar Rooms*. Anheuser-Busch now calls the picture "Custer's Last Fight," but the name "Last Stand" survives. See also R. Taft, "The Pictorial Record of the Old West," pp. 361–390.

gagement, thus reviving old army jealousies. Terry had been dead two years now, but his brother-in-law and aide-de-camp during the campaign, Colonel R. P. Hughes, wrote a critical reply claiming that Custer had disobeyed Terry's order. General James S. Brisbin joined the jackals by printing the order with an alteration which made Custer unquestionably guilty.

Libbie again came gallantly to her husband's defense by publishing the order correctly.* But by this time twenty-one years had passed since the battle, and her recollections began to play tricks — exactly like the memories of Armstrong's enemies. Old grievances had grown in her mind to unreasonable proportions. Not only had Reno and Benteen and Grant connived against her husband, but now the Interior Department had issued guns to the Indians superior to those carried by the soldiers.

There was a modicum of truth in Libbie's statement. At Fort Abraham Lincoln she may have seen the latest model rifles on steamboats headed for the Indian agencies. She knew, too, that Armstrong had picked up superior weapons from the fleeing Indians after the Yellowstone fight in 1873. But such firearms were not generally carried by the red men who killed Custer. An inventory of the guns delivered by the renegades when they surrendered showed many to be muzzleloaders, some flintlocks. Perhaps the Indians withheld their best guns, but large quantities of metallic cartridges were always difficult for them to get, and many Indians carried only bows and arrows.[17]

In 1896, General Nelson A. Miles published his memoirs. He was now commander of the district where the battlefield lay, and he had followed his earlier investigations with an intensive study of the field

---

* Hughes's article appeared in the *Journal of the Military Service Institution,* January, 1896, and is reprinted in W. A. Graham, *Story of the Little Big Horn,* Appendix. Brisbin's fraudulent order is exposed in W. A. Graham, *Custer Myth,* pp. 155–156. An affidavit faked by some Custer supporter is discussed (*ibid.,* pp. 279–282), so both sides were dishonest. See also pp. 141, 301. Terry never complained about Custer after that one unfortunate letter, and Libbie visited him during his last illness. (Letter of E. B. Custer, April 11 [1890] in New York Historical Society, brought to my attention by Sylvester Vigilante.)

and interviews with more participants, both red and white. His book praised Custer and blamed his death on Reno and Benteen.[18]

In 1901 Libbie's three books were consolidated into one volume edited by Mary E. Burt. A completely new book by Libbie might have been popular, but at the age of fifty-seven she had scraped the bottom of her barrel of reminiscences, although she did not admit it. A quarter of a century had passed since the exciting days of her youth, and her interests were diverted by travel and contemplated purchases of that dream house. She moved to Bronxville, bought a lot where she planned to build, and promptly turned her attention to founding a home for girls — preferably impoverished girls from military families.

In 1908, at the age of sixty-four, Mrs. Custer went to Europe again, this time to "motor" around the Continent with friends from Monroe. (Like a true Custer, she never forgot her friends.) Yet always Armstrong was with her in memory. His death brought them closer together than in life. She was hurt when Maggie Calhoun remarried, and died shortly thereafter. On the grave Libbie insisted that only the Custer name should appear. The inscription reads: MARGARET, SISTER OF GEN. GEO. A. CUSTER.[19]

Libbie's closing years were affluent. She traveled around the world, wintered in Florida when so inclined. She served on the boards of hospitals and charitable institutions — the solace of elderly people who like to feel themselves useful. During her seventies and eighties, Libbie mastered a typewriter and apologized for writing personal letters on the plebeian machine. She moved continually — a home on the Grand Concourse, then back to Bronxville again, rooms in the Prince George Hotel on Twenty-eighth Street, summers at Onteora — comfortable quarters, with the bust of Armstrong and with curios she had collected in India, China, and Japan; but never the little place of her dreams.*

Always she welcomed officers from the 7th Cavalry. She cherished every new Custer story, and scribbled on the manuscript of a book

* A list of these souvenirs is at the Custer Battlefield National Monument.

which she never finished. At parties younger women wondered, with little twinges of envy, why a group of men always congregated around her. On the fifty-fifth anniversary of the Battle of the Little Big Horn, newspaper reporters called at her Park Avenue apartment. They found a little gray-haired woman eighty-nine years old. She was interested now in a proposed project to preserve old frontier forts. A year later in her nineties, she still thrilled to the sound of "Garry Owen." Those rowdy cadences set her heart beating like a girl's, made her stand a bit straighter, and toss her head with a proud little jerk.

Libbie was deeply touched when she learned that wives could be buried beside their husbands at West Point. On April 6, 1933,[20] two days before her ninety-second birthday, she joined Armstrong there. It was springtime on the Hudson and her husband had been waiting for a long time — almost fifty-seven years. Hopeful cadet-candidates came to the Academy by train now. The railroad station stood under the granite bluff where the omnibus used to meet steamboat passengers. Airplanes buzzed overhead, but Libbie did not hear them. She lay quietly with her husband on a green hill. Raindrops from April showers sparkled like diamonds in the grass. The blue waters of the Hudson swept past them, and the sky was blue above. For Libbie the long, perfect day had come again. It was all hers, and would be hers for time and for eternity.

Notes

CHAPTER 1

1. E. B. Custer, *Tenting on the Plains,* p. 284; M. Merington, *Custer Story,* p. 4.
2. E. B. Custer, *Tenting on the Plains,* p. 239.
3. Custer to John Chamberlain, April 7, 1860 (Janet Brown collection).
4. D. Hunter, *Before Life Began,* pp. 5–6; R. Hunter, *The Judge Rode a Sorrel Horse,* pp. 16–17.
5. G. A. Custer, *My Life on the Plains* (Quaife ed.), p. xxiv; M. M. Quaife, "Some Monroe Memories," pp. 9–12.
6. M. Merington, *The Custer Story,* p. 7; F. Whittaker, *Complete Life of . . . Custer . . . ,* p. 8.
7. Memo at Custer Battlefield National Monument.
8. Letter to John Chamberlain, May 5, 1860.
9. These boyhood documents were called to my attention by Milton Ronsheim of Cadiz, Ohio.
10. M. Schaff, *Spirit of Old West Point,* p. 2.
11. J. M. Wright, "West Point before the War," p. 14.

CHAPTER 2

1. Record Book (West Point).
2. J. P. Farley, *West Point in the Early Sixties,* picture opposite p. 44.
3. E. B. Custer, *Tenting on the Plains,* p. 320.
4. P. Michie, "Reminiscences," p. 187.

5. M. Schaff, *Spirit of Old West Point,* pp. 40, 68; J. P. Farley, *West Point in the Early Sixties,* p. 78; Michie, "Reminiscences," p. 196.

6. M. Schaff, *Spirit of Old West Point,* pp. 37 ff.

7. Personal account book of Cadet A. R. Buffington, who graduated in 1861 (West Point).

8. E. B. Custer, *Tenting on the Plains,* p. 206.

9. J. H. Wilson, *Under the Old Flag,* I, p. 12.

10. W. L. Fleming, "Jefferson Davis at West Point," p. 263; O. L. Hein, *Memories of Long Ago,* p. 51; M. E. Sergent, "Classmates Divided," p. 34.

11. To John Chamberlain, May 5, 1860 (Janet Brown collection).

12. G. A. Custer, "Battling with the Sioux," p. 92; Sergent, "Classmates Divided," p. 35; J. M. Wright, "West Point before the War," p. 15.

13. M. Schaff, *Spirit of Old West Point,* pp. 193–194.

14. Letter to John Chamberlain, May 5, 1860.

15. J. P. Farley, *West Point in the Early Sixties,* pp. 188–189.

16. Post Orders, No. 5, p. 112 (West Point).

CHAPTER 3

1. Letter to John Chamberlain, April 7, 1860.

2. M. Schaff, *Spirit of Old West Point,* p. 27.

3. To "Brother and Sister," June 30, 1858 (West Point).

4. F. Whittaker, *Complete Life of . . . Custer . . . ,* p. 148.

5. J. P. Farley, *West Point in the Early Sixties,* p. 75; F. Whittaker, *Complete Life of . . . Custer . . . ,* pp. 33, 66.

6. Package #15 (Ms.) at Custer Battlefield National Monument.

7. G. A. Custer, *My Life on the Plains* (Quaife ed.), p. xxv.

8. M. Schaff, *Spirit of Old West Point,* p. 116; J. M. Wright, "West Point before the War," p. 17.

9. To Lydia Reed, May 29, 1860, and fragment of letter to father (West Point).

10. M. Merington, *Custer Story,* p. 8; Wright, "West Point before the War," p. 18; J. B. Washington Ms. One source states that this happened in French class.

11. P. Michie, "Reminiscences," p. 194; F. Whittaker, *Complete Life of . . . Custer . . .* , p. 43.
12. J. M. Wright, "West Point before the War," p. 15.
13. J. H. Wilson, *Under the Old Flag,* I, 369.
14. G. A. Custer, "War Memories," pp. 44–95.
15. M. Schaff, *Spirit of Old West Point,* pp. 180, 183; F. Whittaker, *Complete Life of . . . Custer . . .* , p. 39.
16. J. H. Wilson, *Under the Old Flag,* I, 369; M. Schaff, *Spirit of Old West Point,* p. 168.
17. M. Schaff, *Spirit of Old West Point,* pp. 207–208.
18. F. Whittaker, *Complete Life of . . . Custer . . .* , p. 37.
19. M. Schaff, *Spirit of Old West Point,* p. 84.
20. J. Moore, *Kilpatrick and Our Cavalry,* p. 30; J. M. Wright, "West Point before the War," p. 14.
21. Letter of E. B. Custer to Mrs. Hoxie (no date).
22. May 31, 1861.
23. J. B. Washington Ms.; Michie, "Reminiscences," p. 194.

CHAPTER 4

1. Special Order Book (West Point), M. Schaff, *Spirit of Old West Point,* p. 260; F. Whittaker, *Complete Life of . . . Custer . . .* , p. 44. F. F. Van de Water, in *Glory Hunter,* pp. 31–32, failing to find any record of this trial, concluded that it was never held. In this instance, Van de Water's work, which reveals more thorough research than any Custer book preceding it, demonstrates the danger of assuming that documents do not exist.
2. F. Whittaker, *Complete Life . . . of Custer . . .* , p. 55.
3. K. P. Williams, *Lincoln Finds a General,* I, p. 76; A. G. Brackett, *History of the United States Cavalry,* p. 212.
4. F. Whittaker, *Complete Life . . . of Custer . . .* , pp. 64–65.
5. M. Schaff, *Battle of the Wilderness,* p. 88; K. P. Williams, *Lincoln Finds a General,* p. 94.
6. F. Whittaker, *Complete Life . . . of Custer . . .* , pp. 64–73.
7. John A. Bingham's reminiscences in M. Merington, *Custer Story,* p. 13.

CHAPTER 5

1. F. Whittaker, *Complete Life of . . . Custer* . . . , p. 83.
2. F. Whittaker, *Complete Life of . . . Custer* . . . , p. 87.
3. G. A. Custer, *My Life on the Plains* (Quaife ed.), p. xxiv.
4. M. Merington, *Custer Story,* p. 48; F. Whittaker, *Complete Life of . . . Custer* . . . , p. 90.
5. M. Merington, *Custer Story,* p. 26.
6. F. Denison, *Sabres and Spurs,* p. 56; W. Glazier, *Three Years in the Federal Cavalry,* p. 56.
7. Letter to parents, March 17, 1862; F. Whittaker, . . . *Life* . . . , p. 95.
8. Letter to parents, March 17, 1862.

CHAPTER 6

1. To Lydia Reed, April 11, 1862.
2. To Lydia Reed, April 20, 1862; G. A. Custer, "War Memoirs," p. 685; L. P. Paris, *History of the Civil War,* II, p. 10.
3. O. S. Barrett, *Reminiscences,* p. 11.
4. *O. R.,* I, XI, pt. 1, p. 534; G. A. Custer, "War Memoirs," pp. 686–687.
5. *O. R.,* I, XI, pt. 1, p. 526.
6. *O. R.,* I, XI, pt. 3, p. 140; J. M. Favill, *Diary of a Young Officer,* p. 91.
7. F. Whittaker, *Complete Life of . . . Custer* . . . , p. 105.
8. D. C. Fletcher, *Reminiscences,* p. 139; W. L. Goss, *Recollections,* p. 42; T. L. Livermore, *Numbers & Losses in the Civil War,* p. 80.
9. Letter, Custer to Lydia Reed, May 5, 1862 (West Point). M. Merington, *Custer Story,* pp. 29–30, dates this letter May 15, 1862.
10. O. S. Barrett, *Reminiscences,* p. 12.
11. *O. R.,* I, XI, pt. 1, pp. 153, 639–640.
12. Same, p. 111.
13. McClellan to E. B. Custer, August 6, 1876; F. Whittaker, *Complete Life of . . . Custer* . . . , pp. 113–114; G. B. McClellan, *Own Story,* p. 123.
14. J. H. Wilson, *Under the Old Flag,* I, p. 102; B. Catton, *Mr. Lincoln's Army,* pp. 117–118.

CHAPTER 7

1. *O. R.,* I, XI, pt. 1, pp. 652–653; O. S. Barrett, *Reminiscences,* p. 13.
2. F. Whittaker, *Complete Life of . . . Custer . . . ,* p. 116.
3. *O. R.,* I, XI, pt. 1, p. 654.
4. *O. R.,* I, XI, pt. 1, pp. 153, 651; Barrett, *Reminiscences,* p. 13.
5. He was appointed as of May 28, 1862. *O. R.,* I, XI, pt. 3, pp. 198–199; letter of McClellan to E. B. Custer, August 6, 1876; G. B. McClellan, *Own Story,* pp. 364–365.
6. *O. R.,* I, XI, pt. 1, p. 914. The main secondary sources for these battles are L. P. Paris, *History of the Civil War,* II; W. Swinton, *Campaigns of the Army of the Potomac;* and H. J. Eckenrode and Bryan Conrad, *George B. McClellan,* pp. 73–117.
7. *O. R.,* I, XI, pt. 2, p. 75; W. L. Goss, *Recollections,* p. 48. The quotation has been constructed from these sources.
8. J. M. Favill, *Diary of a Young Officer,* p. 143.
9. Custer to Lydia Reed, July 13, 1862; J. M. Favill, *Diary of a Young Officer,* pp. 130–133; F. Whittaker, *Complete Life of . . . Custer . . . ,* p. 120.
10. F. Whittaker, *Complete Life of . . . Custer . . . ,* p. 121.
11. *O. R.,* I, XI, pt. 2, pp. 947, 954; F. Whittaker, *. . . Life . . . ,* p. 122.
12. E. B. Custer, *Tenting on the Plains,* p. 85, and *Boots and Saddles,* p. 177; M. Merington, *Custer Story,* p. 36; F. Whittaker, *Complete Life of . . . Custer . . . ,* p. 122.

CHAPTER 8

1. J. H. Wilson, *Under the Old Flag,* I, p. 106.
2. K. P. Williams, *Lincoln Finds a General,* I, p. 368.
3. *O. R.,* I, XIX, pt. 1, p. 210; F. W. Palfrey, *Antietam and Fredericksburg,* p. 46.
4. T. L. Livermore, *Numbers & Losses in the Civil War,* p. 92.
5. Letter to Lydia Reed, September 21, 1862, in F. Whittaker, *Complete Life of . . . Custer . . . ,* p. 125–129.
6. Letter to Lydia Reed, September 27, 1862, in M. Merington, *Custer Story,* p. 35, and at West Point. This is a good example of the way the same letter appears differently in different sources.
7. The same letter as Note 6.

8. Quotation constructed from accounts in J. H. Wilson, *Under the Old Flag,* I, p. 126, and F. Whittaker, *Complete Life of . . . Custer . . . ,* p. 133.

CHAPTER 9

1. M. Merington, *Custer Story,* pp. 22, 24.
2. M. Merington, *Custer Story,* pp. 38, 39, 41, 42.
3. E. B. Custer, *Tenting on the Plains,* p. 251.
4. E. B. Custer, *Tenting on the Plains,* p. 73.
5. M. Merington, *Custer Story,* pp. 43–44.
6. M. Merington, p. 235; E. B. Custer, *Tenting on the Plains,* pp. 186, 269.
7. M. Merington, *Custer Story,* pp. 47, 64; F. Whittaker, *Complete Life of . . . Custer . . . ,* p. 208.
8. M. Merington, *Custer Story,* p. 51.
9. F. W. Palfrey, *Antietam and Fredericksburg,* p. 39.
10. Special Order (Custer Battlefield National Monument).
11. F. Whittaker, *Complete Life of . . . Custer . . . ,* p. 148.
12. A. Pleasonton, "Testimony," *Report of the Joint Committee on the Conduct of the War,* p. 28; P. Huey, *True History of the Charge of the Eighth Pennsylvania Cavalry.*
13. Letter to Lydia Reed, May 16, 1862.

CHAPTER 10

1. Letter, G. A. Custer to Judge Christiancy, May 31, 1863.
2. F. Whittaker, *Complete Life of . . . Custer . . . ,* p. 162 fn.
3. Letter of G. A. Custer to Lydia Reed, May 27, 1863 (West Point).
4. Letters to Judge Christiancy and to Lydia Reed, both May 31, 1863 (West Point).
5. To Lydia Reed, June 8, 1863 (West Point); D. M'M. Gregg, "Union Cavalry at Gettysburg," p. 375; F. C. Newhall, "Battle of Beverly Ford," p. 137; K. P. Williams, *Lincoln Finds a General,* II, p. 629.
6. *O. R.,* I, XXVII, pt. 1, p. 1046; H. Norton, *Deeds of Daring,* p. 64; C. D. Rhodes, *History of the Cavalry of the Army of the Potomac,* p. 45.

7. *Harper's Weekly,* July 4, 1863; L. P. Paris, *History of the Civil War,* III, p. 462; G. F. R. Henderson, *Science of War,* p. 270; K. P. Williams, *Lincoln Finds a General,* p. 623. (Paris, III, and Swinton are used as background for this chapter.)

8. *O. R.,* I, XXVII, pt. 1, pp. 903, 905, 1046.

9. F. B. Heitman, *Historical Register of the United States Army,* p. 669.

10. *New York Tribune,* June 24, 1863; J. H. Chamberlayne, *Ham Chamberlayne — Virginian,* p. 188; J. H. Kidd, *Personal Recollections of a Cavalryman,* p. 112.

11. B. W. Crowninshield, *History of the First . . . Massachusetts Cavalry,* p. 144; W. Glazier, *Three Years in the Federal Cavalry,* p. 226.

12. M. Merington, *Custer Story,* p. 55; F. Whittaker, *Complete Life of . . . Custer . . . ,* p. 159.

13. Joseph Gould, *Story of the Forty-eighth . . . Pennsylvania . . . Infantry,* p. 35; K. P. Williams, *Lincoln Finds a General,* p. 662.

14. F. Whittaker, *Complete Life of . . . Custer . . . ,* pp. 161–162.

15. Letter in National Archives.

16. *O. R.,* I, XXVII, pt. 1, p. 167, pt. 3, p. 376; L. M. Boudrye, *Historic Records of the Fifth New York Cavalry,* p. 63; H. J. Hunt, "First Day at Gettysburg," p. 259. The order is at Custer Battlefield National Monument.

17. A. Pleasonton, "Testimony," *Report of the Joint Committee on the Conduct of the War,* pp. 359, 365.

18. M. Merington, *Custer Story,* p. 85; F. Whittaker, *Complete Life of . . . Custer . . . ,* pp. 160, 163, 169–170.

CHAPTER 11

1. *O. R.,* I, XXVII, pt. 1, p. 144; pt. 3, p. 400.

2. J. H. Kidd, *Personal Recollections of a Cavalryman,* pp. 121, 129.

3. *O. R.,* I, XXVII, pt. 1, p. 992; W. Glazier, *Three Years in the Federal Cavalry,* p. 244; J. H. Kidd, *Personal Recollections . . . ,* p. 126; F. Whittaker, *Complete Life of . . . Custer . . . ,* p. 168.

4. *O. R.,* I, XXVII, pt. 1, p. 992; L. N. Boudrye, *Historic Records of the Fifth New York Cavalry,* p. 64; F. Whittaker, *Complete Life of . . . Custer . . .* , pp. 168, 172; J. Moore, *Kilpatrick and Our Cavalry,* p. 85; *History of the Eighteenth Regiment of Cavalry,* p. 87.

5. *O. R.,* I, XXVII, pt. 1, p. 992; W. Brooke Rawle, "The Right Flank at Gettysburg," p. 468 fn.; J. Moore, *Kilpatrick and Our Cavalry,* p. 88.

6. *O. R.,* I, XXVII, pt. 1, pp. 914, 916, 992.

7. J. H. Kidd, *Personal Recollections . . .* , p. 133; G. Meade, *Life and Letters,* II, p. 94.

8. G. F. R. Henderson, *Science of War,* pp. 294–296; J. Moore, *Kilpatrick and Our Cavalry,* p. 92.

9. J. H. Kidd, *Personal Recollections . . .* , p. 135; C. D. Rhodes, *History of the Cavalry of the Army of the Potomac,* p. 67; J. M. Hanson, "The Civil War Custer," p. 27; W. E. Miller, "The Cavalry Battle near Gettysburg," p. 403. Kilpatrick, in his report, considered Custer's act a mistake, not disobedience (*O. R.,* I, XXVII, pt. 1, p. 993).

10. W. Brooke Rawle, "The Right Flank . . . ," p. 468; J. M. Favill, *Diary of a Young Officer,* p. 247; W. Kempster, "Cavalry at Gettysburg," p. 22.

11. C. F. Adams, *Autobiography,* p. 153.

12. J. H. Kidd, *Personal Recollections . . .* , p. 138.

13. W. Brooke Rawle, "The Right Flank . . . ," p. 480; J. H. Kidd, *Personal Recollections . . .* , p. 148.

14. *O. R.,* I. XXVII, pt. 2, p. 725; *History of the Third Pennsylvania Cavalry,* p. 277.

15. W. Brooke Rawle, "The Right Flank . . . ," p. 481; J. H. Kidd, *Personal Recollections . . .* , p. 154; *History of the Third Pennsylvania Cavalry,* p. 278; W. E. Miller, "The Cavalry . . . ," p. 400.

16. *O. R.,* I, XXVII, pt. 2, pp. 697, 724, 725; E. P. Tobie, *History of the First Maine Cavalry,* p. 177.

17. F. Whittaker, *Complete Life of . . . Custer . . .* , p. 180; *O. R.,* I, XXVII, pt. 1, p. 998. Such extravagant language was common at that time. (See *O. R.,* I, XXIX, pt. 1, p. 126).

CHAPTER 12

1. M. E. Sergent, "Classmates Divided," p. 35.
2. H. C. Parsons, "Farnsworth's Charge," p. 394.
3. *O. R.,* I, XXVII, pt. 1, pp. 988, 993, 998, 1005–1006; F. Whittaker, *Complete Life of . . . Custer . . .* , p. 182.
4. F. Whittaker, *Complete Life of . . . Custer . . .* , p. 185; J. C. Andrews, *The North Reports the Civil War,* p. 417.
5. *O. R.,* I, XXVI, pt. 1, p. 144.
6. J. Sedgwick, *Correspondence,* II, p. 138.
7. *O. R.,* I, XXVII, pt. 1, pp. 990, 999; F. Whittaker, *Complete Life of . . . Custer . . .* , p. 188; J. Longstreet, "Lee in Pennsylvania," p. 443.
8. J. H. Kidd, *Personal Recollections,* pp. 184–185.
9. *O. R.,* I, XXVII, pt. 1, pp. 990, 998; *Harper's Weekly,* August 15, 1863; F. Whittaker, *Complete Life of . . . Custer . . .* , p. 189.
10. *O. R.,* I, XXVII, pt. 1, pp. 148, 1004; W. Glazier, *Three Years in the Federal Cavalry,* p. 294; M. T. McMahon, "From Gettysburg to the Coming of Grant," p. 83.
11. To Annette Humphrey, July 19, 1863.
12. *O. R.,* I, XXVII, pt. 1, pp. 1001, 1004; pt. 3, pp. 753, 754.
13. *O. R.,* I, XXVII, pt. 1, p. 1004; pt. 3, p. 792; A. Pleasonton, "Testimony," *Report of the Joint Committee on the Conduct of the War,* p. 364.
14. *O. R.,* I, XXVII, pt. 3, p. 830; *O. R.,* I, XXIX, pt. 1, p. 78; J. M. Crawford, *Mosby and His Men,* p. 254.
15. E. B. Custer, *Tenting on the Plains,* pp. 40, 477; M. Merington, *Custer Story,* p. 61.
16. Letter printed in part in Merington, *Custer Story,* p. 63, and F. Whittaker, *Complete Life of . . . Custer . . .* , p. 206.
17. *O. R.,* I, XXIX, pt. 1, pp. 120, 224; G. G. Benedict, *Vermont in the Civil War,* II, p. 611; F. Whittaker, *Complete Life of . . . Custer . . .* , pp. 193, 194.
18. *O. R.,* I, XXIX, pt. 1, pp. 112, 127; G. R. Agassiz, *Meade's Headquarters,* p. 17.

19. E. B. Custer, *Boots and Saddles,* p. 9; Merington, *Custer Story,* p. 64; F. Whittaker, *Complete Life of . . . Custer . . . ,* pp. 207–211. Custer's statement has been placed in direct quotations. According to one story, Judge Bacon left town to evade the interview.
20. Letter to Lydia Reed, October 25, 1863 (West Point).

CHAPTER 13

1. To Annette Humphrey, October 9, 1863; M. Merington, *Custer Story,* p. 65; F. Whittaker, *Complete Life of . . . Custer . . . ,* pp. 212–213.
2. *O. R.,* I, XXIX, pt. 1, pp. 374, 381, 389, 390; F. Whittaker, *Complete Life of . . . Custer . . . ,* p. 197.
3. *O. R,* I, XXIX, pt. 1, pp. 390, 393, 394; L. N. Boudrye, *Historic Records of the Fifth New York Cavalry,* p. 80; J. Robertson, *Michigan in the War,* p. 588; F. Whittaker, *Complete Life of . . . Custer . . . ,* pp. 201, 213.
4. *O. R.,* I, XXIX, pt. 1, pp. 381, 390; letter to Annette Humphrey, October 12, 1863, in M. Merington, *Custer Story,* pp. 65–66.
5. M. Merington, *Custer Story,* p. 67; F. Whittaker, *Complete Life of . . . Custer . . . ,* p. 214.
6. *O. R.,* I, XXIX, pt. 1, pp. 387, 391, 397; letter to Lydia Reed, November 6, 1863; U. R. Brooks, ed., *Stories of the Confederacy,* pp. 207–208; M. T. McMahon, "From Gettysburg to the Coming of Grant," p. 85; J. M. Hanson, "The Civil War Custer," p. 28; C. D. Rhodes, *History of the Cavalry of the Army of the Potomac,* p. 89; Robertson, *Michigan in the War,* p. 591.
7. M. Merington, *Custer Story,* p. 70; F. Whittaker, *Complete Life of . . . Custer . . . ,* p. 215.
8. Letters from Custer, October 25, November 1, December 7, 1863, a letter fragment, October 29, 1863; all at West Point.
9. Letters from Custer, October 12, 25, November 6, December 7, 1863; *O. R.,* I, XXIX, pt. 1, p. 655.
10. *O. R.,* I, XXIX, pt. 1, pp. 13, 811; Rhodes, *History of the Cavalry . . . ,* p. 93.
11. Letter to Lydia Reed, December 7, 1863 (West Point); Mering-

ton, *Custer Story*, p. 74; F. Whittaker, *Complete Life of* . . . *Custer* . . . , pp. 215–216.

12. M. Merington, *Custer Story*, pp. 74, 75, 77–79.

13. Letters to Christiancy, January 7, 1864 (West Point); letter from Christiancy, January 20, 1864 (Custer Battlefield National Monument).

14. T. E. Wing, *History of Monroe County*, p. 318.

15. M. Merington, *Custer Story*, pp. 84–85. Some statements in letters have been edited slightly.

CHAPTER 14

1. E. B. Custer, *Boots and Saddles*, p. 10, and *Tenting on the Plains*, p. 479; F. Whittaker, *Complete Life of* . . . *Custer* . . . , p. 218.

2. *O. R.*, I, XXXIII, pp. 161, 164, 599; LI, pt. 2, sup. p. 823; *Harper's Weekly*, March 26, 1864; E. B. Custer, *Tenting on the Plains*, p. 480; G. R. Agassiz, *Meade's Headquarters*, p. 77; G. Meade, *Life and Letters*, II, p. 168; M. T. McMahon, "From Gettysburg to the Coming of Grant," p. 94. Custer's reply to Sedgwick has been put in the first person.

3. Statements of Annie Jones, February 2, 1863, March 14, 22, 1864 (National Archives); *Harper's Weekly*, April 4, 1863.

4. *Harper's Weekly*, March 19, 26, 1864; *New York Tribune*, March 4, 1864; E. B. Custer's letter to parents, March 28, 1864.

5. E. B. Custer to Mrs. Hoxie [1880] in Hoxie Papers (Library of Congress).

6. Letter, G. A. Custer to Annette Humphrey, November 1, 1863; to Lydia Reed, December 7, 1863; Jacob Greene to Custer, April 7, 1864; F. Whittaker, *Complete Life of* . . . *Custer* . . . , p. 221.

7. *O. R.*, I, XXXVI, pt. 1, p. 115; W. C. King, *Camp-Fire Sketches and Battle-Field Echoes*, p. 405; T. F. Rodenbough, "Sheridan's Richmond Raid," p. 188.

8. M. Merington, *Custer Story*, pp. 89–93.

9. To E. B. Custer, May 1, 1864.

10. *O. R.*, I, XXXVI, pt. 2, p. 429; A. B. Isham, "Through the Wilderness," p. 198; J. Robertson, *Michigan in the War*, p. 595.

11. *O. R.,* I, XXXVI, pt. 1, p. 803; [F. C. Newhall], *With General Sheridan in Lee's Last Campaign,* p. 228.
12. *O. R.,* I, XXXVI, pt. 1, pp. 774, 788; pt. 2, pp. 466–467; J. M. Favill, *Diary,* p. 291; T. F. Rodenbough, "Sheridan's Richmond Raid," p. 193.

CHAPTER 15

1. *O. R.,* I, XXXVI, pt. 1, pp. 790, 862; J. Robertson, *Michigan in the War,* p. 596; P. H. Sheridan, *Personal Memoirs,* I, p. 373.
2. [F. C. Newhall], *With General Sheridan in Lee's Last Campaign,* p. 228.
3. *O. R.,* I, XXXVI, pt. 1, pp. 790, 813, 818, 847; King, *Camp-Fire Sketches . . . ,* pp. 408–409; M. Schaff, *Battle of the Wilderness,* p. 282.
4. A. B. Isham, "Through the Wilderness to Richmond," p. 215.
5. J. H. Wilson, *Under the Old Flag,* I, p. 407.
6. J. H. Kidd, *Personal Recollections,* p. 308; T. F. Rodenbough, comp., *From Everglade to Cañon,* p. 306; same author, "Sheridan's Richmond Raid," pp. 188, 191; J. H. Wilson, *Under the Old Flag,* I, p. 414.
7. To E. B. Custer, May 14, 1864.
8. M. Merington, *Custer Story,* pp. 97–99.
9. J. H. Wilson, *Under the Old Flag,* I, p. 424.

CHAPTER 16

1. *O. R.,* I, XXXVI, pt. 1, pp. 793, 804, 829, 854, 861; G. R. Agassiz, *Meade's Headquarters,* p. 139.
2. T. F. Rodenbough, "Sheridan's Trevilian Raid," p. 233; F. Whittaker, "General George A. Custer," p. 365.
3. G. A. Custer to E. B. Custer, June 21, 1864; E. B. Custer to Laura Noble, July 18, 1864; E. B. Custer to G. A. Custer, June 10, 1864; M. Merington, *Custer Story,* pp. 105–106.
4. *O. R.,* I, XLIII, pt. 1, pp. 722, 730.
5. G. A. Custer to Lydia Reed, August 24, 1864; *O. R.,* I, XLIII, pt. 1, p. 19; E. B. Custer diary in Merington, *Custer Story,*

p. 130; W. Merritt, "Sheridan in the Shenandoah Valley," p. 502.

6. *O. R.*, I, XLIII, pt. 1, pp. 502, 822, 841; *O. R.*, I, LI, pt. 2, sup., p. 823.

7. *O. R.*, I, XLIII, pt. 1, pp. 816, 921–922, 948; F. Denison, *Sabres and Spurs*, p. 384.

8. E. B. Custer to G. A. Custer, September 6, 1864; M. Merington, *Custer Story*, p. 121; G. A. Custer to Lydia Reed, September 17, 1864; G. A. Custer to Judge Christiancy. September 16, 1864.

9. J. W. De Forest, *A Volunteer's Adventures*, p. 172; R. B. Irwin, *History of the Nineteenth Army Corps*, p. 377.

10. *O. R.*, I, XLIII, pt. 1, pp. 427, 443.

11. *O. R.*, I, XLIII, pt. 1, pp. 454–459.

12. *O. R.*, I, XLIII, pt. 1, pp. 454–459.

13. J. M. Hanson, "The Civil War Custer," p. 29; *Harper's Weekly*, October 8, 1864.

14. H. A. Du Pont, *The Campaign of 1864 in the Valley of Virginia*, p. 138; R. B. Irwin, *History of the Nineteenth* . . . , p. 400.

15. F. Whittaker, *Complete Life of* . . . *Custer* . . . , p. 250, and "General George A. Custer," p. 365.

16. P. H. Sheridan, *Personal Memoirs*, II, pp. 51–52.

17. *O. R.*, I, XLIII, pt. 1, pp. 30–31, 430–431, 520; pt. 2, pp. 320, 327.

18. *O. R.*, I, XLIII, pt. 1, pp. 447, 521, 578; J. M. Hanson, "The Civil War Custer," p. 29; F. Whittaker, *Complete Life of* . . . *Custer* . . . , pp. 256–258; B. W. Crowninshield, *History of the First* . . . *Massachusetts Cavalry*, p. 27.

19. *O. R.*, I, XL, pt. 1, pp. 431, 520–522; *O. R.*, I, XLIII, pt. 1, pp. 521–522; *O. R.*, I, LI, pt. 1, p. 1199; T. F. Rodenbough, comp., *From Everglades to Cañon*, p. 551.

20. R. B. Irwin, *History of the Nineteenth* . . . , p. 409.

21. M. Merington, *Custer Story*, pp. 122–123.

22. G. A. Custer to father, October 16, 1864.

23. *O. R.*, I, XLIII, pt. 1, pp. 522–527; J. W. De Forest, *A Volunteer's Adventures*, p. 229; G. A. Forsyth, "Sheridan's Ride," p. 179; I. Gause, *Four Years with Five Armies*, p. 335; H. P. Moyer, comp., *History of the Seventeenth* . . . *Pennsylvania*

... *Cavalry,* p. 118; R. O'Connor, *Sheridan, the Inevitable,* p. 230.

24. P. H. Sheridan, *Personal Memoirs,* II, p. 89; L. M. Starr, *Bohemian Brigade,* p. 331.

25. *O. R.,* I, XLIII, pt. 1, pp. 53, 59, 435, 547, 582.

26. J. C. Andrews, *The North Reports the Civil War,* p. 607; F. Whittaker, *Complete Life of ... Custer ...,* p. 302.

27. F. Denison, *Sabres and Spurs ...,* p. 415.

28. *O. R.,* I, XLIII, pt. 2, p. 437.

29. M. Merington, *Custer Story,* p. 124.

CHAPTER 17

1. *O. R.,* I, LI, pt. 1, p. 1199; *New York Times,* February 26, 1865; Syracuse, N.Y., *Post-Standard,* August 12, 1920.

2. *O. R.,* I, XXXIX, pt. 3, p. 444.

3. *New York Times,* November 10, 12, 1864.

4. *O. R.,* I, XLIII, pt. 1, p. 508.

5. Petition is at Custer Battlefield National Monument.

6. *O. R.,* I, XLIII, pt. 1, pp. 56, 674–676; pt. 2, pp. 821, 825–826; P. H. Sheridan, *Personal Memoirs,* II, p. 102.

7. E. B. Custer, *Boots and Saddles,* p. 223.

8. Rev. G. Duffield to George Stuart, March 2, 1865 (George H. Stuart Collection).

9. [F. C. Newhall], *With General Sheridan in Lee's Last Campaign,* p. 17.

10. G. A. Custer to Rev. G. Duffield, February 19, 1865.

11. *O. R.,* I, XLVI, pt. 2, pp. 549, 725.

12. Memo, G. A. Custer to Sheridan, March 2, 1865 (Hart Papers); *O. R.,* I, XLVI, pt. 1, pp. 124, 476, 502; pt. 2, pp. 792, 794; P. H. Sheridan, *Personal Memoirs,* II, p. 116; F. Whittaker, *Complete Life of ... Custer ...,* p. 273.

13. *O. R.,* I, XLVI, pt. 1, pp. 124, 477, 503; pt. 2, p. 918; *New York Times,* March 20, 1865; P. Van D. Stern, *An End to Valor,* p. 5. Pennington's account is printed in M. Merington, *Custer Story,* p. 138. Custer was ordered to keep his men out of Charlottesville, by *O. R.,* I, XLVI, pt. 2, p. 834.

14. G. A. Custer to E. Custer, March 16, 1865; *O. R.,* I, XLVI, pt. 2,

p. 982; F. Whittaker, *Complete Life of . . . Custer . . . ,* p. 277.

CHAPTER 18

1. G. A. Custer to E. B. Custer, March 30, 1865; *O. R.,* I, XLVI, pt. 3, p. 234; *New York Times,* April 2, 1865; F. Whittaker, *Complete Life of . . . Custer . . . ,* p. 280.
2. *O. R.,* I, XLVI, pt. 1, p. 1130; H. E. Tremain, *Last Hours of Sheridan's Cavalry,* p. 21.
3. G. A. Townsend, *Campaigns of a Non-Combatant,* p. 320.
4. *O. R.,* I, XLVI, pt. 1, pp. 1103–1104, 1110, 1117; P. Van D. Stern, *An End to Valor,* p. 129. Statements regarding the time of arrival vary from midmorning to 2 P.M.
5. G. A. Townsend, *Campaigns . . . ,* pp. 326, 329; P. Van D. Stern, *An End to Valor,* p. 145.
6. H. Porter, "Five Forks and the Pursuit of Lee," in *Battles and Leaders of the Civil War,* IV, p. 715.
7. *O. R.,* I, XLVI, pt. 1, p. 1131; pt. 3, p. 529; F. B. Heitman, *Historical Register of the United States Army;* M. Merington, *Custer Story,* p. 151; H. E. Tremain, *Last Hours . . . ,* p. 111.
8. *O. R.,* I, XLVI, pt. 1, pp. 1107, 1115, 1258; E. B. Custer, "Beau Sabreur," p. 301; Confederate Soldier, "Custer at the Surrender," pp. 76–77; M. Merington, *Custer Story,* p. 151; H. P. Moyer, comp., *History of the Seventeenth . . . Pennsylvania . . . Cavalry,* p. 315; H. E. Tremain, *Last Hours . . . ,* pp. 144–152; F. Whittaker, *Complete Life of . . . Custer . . . ,* pp. 301–303; B. Catton, *Stillness at Appomattox,* p. 371.
9. *O. R.,* I, XLVI, pt. 3, p. 610; J. M. Hanson, "The Civil War Custer," p. 31; H. Porter, "Five Forks . . . ," in *Battles and Leaders of the Civil War,* IV, p. 721; M. Schaff, *Battle of the Wilderness,* p. 146; H. E. Tremain, *Last Hours . . . ,* p. 155.
10. Kershaw's account in M. Merington, *Custer Story,* p. 153; Confederate Soldier, "Custer at the Surrender," pp. 76–77.
11. *O. R.,* I, XLVI, pt. 1, pp. 1109, 1132; pt. 3, pp. 652, 653; J. Gibbon, "Personal Recollections," p. 939; H. Porter, "Surrender at Appomattox Court House," p. 734; Moyer, comp., *History of*

the Seventeenth, pp. 315, 363, 364; P. Van D. Stern, *An End to Valor,* pp. 236–238; H. E. Tremain, *Last Hours,* p. 227; F. Whittaker, *Complete Life of . . . Custer . . . ,* pp. 305–306.

12. H. E. Tremain, *Last Hours . . . ,* p. 238.

13. Custer's report, *O. R.,* I, XLVI, pt. 1, pp. 1129–1133; Sheridan's report, *O. R.,* I, XLVI, pt. 1, pp. 1101–1110; G. Lemmon, "Story of Appomattox," p. 10; [F. C. Newhall], *With General Sheridan in Lee's Last Campaign,* p. 211; P. H. Sheridan, *Personal Memoirs,* II, p. 193; S. M. Thompson, *Thirteenth . . . New Hampshire . . . Infantry,* p. 586; H. E. Tremain, *Last Hours . . . ,* pp. 239 ff.

14. M. Schaff, *Spirit of Old West Point,* pp. 169–170.

15. J. Gibbon, "Personal Recollections," p. 939; [F. C. Newhall], *With General Sheridan . . . ,* pp. 221–222. M. Merington (*Custer Story,* p. 159) quotes Sheridan as saying, at the Illinois Commandery of Loyal Legion in Chicago, that Custer carried off the table on his head, but Sheridan seems not to have said this in this address.

16. G. A. Custer to Lydia Reed, April 21, 1865 (Custer Battlefield National Monument); M. Merington, *Custer Story,* p. 160.

17. *O. R.,* I, XLVI, pt. 1, pp. 1133–1134; pt. 3, p. 813.

18. G. A. Custer to E. B. Custer, April 11, 1865; *San Francisco Chronicle,* January 12, 1890; M. Merington, *Custer Story,* p. 164.

19. *New York Times,* May 24, 1865; O. L. Hein, *Memories of Long Ago,* p. 37; H. E. Tremain, *Last Hours . . . ,* p. 319; F. Whittaker, *Complete Life of . . . Custer . . . ,* p. 313.

20. To Lydia Reed, April 21, 1865.

CHAPTER 19

1. E. B. Custer, *Tenting on the Plains,* p. 50.

2. *O. R.,* I, LIII, Sup., p. 608; *Congressional Globe, Appendix,* 2nd Sess., 39th Cong. pt. 3, pp. 29–30.

3. G. A. Custer to brother and sister, June 23, 1865 (West Point); E. B. Custer, *Tenting . . . ,* p. 110; M. Merington, *Custer Story,* p. 175.

4. G. A. Custer to brother and sister, June 23, 1865; E. B. Custer, *Tenting* . . . , p. 117.

5. E. B. Custer, *Tenting* . . . , pp. 128, 130, 180.

6. M. Merington, *Custer Story*, pp. 172–174; F. Denison, *Sabres and Spurs*, p. 310. Sheridan's recommendation, dated December 9, 1865, is at Custer Battlefield National Monument.

7. G. A. Custer to the Bacons, October 5, 1865; to brother and sister, October 15, 1865; to Lydia Reed, January 12, 1866; E. B. Custer, *Tenting* . . . , pp. 205, 220, 243. A photograph of the Blind Asylum is at Custer Battlefield National Monument.

8. To Lydia Reed, January 12, February 1, 1866. Custer was mustered out of the Volunteers on January 31, 1866 (National Archives).

9. M. Ronsheim, *Life of Custer*, pp. 23–24.

10. Custer Battlefield National Monument.

CHAPTER 20

1. Service Record in National Archives, Bingham's letter at Custer Battlefield National Monument. F. Whittaker, *Complete Life of* . . . *Custer* . . . , p. 333.

2. To E. B. Custer, March 16, 18, 1866, in M. Merington, *Custer Story*, pp. 178–179.

3. F. Whittaker, *Complete Life of* . . . *Custer* . . . , pp. 340–341.

4. To E. B. Custer, April 3, 14, 1866.

5. M. Merington, *Custer Story*, pp. 187–188.

6. *New York Times*, August 13, 15, 17, 22, 1866; Springfield *Illinois State Register*, August 20, 1866.

7. To Andrew Johnson, August 13, 1866.

8. *New York Times*, August 30, 31, 1866.

9. September 3, 1866.

10. Springfield *Illinois State Journal*, August 28, 1866; M. Sandoz, *Buffalo Hunters*, p. 27.

11. H. K. Beale, *Critical Year*, p. 308; C. G. Bowers, *Tragic Era*, pp. 134–135; G. Welles, *Diary*, II, p. 593.

12. G. F. Milton, *Age of Hate*, p. 363.

13. *New York Times*, September 5, 1866.

14. *New York Times,* September 14, 1866; Springfield *Illinois State Register,* September 4, 18, 1866.
15. Springfield *Illinois State Journal,* September 8, 12, 1866.
16. *New York Times,* September 9, 1866; H. K. Beale, *Critical Year,* p. 366; G. F. Milton, *Age of Hate,* p. 366.
17. *New York Times,* September 11, 12, 14, 1866; *New York Tribune,* September 13, 1866, in L. P. Stryker, *Andrew Johnson,* p. 374; Springfield *Illinois State Journal,* September 13, 1866; *Illinois State Register,* September 12, 1866; H. K. Beale, *Critical Year,* p. 366.
18. *New York Times,* September 18, 19, 1866; M. Ronsheim, *Life of Custer,* p. [23].

CHAPTER 21

1. E. B. Custer, *Tenting on the Plains,* p. 337; M. Ronsheim, *Life of Custer,* pp. 23–24.
2. E. B. Custer, *Tenting . . .* , p. 366; C. G. Leland, *Union Pacific Railway,* p. 43.
3. Box 5, Custer Battlefield National Monument; Godfrey Papers; R. G. Athearn, *William Tecumseh Sherman,* p. 55; C. F. Bates, *Custer's Indian Battles,* p. 8; G. A. Custer, *My Life on the Plains,* p. 48 fn.; telegram from A. J. Smith, March 1, 1867 (National Archives).
4. E. B. Custer, "Beau Sabreur," p. 302; F. Whittaker, *Complete Life . . . of Custer . . .* , p. 332; same author, "General George A. Custer," p. 367.
5. *Harper's Weekly,* December 5, 1868; picture of Myles Keogh, Myrick Collection; F. F. Van de Water, *Glory Hunter,* p. 152; F. Whittaker, *Complete Life . . . of Custer . . .* , p. 604; G. A. Custer, *My Life on the Plains,* p. 173 fn.
6. C. G. Leland, *Memoirs . . .* , p. 333.
7. Interview with T. R. Davis's grandson, Ted Parmelee, Los Angeles; T. R. Davis, *Henry M. Stanley's Indian Campaign,* p. 193, and *With Generals in their Camp Homes,* p. 115.
8. Leland, *Union Pacific Railway,* p. 43.
9. G. A. Custer, *My Life on the Plains,* pp. 39, 51; H. M. Stanley, *My Early Travels and Adventures,* pp. 25, 35, 240.

10. G. A. Custer, *My Life on the Plains,* pp. 58, 64; G. B. Grinnell, *Fighting Cheyennes,* p. 244; H. M. Stanley, *My Early Travels* . . . , pp. 39, 41, 43, 241.
11. E. B. Custer, *Tenting on the Plains,* p. 693; E. S. Watson and Don Russell, "The Battle of the Washita . . . ," p. 104.
12. E. B. Custer, *Tenting on the Plains,* p. 546; C. G. Leland, *Memoirs,* p. 324, H. M. Stanley, *My Early Travels* . . . , pp. 83, 84, 86, 241.
13. Notes of instruction for Custer, June, 1867 (Custer Battlefield National Monument); G. A. Custer, *My Life on the Plains,* p. 132; G. B. Grinnell, *Fighting Cheyennes,* pp. 250–251.
14. E. B. Custer, *Tenting on the Plains,* pp. 653–654.
15. G. A. Custer, *My Life on the Plains,* p. 201 fn.; G. B. Grinnell, *Fighting Cheyennes,* pp. 252–253.

CHAPTER 22

1. E. B. Custer, *Tenting on the Plains,* pp. 699, 702.
2. H. M. Stanley, *My Early Travels and Adventures,* p. 121.
3. M. Merington, *Custer Story,* p. 211.
4. Custer's memos in National Archives and Custer Battlefield National Monument; G. A. Custer, *My Life on the Plains,* p. 212.
5. M. Merington, *Custer Story,* pp. 212, 215.
6. November 20, 1867 (National Archives).

CHAPTER 23

1. R. G. Athearn, *William Tecumseh Sherman,* pp. 213, 223; C. C. Rister, *Border Command,* pp. 77, 91; Paul Wellman, "Sheridan's Operations on Washita," *Dictionary of American History,* V, p. 420.
2. Letters, G. A. Custer to E. B. Custer, October 2, 4, 1868; G. A. Custer, *My Life on the Plains,* p. 217; P. H. Sheridan, *Personal Memoirs,* II, p. 307.
3. Letters, G. A. Custer to E. B. Custer, October 7, 10, 22, 24, 28, November 4, 5, 22, 23, 1868; W. S. Harvey, diary; *Harper's Weekly,* December 5, 1868; DeB. R. Keim, *Sheridan's Troopers,* p. 102; C. C. Rister, *Border Command,* p. 97.
4. Harvey diary; G. A. Custer, *My Life on the Plains,* pp. 282–284,

289, 301. Some of the facts in these sources have been edited into direct quotations.

5. G. A. Custer, *My Life on the Plains,* p. 315.

6. G. A. Forsyth, *Story of the Soldier,* p. 245; C. P. Godfrey, "General Edward S. Godfrey," p. 83.

7. C. J. Brill, *Conquest of the Southern Plains,* pp. 160 n., 173–174; F. S. Dellenbaugh, *George Armstrong Custer,* pp. 128, 132; G. A. Custer, *My Life on the Plains,* pp. 336, 388; C. F. Bates, *Custer's Indian Battles,* p. 14; E. S. Godfrey, "Some Reminiscences of the Battle of the Washita," p. 493; C. P. Godfrey, "General Edward S. Godfrey," p. 75; E. S. Watson and Don Russell, "The Battle of the Washita, or Custer's Massacre?" in which Mr. Russell gives examples of the way in which F. F. Van de Water has taken Custer's statements out of context to malign his character.

8. Harvey diary, November 27, 28, 1868; letter, G. A. Custer to Sheridan, November 28, 1868 (Custer Battlefield National Monument); R. G. Athearn, . . . *Sherman,* p. 272; P. H. Sheridan, *Personal Memoirs,* p. 319; G. A. Custer, . . . *Plains,* p. 397.

CHAPTER 24

1. February 9, 1869.

2. Letter dated December 6, 1868 (Custer Battlefield National Monument).

3. G. A. Custer, *My Life on the Plains,* p. 415.

4. Harvey diary, December 11, 1868; G. A. Custer, *My Life on the Plains,* p. 428; C. C. Rister, *Border Command,* p. 118.

5. S. J. Crawford, *Kansas in the Sixties,* p. 328; G. A. Custer, *My Life on the Plains,* p. 436; DeB. R. Keim, *Sheridan's Troopers,* p. 155. Some of the facts obtained from these accounts have been placed in direct quotations. The text has summarized more complicated negotiations.

6. R. G. Athearn, *William Tecumseh Sherman,* p. 274; E. B. Custer, *Following the Guidon,* p. 53.

7. Letter, G. A. Custer to E. B. Custer, December 26, 1868; P. H. Sheridan, *Personal Memoirs,* II, p. 334.

8. E. B. Custer, *Following the Guidon,* p. 49.

9. G. A. Custer, *My Life on the Plains,* pp. 564 ff.; see note in same by Quaife, p. 596; S. J. Crawford, *Kansas* . . . , pp. 332–334; G. B. Grinnell, *Fighting Cheyennes,* p. 297; C. C. Rister, *Border Command,* p. 142.

10. E. B. Custer, *Following the Guidon,* pp. 50, 64; G. A. Custer, *My Life on the Plains,* p. 509.

11. R. H. McKay, *Little Pills,* p. 9.

12. E. B. Custer, *Tenting on the Plains,* pp. 620–621; photographs of Fort Hays at Custer Battlefield National Monument.

13. Letter, G. A. Custer to Sherman, June 29, 1869; E. B. Custer, *Following the Guidon,* p. 246.

14. Notes on guest hunters as well as on Custer's magazine articles are in Custer Battlefield National Monument. J. E. Parsons and J. S. duMont, *Firearms in the Custer Battle,* p. 20; M. Merington, *Custer Story,* p. 231.

15. Harvey diary, June 11, September 26, 1870; Custer's Service Record (in National Archives) shows his leave began Jan. 11.

16. M. Merington, *Custer Story,* p. 239.

17. February 13, 1871 (Hoxie Papers).

18. M. Merington, *Custer Story,* pp. 234, 236, 237, 242.

19. M. Merington, *Custer Story,* p. 238.

20. M. Merington, *Custer Story,* p. 239.

21. R. G. McMurtry, "Residence of Gen. George A. Custer," pp. 119–123; M. Merington, *Custer Story,* p. 241.

22. Springfield *Illinois State Register,* October 11, 1871; *Louisville* [Ky.] *Times,* January 20, 1949; Service Record (National Archives).

23. C. C. Rister, *Border Command,* p. 167.

24. *Louisville* [Ky.] *Times,* January 20, 1949; C. F. Bates, *Custer's Indian Battles,* p. 22; F. S. Dellenbaugh, *George Armstrong Custer,* p. 47.

25. M. Merington, *Custer Story,* p. 247.

26. E. B. Custer, *Tenting on the Plains,* pp. 317–318; F. Whittaker, *Complete Life of* . . . *Custer* . . . , p. 596; M. Merington, *Custer Story,* p. 244. See also *New York Times,* December 25, 1868.

27. *Louisville* [Ky.] *Times,* January 20, 1949.

28. M. Merington, *Custer Story,* p. 242; F. Whittaker, *Complete Life of . . . Custer . . . ,* p. 632.
29. Service Record (National Archives).

CHAPTER 25

1. E. B. Custer, *Boots and Saddles,* pp. 37–48.
2. Godfrey Papers; R. Bruce, *The Fighting Norths,* p. 20; E. B. Custer, *Boots . . . ,* p. 240; G. B. Grinnell, *Fighting Cheyennes,* p. 343; D. S. Stanley, *Personal Memoirs,* p. 247.
3. E. B. Custer, *Boots . . . ,* p. 69; M. Merington, *Custer Story,* p. 258.
4. E. B. Custer, *Boots . . . ,* pp. 273, 274, 276, 279; D. S. Stanley, *Personal Memoirs,* pp. 240, 246, Appendix p. [239].
5. E. B. Custer, *Boots . . . ,* pp. 90–91; G. A. Custer, "Battling with the Sioux," p. 92.
6. M. Merington, *Custer Story,* pp. 253, 264.
7. G. A. Custer, "Battling with the Sioux," p. 93.
8. E. B. Custer, *Boots . . . ,* p. 208; D. S. Stanley, *Personal Memoirs,* p. 241.
9. G. A. Custer report in E. B. Custer, *Boots . . . ,* p. 288; D. S. Stanley, *Personal Memoirs,* pp. 242, 250, 251.
10. Custer's letter of October 5, 1873, is in J. E. Parsons and J. S. duMont, *Firearms in the Custer Battle.*
11. M. Merington, *Custer Story,* p. 265.
12. E. B. Custer, *Boots . . . ,* p. 98; J. M. De Wolf, *Diary,* April 16, 1876; M. Merington, *Custer Story,* p. 267.

CHAPTER 26

1. Custer to father, December 13, 1873.
2. G. A. Custer, *My Life on the Plains,* p. 609.
3. Letter, Custer to Barrett, May 19, 1874 (Personal Miscellany, MS Division, Library of Congress); Custer to "Insurance Agent," June 24, 1874 (Filson Club, Louisville, Ky.); *Army and Navy Journal,* March 30, 1874; C. C. O'Harra, "Custer's Black Hills Expedition," p. 266.
4. Letter, Custer to Barrett, May 19, 1874; M. Merington, *Custer Story,* pp. 245, 273.

5. The first part of this account of the Black Hills Expedition is based on a letter of Custer to his wife, August 2, 1874, and also on R. Bruce, *The Fighting Norths,* p. 20; E. B. Custer, *Boots and Saddles,* pp. 299–303; W. Ludlow, *Report . . . of the Black Hills,* pp. 32, 54–57, 60; C. C. O'Harra, *Custer's Black Hills Expedition,* pp. 234, 287.

6. C. F. Bates, *Custer's Indian Battles,* p. 23; E. B. Custer, *Boots . . . ,* p. 216; F. Whittaker, *Complete Life of . . . Custer . . . ,* p. 636.

7. M. Merington, *Custer Story,* p. 244.

8. C. T. Brady, *Indian Fights and Fighters,* p. 213; E. B. Custer, "Beau Sabreur," p. 303; E. I. Stewart, *Custer's Luck,* p. 59.

9. Letter of Custer, February 2, 1875 (Johnson Papers); G. F. Milton, *Age of Hate,* p. 669.

10. C. F. Bates, *Custer's Indian Battles,* p. 24; *Index to Reports of Committees,* pp. 154–157; E. I. Stewart, *Custer's Luck,* p. 127.

11. *New York Tribune,* February 29, 1876; *Louisville* [Ky.] *Times,* January 20, 1949; E. B. Custer, *Boots . . . ,* pp. 250–251, and *Tenting on the Plains,* p. 347; F. Whittaker, *Complete Life of . . . Custer . . . ,* p. 635.

12. *The Barren Lands* is imprinted "Cincinnati, 1875," and was published in the *New York Tribune,* January 22, 1876. Further details on the argument over the Washita fight are in G. A. Custer, *My Life on the Plains,* pp. 353 fn., 397, and F. Whittaker, *Complete Life of . . . Custer . . . ,* p. 457.

13. *New York Tribune,* March 3, 7, 30, 1876.

14. Extensions were granted on January 11 and February 5, 1876 (Custer file, National Archives). E. B. Custer, *Boots . . . ,* p. 250; M. Merington, *Custer Story,* p. 277; F. Whittaker, *Complete Life of . . . Custer . . . ,* pp. 635–637.

15. E. B. Custer, *Boots . . . ,* p. 258. *Index to Reports of Committees,* p. 161, notes that Custer was called back to Washington within a week. M. Merington, *Custer Story,* p. 290; F. Whittaker, *Complete Life of . . . Custer . . . ,* pp. 549, 562, 639.

16. W. A. Graham, *Custer Myth,* p. 332.

17. *Manchester Guardian Weekly,* May 23, 1957; O. L. Hein, *Memories,* p. 108.

18. *New York Herald,* March 31, 1876. Statements involving Orvil Grant were published in *New York Tribune,* March 6, 1876; *Index to Reports of Committees,* pp. 155, 161, 234; M. Merington, *Custer Story,* pp. 284, 289; E. I. Stewart, *Custer's Luck,* p. 121; M. Schaff, *Battle of the Wilderness,* p. 45.

19. Arlington, Va., no date given (Hoxie Papers).

20. *New York Times,* April 5, 19, May 5, 1876; E. I. Stewart, *Custer's Luck,* p. 123; F. Whittaker, *Complete Life . . . ,* p. 549.

21. E. B. Custer, *Boots . . . ,* p. 128. The adjutant's refusal is dated March 30, 1876 (Custer file, National Archives).

22. J. I. C. Clarke, *My Life and Memories,* p. 158.

23. Telegram, Sherman to Sheridan, May 2, 1876 (National Archives); Custer's letter to President, May 6, 1876 (Sherman Papers); *New York Tribune,* April 7, 1876; F. Whittaker, *Complete Life of . . . Custer . . . ,* p. 559.

24. *Los Angeles Herald,* May 3, 11, 1876.

25. *Los Angeles Herald,* May 11, 1876.

CHAPTER 27

1. T. M. Coughlan, "The Battle of the Little Big Horn," p. 14; F. Dustin, *The Custer Fight,* p. 19.

2. C. F. Bates, *Custer's Indian Battles,* p. 29; W. A. Graham, *Story of the Little Big Horn,* p. 141; J. M. De Wolf, *Diary,* May 30, 1876; J. McLaughlin, *My Friend the Indian,* p. 126, states that 350 lodges had passed. M. Merington, *Custer Story,* p. 305; A. Terry, diary, June 19, 1876 (Library of Congress).

3. De Wolf, *Diary,* p. 46.

4. J. E. Parsons and J. S. duMont, *Firearms in the Custer Battle,* p. 48.

5. Dustin, *The Custer Fight,* p. 19; De Wolf, *Diary,* p. 52; *Los Angeles Times,* November 8, 1884.

6. F. Whittaker, *Complete Life of . . . Custer . . . ,* pp. 575–576.

7. Copy of letter, George B. Heredeen to wife, January 4, 1878 (Library of Congress); C. F. Bates, *Custer's Indian Battles,* p. 31; W. A. Graham, *Custer Myth,* p. 234.

8. Letter, G. A. Custer to E. B. Custer, June 22, 1876; copy of letter, Bailey to wife, July 4, 1876 (Godfrey Papers); A. Terry, diary,

June 22, 23, 1876; W. A. Graham, *Story of the Little Big Horn,*
pp. xx, 118; J. S. Hutchins, "The Cavalry Campaign Outfit,"
p. 101; Parsons and duMont, *Firearms in the Custer Battle,*
p. 12.

9. The description of the first afternoon's march is based on Ben-
teen's account in the Godfrey Papers. See also Graham, *Custer
Myth,* p. 177; C. F. Bates, *Custer's Indian Battles,* p. 31; W. S.
Edgerly in M. Merington, *Custer Story,* pp. 310, 318–320; E. S.
Godfrey, *Field Diary,* pp. 8–10; T. M. Coughlan, "The Battle
of the Little Big Horn," p. 15.

10. Copy of letter, Bailey to wife, July 4, 1876.

11. E. S. Godfrey, notebook, in Godfrey Papers.

12. T. M. Coughlan, "The Battle of the Little Big Horn," p. 13; W. A.
Graham, *Story of the Little Big Horn,* pp. 24, 122; E. I. Stewart, *Custer's Luck,* p. 139.

13. F. B. Heitman, *Historical Register,* p. 681.

14. E. S. Godfrey, notebook, in Godfrey Papers.

15. Letter of George B. Heredeen to wife, January 4, 1878; W. A.
Graham, comp., *Abstract . . . Reno Court of Inquiry,* p. 108.

16. G. B. Grinnell, *Fighting Cheyennes,* p. 342.

17. E. S. Godfrey, "Death of General Custer," p. 470; R. Taft, "Pictorial Record of . . . Custer's Last Stand," p. 365.

CHAPTER 28

1. G. A. Forsyth, *Story of the Soldier,* p. 328; G. B. McClellan,
Own Story, p. 365; M. Schaff, *Spirit of Old West Point,* p. 209.

2. *New York Times,* July 10, 13, 16, 1876. The cap and sash, now
at Custer Battlefield National Monument, were sent to Libbie
on July 13, 1886. *The Metropolitan* (1876), pub. by Metropolitan Life Insurance Co.

3. F. Whittaker, "General George A. Custer," p. 371.

4. Letter of G. A. Custer to E. B. Custer, April 23, 1876, M. Merington, *Custer Story,* p. 291.

5. F. Whittaker, *Complete Life of . . . Custer . . . ,* pp. 607–608.

6. E. B. Custer, *Tenting on the Plains,* p. 302; C. Wheeler, *Yesterdays,* p. 219.

7. August 11, 1877.

8. *New York Times,* October 11, 1877; *Harper's Weekly,* October 27, 1877.

9. W. A. Graham, comp., *Abstract of* . . . *The Reno Court of Inquiry,* pp. iv, 184, 187, 212, 228, 229, and author, *Story of the Little Big Horn,* pp. 158–162.

10. Letters, E. B. Custer to Vinnie Ream Hoxie, March 15, August 13, September 16, 19, 29, 1879; to Lawrence Barrett, April 6, 1880 (Library of Congress).

11. Notes in Myrick Collection.

12. Letter to Vinnie Ream Hoxie, January 2, 1882; to W. T. Sherman, October 15, 1882.

13. January 2, 1882 (Hoxie Papers).

14. Letters to Vinnie Ream Hoxie, January 13, 1886, June 5, 1888.

15. T. B. Whitman Papers; *Los Angeles Times,* July 5, 1885.

16. Letter, E. B. Custer to Vinnie Ream Hoxie, December 24, 1892; C. Wheeler, *Yesterdays,* pp. 279, 287–288, 313, 317.

17. W. A. Graham, *Custer Myth,* p. 52; J. E. Parsons and J. S. duMont, *Firearms in the Custer Battle,* pp. 33–35.

18. N. A. Miles, *Personal Recollections,* pp. 289–290.

19. For this inscription I am indebted to Mrs. Florence Kirtland, Monroe, Michigan.

20. The *New York Times,* June 26, 1931, tells of interview at Libbie's apartment. April 6, 1933, is the date of Libbie Custer's death, not her burial.

Sources

(The following is a list of works used in citations, not a complete bibliography of the field. Many prominent secondary works helpful to an understanding of Custer are omitted.)

BOOKS AND ARTICLES

ADAMS, CHARLES FRANCIS: *Charles Francis Adams, 1835–1915: An Autobiography* . . . (Boston, 1916).

AGASSIZ, GEORGE R., ed.: *Meade's Headquarters, 1863–1865; Letters of Colonel Theodore Lyman from the Wilderness to Appomattox* (Boston, 1922).

ALEXANDER, E. P.: "Lee at Appomattox," in *Century Magazine,* LXIII, No. 6 (April 1902), pp. 921–931.

ANDREWS, J. CUTLER: *The North Reports the Civil War* (Pittsburgh, *c.* 1955).

ATHEARN, ROBERT G.: *William Tecumseh Sherman and the Settlement of the West* (Norman, Okla., 1956).

BAILLY, EDWARD C.: *Echoes from Custer's Last Fight* (*Military Affairs,* XVII, No. 4 (Winter 1953, pp. 170–180).

BARRETT, ORVEY S.: *Reminiscences, Incidents, Battles, Marches and Camp Life of the Old 4th Michigan Infantry* . . . (Detroit, 1888).

BATES, CHARLES FRANCIS: *Custer's Indian Battles* (Bronxville, N.Y., *c.* 1936).

BEALE, HOWARD K.: *The Critical Year; A Study of Andrew Johnson and Reconstruction* (New York, 1930).

BENEDICT, G. G.: *Vermont in the Civil War* . . . (Burlington, Vt., 1886–1888).

BLISS, GEORGE N.: "Cavalry Service with General Sheridan and Life in Libby Prison," *Personal Narratives of Events in the War of the Rebellion,* 3rd Ser. No. 6 (Rhode Island Soldiers and Sailors Historical Society, 1884).

BOUDRYE, LOUIS N.: *Historic Records of the Fifth New York Cavalry, First Ira Harris Guard* . . . (Albany, 1865).

BOWERS, CLAUDE G.: *The Tragic Era: The Revolution after Lincoln* (Cambridge, Mass.; *c.* 1929).

BRACKETT, ALBERT G.: *History of the United States Cavalry* . . . (New York, 1865).

BRADY, CYRUS TOWNSEND: *Indian Fights and Fighters* . . . (Garden City, 1923).

BRILL, CHARLES J., *Conquest of the Southern Plains; Uncensored Narrative of the Battle of the Washita and Custer's Southern Campaign* (Oklahoma City, *c.* 1938).

BROOKE RAWLE, WILLIAM: "The Right Flank at Gettysburg," in *The Annals of the War* . . . (Philadelphia, 1879), pp. 467–484.

———: "The Second Cavalry Division in the Gettysburg Campaign," in *History of the Third Pennsylvania Cavalry* (Philadelphia, 1905), pp. 261–291.

BROOKS, U. R., ed.: *Stories of the Confederacy* (Columbia, S.C., 1912).

BRUCE, ROBERT: *The Fighting Norths and Pawnee Scouts: Narratives and Reminiscences of Military Service on the Old Frontier* (Lincoln, Neb., *c.* 1932).

CATTON, BRUCE: *Mr. Lincoln's Army* (Garden City, 1951).

———: *A Stillness at Appomattox* (Garden City, 1953).

CHAMBERLAYNE, JOHN HAMPDEN: *Ham Chamberlayne — Virginian; Letters and Papers of an Artillery Officer* . . . (Richmond, 1932). Edited by C. G. Chamberlayne.

CLARKE, JOSEPH I. C.: *My Life and Memories* (New York, 1925).

CONFEDERATE SOLDIER: "Custer at the Surrender," in *Southern Bivouac,* I, No. 2 (July 1885), pp. 76–77.

Congressional Globe: Appendix, 39th Cong., 2nd Sess., pt. 3 (Washington, 1867).

CONRAD, BRYAN. *See* ECKENRODE, H. J.

COUGHLAN, T. M.: "The Battle of the Little Big Horn, A Tactical Study," in *Cavalry Journal,* XLIII, No. 181 (Jan.–Feb. 1934), pp. 13–21.

CRAWFORD, J. MARSHALL: *Mosby and His Men* . . . (New York, 1867).

CRAWFORD, SAMUEL J.: *Kansas in the Sixties* (Chicago, 1911).

CROWNINSHIELD, BENJAMIN W.: *A History of the First Regiment of Massachusetts Cavalry Volunteers* (Boston, 1891).

CULLUM, GEORGE W.: *Biographical Register of the Officers and Graduates of the U.S. Military Academy at West Point* (New York, 1891, 1901).

CUSTER, ELIZABETH BACON: "A Beau Sabreur," in *The Bravest Five Hundred of '61* . . . (New York, 1891), pp. 295–309. Edited by Theo. F. Rodenbough.

———: *"Boots and Saddles"; or, Life in Dakota with General Custer* (New York, 1904). First published in 1885.

———: *The Boy General: Story of the Life of Major-General George A. Custer* (New York, 1901). Edited by Mary E. Burt.

———: *Following the Guidon* (New York, 1890).

———: *Tenting on the Plains; or, General Custer in Kansas and Texas* (New York, 1889).

———: *General Custer at the Battle of the Little Big Horn, June 25, 1876* (New York, printed, not published, 1897).

CUSTER, GEORGE ARMSTRONG: "Battling with the Sioux on the Yellowstone," in *Galaxy,* XXII, No. 1 (July 1876), pp. 91–102, and succeeding issues.

———: *My Life on the Plains* (Chicago, 1952). Edited by Milo Milton Quaife. First edition published New York, 1874.

———: "War Memoirs," in *Galaxy,* XXII, No. 3 (Sept. 1876), pp. 293–299.

CUSTER, MILO: *Custer Genealogies* (Bloomington, Ill., c. 1944).

DAVIS, BURKE, ed. *See* McCLELLAN, H. B.

DAVIS, THEODORE R.: "Henry M. Stanley's Indian Campaign in 1867," in *Westerners Brand Book, 1945–46* (Chicago, 1947), pp. 101–114.

DAVIS, THEODORE R.: "A Summer on the Plains," in *Harper's New Monthly Magazine,* XXXVI, No. CCXIII (February 1868), pp. 292–307.

————: "With Generals in their Camp Homes: General George A. Custer," in *Westerners Brand Book, 1945–46* (Chicago, 1947), pp. 115–130.

DE FOREST, JOHN WILLIAM: *A Volunteer's Adventures; a Union Captain's Record of the Civil War* (New Haven, 1946). Edited by James H. Croushore.

DE LAND, CHARLES EDMUND: *The Sioux Wars (South Dakota Historical Collections,* XV, 1930).

DE WOLF, JAMES M.: *The Diary and Letters of Dr. James M. De Wolf . . . His Record of the Sioux Expedition of 1876 . . .* Reprinted from *North Dakota History,* XXV, Nos. 2–3 (April–July 1958). Edited by Edward S. Luce.

DELLENBAUGH, FREDERICK S.: *George Armstrong Custer* (New York, 1917).

DENISON, FREDERIC: *Sabres and Spurs: The First Regiment Rhode Island Cavalry . . .* (Central Falls, R.I., 1876).

DOANE, GUSTAVUS C.: *Report on the So-called Yellowstone Expedition of 1870* (Sen. Exec. Doc. No. 51, Washington, 1871).

DuMONT, JOHN S.: *See* PARSONS, JOHN E.

DU PONT, H. A.: *The Campaign of 1864 in the Valley of Virginia . . .* (New York, 1925).

DUSTIN, FRED: *The Custer Fight. Some Criticisms of Gen. E. S. Godfrey's "Custer's Last Battle" in the Century Magazine . . . and of Mrs. Elizabeth Custer's Pamphlet . . .* (Hollywood, 1936).

ECKENRODE, H. J., AND BRYAN, CONRAD: *George B. McClellan, the Man Who Saved the Union* (Chapel Hill, 1941).

ELIOT, ELLSWORTH, JR.: *West Point in the Confederacy* (New York, 1941).

FARLEY, JOSEPH PEARSON: *West Point in the Early Sixties* (Troy, N.Y., 1902).

FAVILL, JOSEPH MARSHALL: *The Diary of a Young Officer . . .* (Chicago, 1909).

FLEMING, WALTER L.: "Jefferson Davis at West Point" (reprinted from *Publications of the Mississippi Historical Society,* X, pp. 247–267).

FLETCHER, DANIEL COOLEDGE: *Reminiscences of California and the Civil War* (Ayer, Mass., 1894).

FORSYTH, GEORGE A.: "Sheridan's Ride," in *Harper's New Monthly Magazine,* Vol. 95, No. 566 (July 1897), pp. 165–181.

———: *The Story of the Soldier* (New York, 1900).

FREEMAN, DOUGLAS SOUTHALL: *Lee's Lieutenants: A Study in Command* (New York, 1942–1944).

GAUSE, ISAAC: *Four Years with Five Armies* . . . (New York, 1908).

GERRISH, THEODORE: *Army Life: A Private's Reminiscences of the Civil War* (Portland, Me., *c.* 1882).

GIBBON, JOHN: "Personal Recollections of Appomattox," in *Century Magazine,* LXIII, No. 6 (April 1902), pp. 936–943.

GLAZIER, WILLARD: *Three Years in the Federal Cavalry* (New York, 1873).

GODFREY, CALVIN POMEROY: "General Edward S. Godfrey," in *Ohio Archaeological and Historical Quarterly,* XLIII, No. 1 (Jan. 1934), pp. 61–98.

GODFREY, EDWARD SETTLE: *After the Custer Battle* (*Sources of Northwest History,* No. 29, Montana State University, Missoula). Edited by Albert J. Partoll.

———: "Custer's Last Battle," in *Century Illustrated Monthly Magazine,* XLIII, New Ser. XXI, No. 3 (Jan. 1892), pp. 358–384. Reprinted in 1923, with Mark Kellogg's "Notes," in *Contributions to the Historical Society of Montana,* IX, pp. 144–212.

———: "The Death of General Custer," in *Cavalry Journal,* XXXVI, No. 148 (July 1927), pp. 469–471.

———: *The Field Diary of Lt. Edward Settle Godfrey, Commanding Co. K, 7th Cavalry Regiment under Lt. Colonel George Armstrong Custer in the Sioux Encounter at the Battle of the Little Big Horn* (Portland, Ore., 1957).

———: "Some Reminiscences Including an Account of General Sully's Expedition Against the Southern Plains Indians, 1868," in *Cavalry Journal,* XXXVI, No. 148 (July 1927), pp. 417–425.

GODFREY, EDWARD SETTLE: "Some Reminiscences of the Battle of the Washita," in *Cavalry Journal,* XXXVII, No. 153 (Oct. 1928), pp. 481–500.

GORDON, JOHN B.: *Reminiscences of the Civil War* (New York, 1903).

GOSS, WARREN LEE: *Recollections of a Private. A Story of the Army of the Potomac* (New York, c. 1890).

GOULD, JOSEPH: *The Story of the Forty-eighth; A Record of the Campaigns of the Forty-eighth Regiment Pennsylvania Veteran Volunteer Infantry . . .* (Philadelphia, 1908).

GRAHAM, WILLIAM A., comp.: *Abstract of the Official Record of Proceedings of the Reno Court of Inquiry . . .* (Harrisburg, Pa., 1954).

———: *The Custer Myth, A Source Book of Custeriana . . .* (Harrisburg, Pa., c. 1953).

———: *The Story of the Little Big Horn, Custer's Last Fight* (Harrisburg, Pa., 1952).

GREGG, D. M'M.: "The Union Cavalry at Gettysburg," in *The Annals of the War . . .* (Philadelphia, 1879), pp. 372–379.

GRINNELL, GEORGE BIRD: *The Fighting Cheyennes* (New York, 1915).

HAMLIN, AUGUSTUS C.: "Who Recaptured the Guns at Cedar Creek, October 19, 1864?" in *The Shenandoah Campaigns of 1862 and 1864 and the Appomattox Campaign of 1865* (*Papers of the Military Historical Society of Massachusetts,* VI, pp. 183–208).

HANSON, JOSEPH MILLS: "The Civil War Custer," in *Cavalry Journal,* XLIII, No. 183 (May–June 1934), pp. 24–31.

HAZEN, WILLIAM B.: *Our Barren Lands; the Interior of the United States West of the 100 Meridian, and East of the Sierra Nevada* (Cincinnati, 1875).

———: *Some Corrections of Custer's Life on the Plains* (St. Paul, Minn., 1875).

HEIN, O. L.: *Memories of Long Ago . . .* (New York, 1925).

HEITMAN, F. B.: *Historical Register of the United States Army . . .* (Washington, 1890).

HENDERSON, G. F. R.: *The Science of War . . .* (London, 1905).

History of the Eighteenth Regiment of Cavalry, Pennsylvania Volunteers (New York, 1909).

HUEY, PENNOCK: *A True History of the Charge of the Eighth Pennsylvania Cavalry at Chancellorsville* (Philadelphia, 1883).

HUNT, HENRY J.: "The First Day at Gettysburg," in *Battles and Leaders of the Civil War,* III, pp. 255–284. Also "The Second Day . . . ," in source cited above, pp. 290–313, and, "The Third Day . . . ," pp. 369–385.

HUNTER, DARD: *Before Life Began: 1883–1923* (Cleveland, 1941).

HUNTER, ROBBINS: *The Judge Rode a Sorrel Horse* (New York, 1950).

HUTCHINS, JAMES S.: "The Cavalry Campaign Outfit at the Little Big Horn," in *Military Collector & Historian* (Winter 1956), pp. 91–101.

IMBODEN, JOHN D.: "Lee at Gettysburg," in *Galaxy,* XI (April 1871), pp. 507–513.

Index to Reports of Committees of the House of Representatives for the First Session of the Forty-fourth Congress 1875–'76 (Washington, 1876).

IRWIN, RICHARD B.: *History of the Nineteenth Army Corps* (New York, 1892).

ISHAM, ASA B.: "Through the Wilderness to Richmond," in *Sketches of War History, 1861–1865 . . . Ohio Commandery of the Military Order of the Loyal Legion,* I (Cincinnati, 1888), pp. 198–217.

JONES, VIRGIL CARRINGTON: *Ranger Mosby* (Chapel Hill, 1944).

KEIM, DEB. RANDOLPH: *Sheridan's Troopers on the Borders: A Winter Campaign on the Plains* (Philadelphia, 1891).

KELLOGG, MARK: "Diary," in *The Westerners Brand Book 1945–46* (Chicago, 1947), pp. 83–96.

KIDD: J. H.: *Personal Recollections of a Cavalryman with Custer's Michigan Cavalry Brigade . . .* (Ionia, Mich., 1908).

KING, W. C., comp.: *Camp-Fire Sketches and Battle-field Echoes of '61–5* (Springfield, Mass., 1888).

KOENIG, ARTHUR: *Authentic History of the Indian Campaign which Culminated in "Custer's Last Battle," June 25, 1876* (St. Louis, no date given).

KUHLMAN, CHARLES: *Did Custer Disobey Orders at the Battle of the Little Big Horn? . . .* (Harrisburg, Pa., *c.* 1957).

KUHLMAN, CHARLES: *Legend into History: The Custer Mystery; an Analytical Study of the Battle of the Little Big Horn* (Harrisburg, Pa., 1952).

LELAND, CHARLES GODFREY: *Memoirs . . .* (New York, 1893).
————: *The Union Pacific Railway, Eastern Division . . .* (Philadelphia, 1867).

LEMMON, GEORGE: "Story of Appomattox," in *Washington Post,* March 5, 1899, p. 10.

LIVERMORE, THOMAS L.: *Numbers & Losses in the Civil War in America, 1861–65* (Bloomington, Ind., 1957). Edited by Edward E. Barthell, Jr. First published in 1900.

LONGSTREET, JAMES: *From Manassas to Appomattox; Memoirs . . .* (Philadelphia, 1903). First published in 1896.
————: "Lee in Pennsylvania," in *The Annals of the War . . .* (Philadelphia, 1879), pp. 414–446.

LUCE, EDWARD S. ed.: *See* DE WOLF, JAMES M.

LUDLOW, WILLIAM: *Report of a Reconnaissance of the Black Hills of Dakota, Made in the Summer of 1874* (Washington, 1875).

MARSHALL, CHARLES: "Story of Appomattox," in *Washington Post,* Jan. 29, 1899, p. 20.

McCLELLAN, GEORGE BRINTON: *McClellan's Own Story . . .* (New York, 1887).

McCLELLAN, H. B.: *I Rode with Jeb Stuart* (Bloomington, Ind., c. 1958). Edited by Burke Davis. First published as *Life and Campaigns of Major General J. E. B. Stuart* in 1885.

McCLERNAND, EDWARD J.: "With the Indian and the Buffalo in Montana," in *Cavalry Journal,* XXXVI, No. 146 (Jan. 1927), pp. 7–54.

McKAY, ROBERT H.: *Little Pills: An Army Story . . .* (Pittsburg, Kan., 1918).

McLAUGHLIN, JAMES: *My Friend the Indian* (Boston, 1926).

McMAHON, MARTIN T.: "From Gettysburg to the Coming of Grant," in *Battles and Leaders of the Civil War,* IV, pp. 81–94.

McMURTRY, R. GERALD: "Residence of Gen. George A. Custer in Elizabethtown, 1871–1873," in *A Series of Monographs Concerning the Lincolns and Hardin County, Kentucky* (Elizabethtown, 1938), pp. 119–123. Previously published in *Kentucky Progress Magazine,* V, No. 4 (Summer 1933), pp. 32–33, 50.

MEADE, GEORGE: *The Life and Letters of George Gordon Meade* . . . (New York, 1913).

MERINGTON, MARGUERITE: *The Custer Story; The Life and Intimate Letters of General George A. Custer and His Wife Elizabeth* (New York, 1950).

MERRITT, WESLEY: "Sheridan in the Shenandoah Valley," in *Battles and Leaders of the Civil War,* IV, pp. 500–521.

MICHIE, PETER: "Reminiscences of Cadet and Army Service," in *Personal Recollections of the War of the Rebellion* . . . *New York, Military Order of the Loyal Legion,* 2nd Ser. (New York, 1897), pp. 183–197.

MILES, NELSON A.: *Personal Recollections and Observations of General Nelson A. Miles* . . . (Chicago, 1896).

MILLER, SAMUEL H.: "Yellow Tavern," *Civil War History,* II, No. 1 (March 1956), pp. 57–81.

MILLER, WILLIAM E.: "The Cavalry Battle near Gettysburg," in *Battles and Leaders of the Civil War,* III, pp. 397–406.

MILNER, JOE E., AND EARLE R. FOREST: *California Joe: Noted Scout and Indian Fighter* (Caldwell, Ida., 1935).

MILTON, GEORGE FORT: *The Age of Hate; Andrew Johnson and the Radicals* (New York, 1930).

MOORE, JAMES: *Kilpatrick and Our Cavalry* . . . (New York, 1865).

MOSBY, JOHN S.: *The Memoirs of Colonel John S. Mosby* (Bloomington, Ind., 1959). Edited by Charles Wells Russell. First published in 1917.

MOYER, H. P., comp.: *History of the Seventeenth Regiment Pennsylvania Volunteer Cavalry* . . . [Lebanon, Pa., 1911].

NEWHALL, FREDERIC C.: "The Battle of Beverly Ford," in *The Annals of the War* . . . (Philadelphia, 1879), pp. 134–164.

[Newhall, Frederic C.], *With General Sheridan in Lee's Last Campaign* (Philadelphia, 1866).

NORTON, HENRY: *Deeds of Daring, or History of the Eighth N.Y. Volunteer Cavalry* . . . (Norwich, N.Y., 1889).

O. R. *(Official Records). See The War of the Rebellion.*

O'CONNOR, RICHARD: *Sheridan, the Inevitable* (Indianapolis, 1953).

O'HARRA, CLEOPHAS C.: "Custer's Black Hills Expedition of 1874," in *Black Hills Engineer,* Volume XVII, No. 4, pp. 221–286.

OWEN, WILLIAM MILLER: *In Camp & Battle with the Washington Artillery Battery of New Orleans* (Boston, 1885).

PALFREY, FRANCIS WINTHROP: *The Antietam and Fredericksburg* (New York, 1882).

PARIS, LOUIS PHILIPPE, COMTE DE: *History of the Civil War in America* (Philadelphia, 1875–1888).

PARSONS, H. C.: "Farnsworth's Charge and Death," in *Battles and Leaders of the Civil War,* III, pp. 393–396.

PARSONS, JOHN E., AND JOHN S. DUMONT: *Firearms in the Custer Battle* (Harrisburg, Pa., 1953).

PERRY, MILTON F.: "Come on! Be Quick!" in *True West,* IV, No. 4 (March–April, 1957), pp. 14–15.

PHISTERER, FREDERICK: *New York in the War of the Rebellion, 1861 to 1865* (Albany, 1912).

PLEASONTON, ALFRED: "The Campaign of Gettysburg," in *The Annals of the War* . . . (Philadelphia, 1879), pp. 447–459.

———: *Report of Major General A. Pleasonton, to the Committee on the Conduct of the War,* pp. 1–13. Bound in *Supplemental Report of the Joint Committee on the Conduct of the War,* II (Washington, 1866).

———: "Testimony," in *Report of the Joint Committee on the Conduct of the War, at the Second Session Thirty-eighth Congress,* I, *Army of the Potomac* (Washington, 1865), pp. 26–33, 359–366.

PORTER, HORACE: "Five Forks and the Pursuit of Lee," in *Battles and Leaders of the Civil War,* IV, pp. 708–722.

———: "The Surrender at Appomattox Court House," in *Battles and Leaders of the Civil War,* IV, pp. 729–746.

QUAIFE, MILO MILTON: "Some Monroe Memories," in *Burton Historical Collection Leaflet* (May 1939), pp. 9–12.

———, ed. *See* CUSTER, GEORGE ARMSTRONG, *My Life on the Plains.*

RAWLE, WILLIAM. *See* BROOKE RAWLE.

REMSBURG, JOHN E.: *Charley Reynolds, Soldier, Hunter, Scout and Guide* (Kansas City, 1931).

Review of the Trial of General George Armstrong Custer (Bureau of Military Justice, Washington, D.C.).

RHODES, CHARLES D.: *History of the Cavalry of the Army of the Potomac* . . . (Kansas City, Mo., 1900).

RICKEY, DON: *War in the West; The Indian Campaigns* (Crow Agency, Mont., 1956).

RISTER, CARL COKE: *Border Command, General Phil Sheridan in the West* (Norman, Okla., 1944).

ROBERTSON, JNO., comp.: *Michigan in the War* (Lansing, 1880).

RODENBOUGH, THEO. F., comp.: *From Everglade to Cañon with the Second Dragoons* (New York, 1875).

———: "Sheridan's Richmond Raid," in *Battles and Leaders of the Civil War,* IV, pp. 188–193.

———: "Sheridan's Trevilian Raid," in *Battles and Leaders of the Civil War,* IV, pp. 233–236.

———: *Uncle Sam's Medal of Honor* (New York, *c.* 1886).

RONSHEIM, MILTON, *The Life of Custer* (reprinted from the *Cadiz* [Ohio] *Republican,* 1929).

RUSSELL, DON, "Sixty Years in Bar Rooms; or 'Custer's Last Fight,' " in *Westerners Brand Book* (Chicago, 1946), III, No. 9 (Nov. 1946), pp. 61–68.

———, AND ELMO SOTT WATSON: "The Battle of the Washita, or Horn," in *The Westerners Brand Book* (Chicago, 1944), pp. 81 93.

———, AND ELMO SCOTT WATSON: "The Battle of the Washita, or Custer's Massacre?" in *Westerners Brand Book* (Chicago, 1944), pp. 49–56.

SANDOZ, MARI: *The Buffalo Hunters* . . . (New York, 1954).

SCHAFF, MORRIS: *The Battle of the Wilderness* (Boston, 1910).

———: *The Spirit of Old West Point 1858–1862* (Boston, 1907).

———: *The Sunset of the Confederacy* (Boston, *c.* 1912).

SCRYMSER, JAMES ALEXANDER: *Personal Reminiscences* . . . (no place given, *c.* 1915).

SEDGWICK, JOHN: *Correspondence* . . . (New York, 1902–1903).

SERGENT, MARY ELIZABETH: "Classmates Divided," *American Heritage,* IX, No. 2 (Feb. 1958), pp. 30–35, 86–87.

SHERIDAN, PHILIP H.: *Personal Memoirs* . . . (New York, 1888).

Southern Historical Society Papers, XXV (January–December 1897), pp. 239–244.

STANLEY, DAVID S.: *Personal Memoirs* . . . (Cambridge, Mass., 1917).

STANLEY, HENRY M.: *My Early Travels and Adventures in America and Asia* (New York, 1895).

STARR, LOUIS M.: *Bohemian Brigade; Civil War Newsmen in Action* (New York, 1954).

STERN, PHILIP VAN DOREN: *An End to Valor; the Last Days of the Civil War* (Boston, 1958).

STEWART, EDGAR I.: *Custer's Luck* (Norman, Okla., 1955).

STRYKER, LLOYD PAUL: *Andrew Johnson; A Study in Courage* (New York, 1929).

SWALLOW, W. H.: "The Third Day at Gettysburg," in *Southern Bivouac*, I, No. 9 (Feb. 1886), pp. 562–572.

SWINTON, WILLIAM: *Campaigns of the Army of the Potomac* . . . (New York, 1866).

TAFT, ROBERT: "The Pictorial Record of the Old West, IV, Custer's Last Stand . . ." *The Kansas Historical Quarterly*, XIV, No. 4 (Nov. 1946), pp. 361–390.

THOMPSON, S. MILLETT: *Thirteenth Regiment of New Hampshire Volunteer Infantry in the War of the Rebellion, 1861–1865. A Diary* . . . (Boston, 1888).

TOBIE, EDWARD P.: *History of the First Maine Cavalry, 1861–1865* (Boston, 1887).

TOWNSEND, GEORGE ALFRED: *Campaigns of a Non-combatant* . . . (New York, 1866).

TREMAIN, HENRY EDWIN: *Last Hours of Sheridan's Cavalry* . . . (New York, 1904).

TROBRIAND, REGIS DE: *Four Years with the Army of the Potomac* (Boston, 1889).

UTLEY, ROBERT M.: "The Legend of the Little Big Horn," in *Corral Dust; Potomac Corral of the Westerners*, I, No. 2 (June 1956), pp. 9–12.

VAN DE WATER, FREDERIC F.: *Glory Hunter; A Life of General Custer* (Indianapolis, 1939).

WAGNER, GLENDOLIN D.: *Old Neutriment* (Boston, 1934).

The War of the Rebellion: A Compilation of the Official Records of the Union and Confederate Armies (Washington, 1880–1901).

WELLES, GIDEON: *Diary of Gideon Welles, Secretary of the Navy under Lincoln and Johnson* (Boston, 1911).

WHEELER, CANDACE: *Yesterdays in a Busy Life* (New York, *c.* 1918).

WHITAKER, EDWARD W.: "Story of Appomattox," in *Washington Post*, Jan. 29, 1899, Feb. 12, 1899.

WHITTAKER, FREDERICK: *A Complete Life of Gen. George A. Custer, Major-General of Volunteers, Brevet Major-General U.S. Army, and Lieutenant-Colonel Seventh U.S. Cavalry* (New York, *c.* 1876).

————: "General George A. Custer," in *Galaxy*, XXII, No. 3 (Sept. 1876), pp. 362–371.

WILLIAMS, KENNETH P.: *Lincoln Finds a General; A Military Study of the Civil War* (New York, 1949–1956).

WILLIAMSON, JAMES J.: *Mosby's Rangers: A Record of the Operations of the Forty-third Battalion of Virginia Cavalry from its Organization to the Surrender* (New York, 1909).

WILSON, JAMES HARRISON: *Under the Old Flag; Recollections of Military Operations in the War for the Union, the Spanish War, the Boxer Rebellion, etc.* (New York, 1912).

WING, TALCOTT E.: *History of Monroe County, Michigan* (New York, 1890).

WRIGHT, J. M.: "West Point before the War," in *Southern Bivouac*, IV, No. 1 (June 1885), pp. 13–21.

NEWSPAPERS

Harper's Weekly

Los Angeles Times
Louisville [Kentucky] *Times*

Manchester Guardian Weekly

New York Times
New York Tribune
New York World

Putnam County [Ohio] *Gazette*
San Francisco Chronicle
Springfield *Illinois State Journal*
Springfield *Illinois State Register*
Syracuse, New York, *Post-Standard*
Washington [D.C.] *Post*

MANUSCRIPTS

BROWN, JANET E.: Personal collection (Endicott, N.Y.).

CAMP, W. M.: Typewritten extracts from letters to Mrs. Custer (West Point).

CUSTER, ELIZABETH B., AND GEORGE A., manuscripts. Custer Battlefield National Monument, Detroit Public Library, Lincoln Memorial University, Monroe County [Mich.] Historical Society, New York Historical Society, United States Military Academy, Yale University Library.

GODFREY, E. S.: Papers (Library of Congress).

GREENE, JACOB: Letter to G. A. Custer, April 7, 1864 (Yale University Library).

GRIERSON, BENJAMIN: Letter of July 16, 1878 (Illinois State Historical Library).

HART, C. C.: Autograph collection (Library of Congress).

HARVEY, WINFRED S.: Diary — typewritten copy (Library of Congress).

HASKELL, JOHN CHERES: "Reminiscences of the Confederate War, 1861-1865" — typescript (Virginia Historical Society).

HOLLAND, DUDLEY: "Reminiscences" — typescript (Cadiz, Ohio).

HOXIE, VINNIE REAM: Correspondence (Library of Congress).

JOHNSON, ANDREW: Papers (Library of Congress).

JONES, ANNIE E.: Record in Provost Marshal's file (National Archives).

MYRICK, HERBERT: Collection (Henry E. Huntington Library).

PARMELEE, TED: Collection of Theodore R. Davis's Custeriana (Los Angeles).

"PERSONAL MISCELLANY" (Library of Congress).

Sherman, William T.: Papers (Library of Congress).
Stuart, George H.: Collection (Library of Congress).

Terry, Alfred: Diary (Library of Congress).

Washington, James Barroll: Manuscripts (United States Military Academy).
Whitmore, T. B.: Collection (Henry E. Huntington Library).

Acknowledgments

My indebtedness to students in the Custer field is somewhat akin to the 7th Cavalry's indebtedness to General Custer. For information on the Boy General's early life I received cordial co-operation from MILTON RONSHEIM of Cadiz, Ohio, who knows more than anyone else about Armstrong's boyhood in Ohio. I was also helped in this field by the generosity of MISS JANET BROWN of Endicott, New York, and by DARD HUNTER of Chillicothe, Ohio. CARLETON CUSTER PIERCE, JR., Lieutenant Commander, USNR (Ret.), gave me invaluable help on the Custer genealogy. I am also indebted to MRS. RICHARD S. FISHER, my wife's sister, of Fostoria, Ohio, for driving us with skill and enthusiasm to Custer home sites in the Middle West.

For details on the life of Custer in Monroe, Michigan, I want to express my great obligation to DR. LAWRENCE FROST, whose intensive study has made him one of the best informed scholars on Custer's entire life. DR. MILO M. QUAIFE, editor of the *Burton Historical Collection* in Detroit, graciously gave me his time and the product of his resourceful research. MRS. FLORENCE KIRTLAND, in the Monroe County Historical Society, told me personal anecdotes about the town's early history. DOROTHY V. MARTIN, curator of manuscripts in the Detroit Public Library, furnished me with details concerning the Custer documents in her charge.

At the United States Military Academy, West Point, I received cordial help and courtesy in both the Library and the Museum, from COLONEL WILLIAM JACKSON MORTON, DR. SIDNEY FOREMAN, J. M. O'DONNELL, and KENNETH RAPP. In the rare book room MRS. LOUISE HOROBIN showed me documents heretofore unused. LIEUTENANT

COLONEL JOHN R. ELTING gave me the benefit of his definitive technical knowledge of the Battle of Gettysburg. MISS ELIZABETH SERGENT, of Middletown, New York, shared with me her vast knowledge of Civil War cadet life.

In Washington, DAVID C. MEARNS, Chief of the Manuscript Division, Library of Congress, and VICTOR GONDOS, JR., Archivist in Charge of the Old Army Branch of the National Archives, furnished me with invaluable Custer documents. The Misses JOSEPHINE COBB and VIRGINIA DAIKER helped me unstintingly with the pictures in their files at the National Archives and the Library of Congress, respectively. PAUL GANTT, former Tally Man for the Westerners Potomac Corral, has been a real rustler (in the best sense of the word), rounding up strays on the Custer range.

Odd details concerning Custer in the Civil War came to me from those vivid writers in the field, PHILIP VAN DOREN STERN, BURKE DAVIS, and COLONEL JOHN M. VIRDEN. HOWSON W. COLE furnished me with photostats of manuscript material in the Virginia Historical Society archives. SYLVESTER VIGILANTE sent me his collection of Custer clippings, and helped me with the same enthusiasm which he used to show when he superintended the American History Room in the New York Public Library. SAMUEL E. GALLO, associate editor, Publications Division, Metropolitan Life Insurance Company, New York, supplied me with data and photostats concerning Custer's business with that firm. MRS. DOROTHY THOMAS CULLEN spent her valuable time checking records in the Filson Club Library in Louisville, Kentucky. WILLIAM E. TAYLOR, editor of the *Lincoln Herald,* typed for me a copy of the fragment of a Custer letter in the Lincoln Memorial University Library. DON RUSSELL, expert in the Custer field, helped me locate Custer paintings.

Mari Sandoz has been most generous in giving me the sources of Custer-Indian relations. DON RICKEY, JR., Executive-Secretary, Custer Battlefield Historical and Museum Association, was extremely helpful when my wife and I visited the National Monument, and he has since sent me copies of both pictures and documents. MAJOR EDWARD S. LUCE, former Superintendent, Custer Battlefield National Monument, has been untiring in answering my letters. As a 7th Cavalryman, he knew Mrs. Custer personally. In Santa Barbara, the widow of another 7th Cavalryman, MRS. CLYDE SIMPSON, when a little girl also knew Mrs. Custer and has given me many personal touches on her character. Also in Santa Barbara, MRS. ELMER T. MERRILL has called my attention to obscure Custer citations.

HARRY McGUIRE presented me with a rare publication on Custer's Black Hills expedition. ROBERT UTLEY, HUGH W. SCHICK, EDGAR I. STEWART, MICHAEL HARRISON, and HOFFMAN BIRNEY — all experts in Custeriana — generously replied to my written inquiries. COLONEL GERALD E. CRONIN typed a long extract about Custer for me. I want also to thank PETER WYNNE for sending me a clipping concerning Custer's last trip to New York, which would otherwise have been overlooked. Prompt and enlightening replies to my queries have been sent by W. H. HUTCHINSON of Chico, California; R. GERALD Mc-MURTRY, Director of the Lincoln National Life Foundation at Fort Wayne, Indiana; CAPTAIN GEORGE A. CUSTER, 19th Battle Group, U. S. Army; DONALD JACKSON, Editor of the University of Illinois Press; E. S. SUTTON, Benkelman, Nebraska; COLONEL GEORGE B. CAMPBELL, South Chatham, Massachusetts; and TOM McCLARY of Langhorne, Pennsylvania.

TED PARMELEE, in Los Angeles, graciously allowed me to examine the notes and sketches made by his grandfather, war correspondent Theo. R. Davis. In the Illinois State Historical Library, the ever-resourceful MARGARET FLINT called my attention to a letter concerning Custer; and MRS. L. J. COLLAMORE showed me a derringer allegedly owned by Custer. At the Henry E. Huntington Library in San Marino, California, I am indebted to the skillful advice of the Misses NORMA CUTHBERT and HAYDÉE NOYA. At the Library of the University of California, Santa Barbara, Librarian DONALD C. DAVIDSON has been exceptionally helpful in response to my numerous requests. The outstanding and ever-growing Wyles Collection of Civil War and Western Americana publications, which is a part of this Library, has been indispensable. I also want to express my sincere appreciation to MRS. VIOLET SHUE, MRS. MARTHA PETERSON, and to JOHN J. MESCALL, all members of the Library staff, who have helped me with many a problem. PROFESSOR RUSSELL BUCHANAN, of the History Department, has been most thoughtful in giving me Custer citations unearthed in his own research. For typing the entire text with

Custerlike dash when time was short, and with unCusterlike accuracy, I want to thank Mrs. LUELLA HOWARD.

And finally, for those readers who turn to the last paragraph to see what the author says about his wife, let me say that MILDRED MONAGHAN has read the entire manuscript and notes with her usual editorial skill, and has also typed the bibliography and footnotes. Carrying the guidon for the entire book, her gay companionship makes a writer forget the hardships of his task and remember only the prospect of seeing the finished volume.

J. M.

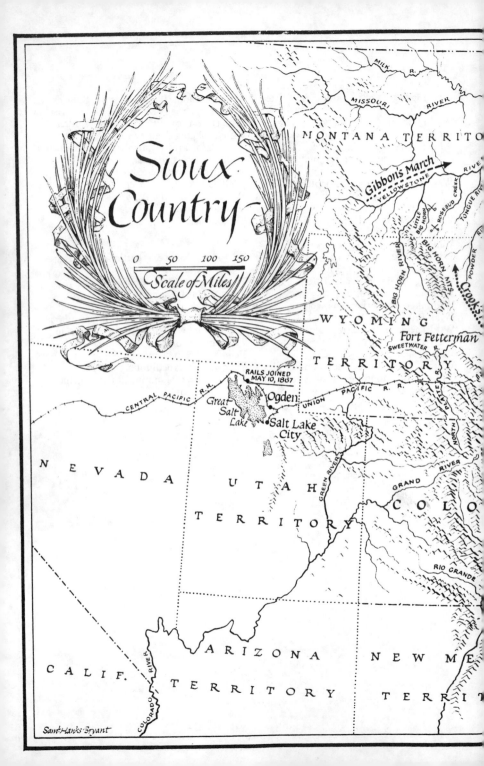

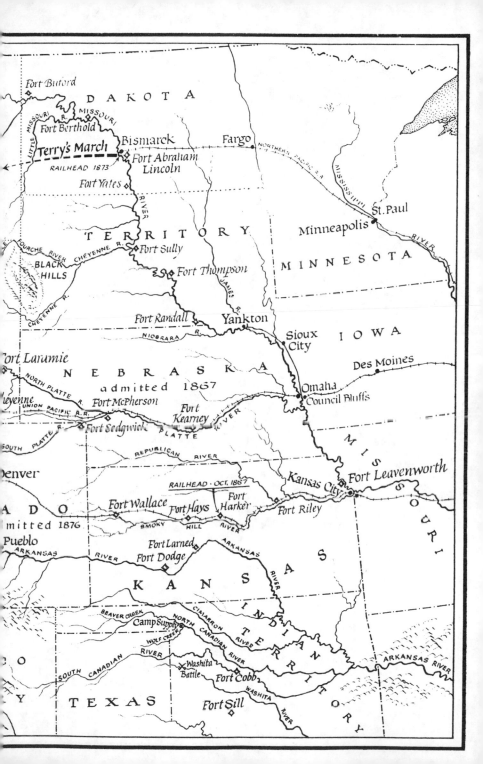